The history of the Armenian people, from the remotest times to the present day

J de 1857-1924 Morgan

Nabu Public Domain Reprints:

You are holding a reproduction of an original work published before 1923 that is in the public domain in the United States of America, and possibly other countries. You may freely copy and distribute this work as no entity (individual or corporate) has a copyright on the body of the work. This book may contain prior copyright references, and library stamps (as most of these works were scanned from library copies). These have been scanned and retained as part of the historical artifact.

This book may have occasional imperfections such as missing or blurred pages, poor pictures, errant marks, etc. that were either part of the original artifact, or were introduced by the scanning process. We believe this work is culturally important, and despite the imperfections, have elected to bring it back into print as part of our continuing commitment to the preservation of printed works worldwide. We appreciate your understanding of the imperfections in the preservation process, and hope you enjoy this valuable book.

Jacques de Morgan

Former Director-General of the Egyptian
Department of Archaeology and former General
Delegate in Persia of the French
Ministry of Education

The HISTORY OF THE
ARMENIAN PEOPLE

From the Remotest Times to the Present Day

Preface by GUSTAVE SCHLUMBERGER
*of the Academy of Ancient
Monuments and of Literature*

> Victrix causa diis placuit,
> sed victa Catoni.
> (*Lucan, Pharsala, I.* 128)

Illustrated With 296 Maps, Plans, and Documentary Sketches
by the Author.

Translated by
ERNEST F. BARRY

DEDICATION

To you, Armenians, I dedicate this book, in memory of those happy days of my youth spent in your picturesque mountain villages, in your enchanting forests, among your flower-spangled meadows all glistening in the beautiful Eastern sunshine.

May this story of the deeds of your forefathers bring to your thought the dauntless and upright men of the past who have bequeathed you their nobility of heart and their unconquerable love of national freedom, and remind you of your ancient lineage, one of the most ancient among the illustrious peoples of the earth, also of the twenty-five hundred years that your fathers have valiantly struggled to uphold the honor of your great Haïk.

May this dedication recall to some among you the traveler who found such charm in your delightful country-side, in the silvery laughter of your children, the happy songs of your shepherds, your village festivals, the zourna of your country-folk, and the singing of your maidens.

O martyred people! may you, by the time this book appears, see the dawn of your final day of freedom: may you with your poet Tchobanian sing:

Behold the fire springing anew from out the night;
   The redding glow of the mountain tops;
. . .
   'Tis the sweetest hour of all,
      the lovely reawakening to Life!

PREFACE

During this seemingly endless war, the worst ever to afflict mankind, Armenia has undoubtedly been the most unfortunate of all lands, the most racked and tortured, more so even than Belgium, more so than Serbia! Victim of the frightful massacres by the Turks, subjected to the cruelest horrors, partly delivered by the Russians and then woefully abandoned by them, Armenia has seen her fine and industrious rural population decimated to an unthinkable extent through a most abominable series of slaughters. Not only is she the unhappiest of nations, but no national history is so little known as is hers, despite the fact that this history was once so famous. The reason for this is that for several centuries Armenia has been constantly held down beneath the most unbearable of servitudes, the bloody Ottoman yoke. In our western civilization hardly any but a very few scholars know the early history of the Armenians, those ancient and medieval times when this then warlike race played a most important rôle in the hinterland of the Eastern world, first the Roman and then the Christian.

A few noble-minded men of this long and sorely tried nation, along with some French friends devoted to their cause, felt it urgent to bring Armenia's hitherto neglected history to the knowledge of the general French public and that of our Allies, through a published work of high standing and practical value. This they deemed one of the best ways to interest the world, and France in particular, in the salvation of so worthy a people. These friends of Armenia, choosing as spokesman one of the best among them, the great patriot Archag Tchobanian, kindly asked my advice as to whom they should appeal to carry out this difficult task. One name came at once to my thought. that of my friend Jacques de Morgan, the intrepid explorer, the scholarly and enthusiastic traveler and great archaeologist, renowned for his excavations at Susa and in Egypt. No one is better acquainted with the vast regions around Armenia, and with Armenia itself, which he has traveled over more than anyone. No one has more carefully studied the mysterious beginnings and the history of those races that settled over the magnificent lands south of the Caucasus. Many years of incessant labor had impaired his health, yet when upon my advice my Armenian friends asked him to write the history of their nation and to compass its glorious but forgotten annals in a volume of striking interest, to be widely disseminated in behalf of this sacred cause, he at once accepted, despite his poor health and comparative reclusion. He set to work immediately, happy to be able still to serve the sublime cause of oppressed peoples. In two years of ardent labor he completed this important work, of such great interest to a vast public so lacking in knowledge about Armenia. I have been done the great honor of being asked to write a few introductory lines to this volume. For this honor I am perhaps indebted to my own works on the Crusades and Byzantine history, in which I so often had to refer to the valorous deeds in the East of the illustrious Armenian race. "This is the first time," wrote Jacques de Morgan to me,, "that I am not writing the preface myself to one of my books!" I accepted, however, this pleasurable task, with the stated intention of writing briefly, not to re-introduce to the public my friend Morgan already so well known, but if possible to draw the further attention of all the allied nations to the unhappy Armenian people and to the abominable injustice they have endured for centuries.

I fondly hope that very many French people, and very many of our allies, will read this admirable and clear outline, so understandingly set forth, of the history of Armenia, a history of centuries of valor, of energy, and of suffering, lived under the shadow of the two mountains of Ararat, the giants that tower over the land. For my part, I feel that of all the different periods of this people's constantly sublime and tragic history, none offers more interest than that of the Armenian nation during the Crusades and the large part their doughty sovereigns took by the side of the Latin princes for the cause of Christendom overseas. I wish this splendid volume the very great success it deserves. May it contribute, upon the final victory now so near, towards the entry of Armenia, freed from the unbearable Turkish yoke, into the rightful and definite place to which she is entitled in the future Society of Nations!

GUSTAVE SCHLUMBERGER

September, 1918.

FOREWORD

To my friend Gustave Schlumberger, member of the Institute of France, the eminent Byzantinist, and to the great Armenian poet Archag Tchobanian, I am indebted for the idea of writing this history of Armenia. It was with some hesitation that I undertook so bold and, I do not mind saying, arduous task. Arduous on account of the multiplicity and unfortunate tangle of sources of information, and of the fact that these are available so often only in Armenian, a fact that closed to me a number of doors. However, at my friends' urgent request, I set about the work, and endeavored to write a history which should be within the range of all readers without departing from the strict limits of accurate scholarship. At the same time I crave the reader's indulgence because for many reasons outside the author's will it is necessarily incomplete For one thing, the storehouses of data in the libraries of Russia, the Caucasus, and Constantinople, are not at my disposal, and also there is so much written in languages I do not know and not yet translated, consequently unavailable. As for archaeological material, it is practically non-existent. In Russian Armenia the excavations which I began in 1887-88 were subsequently forbidden by the Imperial Government, and have hardly yet been resumed by a Russian Commission,—whilst in Turkish Armenia due to the innumerable difficulties raised by the Ottoman government no searches have been attempted beyond a few excavations of small extent at Van. We are consequently obliged to fall back, so far as the earliest periods are concerned, on the statements of classical Greek and Latin authors, minus any archaeological support.

As with the history of all Oriental peoples, especially in the Middle Ages, the annals of Armenia are extremely complex. The interlaced events are not only intimately related to the evolution of the peoples of Asia, but also frequently depend on the politics of western nations; so that one must often deal with general history to explain the cause and effect of purely Armenian happenings. As for the facts themselves, the relevant documents are in most cases very widely scattered, spread among the histories and chronicles of foreign nations. They had to be discovered, discussed, and compared,—a task frequently difficult, they being often narrated differently by the various chroniclers.

As early as 1889 I was interested in Armenian history, and I made a brief incursion into this interesting subject in a volume entitled Mission scientifique au Caucase, Études archéologiques et historiques. Tome II. Recherches sur les origines des peuples du Caucase. *But, as the title shows, this research was not restricted to the Armenians, and the history of Armenia was only included in its main aspects, my attention being more particularly directed to the questions as to the origins of the Kartvelian peoples*

Nevertheless, I had examined the matter of Armenia very carefully both as regards its records and the character of the Armenian people, whom I knew from having lived a long time among them. These are the reasons why Messrs G Schlumberger and A Tchobanian urged me to write, and why I yielded to their wishes

Moreover, in the present circumstances, writing a history of Armenia is not only in the interests of science, but it is fulfilling a duty to humanity, to a people far too little known, remembered only for its woes, and deserving of a happier destiny.

During the nearly thirty years that have elapsed since my book on the Caucasus appeared, numerous works have dealt with the question of the Armenian people's first beginnings, for the study of mankind's earliest times has actively engaged men's thoughts and the Armenians have not been left out in these investigations. However, a few books in particular are specially to be commended for the safe scientific method their authors have followed, they all reach the same conclusions from different viewpoints. A MEILLET, in his Grammaire comparée de l'Arménien classique (1903), *deduces from his analysis of the language irrefutable proofs of the Indo-European origin of the people; Messrs. Noel DOLENS and A KHATCH in their* Histoire des anciens Arméniens (1907) *and M. Kevork ASLAN in his* Études sur le Peuple arménien (1909) *all vigorously espouse and clarify my own arguments of 1889, and so dispose of the main problem*

While I was finally reviewing the manuscript of the present History of the Armenian People, *there appeared (1917) in Rome a book of some importance by J SANDALGIAN,* Histoire documentaire de l'Arménie des temps du paganisme, *in which the writer arrives at conclusions contrary* to those of Meillet, N Dolens, A. Khatch, and K. Aslan Unfortunately the author of this voluminous work has accepted deceiving etymological analogies that have led him astray from scientific conclusions.

The sources of Armenian history are very numerous; they divide naturally into three classes, according to the periods The chronicles of the Ararat region go back to very remote antiquity The first events there are related in the Ninivite inscriptions and in those of Urartu (Van), but antedate considerably the arrival of the Armenians on the plateau of Erzerum To discuss the peoples conquered and assimilated by the later arrivals would be to take up the history of Western Asia from the 15th or 10th centuries B C., thus going outside the framework of this volume The reader will find in the Histoire ancienne des Peuples de l'Orient, by G. MASPERO, and in my Premières Civilisations, all the guidance he may desire on these questions; I shall therefore deal with them only indirectly.

Regarding the very earliest times of the Armenians, we have in the West: the Achaemenian inscriptions of Behistun, (published and translated by J OPPERT), HERODOTUS, the narratives of XENOPHON, and the traditions handed down to us by PLINY, STRABO, and PTOLEMY; also in the East, the writings of MOSES of KHOREN with a few passages from other Eastern authors.

As we enter the Alexandrian era we are more abundantly documented, for both Greek and Latin writers tell us, chiefly during the Seleucidan period, of the wars waged by the Senate of the Eternal City against the rulers of Syria, Pontus, and Armenia ARRIAN, DIODORUS OF SICILY, STRABO, APPIAN, JUSTIN, JOSEPHUS, PLINY, PLUTARCH, TACITUS, SPARTIAN, SUETONIUS, DION CASSIUS, EUTROPIUS, FLORUS, VELLEIUS PATERCULUS, are authoritative not only for data on the Seleucidan period but also for our knowledge of events in the Parthian era. These Western writers enable us to verify and fill in the statements left us by AGANTHANGELUS, by MOSES OF KHOREN, and other Eastern authors, whose relation of happenings they did not witness are often questionable.

During the time of the Roman Empire, when the legions were constantly fighting the Arsacid Persians and waging war in Armenia, the various emperors caused coins to be struck commemorating the chief political or military events in the East. These coins are sometimes very useful in accurately establishing dates.

Unfortunately not a single one remains of the many historical works *that were written in the Pehlevi language under the Sassanid kings. For that period our chief sources are Armenian, Syrian, Latin, and Greek* MOSES OF KHOREN, EVAGRIUS, JOHN MAMIGONIAN, AGATHANGELUS, SOZOMEN, MICHAEL THE SYRIAN, FAUSTUS, EUSEBIUS, ZENOBIUS OF GLAK, ELISHA VARTABED, SEBEOS, LAZARUS OF PHARP, AMMIAN MARCELLINUS, *are the most important authorities.*

For the time of the Bagratides dynasty we come to MATTHEW OF EDESSA, *Catholicos* JOHN VI, ASSOGHIK, TH. ARTZRUNI, SAMUEL OF ANI, ARISTACES OF LASTIVERT, *the Arabian historians* MAKRISI *and* IBN-AL-ATHYR, *along with others, and the Greek chroniclers* CEDRENUS, ZONARAS, GLYCAS, *etc.*

In writing the history of Armeno-Cilicia (New Armenia), I have drawn mainly on Historiens des Croisades, documents arméniens, *by* E. DULAURIER, *and on* Sissouan, *by* L. ALISHAN.

Finally, for modern times, I have consulted the books and numerous pamphlets published of late years, such as A. J. TOYNBEE, The Murder of a Nation, *A.* TCHOBANIAN, Chants populaires arméniens (Introduction), l'Arménie sous le joug turc; Les publications du Comité arménien d'Angleterre, de New York; *E* DOUMERGUE, L'Arménie, les Massacres et la Question d'Orient, *K. J.* BASMADJIAN, Histoire moderne des Arméniens; *Viscount* BRYCE, The Treatment of Armenians in the Ottoman Empire, 1915-1916; *Marcel* LEART, La Question arménienne à la lumière des documents, *etc.*

To these special works should be added some writings of a more general nature, such as: H.F.B. LYNCH, Armenia; MICHAEL CHAMICH, History of Armenia; *Fr.* TOURNEBISE, Histoire politique et religieuse de l'Arménie; *Viscount* BRYCE, Transcaucasia and Ararat; *Noel and Harold* BUXTON, Travels and Politics in Armenia; *Reinhold* RÖHRICHT, Geschichte des Königreichs Jerusalem; SAINT-MARTIN, Mémoires sur l'Arménie; *Noel* DOLENS *and A.* KHATCH, Histoire des anciens Arméniens, *Geneva, 1907;* KEVORK ASLAN, Études historiques sur le peuple arménien, *Paris 1909, id.,* L'Arménie et les Arméniens, *Constantinople, 1914.*

As regards chronology, I have made use of the very thorough work by K. J. BASMADJIAN, Chronologie de l'Histoire de l'Arménie, *and in my survey of religious questions, I have in addition to the above works taken largely from the article of R.* JANIN *in* Les échos d'Orient: Les Arméniens, *also* L'Église arménienne *by Mgr. M.* ORMANIAN.

Finally, the writing and valuable advice of A. Tchobanian have been my main source in acquainting my readers with Armenian literature and poetry.

Besides these main sources I have also consulted a large number of scattered documents in various reviews and newspapers.

My acquaintance with the country and with Eastern life has been moreover very helpful to me me in compiling this work, enabling me often to understand the cause and effect of events. Writing a history has meant going into innumerable details, but in regard to each principal period I have striven to show the main lines of the evolution of the Armenian people and their relation to the outside world at each period, for from the remotest times Armenia by reason of its geographical position had a very large rôle to play in the outlook of the major powers concerning Western Asia

The reader will perhaps be often puzzled by the seemingly uncouth names and places in the volume These I have had to use, however, for we must not forget that throughout the centuries we have here to deal with strictly Oriental nomenclatures, in the Armenian, Arabic, ancient and modern Persian, Turkish, Kurdish, and Georgian languages. These names, so strange to European ears, become much simpler when their meaning is known. Vagharschapat, for instance, means "built by Valarsace;" Sarkis is "Sergius"; Karapet, "forerunner"; Alagheuz, "blue eye"; Arpa-tchai, "barley river"; Gheuk-tchai, "blue river"; while Vramchapouh is the Armenian pronunciation of the Persian (Sassanides) double name Varahran-Chapour (Sapor), and so on. Sometimes also the names assume the most varied forms; George I, king of Iberia (Georgia) becomes, according to different writers and countries, Gorigè, Korkè, Kéorké, Kéorki, Giorgi, Korike, Kourken. Therefore the sounds I have had to keep to, in order to preserve the linguistic character of proper names, should not look too formidable. Their use was unavoidable.

The geography of Western Asia is not generally known beyond its main outlines, and here again the reader will be confronted with unavoidable difficulties. But they have been mine also, for they have necessitated much research on my part, the forms which the geographical names assume being so numerous. Erzerum of the Turks, or Qaliqala, is the Theodosiopolis of the Byzantines; the Armenians call it Karin. The kingdom of Albania is Aghouania, the Aghouanq of the Armenians; Azerbaïdjan of the Turks and Persians is Atrpatakan in Armenian, Atropatenes in Greek, not to speak of its names in Achaemenian and

Pehlevi. But, for the reader's guidance, I have generally indicated in footnotes the names most commonly found on current maps, and have not hesitated to repeat myself occasionally to save having to turn back to preceding pages; and in addition I have illustrated my text with a large number of maps drawn most carefully by myself, containing just the data needed for each particular period

Though the reader probably knows the history of the principal Asiatic peoples, I have referred to their chief historical events and dates wherever I have thought it helpful to clarify the story. No one is expected to know the order of succession of the Caliphs, or the Sassanid kings of Persia, any more than that of the Byzantine emperors; and as for historical concordances, they are even less known, and ignorance in these connections is definitely excusable I must confess, moreover, very frankly that had I to read the history of China, I should be grateful if the author explained to me innumerable details of geography, language, and chronology.

To give more color to my narrative of subjects and events so unfamiliar to European readers, I have illustrated my text with all the interesting documentation I have been able to obtain, such as coins, seals, autographs, signatures of rulers, coats of arms, archaeological objects, ruins of castles and towns, the most notable structural remains, etc. I have added topographical plans and sketches, all from the most varied sources, and I have made it my care to draw all these illustrations myself and to prepare the drafts for the map-specialist. In my published scientific works I have always avoided so far as possible relying on professional draughtsmen for my illustrations, because despite their skill they do not attain to the absolute documentary accuracy needed to convey the author's exact purpose. My illustrations, it is true, are far from the professional perfection of a skilled draughtsman, but I trust the reader will overlook this as he realizes the truly scientific character of my documentation

In the appendix to this volume will be found chronological tables.

I have thus endeavored to assist in every way possible the perusal of this book, and I hope, as I commit it to press, that it will acquaint very many people with the background and glorious history of a nation of whom so little is known beyond the fact of its long martyrdom under the Turkish yoke These pages will show the world how little the Armenian people deserved the terrible fate that has hitherto been their cruel lot.

The two Ararats, as seen from the valley of the Araxes

CHAPTER I

PHYSICAL FEATURES OF ARMENIA — GEOGRAPHY — GENERALITIES

ARARAT   In the regions of Ararat, in that land of mystery in which earliest tradition locates our nebulous human origin, the Armenians have dwelt for about twenty-five centuries. In this mountain mass, in this welter of great peaks, the Armenian people planted themselves, on this soil they became a nation. But the land was already sacred, a land renowned to the peoples of ancient times, for to their religious sentiment this was the scene of mankind's rebirth following the most awful cataclysm that through the dim corridor of memory has remained in the minds of men through countless generations.

In the imagination of the ancients, Ararat seemed a wonder, the work of a supernatural power, and the colossus became sacred, the abode of genii known as "Dragon's Sons." (1) Its snowy summit was associated with the dim memories of forgotten ages, with stories enhanced by tradition, and Ararat, the work of divine hands, stood in contrast to that other fabulous tower which mortals had sought in vain to build to heaven. Such power and grandeur, such commanding poetry, emanate from the volcano's

---

(1) Vichapazunk.

majesty, that simple minds have ever been struck with overwhelming awe and admiration in the presence of this natural wonder, when in the midst of the night's darkness, the Giant's summit shines forth in all its luminous glory. This is the moment when Ararat, the messenger of the powers of heaven, announces to men that the God of Zoroaster is getting ready to cause his golden disk to rise upon the old world. The Masis (1) is the wonder mountain of Western Asia, towering over, crushing all around it, seeming to have been forged by Vulcan to discomfit the soul of the beholder.

When towards the east the sky is aglow with the fires that herald the dawn, while all Armenia is still slumbering deep in darkness, a blood-colored patch appears in the cloud, bright as the steel aglow on the blacksmith's anvil. Slowly this patch spreads, lengthens, and takes the form of the sharp-pointed head of a giant arrow, directed threateningly to heaven. This is the snowy peak of Great Ararat, made crimson by the first rays of the sun, while the orb itself, still hidden to mortals, announces its coming by the gleams it sheds in the cloud beyond the Black Mountains. (2) Only the Giant's summit is lit with the ardent glow of dawn: it seems to melt and pass slowly away while Phoebus' chariot rises on the horizon.

To the left of the Giant rises another peak, lower but just as sharp in outline, and also bathed in blood, namely, the Lesser Ararat. It likewise is touched by the first glows of daylight, and this vision, evocative of the time when the two craters together belched forth flames and lava (3), soon disappears. Then, towards the west, there comes soon into view the summit of another extinct volcano, the brother of the two Ararats, the Alagheuz (4) whose eternal snow appears pink in the now azured sky and stands out against the dark huddle of the mountains of West-

THE ALAGHEUZ

---

(1) Name given by the Armenians to Ararat, the Arghi-dagh of the Turks, the Kouh-i-Nouh (mountain of Noah's ark) of the Persians.
(2) The Qara-dagh and the Qara-bagh.
(3) In Turkish: Ala-gheuz (Blue Eye); in Armenian: Aragadz.
(4) The table-land of Iran and that of Erzeroum emerged at the end of the tertiary period, together with the volcanoes (Ararat, Alagheuz, Lelwar, etc; Savalan, Sahend, Demavend, etc.) During the latter part of this geological period (Plaisancian), Azerbaidjan and the adjoining regions, not yet raised, enjoyed a climate similar to that of the present tropical zones, and maintained the elephant, the rhinoceros, and all the animals of warm and moist lands (fossil fauna of Maragha). At the end of the Pliocene period the raised surfaces were formed, and during the quaternary period, Iran, Armenia, and the Caucasus were covered with snow. The volcanoes remained active long after their first eruptions and lasted perhaps until men peopled these regions freed from snow. (Cf. J. DE MORGAN, Les Premieres Civilisations, p 57 sq, 91 sq, 164 sq.).

ern Armenia Gradually, hundreds of peaks come out of the darkness, announcing to every valley the coming of Day, while shadow and morning mist still surround the whole Araxes plain, including Erivan, the ancient town founded by King Ervand, and Etchmiadzin, the holy city of the Armenians. In the distance are heard the church bells ringing the Angelus, the bleating of herds leaving the villages, the singing of shepherds, the barking of dogs· Armenia is awaking to return to its daily labors in its fertile fields.

Now the sun pours its joyous smile on the workers who have been up before dawn, dispels the shades of the mist, tinges with blue the light smoke hovering over the villages, and sends forth its waves of warmth. Women clad in blue or red, carrying a jar on head or shoulder, come out chattering from their houses of yellow clay, while the men, wearing heavy sheepskin caps like the Tartars, come and go, take the horses to water, and lead the oxen to the plow. Heedless of Nature's awakening, they sing, chant love-songs or old legends preserved by the minstrels, and do not even look at the Giant majestically standing beyond the plain, an object of admiration for the traveler, but of no concern to the countryman who has seen it ever since he was born.

Ararat (1) whose summit stands in the clouds like an immense regular cone, is over 13,000 feet (2) higher than the waters of the Araxes. Its barren sides, burned and furrowed by lava outflows, incline abruptly downward in slopes covered with crumbling scoria and fragments of volcanic bombs. No abutment, no minor mountain, hides the Giant's base to take away from its grandeur It stands in isolation, as though it had risen at one thrust from the bowels of the earth by the force of an almighty fiat. Beside it stands the Lesser Ararat which, despite its tremendous stature (3) gives one the impression of a child alongside its father, waiting on his orders. About twelve miles, as the crow flies, is the distance to the top of the Great Ararat from the bed of the Araxes; consequently the mountain seems to crush with all its weight the valley of Erivan: a sight unequaled, if not in the universe, at least in the Old World For Mont-Blanc (4), Kazbek (5), Demavend (6), Everest (7), and almost all the highest summits in our own lands, rise from huge bases

	Alt.		Alt.
(1)	16,930 ft.	(5)	16,545 ft.
(2)	14,140 ft.	(6)	19,950 ft.
(3)	13,220 ft.	(7)	29,000 ft.
(4)	15,780 ft.		

surrounded by large peaks, so that much of their majesty is lost to the spectator. The Elburz Mountain (8) alone, seen from the Russian steppes, appears in all its magnificence, although resting on an enormous pedestal.

To the south of Armenia, in the Kurdish chain forming the border of Iran, are numerous heights varying from 13,000 to 16,500 feet, but all these peaks are enclosed among very high mountains, so that they are lost in the ensemble of that gigantic wall and never drew the attention of the early inhabitants: Zagros (1) overlooking Bagdad, Zerd è Kouh (2) the snow of which is seen from everywhere in Susiana, have not played in popular imagination the part they should. Demavend alone, among these ancient civilizations, Demavend, the "Mountain of the Genii," is comparable to Ararat as regards the impression made on the traveler. But although this peak is about 3,330 feet higher than the Armenian volcano, it does not strike one so forcibly because it stands in the middle of the Elburz, a chain higher than the Alps. Ararat itself when viewed fro mthe south, from Khoï or Bayazid, does not give that feeling of grandeur one has when looking at it from Erivan or Vagharchapat. (3)

Ararat rises in the centre of Greater Armenia, it overlooks on the east the region of Lake Urumiah, (4) the Atropatenes of the ancients (5), on the south the region of Lake Van (6), the Urartu (7), on the west and south-west the watersheds of the Tigris, the Euphrates, and the Araxes, rivers whose names are linked with that of the cradle of mankind. The Masis reigns over these celebrated regions, just as the Kazbek does over the two slopes of the great Caucasian wall, as the Demavend is seen over the Caspian Sea and the land of the Iranians, and as the great peaks of the Himalayas stand supreme between the frozen tablelands of Tibet and the rich plains of India.

In all lands, the sight of giant mountains has always aroused mystical feelings in peoples' souls, and just as Fuji-yama is sacred to the Japanese, and Mt Olympus became the abode of the Greek gods, so in our time Ararat is still a holy site both to Christians and Moslems. Even prior to

---

(8) 18.525 ft
(1) Delaho Kouh in southern Kurdistan.
(2) In the country of the Bakthyaris.
(3) Etchmiadzin, founded and built by King Valarsace (Vagharchak).
(4) Alt. 4,000 ft.
(5) Azerbadjan
(6) 5 400 ft
(7) The Ararat of the Bible is the same name as Ourartsa in Assyrian.

the arrival of the Armenian Haik in the region, the volcano was undoubtedly deified by the people dwelling under its shadow (8)

As always happens to the heritage of peoples for many centuries deprived of political independence, Armenia is today without precisely defined frontiers, both in its districts ruled by the Czar and those in Persian or Ottoman territory. Tiflis, in ancient times the capital of the kings of Karthli, (1) contains today many Armenian families, and so do Maku, Batum, Trebizond, etc. In ancient times, as in the Middle Ages, during the different periods of Armenian independence, the frontiers of Greater and Lesser Armenia were exceedingly unsettled; nevertheless, as regards the Transcaucasian regions, the mountains to the south of the Kura river should be considered as belonging to the Armenian domain, while the valley of the Cyrus (2) keeps its Georgian nationality.

Not many years ago, the traveler going from Tiflis (3) to Erivan (4), used to cross the highest and most picturesque part of the massif of the Lesser Caucasus After leaving the capital of Karthli, he first followed down the Cyrus right bank; then, leaving the Georgian river at its junction with the Akstafa-tchai, he ascended the valley of the latter torrent as far as the village of Delidjan, inside the northern districts of Armenia. There, at the mountain pass near the village, he left behind the Kura watershed and entered into that of the Araxes Then, along the shore of the great Transcaucasian lake (5), he reached Yelenovka, a small Russian village from where one goes down to Erivan by the valley of the Zenghi-tchai (6), the river feeding the Araxes from the lake's overflow.

This journey from Akstafa to Erivan, formerly undertaken by carriage, was one of the most delightful drives one could take among the picturesque mountains of the Lesser Caucasus The road, today very neglected, winds amid wild and endlessly changing scenery. Sometimes

---

(8) Near the natural deposits of volcanic glass at the foot of the Alagheuz, I found locations of cut obsidian that must be ascribed to neolithic workmanship. Some of the objects belong apparently, however, to the quaternary (Magdalenian) period; these are the oldest traces of man in this region, which in the glacial period was certainly not inhabited, any more than was the whole of the Iran plateau, or the tablelands of Armenia and Transcaucasia.
(1) Native name for Georgia
(2) Ancient name for the river Kura.
(3) Alt. 1.475 ft.
(4) Alt. 2.800 ft
(5) Gheuk-tchai in Turkish, Goktcha in Russian, Sevan in Armenian. Alt. 6,330.
(6) River Zangui in Armenian.

it climbs forest-covered slopes, then it slips through bare rocks, or creeps along the foot of basaltic cliffs, of many-hued lava-flows, of swollen scoria or beds of black red-veined obsidian, the volcanic glass sparkling in the sunlight. Further on it sinks into deep and forbidding gorges brightened only by the bubbling waters of countless torrents, and now and then, fastened like an eagle's nest to the mountain-side, there appears a village of clay dwellings terraced with beaten earth and inhabited by hospitable farm folk, mostly Armenians. Apart from this road, or "causeway" as the Russians call it, there are only mule-paths from village to village, just as in the Middle Ages and in the earliest times.

THE GHEUK-TCHAI OR SEVANGA
Lake Sevanga (1), one of the largest and finest in the Old World, the fresh blue water of which is ever transparent, is about 44 miles long and 19 at its widest point. An amphitheatre of verdant mountains, rising over 3,000 feet high, encircles it and feeds it from a thousand streams, watering the many villages on its shore. The lakeside dwellers live off their crops and to a lesser extent off their fishing, for the Gheuk-tchaï is very deep and well-stocked, being noted for its fine trout

During the summer the Sevanga region is delightfully cool and the countryside rich and smiling, but as soon as the cold sets in and the north wind strips the trees, the land situated as it is over 6,000 feet above sea-level is covered with a thick pall of snow, the surface of the freshwater lake is ice-bound, and the peasant stays inside his village. The herds go underground, while around every dwelling, underneath the snow, stand piles of wood, argols (manure-fuel), and straw needed to weather the frosts. The village is as though dead, for four or five months of the year. All is buried under the great white shroud, and the site of the locality is indistinguishable save for the light wreaths of smoke that seem to issue from the frozen bowels of the earth.

In the days of the carriage-drive from Tiflis to Erivan, should the traveler arriving from Tchoubouqlou and Yelenovka be fortunate enough to reach the village of Akhta a few moments ere the break of dawn, he was met with the awe-inspiring spectacle of Ararat ablaze, a scene which would remain with him as the most marvelous human eye could witness But this wonderful road is today forsaken, now that a prosaic railroad

---
(1) Lake Sevan, formerly called Lake Gegham.

links the capital of Georgia to that of Azerbaidjan via Alexandropol and Erivan. Progress has swept along these enchanting mountains, and the wayfarer no longer sees Lake Sevanga, he no longer witnesses the sunrise over Ararat, nor does he now behold the awful gorges of Dariall (2), nor the glaciers of the Kazbak, the monarch of the Caucasus, now that the "Grouzinskéaya-daroga" is no more the great thoroughfare between the northern steppes and Transcaucasia.

The Imperial government has laid down some roads in the Armenian mountains, but these roads have nearly all been built for political or strategic reasons, and the bulk of the country has still to put up with its old-time means of communication. However much one may regret this from a commercial standpoint, it is quite an advantage as regards the preservation of the ancestral traditions, customs, sentiments, and language of the inhabitants, and it is due to this isolation that Armenian communities have been able to keep intact their national spirit. Secluded in their deep valleys, amidst their forests, and surrounded by often impassible heights, these mountaineers live happily, richly endowed by nature, and seldom leave their natal roof, unless it be for a pilgrimage to Etchmiadzin. This secluded existence, this life away from the world, is the lot of all Eastern peasants; consequently one finds among them family sentiment far more strongly developed than it is among our own country-people, who are losing it more and more under outside influences.

THE ARAXES The Araxes, which is fed by the streams of the southern slopes of the Little Caucasus and runs at the foot of Ararat, is the great river of northern Armenia. It takes its rise in the mountains overlooking the east of Erzerum (1), 9 miles from that city. Its waters come down from Palandeukendagh (2) and Karghabazar-dagh (3), mountains belonging to the divide between the versants of the Persian Gulf and the Caspian Sea, for it is near Erzerum that the western Euphrates itself takes its rise.

Not so far along its course the Araxes is joined by a larger tributary than itself, the Pasin-sou, which comes down from a fertile but cold and bare tableland, recently made famous by the victories of the Russian army over the Turks.

---

(2) The "Gate of the Alans" of the ancients.
(1) Theodosiopolis of the Greeks and Romans, Garin of the Armenians.
(2) Alt. 10,335 ft.
(3) Alt. 8,300 ft.

Leaving these gloomy solitudes, the Araxes makes its way through a labyrinth of mountains, for the most part wooded, and flows to the east in a dashing torrent, the muddy waters of which rush through deep gorges, fall in cascades, and thus drop 5,000 feet before reaching the plain of Erivan. On this plain, in a vastly wider valley, the river receives a number of tributaries from the northern mountains, among them being the Arpa-tchaï (1), the Ani, the Silav, the Karpi-tchaï or Abaransou which waters Etchmiadzin, and the Zenghi-tchaï flowing from lake Sevanga past Erivan. Likewise the snows of Ararat, of Alagheuz and of all the great mountains of Armenian Caucasus send down thousands of springs and streams which keep cool the valleys and dales during the summer heat, water the orchards and fields, and only join the Araxes at the time of the heavy Spring rains.

Formerly all the mountains in northern Armenia were covered with forests, both north and south of the Araxes. Today, however, there are to be seen in these parts only scanty bushes, which the shepherds rob year by year, cutting down, every spring, the new growth to feed their herds. As for the valleys, they are all extremely fertile due to the abundance of water and the warmth of the sun in this latitude (2). In the dales, the vegetation is nearly always ahead of that of the country just outside Erivan, because although well sheltered from the north wind, the latter wide plain suffers hard winters. The vine and fruit-trees grow here, however, in abundance, and from the vineyards of the Masis there are still made those excellent wines of which we are told the patriarch Noah imbibed to excess.

THE PLAIN OF ERIVAN The middle valley of the Araxes has always played a considerable part in the national life of the Armenians. At the foot of Ararat, not far from the left bank of the Araxes, is the chief seat of the Armenian Church, at Etchmiadzin. In this neighborhood also stood the ancient capitals, Armavir and Artaxata, and in the Middle Ages Ani, the residence of the last sovereigns of Greater Armenia. Here too the Persians fortified Erivan, to guard the possessions of the Shah-àn-Shah north of the Araxes. Erivan became Russian in 1828, and today its population is almost entirely Armenian.

The historian Lazarus of Pharp (3) has left us a charming descrip-

---
(1) Barley river.
(2) Lat. N. 40° (Taranto, Sardinia, Valencia, Lisbon).
(3) Transl. *vide* LANGLOIS, Hist. Arm., Vol. II, p. 263.

tion of the province of Erivan in the fifth century of our era and of the life led by the Armenian lords at that time:

".... The magnificent, renowned, and illustrious province of "Ararat produces every kind of plant; a fertile and fruitful province, "abounding in useful things, and well supplied with all that man needs "for a life of happiness and bliss. Its plains are vast and teem with game; "the surrounding mountains, pleasantly situated and offering abundant "pasture land, are full of ruminant, cloven-footed, and other animals. "From its mountain-tops flow plentiful streams that water the fields "needing no fertilizing; thus the city is assured of abundant bread and "wine, delicious sweet-tasting vegetables, and a variety of oil-yielding "seeds, for its large population. As one looks for the first time in the "direction of the mountain slopes and the smooth surfaces of the hills, "the multicolored flowers appear like embroidered cloth; their fertile "seeds enrich the sweet-smelling pastures where the abundant grass feeds "countless herds of donkeys and untamed deer. The scented flowers "exhale a keen fragrance that is health-giving both to the skillful bowmen "and huntsmen, and to the shepherds dwelling in the open field; the "atmosphere is strengthening and bracing to the mind.

". . These fields are found not only to provide for men's needs, "but they disclose to ardent seekers treasures in the bosom of the earth, "procuring, for profit and mundane enjoyment, also for regal display and "the royal exchequer, gold, copper, iron, and precious stones that the "craftsmen turn into majestic ornaments for monarchs, into jewels spark- "ling on tiaras, or into crowns or gold embroidery for vestments.

".... The rivers provide the table with fish of many kinds, both "large and small, and of all sorts of shapes and tastes ... The soil also "feeds innumerable birds for the pleasure and amusement of the hunting "noblemen, coveys of sweetly cooing partridges and francolins, fond of "steep places, hide in the rocks and nest in the nooks; while families of "wild birds, fat and appetizing, frequent all reedy places and hide in the "groves and bushes, and large fat aquatic birds feed on seeds and water- "weeds, together with countless other land and water fowl. Here the "satraps with their highborn offspring enjoy hunting with trap or net; "others pursue the wild ass or the deer, discussing bowmen and marksman- "ship among themselves; others again gallop after herds of stags and "buffaloes and excel as archers; still others armed like gladiators with "daggers drive large herds of boars down steep inclines and kill them

"Some of the satrap's sons with their tutors and friends supplement the "return banquet with various birds caught by the sparrow-hawk; everyone "thus comes happily laden from the hunt. The fishermen's children, "catching fish and swimming in the water, await the noblemen's return "as is customary, and running to meet them present them with their "catch, and with various wild birds and eggs they have found in the "river-islands The satraps, accepting with pleasure a part of their "offerings, reciprocate with a bountiful gift from what they have taken "hunting. Thus all, laden with good things, go to their homes. It is a "sight, for those who love fish and viands, to behold each festal board "piled high with the produce of the hunt.

QARA-BAGH & QARA-DAGH Leaving the plain of Erivan, the Araxes river bends off to the south-east and cuts the southern edge of the mountainous massif of which Lake Sevan is the centre. It passes then into very narrow gorges, leaving to its left Qara-bagh, or Black Garden, which is on Russian territory, and to its right Qara-dagh (the Black Mountain) belonging to Persia. In this region stood, before our era, the city of Naxuana.

Towards Julfa, the frontier station of the railroad that has for the last few years connected Tiflis and Tabriz, the valley is still some miles wide; but downstream it shrinks gradually until it soon narrows to the limits of the river-bed, the Araxes flowing most of the time alongside cliffs, hemmed in by high mountains Here and there, torrents rushing down steep slopes form small alluvial deltas in the main valley, whereon well-sheltered from the wind there grows the most luxuriant vegetation Wheat grows in these gorges surprisingly well, while vine-branches entwine the tallest trees, reach the top of huge-trunked walnut-trees, and spread out into gigantic wreaths above impenetrable thickets of centuries of growth. The villages are lost to sight under the verdure, buried in veritable forests of fruit-trees,—incomparable orchards replete with peach-trees, plum-trees, apricot-trees, fig-trees, pomegranate-trees, apple-trees, and pear-trees, bringing rich harvests to the inhabitants who dry the fruit in the sun and export it (not without considerable difficulty) to the towns of Azerbaidjan and Transcaucasia.

Each small valley of any note has its little town or hamlet; the houses, however, cleave to the rocks, for there is little ground available for cultivation, and it has to be most carefully parceled out and arranged in terraces upheld by walls of dry stones. The mountain torrents diverted at high altitudes send, through countless streamlets, their water to the smallest plot of land, cooling and enriching the earth.

These oases are often at quite a distance from one another, and their inhabitants are dependent for inter-communication on the good pleasure of the torrent. Today as in ancient times, they make for themselves in their villages all the necessities of life, woolen and cotton cloth, farming instruments, horse-saddles, pottery, and copper utensils. Nature provides them with cereals, vegetables, fruit, and cotton. The herds feeding on their mountains supply them with wool, meat, dairy products, and hides. Game abounds, and living in such affluence, they disdain the fish which swarm in the Araxes,—carp, salmon, sturgeon, all of them sometimes of giant size. As for their needs from outside, these are restricted to fire-arms, cartridges, powder, and salt. Such people are poor, some may say, because they have but little money, but really they are rich, very rich, for they fear neither hunger nor cold, and their needs are more bountifully supplied than those of our own townfolk at home.

At Qara-dagh as well as at Qara-bagh, the highest parts of the country are sometimes terribly bare; one sees hardly any but a few weakly fruit-trees around the villages, and for lack of wood the people are obliged to burn dried manure. However, in these regions of rigorous climate, most often fog-covered and wrapped in clouds, rains are frequent and the dew falls every day, ensuring abundant cereal crops which, with the care of the herds, form the mountaineers' sole occupation. There is nothing gloomier than these high tablelands, that are the same in all latitudes. Even in midsummer it is icy cold at night, and the damp piercing; the bare hills follow one another as far as the eye can reach, and the very few trees one finds bending before the wind around the villages remind one of the sparse woods of our ocean coasts in the parts of Brittany most exposed to the storms, or of the steppes in southern Russia.

Elsewhere, whether on Persian or Russian territory, the heights are covered with forests;—in the eastern Qara-dagh, for instance, where there are Armenian colonies; but in those districts too, the cultivation, restricted to the small valleys, is that of the colder countries. The vine grows with difficulty at these altitudes and can only endure the big winter frosts by being hidden underground for four or five months of the year,— as is the case moreover throughout the tableland of Iran. Due to the forests, that retain the moisture, springs abound. A small district to the east of lake Sevan is called Kirk-boulaq, "forty springs", on account of the many streams carrying their clear water from its mountains to the Gheuk-tchai, and this term would well fit many of the cantons of Qara-dagh, of the region of Kars, of that of the Joruk and many other districts of Armenia.

But Qara-bagh, a medley of wooded mountains, of abrupt peaks, and bare plateaus, with only the valleys at all fertile, is a region of very limited resources, where the inhabitants are necessarily restricted to the limits set by the scanty amount of soil fit for cultivation. Some writers, however, who surely have never gone outside their atlas, have considered this massif as the cradle of the whole Aryan race. This hypothesis is untenable, not only because Qara-bagh lacks space for any such expansion of a human family of this size, but also because all the data obtainable from languages, history, and archaeology, contradict it (1)

We shall see in the next chapter that before the arrival of the Armenians and the Tartars in these mountains, the peoples inhabiting them belonged most probably to an ethnic group that was non-Semitic and non-Aryan, akin to the Kartvelian family, i.e. to the Georgians, the Mingrelians, the Lazi, and other Caucasians of ancient stock, and that the same thing holds for most nations of the north of Western Asia, that the Urartaeans, the people of Nairi, the tribes who preceded the Iranians in Atropatenes, probably belonged to one and the same ethnic group. Those among these people who were not absorbed by the Semitic conquerors of Assyria, the Medes or the Armenians, were concentrated in the valleys and mountains of the Cyrus, of the Phasis, or the Joruk, and occupy the countries in which they are still to be found today. (2)

Archaeological discoveries prove that there were some Aryan invasions across the Lesser Caucasus in very ancient times, but those movements of people left no lasting colonies apart from that of the Ossetes from the south who took up their abode in the center of the Great Caucasus. These Aryans came from quite distant regions, some by the southern shore of the Caspian Sea, by the Derbend pass (3), others by the defile of Dariall. They all originated, however, from populations to the north-east, very far from Qara-bagh.

---

(1) In my Premieres Civilisations (p. 58 sq.), in 1909, I discussed this interesting question with all its ramifications.
(2) Cf. J. DE MORGAN, *Recherches sur les Origines des peuples du Caucase*, (1889), in which work I went in great detail into these movements of population in Transcaucasia, Persia and Armenia.
(3) In Persian. "which closes the door."

Some writers have imagined the Araxes valley to be one of the great highways that armies and migrations have been wont to follow, but that is an unfounded supposition, for even still today that route is impassable, and caravans consisting of a few mules only get into serious difficulties when they venture onto either of the river's banks. The massif crossed by the Araxes forms an almost impossible barrier between the lower valley and the middle section of the river, and served eminently as a natural protection for the Armenian capitals located in the country of Ararat; consequently, the men occupying the plain of Erivan have always striven to gain dominion over the inhabitants of these mountains.

THE PLAIN OF MOUGHAN Continuing its course, the Araxes, on leaving the above gorges, widens its valley and then comes out into a vast plain, the steppe of Moughan,— first being joined, however, on its right (3) by the Qara-Sou (4), a tributary from the plateau of Ardebil (5). In this low-lying plain the Araxes joins the Kura, and the two rivers, mingling as one, meander across their own alluvial soil before emptying their waters into the Caspian Sea (6). The Moughan plain, not the Araxes valley, was the former great thoroughfare between the civilized States of Asia and Eastern Europe, and it was also over this plain that the nomad tribes pouring into Transcaucasia by the passes of Derbend or those of Dariall were able to bear down on the old Asiatic empires. Both Persians and Romans, however, kept jealous watch always on the Caspian Gates and the "Gate of the Alans" (7). From Iberia, the legions reached the passes by going down the valley of the Cyrus, whilst from Iran this very important point was reached by way of the plateau of Ardebil, the valley of Qara-Sou (the country of the Cadusii), the steppe of Moughan, and Baku—the city of the Caspi, then renowned for its temple of fire, as it is today for its oil fields. The two rival powers, Rome and Persia, had agreed to a joint watch of the gateways to the East, but their concern did not extend to Armenia nor to the movement of armies and peoples between the northern steppes and Asia.

---

(3) Alt. of junction at Sudjeil: 623 ft.
(4) In Turkish: The Black River.
(5) Alt. 4,265 ft.
(6) The level of the Caspian is 88 feet below sea-level.
(7) Derbend and Dariall (Der-i-Alan, in Persian, the Gate of the Alans).

AZERBAIDJAN To the south-east of Ararat stretches the present Persian province of Azerbaïdjan, the Atropatenes of the ancient Persians, formerly the land of the Medes, and today inhabited by Turks, Armenians, Kurds, Mazdeans, and Chaldeans. Here Zoroaster is said to have been born, and it is here that originated the religion of the Avesta, a thousand years or so before the Ascanian people arrived in the Masis region. (1)

This province is fertile in some parts of its plains and in its valleys, but dry and barren in its mountains. It is an immense inland basin, the bottom of which is lake Urumiah (2), with Ararat in the north-west, and Sahend, a large volcanic cone with extinct crater, to the east. The chain of Kurdistan bounds Azerbaïdjan on the west, while to the east this province connects with the Iranian tableland properly speaking by the high valley of the Kizil-Ouzen or Sefidroud, the largest river in Persia, running into the Caspian Sea.

Lake Urumiah is fed by many streams and a few large rivers. (This lake was known to the ancients by the name of Mateanas.) Many of its tributaries, however, carry salt water, so that by degrees the lake has become a vast reservoir of salt which like the Dead Sea contains no life. In the dry season when its level sinks, it is ringed with saline deposits as white as snow, which shining in the burning sun, form a dazzling belt all around the blue surface of Mateanas.

In reality, Azerbaidjan like all the Persian plateau is a vast desert with very many scattered oases. Each spring, each stream, very skillfully diverted by the natives, spreads fertility through this wilderness. But, beyond the fields made arable by watering, there is only stony sunburnt ground, growing just a few scanty prickly plants. The mountains are dry, bare, often impregnated with salt, sometimes covered with patches of motley flowers of the brightest hues. Ruddy heights overlook the city of Tabriz. Elsewhere the hillsides show tiers of clay,—grey, white, yellow, purple, and green,—intermingled with beds of sandstone or limestone

---

(1) In northern Azerbaïdjan, there are no traces of neolithic man; the oldest burial places are dolmens of the Bronze Age; iron is found from the beginning of the 12th century B.C. Later, burial sites give way to Mazdean frames for exposing dead bodies. This change took place apparently about the 8th century at the time that Zoroaster's religion spread in Atropatenes, and the Median empire was formed. Hence, no further tombs are found until Moslem burial sites appear. (Cf. J. DE MORGAN, *Mission scientifique en Perse*, vol. IV, 1st part; H. DE MORGAN, *Memoires de la Delegation scientifique en Perse*, vol. VIII, p. 251 sq.).

(2) Alt. 4,000 ft.

as multicolored as an artist's palette. Then towards the Sahend are found thick flows of dark lava, and at the foot of that volcano immense heaps of yellowish phosphorites containing a medley of remains of entirely lost fauna: (1) elephants, rhinoceros, huge boars, prehistoric horses, monkeys, giant tortoises, and large birds, which lived hereabouts in the tertiary period. Whereas this was before the upheaval of the Iran plateau, when these lands scarcely emerged from the ocean had a climate like that of India today, here and there one finds, on this chaotic desert tableland, green valleys forested with poplars, white-trunked tebrizis, with compact upright branches; these trees planted in profusion are the country's only source of wood for building and heating. Tall, slim, and pale-leaved, their colorful forms add an original and cheerful note to the otherwise gloomy landscapes of Azerbaïdjan.

On the heights, on Sahend, and in the Kurdistan chain, are the summer pasture-lands of the nomads which have caused constant strife and barbarous wars between neighboring tribes for centuries and centuries. Down on the plain, however, it is over spring and streams that villages quarrel, for in these lands the smallest stream is looked on as most precious property; no single drop of water it supplies is wasted, and the Turkish, Persians, and Armenian farmers are pastmasters in the science of irrigation. Both the distribution of the water supply and the apportionment of pasture-land, it is true, are governed by customs dating back to the first settlements of the region; nevertheless respect for these customs rests upon force, and generally might is right.

The chief towns of the Medes in Atropatenes, Gazaka and Phraaspa, were situated far to the south in what were at that time the populous districts of Moukri and Gherrous in present-day Kurdistan, whereas the north was more sparsely inhabited, not offering sufficient natural resources for a large population.

PERSIAN KURDISTAN Between Dilman and Ouchnouw, on the western shore of lake Urumiah, at the foot of the Kurdish mountains abounding in streams, the whole country is verdant, and the highlands, shaded by forests, are

---

(1) Cf. R. DE MECQUENEM, *Annales de la Delegation scientifique en Perse*, concerning the fossil vertebrata of the Maragha deposit.

THE TOWN OF SAMOSATA AND THE EUPHRATES (Allegorical figure on an old coin.)

covered with fat pastures. The same is true of the region of the river Kialvi (the lower Zab), and all the western slope of these mountains, in Ottoman territory, is likewise wooded, well watered, and fertile in the valleys. But these districts have always been in the possession of the Medes or their descendants, the Kurds, and if they had sought to venture into them, the Armenians would have come up against countless difficulties. They therefore turned away from the mountains and colonized only the plain, around Dilman, Salmas, and Urumiah. The Ghâdertchaï is their extreme limit in the south.

The Armenians did not find in Atropatenes the same facilities to expand that they found in the countries north, west, and south-west of Ararat, and moreover they met, on the shores of lake Urumiah and in the region of the upper Zab, with the resistance of a powerful and warlike people. On the other hand, in Transcaucasia the older populations were divided, and to the west the Assyrian and Urartian provinces, disorganized by the downfall of their capital cities, were incapable of resistance. Armenian expansion in Atropatenes was therefore very limited; there were a few settlements, but these farming colonies were never more than sporadic, and the chief centers of the nation in Persia developed only later in the towns where commerce and industry gave the newcomers means of livelihood.

THE PLATEAU OF ERZERUM

To the west and south-west of the Masis stretches Turkish Armenia, the largest of the three modern political divisions of the Ascanian people. Its chief center is on a very high plateau containing today the towns of Erzerum (1), Van (2), ancient Thospia, Bitlis (3), ancient Batatesa, Mouch (4), all names renowned in history; the center of this province is the Bin-Gheul-dagh (5), a very squat mountain sending forth many streams through its countless gullies. It is on this plateau commanding the whole of Western Asia that the

---

(1) Alt. 6,168 ft.
(2) Alt. 5,413 ft.
(3) Alt. 5,020 ft.
(4) Alt. 4,593 ft.
(5) Alt. 10,500 ft.

most famous rivers of early legends take their rise. The Araxes, just mentioned, the western Euphrates (or Qara-tchaï in Turkish) which rises not more than 25 miles north of the city of Erzerum near the village of Kizail-Kilissa (1), the eastern Euphrates or Mourad-tchaï, the ancient Arsanias, flowing down from the Agri-dagh (2), the height forming the frontier outpost of Russian territory prior to 1914, and finally the Tigris composed of a hundred or more streams issuing from the great land eleva-

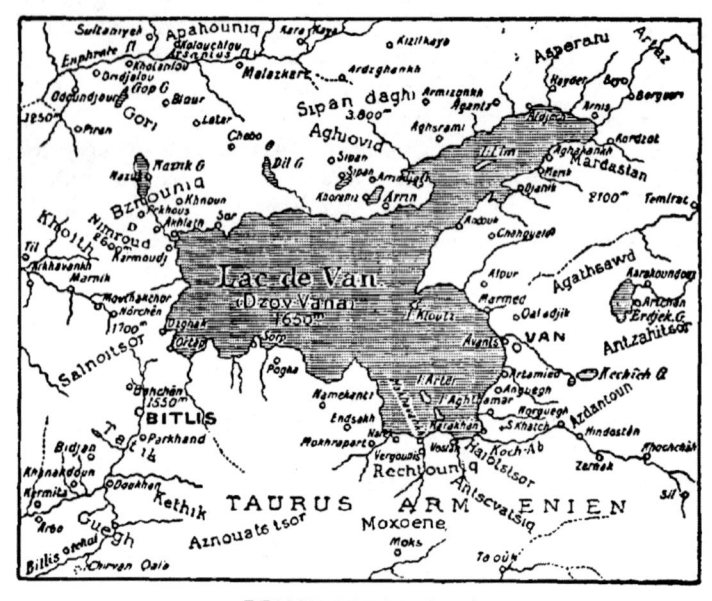

REGION OF LAKE VAN

tion situated to the south of lake Van, namely, the Armenian Taurus.

Just as each Russian and Persian province of Armenia has its lake, so has Turkish Armenia,—the Dzov Vana of the Armenians, the lake Van of the Turks and Europeans, and the Thospitis (3) of the ancient world, a vast sheet of slightly salty water, 75 miles long, and 56 wide in its

---

(1) The Yellow Church, in Turkish. Alt. 7,440 ft.
(2) Alt. 10,630 ft.
(3) Alt. 5,413 ft.

southern part, fed by the massif of Ararat, the Kurdistan chain, and the Armenian Taurus. Here formerly, on the eastern shore of lake Thospitis stood the capital of the kings of Urartu, and here upon the rocks the Sardur and Argistis dynasties engraved the story of their exploits against their terrible subjects of Ashur, against the inhabitants of Media. The territories of these rulers then extended from the regions around Gheuk-tchai on the north and the Kurdistan mountains on the east, as far as and sometimes beyond the Armenian Taurus on the south. These lords of Uraitu were mighty monarchs; they waged unceasing war often victoriously, against their eastern and southern neighbors. Their country, moreover, despite its cold climate due to high altitudes, produced all the supplies needful for the life of a State in those times. Its valleys are fertile, its pasture-lands rich, and its mountains well wooded and abounding in metals.

If the traveler crosses the pass of Kel-i-chin (1) by the path leading from Ouchnouw to Revandouz, he enters Turkish Kurdistan, an uncultivated but physically favored land, covered with immense forests of sweet acorn-bearing oak-trees. Whereas if he leaves Persia by the passes of Khoï, he meets only with meadows and well watered farm-lands. This is because in spite of its centuries and centuries of neglect, in spite of a lamentable government, the region is still one of the most fertile of Asiatic Turkey, thanks to the industry of the Armenians who since they arrived in the land have always striven to develop the natural riches of the soil. The new-comers alone endeavored to improve their native land, whereas the pillaging Kurds and the lazy Kartvelians made no attempt to enhance their province, and the only ambition of the Arabian or Turkish masters was to live off the work of their Christian serfs.

LAZITAN AND THE PONTIC ALPS

To the north-west of the Armenian plateau, the river Tcharoukh of the Turks, the Jorokh of the Armenians, makes a deep separation between the lands of the Christian Aryans and those of the Moslem Lazi. This stream, rising in the neighborhood of Baibourt (2), runs parallel to the Black Sea coast, crosses the Parkhal mountains, the ancient Paryadres, near Artvin (3) and empties itself into

---

(1) In Kurdish: the Blue Stone, a name taken from a stele of diorite rock placed there once by a king of Urartu.
(2) Alt 5,085 ft.
(3) Alt. 2,100 ft.

the Black Sea a little to the south-west of Batum, after traveling about 220 miles. It is a rushing torrent from its source to its mouth; at a hundred or more different points it has dug itself deep and impassable gorges, and following its valley it is easy to understand the important part it played as a ditch dug by Nature between the Armenian States and the Greco-Roman territory of the Pontus.

Formerly the Pontic Alps north of the Tcharoukh belonged to tribes called the Macrones and the Moschi; today the Lazi occupy these mountains, and it is quite certain that the Lazi are none other than the descendants of the tribes that Xenophon's Greeks once visited, for these people, speaking a Caucasian tongue, undoubtedly are still dwelling in the land of their ancestors.

There is nothing more interesting, for anyone who is fortunate enough to be able to visit Lazistan and to read once more the *Anabasis* as he makes his way through this mountain chaos, than to observe the customs of these uncivilized peoples. Except for their religious beliefs, no change has come to the life of these mountaineers during the twenty-five centuries separating us from the time of Cyrus the Younger. The villages are still today as they were when the Ten Thousand passed through, and the people have remained just as fierce and inhospitable as they were in the past. On this side Armenian expansion came up against the precipices of the Tcharoukh, and at the giant wall of the Pontic Alps (of which many peaks reach 13,000 feet) met with inpenetrable forests and, above all, with warlike, energetic inhabitants absolutely determined to drive back any foreign intruders.

It is because of the Lazi on her north-west border that Armenia never had any outlet to the sea, and this impossibility of having direct communication with the centers of Greek civilization played an important and baneful rôle in her destiny. For had they been in possession of the coast, had they settled at the mouth of the Tcharoukh, at Rizeh, or at Trebizond, the Armenians would have been able to take part in the general life of the Greek world and Armenia would have formed a great State able to resist the mighty Eastern and Western empires centuries before the Romans appeared in Western Asia. To understand what Armenia would have become in Roman times for instance, one need only read the annals remaining to us of the great Mithidrates and other rulers of his dynasty; for the kings of the Pontus accomplished great feats, and yet the people under them were less gifted than the Armenian nation.

CLIMATE OF THE ARMENIAN PLATEAU

Like all high-lying lands, the climate of the plateau of Erzerum is very severe. The winter is frigid, and the very deep snow remains on the ground for months. On the other hand, due to the latitude, the summers are torrid, and the great heat in conjunction with the plenteous water supply and the natural fertility of the soil, make Armenia a fruitful land.

As in the northern plains of Europe, vegetation grows very fast, and it can be said that, like in Scandinavia, "you can hear the wheat grow."

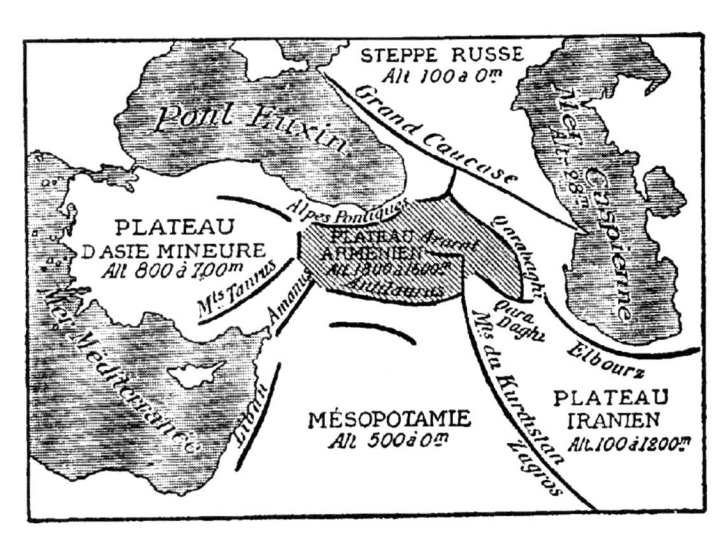

POSITION OF THE ARMENIAN PLATEAU COMPARED TO
NEIGHBORING COUNTRIES

As for the orchards, they are as fruitful as any of our European gardens, for the snow covering the mountain-tops both in Kurdistan and in the Armenian Taurus remains throughout the summer and the gardens can be well watered during the whole dry season.

To the north of Erzerum, in the upper part of the western Euphrates, are immense marshes locally called "sazluk." These expanses of stagnant water were once more extensive still, before men cut down the forests and stripped most of the hillsides. These earlier marshes have left in most of the valleys a black humus that is rich in organic remains and yields without manuring luxuriant yearly crops.

THE ARMENIAN STRONGHOLD But the unusual position of the Armenian plateau affects not only the climate of the region and the soil's generous productivity; it gives its inhabitants a place of special importance from a political and military standpoint, with regard to the districts of Iran and the large Turkish valleys lying below the level of this massif. Armenia is in itself a veritable fortress commanding all Western Asia together with the great arteries of the two Euphrates and the Tigris rivers. This prime characteristic has always made it a citadel coveted by neighboring States. Assyria was for very many centuries at war with the rulers of Van, when the kings of Urartu controlled the mountain region that later became

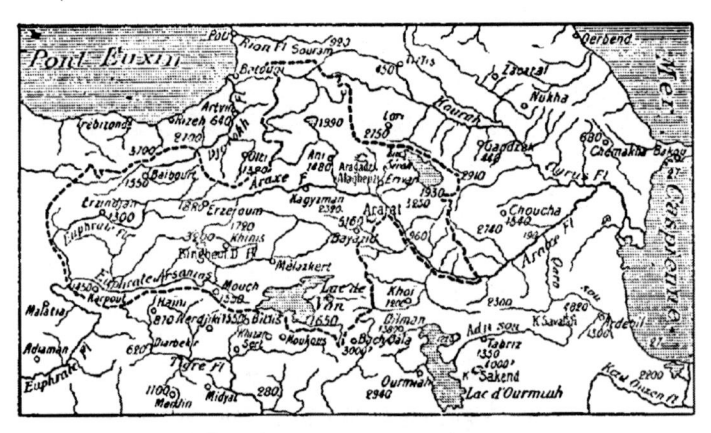

THE ARMENIAN STRONGHOLD

the realm of the Armenians. A formidable wall, the Taurus of Armenia, standing between the Ninivites and their northern enemies, then protected the kingdom of Van against the assaults of Ashur. Later on, when the Parthians and Sassanids were contending with the Romans for the

— 35 —

overlordship of Armenia, the ramparts of Roman territory were at Nisibis, Tigranocerta, and Amida, at the southern foot of the Armenian Taurus, but the political center and strategic base were further north on the plateau itself. The great Theodosius (1) had no illusions regarding the importance of the Armenian citadel, when he ordered one of his legates to build right in the middle of this region the city of Erzerum which ever since has been the heart of Armenia. Moses of Khoren (2) has left us an account of the founding of Theodosiopolis (Erzerum) along with a description of the site selected by the Romans:

"General Anatolus, upon receiving the order from the Emperor, "came into our land; he traveled over many of our provinces and de-"cided to build in the District of Karin, (1) the center of the country, "possessing a well-watered, rich, and fertile soil. This center is not very "far from where the springs of one part of the Euphrates take their rise, "and these springs in their quiet flow spread out into a vast marsh or "inland sea. (2) There were great quantities of fish and of all kinds of "birds, and the inhabitants lived entirely on eggs. The edges of this marsh "are covered with rushes and reeds. The plains grow grass and seed-"fruits. The mountains abound with cloven-footed and ruminating an-"imals. The herds breed rapidly, are large and strong, and fatten won-"derfully.

"At the foot of this pleasant mountain (3) are many clear springs. "This is the point which Anatolus chose for the site of the city; he sur-"rounded it with a wide ditch, laid very deep the foundations of the "walls, and erected on the ramparts a number of tall and tremendous "towers, the first of which he called Theodosia in honor of Theodosius. "Further out he built other towers with projections like ships' prows, and "he also dug passages opposite the mountain. He did the same on the "side of the plain towards the north; and both on the east and on the "west he constructed round-shaped towers. In the middle of the city, on "an eminence, he built a number of warehouses, and called the spot "Augusteum in honor of Augustus (Theodosius). He conveyed water

---

(1) 379-395 A.D.
(2) Vol. III, LIX; transl vol. II, p. 166.
(1) Caranitis of Pliny.
(2) Sazlouk of the Turks, i.e. place of the reeds
(3) Top dagh or "Cannon mountain", of the Turks; sourp-khatch or "the holy cross" of the Armenians.

"to different points by underground conduits He filled the city with arms "and troops, and gave it the name of Theodosiopolis, so that its name "should immortalize that of Theodosius. Finally, Anatolus erected edifices "of freestone over the thermal springs. (4)

The perpetual wars which the Armenian people had to wage to preserve their independence, together with the harshness of their native climate, made them a race of sturdy, hardy, and brave warriors, whose love of country and national freedom increased in proportion as they shed their blood preserving their heritage To this special situation of Armenia is due the ardent patriotism in the heart of every Armenian. It is also the reason why for centuries the kingdom of Urartu lasted, while all the great Eastern States fell successively, under the Assyrian assault. In this history, the reader will see the Armenian nation ever fighting to keep their land, their freedom, their traditions, and their religion, and ever being attacked from every point of the compass because fate had placed them in the most vital strategic position of all Asia.

During the great wars of the Romans and the Byzantines against the Persians, hostilities almost always broke out in Armenia where, if the Empire was directing its chief effort against Ctesiphon, the Armenian armies fighting alongside the legions constituted a threat on the north to the King of Kings, compelling him to divide his army. Was not the capture of Erzerum by the Russians in 1878, and again recently, regarded as a fatal blow to Turkey? This peculiar position of the Armenian homeland explains not only the main phases of this valiant people's history, but their development of physical and moral character.

SOUTHERN ARMENIA Although at different periods the Armenian domain greatly varied in extent, it appears (except for the time of Tigranes the Great) never to have gone further south than the left bank of the Tigris between Diarbekir and Djeziret-ibn-Omar, and in the Armenian Taurus the Armenians seem to be a minority compared to the Kurdish population. Moreover the vast mountain massif of the Djoudi-dagh at the south of lake Van has hardly been explored geographically A few travelers at the most have noted the general direction of the main streams running down from it. Two large rivers, tributaries of the Tigris, take their rise in these mountains.

---

(4) Cf PROCOPIUS, *De Aedif.*, vol. III, p. 5. Karin of the Armenians, Erzerum of the Turks (Arz-Rum or Arz-er-Rum, "the citadel of the Greeks").

namely, the Bohtân-tchaï into which there runs the Bitlis torrent, and the Khabour, issuing from the heights of the Persian frontier, at about the latitude of Dilman. Between these two rivers the maps show nothing; the reason is that this massif is inhabited by the most inhospitable tribes of these parts, by the notorious massacring Kurds who, let loose in recent years against the Armenians, descended on Bitlis, Van, and Mouch, with their adjacent countryside, and spread death and devastation in the villages and towns.

All the mountain region of the left bank of the Tigris, from Diarbekir to the outskirts of Bagdad, is still steeped in the most frightful savagery. Every valley, every little district, has its independent Kurdish tribe, often at war with its neighbors. They are all more or less emancipated from Turkish or Persian authority; many have never been subdued. So much is this the case that officials of the Shah or the Sultan hardly ever venture into this labyrinth of mountains, rocks, forests, precipices, and deep gorges, where the Kurds, far from the outside world and sure of impunity for their crimes, live to themselves on their loot, maintain the fierce instincts of their ancestors, the Carducii, and repulse any foreign interference, be the intruders coreligionists or not. One can easily understand the enthusiasm with which the bloody orders of Abdul-Hamid and the Young Turks were greeted in these mountains; it was a terrible revival of barbarity, a delirium of murder, pillage, and sadism.

TURKISH KURDISTAN The center of Kurdistan is indeed in this vast region, where the tribes, (whose annals have been written by Sherif nâmeh) (1), have kept their ancient character and customs with undiminished harshness and abandon. These clans encroach widely on Persian territory, towards Moukri, Serdecht, and Sineh, in the Avroman region; but they occupy mainly the Armenian Taurus and the mountains from which flow the two Zab rivers, the Zâb-âla or upper Zab (2), and the Zâb-el-asfal, or lower Zab (3) This country is one of the chief recruiting sources for the Turkish government of its famous Hamidiyehs, notorious for the horrors they commit daily against Christians.

---

(1) Cf. Transl. Desire CHAMROY (St. Petersburg).
(2) Zabas major
(3) Zabas minor

WESTERN ARMENIA Towards the west, in the valleys of the two Euphrates, the Armenians expanded more vigorously than towards the south. There, in the regions once crossed by their forefathers as they made their way to Ararat, they founded very many flourishing colonies, both in the open country and in the small towns and cities. One need mention only the "Armenistans" of Erzindjan on the eastern Euphrates and Kharput on the Arsanias, to have a proper idea of the expansive force of the Armenian race. The scattered colonies linking Greater Armenia with Armeno-Cilicia are very numerous; they constitute a sort of archipelago between Erzerum and the mountains of the Amanus Everywhere on this long route, these Christians founded villages deep in Moslem lands, and they parceled out the soil, in spite of the dangerous proximity of Kurds, Turks, and Circassians. Most of the tributaries of the Euphrates run in fertile valleys, and these lands had been generally abandoned when gradually during the centuries the Armenians came and developed them.

In the principal valley, the arable lands do not follow accurately the river banks, but crop up in islets of all sizes, running like a string of oases from one bank of the river to the other according to the whim of the current Elsewhere the river forms rapids, and rushes through deep gorges which are often flanked with high cliffs. One of these gorges, the Kamagh-Boghaz (1) recently acquired sad renown. Turks and Kurds, at the orders of their Stamboul masters, massacred thousands of Armenian women, children, and old folk, a harmless multitude driven out of their towns and villages and pushed forward like cattle to these rocks, the scene of their martyrdom. Many of these unfortunate people, rather than wait for the fate their executioners had for them, put an end to their sufferings in the turbulent waters of the Euphrates.

The Euphrates is not navigable throughout its upper course, either its western or its eastern branch (2). Only after Biredjik, or rather after Meskeneh, (3) can boats be used. Above this spot, the river runs violently in a bed full of rocks and interrupted by falls and rapids.

Usually vessels leaving Meseknch go adrift down the river, not without some difficulty, and stop at Feloudja (4), a small village near Bag-

---
(1) Alt 3,510 ft. at 25 miles downstream from Erzindjan where the altitude is about 4,250 ft
(2) The junction of the two Euphrates (alt. 2,300 ft.) is 22 miles south-east of Arabkir and 25 miles west of Kharput.
(3) A place on the left river, 38 miles west of Aleppo.
(4) At 38 miles west of Bagdad.

dad; the Euphrates current is so strong that no boat can go upstream. On arriving at Feloudja these vessels unload their goods, and are then taken to pieces, and the wood is taken on camels to the capital of the Caliphs and there offered for sale. As for the crew, they have a twenty or twenty-five-day journey overland back to their country.

On the middle Tigris, navigation, downstream only of course, is carried on by means of keleks or rafts of planks held together by a cross-work of tree-branches and supported by inflated water-skins. This mode of transportation is as old as history itself in these lands, and is depicted in Assyrian carvings. It is used between Diarbekir and Bagdad, for only beyond Samara or Eski-Bagdad, not far from Harun-al-Raschid's city, is two-way navigation on the Tigris possible for boats and shallow-draught steamers

Thus we see that the rivers coming down from the Erzerum plateau never served the Armenians in their political or commercial expansion to the south and south-west This fact not only has an important bearing on the growth of the Armenian people's outward connections, but it played a vital part in the history of Western Asia, first in checking the westward movement of Chaldean civilization, and then by confining the regions of the two great rivers to outlets on the East, i.e. towards still barbaric countries, and this at the time when the Mediterranean countries had become the center of human progress.

When Julian the Philosopher left Antioch at the head of his army to attack the Persians, he took the road to Ctesiphon, following the left bank of the Euphrates, whilst the ships laden with his troops' military supplies were carried downstream, and when he reached Sapor's capital, knowing that none of his vessels could return to Syria, he set fire to the fleet. The return journey of the legions, after their Emperor's death, was a downright disaster.

When King Chosroes went out against the Roman provinces of Syria, against Antioch or Jerusalem, he and his transports moved overland, and so it was always whenever Asiatics set out to conquer Phoenicia or Egypt. The inhabitants of Coelo-Syria seem to have been in the best position, but it was still a precarious privilege, for the forty days march at least (1) between Antioch and Ctesiphon, offered serious difficulties whether for advancing armies or for trade-caravans, on these sometimes torrid, sometimes frigid deserts. These same difficulties blocked all northern peoples in their desire to obtain lands enjoying milder climates. The Armenians were

---

(1) **About 600 miles.**

no exception to the general law; they stopped at the latitude of the middle Tigris and only occasionally, at the time of the conquests of Tigranes the Great, did they push as far as the northern limits of the Sindjar. The unfortunates who today are suffering thirst in the desert near Deïr-el-Zor and Damascus, driven from their native land by the Turks into these wastes whence there is no return, are parked in districts that were never known to the Armenians.

FRONTIERS OF ARMENIA   At different times, the extent of the Armenian homeland has varied greatly. The Achaemenian inscriptions (1) show this nation as already settled on the Erzerum plateau; but only in the first centuries of our era was its geographical position accurately stated in writings remaining extant. The geographer Strabo (2) has left us quite a clear idea of what Armenia consisted of in his time. (3)

"Protected on the south by the [Armenian] Taurus," he wrote, "Armenia is bordered on the east by Greater Media [the Kurdistan of "Moukri and Sineh] and by Atropatenes [Azerbaïdjan]. To the north "it is bounded partly by the portion of the Parachoathras chain situated

ARMENIA IN ROMAN TIMES

---

(1) Trilingual inscriptions of Darius at Bisoutun (Behistun).
(2) Strabo died in the reign of Tiberius (A.D. 14-37).
(3) STRABO, Geogr. vol. XI, p. XIV-I.

"above the Caspian Sea [western Elburz], by Albania [Daghestan] and
"Iberia [Georgia],—together with the Caucasus that includes these two
"latter provinces and which, connecting on the very frontiers of Armenia
"with the Moschian and Colchaean mountains [eastern Lesser Caucasus]
"extends actually into the lands of the Tibareni [towards Qara-Hissar]
"and by Mount Paryadres [Pontic Alps of Lazistan] and the Skydises
"[towards Kharput] as far as Lesser Armenia [to the west of the western
"Euphrates] and the valley of the Euphrates, which prolongs the separa-
"tion between Armenia on the one side and Cappadocia [Sivas] and
"Commagene [east of the Amanus] on the other."

According to his invariable custom, the Cappadocian geographer not only describes the appearance of the country (which has, moreover, undergone no great change for the last two thousand years), but he sets forth also, briefly, the progress made by the Armenians in their country from the time the Persians were subdued by the armies of Alexander the Great to the date of his incomparable work.

"The Kingdom of Armenia," he says, "owed its extension chiefly to
"the conquests of Artaxias and Zariadras, former lieutenants of Antiochus
"the Great, who on the fall of their master were called to reign, the one
"over Sophene [the eastern bank of the Euphrates], Antisene, Oromandris,
"and the surrounding districts [Erzerum plateau],—the other over the
"province of Artaxata [Erivan province]. These two by their united
"efforts captured in succession: Caspiana [the plain of Moughan and
"region of Baku] from the Medes; Phaunitis and Bassoropeda [northern
"slope of the Lesser Caucasus] from the Iberians; the whole foot of Mt.
"Paryadres [Pontic Alps] together with Chorzene [between the two
"branches of the upper Euphrates], and beyond the Cyrus, Gogarene
"[Gougarq or Gougarkh of the Armenians] from the Chalybi and the
"Mossinaecians; Carenitis and Derxene [high western Euphrates] two
"provinces today adjacent to Lesser Armenia if not parts thereof, from
"the Cataones; Akilisene [north part of Commagene] and all the dis-
"tricts of the Anti-Taurus from the Syrians; and finally Taronitis [Taron
"of the Armenians, south of Lake Van],—all of which countries, on ac-
"count of this grouping together under one rule speak today the same
"language."

Undoubtedly the Armenians' glorious periods under Artaxias and Zariadras, and Tigranes the Great, are those of their country's greatest expansion. Numerous colonies were founded in the vast States of those rulers, colonies so large and that became so prosperous that the Armenian language was spoken throughout the provinces listed by Strabo. Most of the Armenians' present-day centers certainly owe their origin to the above conquests, for they are all within the regions mentioned by the Greek geographer, and any other colonies founded in various valleys after the first century of our era were, as regards Greater or Lesser Armenia, attributable only to the older homelands.

THE PROVINCES OF ARMENIA The subdivisions of Armenia have varied at different periods, and their names have undergone changes. In most provinces the Greco-Latin names were succeeded by the Armenian ones of native writers. The latter are very little known, and need to be explained and their corresponding ancient or modern districts indicated.

Greater Armenia consisted in the Middle Ages of fifteen provinces, the frontiers of which have greatly varied but which on the whole correspond to definite regions:

1) Upper Armenia, comprising Derxene and Akilisene of ancient times, included the region of the upper Jorokh and upper Euphrates, where we find today the towns of Baïbourt, Gumuch-Hâné, and Erzindjan.

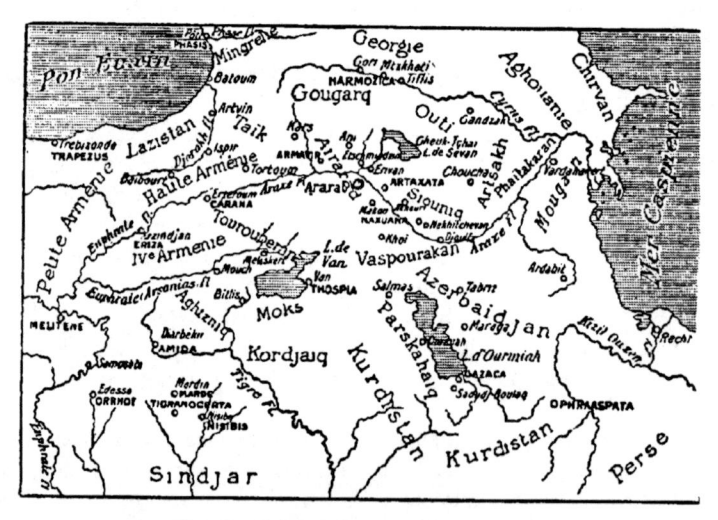

PROVINCES OF GREATER ARMENIA

2) Sophene, or Fourth Armenia of the Greeks, bounded on the west by the middle Euphrates, and crossed by the eastern Euphrates (the Arsanias). Its chief city today is Kharput.

3) Aghtznik, extending south to the upper Tigris (Diarbekir), included Arzanene (Arm-Aitzn), the cities of Martyropolis and Tigranocerta,—and today the town of Mouch.

4) Tourouberan, the ancient Chorzianene, comprises the whole Erzerum region as far as the north shore of lake Van.

5) Mock, or ancient Gordyene, probably the Moxoene of Ammian Marcellinus, including the northern slope of the Armenian Taurus, as far as lake Van, with Bitlis and Van as its towns.

6) Kordjaiq, on the left bank of the Tigris, south of the Armenian Taurus, as far as the upper Zab. Djeziret-ibn-Omar is the chief town of the region today.

7) Parskahaiq, or Perso-Armenia, a region straddling the Kurdistan chain, belonging today partly to Persia;—includes Salmas, Urumiah, and the western bank of lake Urumiah.

8) Vaspourakan, to the south-east of Ararat (Persia and Turkey) with the towns of Maiand, Khoi, and Bayazid.

9) Siouniq, the Sissakan of the Persians, Syrians, and Arabs, to the north of the Araxes, includes the Russian mountain districts of Chahrour, Daralagheuz, Djahouk, and Ghapan, and the towns of Nakhitchevan, Djulfa, and Ordubad.

10) Artsakh or Qara-bagh of our time, with Choucha its chief town.

11) Paitakaran comprising the promontory formed by the junction of the Kurah and Araxes rivers in the middle of the Moughan plain. In this direction the Armenians sometimes pushed temporarily as far as the Caspian shore.

12) Outi, comprising the northern slope of the mountains of Gheuk-

tchaï (Russian districts of Kazakhi, Chamchadil and Airioun) as far as the bank of the Cyrus, with Iclisavetopol (Gandzek) its chief modern town. The Greeks called this province Otene.

13) Gougarq, the Gogarene of the Greeks, a mountainous country on the upper course of the Cyrus, north of the Araxes, the region of Kars, Alexandropol, Ardahan, and Artvin.

14) Taiq, a district situated between that of Erzerum and the right bank of the Jorokh.

15) Aïrarat (Ararat), the great Armenian center of Erivan and Etchmiadzin. Here stood the cities of Artaxata, Armavir, Bagaran, and Ani.

GREATER AND LESSER ARMENIA

As we have seen, the ancient world divided Armenia into two distinct States, Armenia Major or Greater Armenia and Armenia Minor or Lesser Armenia. The latter was bounded on the north by the kingdom of Pontus, on the south by Cappadocia, and on the west by the district of Polemon. It included the regions to the left of the western Euphrates as far up as its junction with the Arsanias. This State had therefore nothing to do with Armeno-Cilicia, which did not exist until the 11th century of our era. The name of Lesser Armenia cannot, consequently, be applied to the Rupenian kingdom for which the name of New Armenia is much more appropriate.

NEW ARMENIA OR SISSOUAN

At the present time, we find the Armenian population decreasing as, leaving Erzerum, we go towards the Euphrates, and increasing as we leave the right bank of the Euphrates and descend from Kharput towards the Cilician shores of the Mediterranean. The reason is that we are now entering the last of the Armenian kingdoms, New Armenia, called Sissouan by the natives. Most European writers call it Armeno-Cilicia, but improperly so, for in the attempt thus to join together two periods of the country's history, they are committing a grievous anachronism.

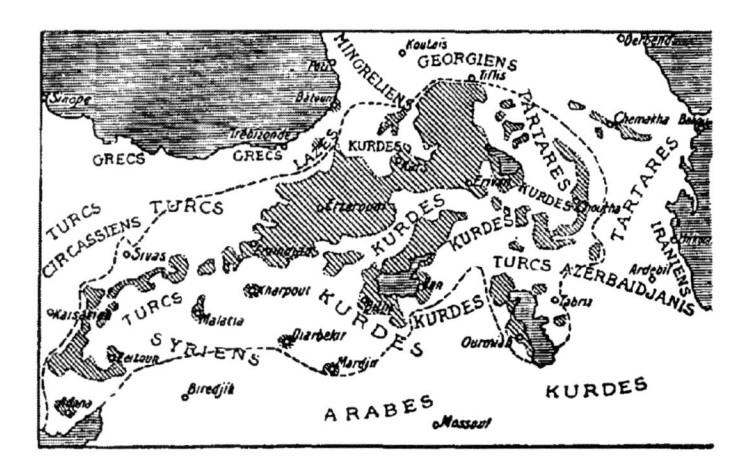

MAP OF THE REGIONS OF WESTERN ASIA INHABITED BY THE ARMENIANS

..... Regions inhabited by the Armenians.
(Shaded) :—Districts where the Armenians are more than a third of the population.

Marasch, Zeitoun, Adana, Sis, Hadjin, Dortyol, etc. are the chief Christian centers of this country. In those valleys, on the southern slope of the great Asiatic peninsula, are preserved to this day the remains of the Armenian population over whom reigned, after the Rupenian founders of the kingdom became extinct, the French dynasty of Lusignan,

New Armenia, which came into existence shortly after the disaster of the Bagratids of Ani, had like all eastern States its days of good and ill fortune, and its frontiers varied according to the success attending its arms. Nevertheless its average extent was at least equal to that of the smaller European countries such as Switzerland, Belgium, Holland, or Denmark.

New Armenia occupied a little over 300 miles of the Mediterranean coast, from the Gulf of Alexandretta to near the mouth of the river known to the ancients as the Melas, and to the Turks as the Manargaï-tchaï. Its northern borders, which were always rather vague, seem to have been the Taurus watershed, whilst the Amanus Mountains were its eastern frontier.

Large streams water the plains lying between the two chains, as well as the coastal region. On the west there is first the Gheuk-sou (or blue water), the Calycadmus of ancient times; then, further east, the river Tarsus or Saïhoum, the former Sarus, and the river Djihan, known to the Greeks as the Pyramis, not to speak of a large number of rivulets descending from the Taurus and Amanus chains.

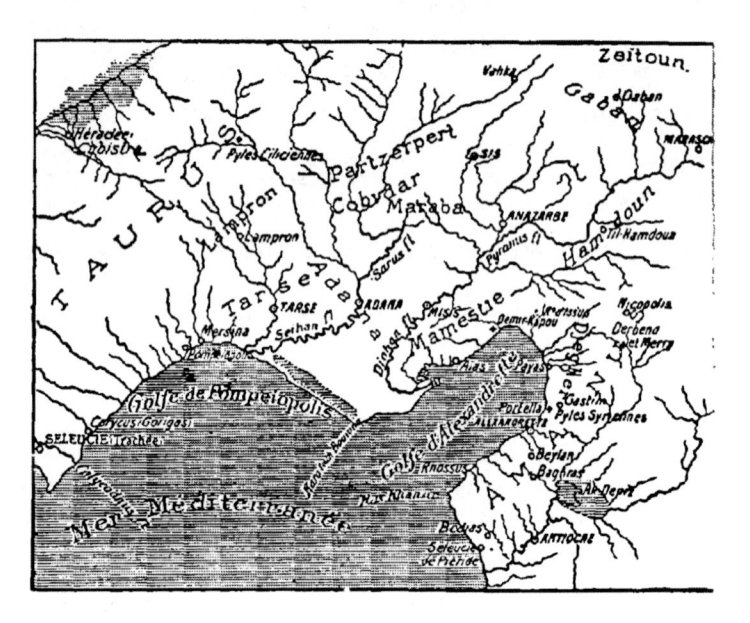

MAP OF CILICIA

It has so happened that the Armenians have always been connected with lands of fame, for, after losing their independence in their Ararat homeland, they settled around the famous Cilician Gates through which Alexander the Great passed, on his way to his victory in Issus that was to spread Greek civilization throughout the world.

The new home then chosen by the Armenians is a land blessed of heaven; abundantly watered, the fertility of its plains, the coolness of its southward-exposed valleys, make it a veritable paradise on earth. In

Cilicia, as moreover in Syria, everything grows in profusion: the vine, the olive-tree, the pomegranate and orange trees, fill the orchards along with every variety of our European fruit-trees. The farmer has two crops yearly, and the mountains also, above their shaded sides of century-old forests of cedar and pine, have rich grass-lands on their summits that are often over thirteen thousand feet high. Only indeed some evil genius could have surrendered these regions to the indifference of the Turks, cutting short the development of such bountiful natural riches.

THE RIVER CYDNUS
(Allegorical figure on an old coin.)

For the first time in the course of their long national existence, the Armenians of Cilicia were able to maintain direct intercourse by sea with the peoples of the west, and if fate had allowed they would have developed in a parallel direction and under the same influences as the peoples of Europe. During the Crusades, the Armenian people, though of Eastern origin, developed rapidly and parted company with the Byzantine world which for so many centuries had hindered their progress, and which perished, the victim of its own obstinacy and ancient prejudices.

THE RIVER AND CITY OF TARSUS
(Allegorical figure on a coin of Emperor Commodus.)

But the Armenians were not the only possessors of the rich lands of Cilicia. Before they arrived, the country was already inhabited, and after their own kingdom fell, the Turkish rulers encouraged Moslems to settle in the region. Today in the valleys and plains are to be found not only Armenians but Turks, Kurds (9th century emigrants), Arabs, and, in the mountains, Turkoman nomads along with uncivilized tribes of unknown origin. There are also half-breeds, part Armenian and part Kurd, who have become Moslems and never leave the mountains and forests. Due to this mixture of uncivilized clans, there is very little security in the Taurus and the Amanus mountains.

THE RIVER PYRAMIS
(Allegorical figure on an old coin.)

THE THREE ARMENIAS

Consequently, the regions inhabited by the Armenian nation consist historically speaking of three distinct parts, the first two of which, Greater and Lesser Armenia, dating from ancient times, are often merged subsequent to Alexander the Great, while the third, New Armenia, dates from the Middle Ages. It follows, therefore, that the history of the Armenians divides into phases that correspond to its geographical sections. The first part comprises the annals of Ancient Armenia (Greater and Lesser) and starts with the Achaemenian period (6th century B.C.) and continues until the Moslem conquests of the 10th century of our era. The second part deals with New Armenia, the records of which cover several centuries of the Middle Ages and are contemporaneous with the Crusades. Finally for both Armenias there comes the period of martyrdom, of the Mohammedan yoke, which still exists, alas! The very conditions under which the Armenian people have existed throughout the centuries, account for the fact that although mostly at the present time quartered in their ancient territory of Ararat, they are also spread out, more or less densely according to location, from the banks of the Kurah to the shores of Cilicia, and from the Black Sea coast to the borders of the Mesopotamian desert.

THE CITY OF ANAZARBUS
(Allegorical figure on an old coin)

CHAPTER II

Origin of the Armenian people. — Sojourn of the Armeno-Phrygians in Thrace. — Their crossing into Asia. — Their march to the Ararat country. — Conquest of the Erzerum plateau. — The Haikian patriarchs. — The legendary dynasty. — Median ascendency. — The kingdom of Armenia under Achaemenian suzerainty. — The Macedonian conquest. — The dynasty of Phraataphernes. — Rule of the Seleucids of Syria.

We are indebted to narratives of ancient writers, interpreted in the light of inscriptions and archaeological research, for our success of recent years in disentangling at great pains the earliest movements of the great peoples of antiquity from the mass of legends surrounding them. This fresh light on those beginnings presents in a new aspect humanity's stirrings at the dawn of modern civilization. The first strivings of Chaldaea, of Elam, and of Egypt are revealed with sufficient clarity to warrant the assertion today that six or seven thousand years have elapsed since the start of our own civilization and that its first beneficent waves emanated from those Asiatic and African homes. Men then had just discovered how to record their thoughts in writing and were emerging from the barbaric era wherein memory had no aid beyond rudimentary representations of objects considered worthy of remembrance.

But although those nations that were able to write have handed down to us the story of their early pulsations, it is unfortunately not so as regards all peoples. The Greeks and the Italiotes were quite late in the adoption of writing, and to many nations this ability, the most needed for the spread of progress, remained unknown until the beginning of the Christian era, in some cases to this day. The Armenians are among those who long remained in ignorance of writing, and did we not have some scattered indications concerning their existence, from stray mentions by non-Armenian writers, we should be utterly without knowledge of their origin, just as we are today with regard to the Pelasgians, the Etruscans, the Basques, and so many other peoples whose names crop up constantly in history. Fortunately some passages of Herodotus, clear and exact like all that that great historian wrote, give us valuable affirmations concerning the beginnings of the Armenian people, and assist us in assessing the information we can glean from later writers, from archaeology, or from general historical data.

ARMENIAN BEGINNINGS In his enumeration of the Persian army, at the time the Great King crossed the Hellespont on his onward march to Attica, Herodotus states concerning the contingents which Xerxes was given by Armenia:

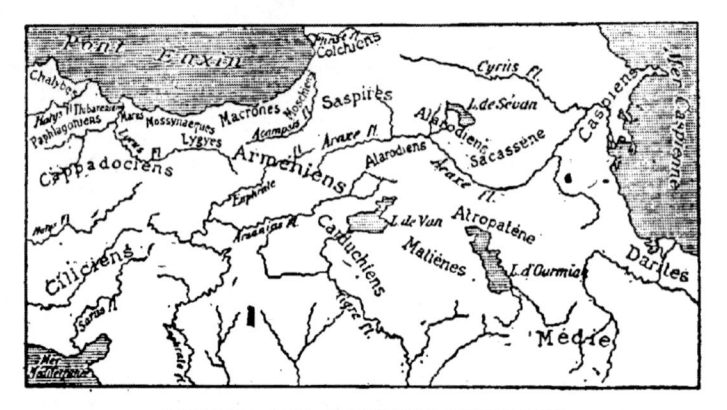

ARMENIA AND ADJOINING COUNTRIES
(according to Herodotus)

"The Armenians were armed like the Phrygians of whom they are "a colony (1)."

And, a few lines above:

"According to the Macedonians, the Phrygians were called Briges "so long as they remained in Europe and dwelled with them; but when "they crossed into Asia they changed their name along with their country "and took that of Phrygians."

We know how accurate were the statements of the Father of history,

---

(1) HERODOTUS, VII, 73.

and all the care he took in collecting historic lore, also how scrupulously he quoted his authorities. In this case as elsewhere, when he speaks of oral traditions, his statements cannot be doubted.

The definiteness with which Herodotus wrote concerning the Armeno-Phrygians shows his full reliance on the past memories of the Macedonians, although such traditions were already quite ancient, dating then a thousand years back. But the Macedonians had known the Phrygians in their midst before they left for Asia, and they must certainly have maintained intercourse with these people who, there is every reason to believe, were related to them. The Armenians were then a section only, a tribe of the Briges, and following the destiny of the whole nation, they emigrated with them. Phrygians, Armenians, and Macedonians, all belonged to the great Aryan family.

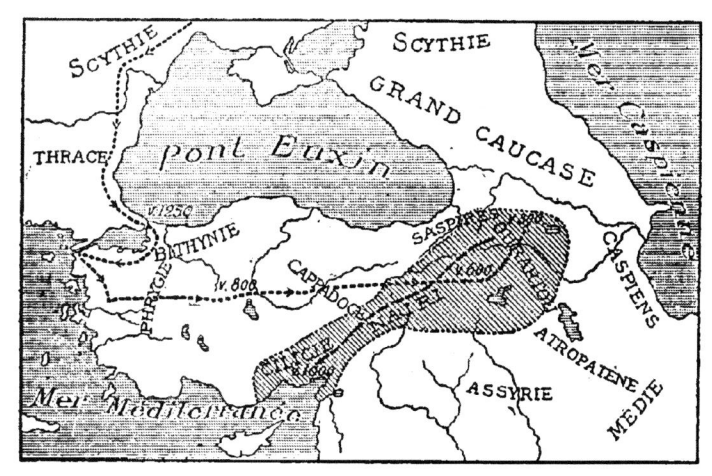

MIGRATIONS OF THE ARMENIANS

1st migration ca. 1250-300 B.C.
2nd migration ca. A.D. 1000
(The shading shows roughly the regions peopled today by the Armenians.)

The passing of the Armenians through the Balkans is recorded in the history of Armenia of the patriarch John VI (1); for, although that writer's statements are manifestly based on a desire to link the early

---

(1) Transl. E. BORE, *Arménie*, p. 74

Armenians to the Bible, it is none the less true that, accepting the theories of Biblical expositors who identify Torgom with Thrace (because of the similar consonantal sequence of the two names), the patriarch John was thus led to record his fellow-countrymen as having once lived in Macedonia, a memory still extant probably in his time in the traditions of the Armenian people. Perhaps John even had access to very ancient writings, since lost; in any case the traditions recorded by Herodotus together with many historical facts subsequent to the migration of the Armenians corroborate his opinion, as also do the affinities of language between this race and the other Aryan peoples who at that period took part in the invasions of Thrace, Asia Minor, and the eastern Mediterranean regions.

Leaving the Balkan peninsula, where they were lost among the other Indo-European hordes (who probably came from Central Asia viâ the Russian plains and the Danube valley), the Armenians crossed the Bosphorus, as Pliny affirms on the authority of ancient tradition (1). The names of the two Ascanian lakes, the one in Bithynia and the other in Pisidia (2), that of the Ascanian port (3), perhaps also that of the Ascanian Island (4), are undoubtedly so many sign-posts left by the migrations of Askenazou, the Ashkenaz of the Bible, i e by the Phrygians including the Armenians.

CENTURIES B C. XII - VIII This took place twelve or thirteen hundred years before our era, at the time the Hellenic world was so confused; but before the 8th century, the Phrygians and Armenians had already split, and the latter leaving their kinsmen in the mountains at the source of the Halys, had already advanced towards Cappadocia, taking advantage of the neglect this region was in since the fall of the Hittite empire.

We do not know why the Armenians on crossing the Euphrates moved on to the Ararat region preferably, but we know that about

---

(1) PLINY, Nat Hist., V. 40.
(2) STRABO. XII — PLINY, Nat Hist XXXI, 10 Lake Isnik (Bithynia). and lake Burdur (Pisidia).
(3) PLINY, Nat. Hist V. 32.
(4) PLINY, Nat Hist, V 38 (in the Cyclades).

the time of their migration important moves were taking place in Asia Minor and the sea-coasts. The Hellenes were spreading all over the Black Sea shore, founding trading-posts and colonies; Trebizond & Sinope both date from this period (5). The kingdom of Urartu was disappearing (6), Nineveh even was falling (7), whilst the Scythians were ravaging all Western Asia. May not the settlement of the Armenians in their new homeland have been facilitated by the invasion of the northern hordes who perhaps were akin to them? It would seem plausible, for these invaders had just crushed the biggest States and sown ruin and desolation among the former tributaries of Assur. "There are Meshech and Tubal," cried Ezekiel, "and their graves are round about them." And this frightful disorder was most auspicious for the realization of the Haïkanians' ambitions.

THE IRANIANS 8TH CENT. B.C. At this period, about the end of the 8th century B C., the Median power appeared in the Eastern political world. In 713, Sargon subdued the small State of Dayakkou (Deïokes), and the successor of this Iranian ruler, Fravarti (Fraortes), annexed to his kingdom Persia proper, i.e. the countries south and south-east of Ecbatana. The new king of the Medes had regained advantage over the Assyrians and was harrying them so closely that he died under the very walls of Nineveh that he was besieging.

With Cyaxares (Huvach-Chatra), Media reached the zenith of its power, and, after the downfall of the Assyrian empire, this king and his ally Nebuchadnezzar, king of Babylon, shared Asia between them. Ecbatana kept Assyria proper, seized the kingdom of Urartu, extended its sway over all the northern countries, and its armies advancing to the river Halys attacked even the kings of Lydia (585 B.C.).

When in 559 the crown passed from the Medes to the Persians, the Armenians, already settled on the Erzerum plateau, were treated sim-

---

(5) Trebizond was founded 756 B.C. and Sinope about 780 B.C. by the Milesians.
(6) Sardur III, who was apparently the last king of Urartu, sent an embassy to Assurbanipal about 644 B.C.
(7) 606 B C.

— 54 —

ilarly to other peoples brought under Cyaxares' rule; the Achaemenids placed them in their 13th Satrapy, whilst the Urartaeans were joined to the Matians and the Saspires to form the 18th province. The text of Herodotus makes clear that in the 6th century the Armenians had not yet assimilated the Vannic population.

Coins ASCRIBED TO KING CROESUS OF LYDIA

Some writers consider that the Armenians might be descended from the former subjects of the Argistis and Sardur monarchs. This hypothesis is contradicted by the above facts; it sets aside, moreover, both tradition and linguistic data. The two peoples were clearly distinct and had nothing in common. The Aryans, who were newcomers, caused the older inhabitants of Naïri and Van whom they gradually assimilated to lose their national characteristics and language, and soon all that remained of the once mighty Urartaeans were a few proper names preserved in the Armenian language. "The princely families of "Armenia, such as the Rechtuni, the Manavaz, the Biznuni, the Arz-"eruni—who reigned over the Van country until the 11th century of our "era, have kept the names of Rousas, Menuas, Ishpuinis, Argistis, de-"rived from the ancient kings of Biaïna. The fall of the kingdom of "Urartu did not therefore entail the disappearance of its vassals, who "were gathered into the main body of the Armenians, while keeping their "seignorial privileges." (1).

This survival of names belonging to lost tongues in the speech of new-comers, is a logical phenomenon, and examples are plentiful in all languages. Latin contains a good number of Etruscan words, and in French we find names derived from Celtic and Ligurian vocabularies, as well, we may be sure, as those of people of the Stone Age.

More than any other, the Armenian vocabulary presents great difficulties. Into this language there have entered terms from all the following tongues; Assyrian, Hebrew, Median, Kartvelian (Georgian, Mingrelian, Lazian), Urartaean (of Naïri), Scythian, Greek, Arabic,

---

(1) KEVORK ASLAN, *Etudes historiques du peuple arménien*, p. DF.

Turkish, Mongolian, Persian (old and modern), Kurdish, Latin, Russian, and others. In analyzing the Kurdish vocabularies, (2) I have found in each dialect a large non-Aryan residue of indispensable elements, derived undoubtedly from lost languages, and the same thing is true with the Armenian

This mixture of the Armenians with the more ancient populations to form the final nation deserves some consideration, necessitating our turning back to what composed the peoples of Western Asia in the Assyrian period.

We have little authentic information as to the ethnic composition of the peoples living in Western Asia before it was invaded in the south by the Semitic element The only languages in which any inscriptions have come down to us are the Sumerian and the Elamite in the south, the Hittite in the west, and the Vannic in the north These tongues are neither Semitic nor Aryan; they belong to the group termed Turanian in which all non-Semitic and non-Aryan material has long been classified. Of these four languages, two only have yielded to scientific analysis, viz; the Elamite and the Vannic.

The Elamite, well known today through my own discoveries and the research of V Scheil in the Susian texts, is shown by the latter to cover a duration of about two thousand years It was still spoken by the Achaemenean Persians. The monosyllabic roots in Elamite are agglutinative, and the only reason that the resulting words can still be inflected simply, is that the agglutinative language has been influenced by a higher form of speech (the Semitic languages) from which it has borrowed the idea of inflection without appropriating the forms thereof

The same is the case with Vannic, spoken in the Ararat regions (Urartu) in Assyrian times and quite distinct from the Semitic languages.

These data together with the many proper names found in the Assyrian texts show that twenty centuries B C. the greater part of Western Asia was inhabited by a non-Semitic and non-Aryan group of peoples. I do not mean by the word "group" that the languages spoken by these various peoples were inter-related, far from it, but I classify these non-Semitic and non-Aryan peoples as speaking languages less developed than those of the Semitic invaders The numerous Kartvelian tongues are apparently the last representatives today of that ethnic collection

---

(2 *Mission scientifique en Perse*, Vol V, 1st part. (Paris, 1904).

which some writers have called by the vague name of white allophylians. Meillet, in his *Grammaire comparée de l'arménien classique,* calls attention to grammatical affinities of Armenian with the Caucasian languages, these affinities have come about through contact with native populations in very early times, which is only natural.

The first attempt to analyze scientifically the Georgian language is contained in an article by J. A. Gatteyrias; (1) and the learned translator of the Vannic inscriptions, Professor A. H. Sayce (2), recognized real connections between the language of Urartu and the speech of the Kartvelians. So that, on the one hand, Armenian contains Vannic terms and Kartvelian forms, and on the other, Vannic is not unconnected with the Caucasian tongues. These facts established by eminent linguists support the hypothesis that the ancient inhabitants of Western Asia who were partly absorbed by the Armenians belonged to the same linguistic group as the modern Caucasians.

The Assyrians described as "Peoples of Nairi" all the nations living between the sources of the river Halys and lake Urumiah as well as those dwelling further north, and did not confuse this group with the Mouchkou (Moschi), the Khâti or Hittites, Koummoukh (Commagene), and the Kourkhi, stationed further south. They recognized therefore the ethnic connections of these populations. Urartu was the chief of all the Nairi Kingdoms. Lake Van was called the Nairi Sea, and the rulers of Dhouspana (Van) extended their sovereignty over the regions of Noummé (Erzerum), Kirouri (Mouch-Bitlis), Biaina (Van), Mouazir (Bitlis-Salmas), Ahkouza (Qara-bagh-Erivan), and towards the north in the Lesser Caucasus chain. These are the very countries which the Armenians later conquered and made their realm. As for the people of Nairi, it is certain that they did not disappear. Some of them may have withdrawn into the mountains, but they were mostly absorbed by the new Aryan element, which was much more developed than the ancient inhabitants of Asia. The languages were lost and with their disappearance the memory of what Nairi was under the kings of Urartu gradually faded out.

Some traditions, however, were still extant in the first centuries of our era, for Moses of Khoren has left us a curious description of the city

---

(1) *Revue de Linguistique et de Philologie comparée,* Vol. XIV, July 1881, p. 275-311.
(2) *The Cuneiform Inscriptions,* of Van, p. 411.

of Van and the works carried out by the kings of Urartu in Dhouspas, their capital, which works he attributes to the legendary Queen Semiramis. (1).

TRADITIONS CONCERNING THE KINGDOM OF URARTU

VANNIC WINGED BULL
(British Museum)

"Semiramis," he wrote, "having visited "many sites, arrived from the east at the "shore of the Salt Lake; she saw on its bank an "oblong hill exposed to the west throughout "its length, curving somewhat on the north. "To the south a grotto standing straight up "to the sky, while a little further southward "she saw a flat valley, which, bordered on "the east by the mountain and lengthening "and broadening out towards the lake, had "a glorious appearance. Across these "grounds, pure water coming down from "the mountain in gullies and valleys and "collecting at the foot of the mountains, "ran in veritable rivers. Right and left of "these waters stood numerous villages in "the valley, and to the east of this smiling "hill, rose a small mountain.

" . . . . . Semiramis first had a cause-"way built along the river, with blocks of "rock cemented together with lime and "sand, a gigantic undertaking both in extent and height, and which, it is "said, still exists today. (2). This causeway, several stadia long, reaches to "the town . . . By continuous labor, the Queen finished these wonderful "works in a few years and had them surrounded with strong walls and "brass gates. She built also in the city many magnificent palaces, adorned "with different stones of many colors, two or three stories high, each "one with a desirable southern aspect. She distinguished between the quart-"ers of the city by bright colors, divided them into wide streets, and built ap-"propriate hot baths in the center of the town, admirably fashioned. Di-"verting part of the river-water into the city, she had it canalized wher-"ever needed and for the watering of gardens and terraces . . . All parts of

---

(1) *Hist. d'Arm.* I, 16.
(2) 4th century A.D.

"the city were adorned by her with fine buildings and leafy trees bearing "varieties of fruits and foliage. She made the walled section of the city "magnificent and glorious on all sides, and drew inside an immense popula- "tion.

" .... Semiramis garrisoned the tops of the walls, arranged entrances "difficult of access, and erected a royal palace with terrible dungeons.

"On the eastern side of the grotto, where the stone is still so hard "that it has a keen edge, were built palaces, rooms, cellars for treasure- "houses, and long galleries. No one knows how ever these marvellous "constructions were raised. On all the stone surfaces are many inscrip- "tions, chiselled as though on wax. All who behold such marvellous "achievement are in wonderment,—but we will say no more. In many "other districts of Armenia the Queen caused to be carved on stone the "record of different events; at many points she had steles erected, similarly "inscribed.

Such, according to tradition, was how in the first centuries of our era the Armenians thought of the city of Van, in the district of Tosp, province of Vaspouraken. A thousand years had elapsed since the fall of the Urartu kingdom, the inscriptions of the rulers of Ararat were no longer understood by anyone, and the history of Assyria's mighty enemies was lost in the mists of oblivion. There was no remembrance even that a great independent kingdom had existed on the plateau before the arrival of the Armenian patriarch and his companions-in-arms. Imposing ruins at Van remained to excite the imagination of travelers. Moses of Khoren visited them, and has handed us down the legends that were current regarding them in his day.

MIGRATIONS OF THE ARMENIANS In any case, documents we possess show that the Armenian advance from Cappadocia to the plateau of Erzerum took place during the 8th and 7th centuries B.C., and that at least six hundred years before our era, the nation already occupied some of the districts in the neighborhood of Ararat and lake Van (1). In their march eastward,

---

(1) Until recently it was believed that the Armenian exodus from Phrygia took place about the end of the 7th century B.C. (Maspero), but we must move back considerably the date of this event, for (according to Belck and Lehmann) an inscription of Menouas (828-784) places them in Cappadocia in the 8th century (N. DOLENS & A. KHATCH, *Hist. anc. des Arm*, p. 34). However the migration may have been in several waves, some Armenian tribes still dwelling in Cappadocia while others had gone forward to the east. Moreover, the reading of Urmani or Armeni on the Maltai inscription is still in doubt. (Cf. S. Ac. *Wissensch.*, Berlin, 1900, p. 621).

the Armenians had driven back the Mouchkou and Khaldis tribes, as also other clans of the Naïri land mentioned in the Assyrian inscriptions as living in the valleys of the upper Euphrates.

It is probable, as we have just seen, that the Naïri peoples belonged to the same racial stock as the Lazi, the Mingrelians, and Georgians of our time. Some of these nations were absorbed by the Armenians, and

ARMENIA AND NEIGHBORING COUNTRIES ACCORDING TO THE ASSYRIANS

the others who withdrew before them into the north, seem to have remained ever since unchanged; they took with them in their hearts a hatred of the invader, and this ill-will has persisted throughout the centuries, ever apparent in the hostility of the Caucasians to the usurpers of the land of their forefathers. This enmity the Georgians still cherished some years ago, even though the memory of their erstwhile misfortunes had so long disappeared.

It is noticeable that the Kartvelians have remained divided into clans speaking different dialects of the same linguistic group, with no political connection with one another, and often mutually hostile as they used to be in the time of the kings of Urartu. This persistance in speech and traditions leads us to believe that in the Caucasians we see today the remains of the primitive peoples conquered by the Armenians.

The results of the great revolutions which at the beginning of history disquieted Asia are not at all clear to us; our only source of knowledge, the Assyrian inscriptions, stop short with the downfall of Nineveh, and there remained in Urartu no more rulers able to continue the recording of deeds and events such as the Argistis and Sardur kings formerly engraved on the rocks of Van As for all those peoples who were destitute of the art of writing, they receded into the oblivion from which for a few centuries they were rescued by the triumphant inscriptions of the Ninivite monarchs. Thereafter a thick fog descends on Asiatic history, and this mist lasts until the Achaemenids ascend the Persian throne.

The beginnings of the Armenian people in the Masis land are dimly recorded by Moses of Khoren (1), but as the documentation that this writer states he obtained from Mar-Apas-Katina (2) was systematically garbled by himself, it is very difficult to utilize the names he gives to the early heroes of Armenia. Haik, who apparently led the nation in their march from Cappadocia to the Ararat country, is said to have had four sons: Cadmos, Khor, Manawaz, and Armenak. The last-named, one of the heroes of the nation, (3) had a son called Aramaïs, the ancestor of Amasia, father of Kegham, who begat Harma, the father of Aram.

The Assyrian empire, as we have seen, had been destroyed and replaced by that of the Medes. We know that the latter extended their empire to the river Halys, to the borders of the territory of Croesus, for at that period the kingdom of Lydia took in all Asia Minor except Lycia and Cilicia (558 B.C.). Perhaps the domination of the Mermnads caused the Armenians to leave Phrygia; in any case they were already on the Erzerum plateau when the sceptre passed from the hands of the Medes to that of the Persians. Cyrus took only three years (549-546) to subdue the northern lands and conquer ancient Urartu together with all Asia Minor, and it is likely that the Armenians had to endure the Median yoke

---

(1) The chief Armenian historian, who lived at the end of the 4th century of our era. (Cf V LANGLOIS. *Hist. Armén.* Transl Paris, 1869, Vol II, p. 47).

(2) Mar-Ibas (or Apas) Katina (in Syriac, *the subtle one*), according to Moses of Khoren, was commissioned by king Vagharchak (Valarsace) of Armenia about 149 B C to search in the records of the southern Semites for everything relating to the ancient history of the Armenians. This statement is, moreover, very questionable, and it is believed today that no such person ever existed, and Moses used him each time as a mouthpiece for the traditions and legends still current in his day.

(3) The Armenians call themselves *Haikians*. As for the name *Armenia, Arminia, Armaniya*, of foreign extraction, this is apparently an appellation of a part of the country subsequently taken to comprise all of it. Haik is the eponym of the race of people entitled Hay or Haikazn (descendants of Haik).

prior to that of the Persians, for in all probability they established themselves towards the end of the period of confusion following the Ninivite downfall and preceding the accession of the Achaemenids.

LEGENDARY DYNASTIES   According to Moses of Khoren, Haik, (1) the hero who gave his name to the race, was the son of Thorgom, the son of Thiraz, the son of Gomer, the son of Japhet.

This genealogy which is entirely Biblical, perhaps corresponds to general ethnic fact, but it should not be considered as based on Armenian traditions, and therefore as corroborative of the tabulation of peoples in Genesis. Moses of Khoren confesses that he himself made it out "from what he had discovered as certain in the ancient Histories, and to the best of his ability." These last words set the seal of improbability on all his narratives of events with which that writer was not contemporary.

The first four names of this genealogical list are taken from Genesis, there is no doubt, and these borrowings took place in the first centuries of our era, when Armenia was becoming Christian, for the altered form of Thorgom, from Tôgharmah, is found nowhere except in the Greek version of the Bible, called the Septuagint. It was, therefore, from that version of the Scriptures that the first Armenian chronologists took the family tree which they adopted. Besides, with the newly converted Christians, the general tendency was to link up their racial origin with the Bible, and the non-Aryan Georgians, who were completely foreign to the Armenians, did not hesitate about the same time to call themselves like-

ETHNOGRAPHY OF WESTERN ASIA
(from Genesis, ch. X)

---

(1) The name of Haik has given rise to much research and study. All the resources of etymology have been invoked, often beyond permissible scientific limits, and none of the proposed solutions are acceptable. The most rational is the supposition that Hay (pati) means *chief*, as Hayr (pater) means paternal authority. It is impossible to give any date to this legendary person who undoubtedly was one of the great leaders of the Armenian people, but whose role has certainly been enlarged by tradition, as is the case with all heroes. It would seem best therefore to leave to Haik his mystical value and to use his name only as a symbol of the origin and displacements of the Armenians previous to their forming a nation in the Ararat region. Ohannes in Chaldea, Menes in Egypt, Abraham among the Jews, Romulus with the Latins, are hardly any more definite as figures than is Haik to the Armenians; each nation attributing to a single head its birth-throes.

wise the sons of Thargamos. The juxtaposition of these two pseudo-traditions shows what credence can be given to the stories of the early Christian historians concerning national origins. (1).

In a curious passage of his History, Moses of Khoren (2), thoroughly imbued with his readings, indulges in a strange mixing of heathen and Biblical traditions: (3).

"Terrible, extraordinary," (he writes), "were the first gods, who "created the chief blessings of this world, the principles of the Universe and "of human reproduction The race of the Giants stood out apart, a race "endowed with terrible strength, a race invincible and of enormous stat-"ure. They in their pride conceived and brought forth the plan to build "the tower [Babel]. They had set themselves to the task, but a furious "and heaven-sent wind, the breath of the wrath of the gods, overturned "the edifice. The gods, having given each of these men a language that "the rest understood not, spread trouble and confusion among them. "One of these men was Haik of the seed of Japhetos, a famous chieftain, "mighty and skillful to draw the bow. (4)"

But Moses did not confine himself to these fables, he also republished an old tradition peculiar to the Armenian nation, a narrative that agrees on the whole with the Macedonian legends handed down to us through Herodotus.

"As for Haik," wrote the Syrian historian, (5) "he went off with "the others of his company to the north-east, and settled on a plain "called Hark (6) or the plain of the Fathers, i e. the fathers of the race "of Thorgom Then he built a village which he called Haikaschen, mean-"ing *built by Haik*. In the center of this plateau (7), near a mountain "of great width of base (8), some men were already settled, and these "willingly put themselves under the hero."

(1) See *inter alia*, JORNANDES: *De la Succession des temps*, a book in which the writer commits the same abuse of Biblical tradition.
(2) According to Mar-Apas-Katina (Cf V. LANGLOIS, *op. cit*, Vol. I, p. 15).
(3) The date at which Mar-Apas Katina is supposed to have lived, if he ever did, is uncertain This writer found, according to Moses of Khoren, in the archives of the Persian kings a manuscript translated from Chaldean into Greek by order of Alexander the Great, *History of the First Ancestors*. The book of Mar-Apas-Katina was said to have been translated into Syriac, then into Armenian, before being summarized by Moses of Khoren Quatremère considers that the *History of the First Ancestors* was only the work of Berosis.
(4) We know that the tower of Babel was the giant Ziggurat, the ruins of which still stand on the site of Babylon
(5) Transl. V. LANGLOIS, vol. I, p 17.
(6) District of Hark, in Dourouperan.
(7) Plateau of Erzerum.
(8) Rather the Bin-Gheul, than Ararat.

One could hardly sum up more succinctly in a few lines the history of the migration of the Armenians from Cappadocia to the land where they still live today.

Starting from the old Chaldeo-Hebrew legends and drawing as their fancy dictated on the Semitic traditions, the Armenians, following the example of the so-called Mar-Apas-Katina, related in their writings that an invasion by Belus took place in the Erzerum and Van regions for the purpose of putting an end to Haik's conquests. No mention is made of the Assyrians, the Medes, the Urartians, or of the Nairi peoples; Belus personifies all the opposition which the new-comers met with. (1) But, they add, Belus was defeated and killed in the battle of Haiotztor, and this event is placed by the native chronologists at 2350 B.C. (2) This date needs to be brought down about eighteen hundred years, to give any likelihood to the narrative, for in the 24th century B.C. the ancestors of the Armenians were certainly still mingled with their Aryan brothers in the Indo-European cradle-land and were far from the Danube and the Thracian mountains. The Assyrian empire and the kingdom of Urartu were not yet born, and the Semites of Chaldaea were still stationed in southern Mesopotamia and the seaboard.

On the one hand, in this fanciful and confused rehearsal of the struggles the Armenians had to maintain to conquer their new domain, we certainly see the remembrance of the opposition put up against the advancing newcomers by the newly emancipated vassals of Assyria, and doubtless by the Urartaeans. On the other hand, the Ninivite kingdom although tottering remained unfallen for some years yet (3), and the kings of Assur, very disquieted by the Median tribes uniting in a single State, and threatened by the Babylonians, in addition to the anxiety caused by the Scythians entering the Asiatic scene, could not bear to have fresh adversaries encamped on their Empire's northern borders.

---

(1) To the early Armenian chroniclers, Chamiram (Semiramis) symbolized Assyria, as Ara did the lands of Nairi and Urartu.

(2) The first Armenian chronologists show Haik as followed by thirty-six patriarchs (2350-870 B.C.). Then, seventeen kings ruled, from 870 to 330 B.C. But recent books give the names of these people only for the record. (Cf. at the end of this volume, in the Appendix, the list of legendary patriarchs and kings, according to K. J. BASMADJIAN, Chron. de l'Hist. de l'Armenie, in Revue de l'Orient chrétien, vol. XIX, 1914.)

(3) The name of the Armenians does not appear in the Assyrian inscriptions. We must conclude that the conquest of Armenia by Haik took place in the last days of the Assur monarchy only, perhaps even a little later than the fall of Assyria.

They failed, however, and "Belus having been vanquished and killed by Haik", the Armenians were able to establish their dominion over the Erzerum regions.

THE SCYTHIANS The occupation of Western Asia by the Scythians lasted, according to Herodotus, twenty-eight years, that of Armenia and Transcaucasia by them was certainly much longer, for the hordes from the north had only a single road whereby to join the bulk of their nation, and this road passed by the gorges of Derbend or the so-called Gate of the Alans (1). Few of them, however, returned to their northern steppes; they mostly settled in the districts of the upper Halys river and of the river Thermodon and gradually disappeared, lost in the adjacent nations, the Cappadocians, the Phrygians, the Armenians, Moschi, and Tibarenes. We find no trace, however, in Armenian chronicles of any Scythian domination, and this silence leads us to suppose either that the Armenians were related to the northern nomads or that they made their migration to the east after the scourge had past. In the first case, far from being hostile to Haïk's warriors, the Scythians would have helped them realize their aims. In the second, the Armenians would only have taken advantage of the general disorder that followed this invasion.

CONQUEST OF ARMENIA BY HAIK We have seen that the Armenians arrived in Thrace at the same time as other branches of the Aryan family, and that all these peoples came from the East via the Russian steppes. Nations belonging to the same ethnic group ascended at the same time the valley of the Danube and reached western Europe, whilst others spread over the countries of central Europe. The Ligurians and our ancestors the Gauls no doubt belonged to one of these tidal waves of humanity, for they had already been long settled in the west of the old world when, six hundred years B.C., the Greeks came into contact with them on the Mediterranean coast.

That was the time of those invasions the various elements of which

---

(1) Gorges of the Dariall in Ossetia, in the center of the Greater Caucasus.

went to make up the world of our classical ancient times, a world which developed for a period of two thousand years, from the 15th century B C to the 5th century of our era, and which finally achieved world leadership. For although two thousand years later other waves, also from the East and over the same roads, changed for a time the face of the old world, sowing ruin and plunging Europe back into barbarism, yet the elements of the first invasions survived and gave birth to our modern States, to those nations which in the last few centuries have carried their impetus to the four corners of the globe

During the disorders that reigned in Asia, the Armenians, established in their newly conquered homeland, remained unshakable, and by their courage preserved to this day their nationality, language, and customs, —whereas almost all the peoples whom they had known in their early days disappeared from the earth Their brothers, the Phrygians, are only now a dim memory Alone among their contemporaries, the Hellenes, the Italiotes, and the Gauls overcame the cataclysms, not however without receiving many admixtures and forsaking many of their former customs But apart from the Greeks, we must not seek any kinship with the Armenians in modern nations, only in those nations that were brought from the northern steppes to the Mediterranean shores by the same tidal wave that carried the ancestors of Haik to Thrace And those peoples have unfortunately for the most part been engulfed for very many centuries in the darkness of oblivion

Such in their main lines are the beginnings of the Armenian people. We have sufficient documentation to ascertain satisfactorily the chief phases of the development of this ancient nation, but not to permit of detailed accounts. It is certain, nevertheless, that the proud lineage of the race goes back to over three thousand years ago and is considerably more ancient than that of most European peoples India and China, despite their fanciful legends, hardly show such remote beginnings Only the old nations of Western Asia, the Syrians, the Chaldeans, the Kurds (Medes), and in North Africa, the Egyptians, have more ancient ancestral records As for the Persians, their political life did not begin until about the time that Armenia achieved statehood, and Rome was not founded until the time that Haik's people were leaving Cappadocia.

THE ARMENIAN LANGUAGE

Armenian is an Indo-European language (1), i e it belongs to the western branch of the Aryan family, and evolved in a parallel direction with Greek and other tongues, most of them now lost, that were spoken in the central and eastern Mediterranean world about 1,000 B.C. But, due to the Armenians settling in the Ararat regions, their language, while keeping its main grammatical forms, became permeated with very many elements taken from subject peoples, from the various overlords of Armenia, and from neighboring nations The successive sway of Medes, Achaemenian Persians, Parthians, Sassanids, Macedonians, Byzantines, Arabs, and Turks has given fresh verbal roots to the Armenian vocabulary, but the general characteristics of the language remain (2) There are no inscriptions to show us the ancient form of Armenian, and the primitive tongue can be reconstituted only theoretically, because until the Christian era the Armenians had no writing Their Phrygian brothers were better advised in this respect, but when the latter under Hellenic influence adopted writing, the Armenians had probably already separated from them

Moses of Khoren complains bitterly of the ignorance his countrymen were in prior to their conversion to Christianity and explains it by the fact that they had no written language of their own We know therefore for certain that the Armenians did not have, during their migrations,

---

(1) Until a few years ago there was the greatest confusion generally as to the ethnical character of the peoples who lived in western Asia in ancient times Some writers on the strength of superficially noted physical features, looked on the Armenians as Semitic others classed them with the Urartaeans or the Hittites Renan (*Hist des Langues semitiques*, vol I, p 11, par 1) rightly considers the ancestors of the Armenians to have been in all probability settlers of Indo-Germanic origin. but he thinks they went from Babylon to occupy a land populated by Semitic people J. Oppert (*La Peuple et la Langue des Medes*) writing at about the same time ascribed to the Medes the lines on the third column of the trilingual Achaemenean inscriptions, whereas actually these were in the Neo Susian language, the ancient form of which has been made known of late years by the many inscriptions discovered at Susa Thanks to the Assyrian and Old Persian versions of these valuable trilingual inscriptions, J Oppert had been able, not only to give us a correct translation of the neo-Susian texts, but also to set forth the grammatical rules and glossary of this non-Aryan and non-Semitic language But then, not knowing its authors, he ascribed it to the Medes who as we know today were Indo-Iranians like the Persians These errors, which were then common, have been a great hindrance to understanding the historical facts

(2) *Vide* the *Grammair critique de l'arménien moderne* (Vienna, 1903) of M MEILLET, a basic and authoritative work on the origin of the Armenian language The writer in his introduction admits that after the 6th or 7th centuries B C this language borrowed much from a non cognate tongue. He thinks these borrowings are from the speech of the "old inhabitants"

the means of recording their thought. No doubt when they were in Cappadocia, they knew the Hittite hieroglyphics (2) but the latter system of writing, full of ideograms, did not lend itself to phonetic transcription. Agathangelus, Moses of Khoren, Lazarus of Pharp, agree with Diodorus of Sicily and Polyaenus, in stating that for drawing up deeds, for correspondence, and the documents needed for daily life, the Armenians for a long time used Greek, Persian (Pehlevi), and Syriac letters. They perhaps tried to use the Persian cuneiforms which are known to be phonetic derivatives of the Chaldeo-Assyrian system, seeing that ideographic signs had been used in Urartu as well as by several non-Semitic peoples of Western Asia. But this attempt, if it was made was short-lived, and the example shown by the Persians does not seem to have been followed by the Armenians, the Medes, the Kartvelians, or the Naïri peoples. We indeed possess no inscriptions left by these nations.

The Russian archaeological Commission discovered in 1900 near Ani, on a vase in a cemetery, a curious hieroglyphic or pictographic inscription which seems to be of great antiquity and which appears to show that before the time of the Vannic cuneiforms in this region, perhaps during the period of the Urartu kingdom, the predecessors of the Armenians in the plain of Erivan used a very primitive graphic system. This attempt does not seem to have been followed up, for it is an isolated case. It proves, however, that from the remotest times the peoples of Transcaucasia felt the need of expressing their thought. The revolutions that occurred prevented the development of this primitive conception, which we only mention for the record.

HIEROGLYPHIC INSCRIPTION AT ANI

At the time Haïk arrived in Armenia, a phonetic writing which was to have a famous future was already in current use in Western Asia, viz. the

---

(2) The recent German excavations at Boghaz-Keuï have brought to light a large number of slate tablets with cuneiform characters in the Hittite language, and from certain words Winckler deduces in the latter the existence of Indo-European connections. If this be so the Hittites would be the first precursors of the Aryan migrations; but these linguistic resemblances are too uncertain to be accepted. Besides, the Hittite system of hieroglyphics is known to be independent of the Egyptian, and it would be strange for an Aryan people to work out for themselves a system of ideographic writing without any of their fellow-Aryans having the same idea.

Aramaean alphabet. Originating in Phoenicia, it had spread into Assyria and Chaldaea for current documentary purposes, and had also reached Arabia, developing differently in each country. Undoubtedly the Armenians knew this writing, but it was created for Semitic languages in which the consonants play the chief part, and the Aramaean alphabet was unsuited to the sounds of the Aryan languages which have inflections mainly based on vowels; the Armeno-Phrygians, unlike the Greeks, did not know how to complete it to fit their need. The Persians were more far-seeing; they composed the Zend alphabet to transcribe the sacred books of the Avesta. This innovation, however, was at a much later period, subsequent to the formation of the Pehlevi language.

Philostrates states that in the time of Arsaces (150 B.C.) the Armenians had a system of writing of their own, but this assertion, which contradicts all that Moses of Khoren says on the subject, has no inscriptions to support it, and seems inadmissible.

The Armenian language, basically, constructively, and as regards its roots, is definitely Indo-European, a point that must be emphasized. It differs from the eastern Aryan group, i.e. from the tongues of Iran, Old Persian, Zend, Pehlevi, Kurdish, Ossetian, etc. in the same way as do European languages. However, in its various provincial forms, it is today frequently mixed with Semitic, Caucasian, Iranian, and Altaic elements, due to the long contact that the descendants of Haïk's warriors had with populations speaking languages of those groups. The Persian-Pehlevi language, among others, on account of the domination of the Parthians and the Sassanids, has left very many traces in the vocabulary. As for medieval Armenian and the modern literary language, which are much purer in this respect, they are on account of their flexibility first-class mediums of thought. The Armenian language has thus been very well preserved throughout the centuries, at least in its grammatical forms, despite the vicissitudes of the people who speak it. Like all forms of speech, it has just developed.

RELIGION OF THE ARMENIANS Together with the tradition of language, of capital importance to the preservation of national character, there were the ancestral religious beliefs of the Armenians. They certainly had a national Pantheon, and in all probability it was very nearly akin to that of the Phrygians and fitted in with the religious ideas of the whole group of Indo-European peoples (1) Finding themselves, however, through their conquests in contact with the Semites of Assyria, the sons of Haik adopted some of their southern neighbors' divinities (2). The god Barchamin mentioned by Moses of Khoren, and called Barcham the Assyrian by Anania of Chirak, is none other than the Parchimnia of the Semites The statue of this god, long worshipped throughout Armenia, was one day carried into Mesopotamia by Tigranes II, the son of Artashes. In another place, in the town of Erez, stood the golden image of the goddess Anahit, the Semitic Anahita, and according to Pliny, this statue was worshipped both by Asiatic and western peoples The precious idol was among the booty captured from the Parthians by Marcus Aurelius, and ended up by being destroyed by Tiridates when Christianity was introduced into Armenia

In the village of Thil stood the statue of the great Chaldaean goddess Nana, assimilated to the Artemis of the Greeks, and when in subsequent centuries, under Persian influences, the Armenians accepted officially the Mazdean religion, Ahoura-Mazda was given by them the name of the "Father of the Gods" Losing his Iranian qualities, he became a sort of Zeus in relation to the ancestral divinities.

This conversion of Armenia to the Zoroastrian cult, which seems to have been only very superficial, did not shut out the gods worshiped by Haik's warriors; Persian influence, along with the fear of a Sassanid invasion, made the conversion necessary. The inclusion of Barchamin, Anaita, Nana, and other Semitic gods in the Armenians' holy places was due also to the need on the part of the rulers to help onward the assimilation of the peoples whose lands they had invaded These gods of Semitic origin were worshipped among all of Assyria's vassals, and it was necessary not to wound the religious convictions of the subdued nations. The great god of Urartu, Khaldis, very probably had likewise his altars beside those of Bagdias, the Phrygian Jupiter

In short, the Armenian pantheon in the century prior to the introduction of Christianity among this people, was derived from a variety of sources To the ancestral gods were added those of Persia, of the Mesopotamian Semites, of Syria, and of the Greek pantheon, —but in

---

(1) Strabo (vol XI, p 19) tells us that in the temples of Acilicene, the Armenians observed mysteries resembling those of the Hellenes
(2) This hospitality to foreign gods was widely practised by the Romans

most cases these divinities represented assimilations rather than innovations. Among all Indo-Europeans the deities were extremely numerous, and so the Armenians easily found room in their pantheon for the gods of their neighbors, of their overlords, and of the nations they themselves subdued. The names of their gods are almost all Iranian. The offspring of Ormazd (Ahura-Mazda), originally seven in number, later numbered ten. Mihr, Anahit, Nanea, Barchamin, Astlik, Tiûr, are the chief ones, followed by Vahakn and Spandaramat. But ranking above all the gods was Vanatûr, the god of the New Year who lavished his blessings on men, and whose supposed existence, peculiar to the Armenian people, seems to go back to the earliest days of their nation. In addition, the naturistic beliefs of the Indo-Europeans had under Persian influence become personified in Armenia in the form of good and evil genii.

Hellenism brought no new gods, but a number of assimilations, most of them quite relative. Ormazd became Zeus, Mihr was confused with Hephaestus, Anahit with Artemis, Nana with Athena, Astlik with Aphrodite, Tiûr with Helios, Vahakn with Heracles or Ares, etc. As for the beliefs themselves, they seem to have undergone little change.

Every province, every district, had its local god or its protecting deities. The chief temple of Anahit was at Eriza (Erzindjan), but this goddess also had holy places at Armavir, Artaxata, in the district of Taròn, and elsewhere. Astlik, the goddess of Pleasure, was worshipped on the shores of lake Van.

PAGAN BAS-RELIEF AT BAGREVANT, NEAR BAYAZID

We have very little information as to the original religious ideas of the Armenians, but there are some indications that like most of their fellow-Aryans they started with Nature worship, which gradually was transformed to produce the national Pantheon. In any case, reverence for the ancestral gods was so deeply rooted in the people, that it survived despite all temptations and attacks. This tenacity of religious convictions, moreover has never weakened among the Armenians since the time of Christianity, for few nations have had the strength to keep their faith so much alive for centuries and centuries, amid the most terrible persecutions.

PERSIAN PERIOD When he became master of the Persians and the Medes, Darius I. the son of Hystaspes, had to assume the heavy task of strengthening and organizing the empire of Cyrus, and anxiety concerning the borders of his dominions compelled him to seize the Armenian stronghold. He had to have rule over the Erzerum plateau, not only to avert dangers that might arise from that mountain massif if it remained held by an energetic and independent people, but also to keep in check the turbulent tribes of the Phasis and Cyrus valleys, and to control the northern hordes who were a standing threat. The barrier of the Greater Caucasus stood like a formidable wall against the Scythians of whom Western Asia had terrible memories, but it was necessary to hold the foot of this rampart and close the Caspian Gates and Dariall. He had then first of all to make sure of Armenia. Once Armenia was occupied, the Great King's only remaining frontier care was on the Oxus, the steppes of which were then inhabited by the famous Massagetes, in whose territory Cyrus lost his life, and by other no less formidable Scythian nations

But this great Persian State, so speedily founded by Cyrus, was based on feudal principles. Each people had kept its laws and its hereditary rulers, and consequently the palace revolution which resulted after Cyrus' death in Darius' accession reverberated among the vassals of the Empire and revolts broke out in most of the provinces. Armenia, in the hope of gaining freedom, joined the coalition of the northern peoples, and was perhaps even its instigator

The Persians fought bitterly against the Armenians, judging by the accounts on the famous stele of Bisoutoun (1), the only inscription of note that remains to us concerning the wars that resulted in the empire of the Achaemenids.

Darius I. relates himself the campaigns he had to conduct to overcome the obstinate resistance of the Armenians whose country though included in his dominions certainly still enjoyed considerable independence.

There is reason to believe that, either by force or by stratagem, the Persians succeeded in dividing the Armenians. The political structure of the latter was also on the feudal system, for it was an Armenian in the service of the Achaemenids, surely a traitor to his country, that the King

---

(1) Bi-soutoun (without columns), the modern name of Behistoun (in Persian, Baghistana). These inscriptions were carved about 500 B C. by order of Darius I. son of Hystaspes.

commissioned to crush a national uprising, called by him a revolt. The tiara of a Satrapy was no doubt to be the felon's reward.

The record in stone reads thus:

"And Darius, the King, said: An Armenian named Dadarses, my "servant, I sent into Armenia. I spoke in this "manner to him: "Go against the army of the "rebels that say they are not mine; kill them!" "Then Dadarses set forth. When he arrived "in Armenia, the rebels massed together and "went out against Dadarses to battle. Then "Dadarses fought them. There was a fortress "named Zura in Armenia. There Ormazd was "my support. By the favor of Ormazd my "army killed many of the rebels' army. This was the eighth day of the "month Thuravashara [May-June, 519 B.C.] that this battle was fought "(2)."

DOUBLE GOLDEN DARIC OF THE ACHAEMENIDS

A second encounter took place near the city named Tigra (June 519), and a third one the same month against a fortress called Ethyama. But in his narratives, Darius speaks only of the losses sustained by the enemy, without saying if his troops were victorious.

It seems likely, however, that the Persians under Dadarses did not meet with all the success expected by the King of Kings, or else this person who was undoubtedly an Armenian prince fell under his suspicion, for shortly after the above expedition Darius replaced him by a Persian general named Omises.

On their side, the Armenians apparently advanced to well beyond their frontier, and were subsequently the victors in the campaign against Darius. It was indeed in Assyria, probably in the southern buttresses of the Armenian Taurus that Omises met and defeated the insurgents towards the end of that year. A decisive battle seems according to the inscriptions to have been fought in May 518 B.C. in a district called Antyarus, a location we cannot identify. However, the Achaemenean statements contradict the facts as a whole, for Omises, afraid to commit himself and enter enemy territory, perhaps because of reverses, deemed it wiser to wait for his master, then engaged in besieging Babylon, to come and pacify in person the north of his empire.

---

(2) Transl. J. Oppert, in *Le Peuple et la Langue des Medes*, p. 127 sq.

These battles of the armies of Darius I against the Armenians are the oldest records of Armenian prowess that have come down to us, but before them there were certainly some expeditions of Cyrus into the Ararat massif. These wars succeeded long efforts on the part of Haik's descendants to conquer their new homeland, so that about 520 B.C. the Armenian people had already acquired much experience in the art of war. According to the testimony of the Achaemenids themselves, it was the Persians who had to repulse attacks, and not the Armenians who were obliged to drive back from their land the soldiers of Omises.

These few lines, written by their enemy, are entirely to the credit of the Armenian nation. They show this people, two centuries after their settling in their land, a regularly constituted State, conscious of sufficient strength to dare to cross swords with the cohorts of the Immortals. Perhaps also this uprising was a coalition of the northern peoples seeking to compel Darius to raise the siege of Babylon. In any case, the campaign of Omises and the way his undertaking terminated, place Armenia at the end of the 6th century B.C. in the position of a Power playing a very important part in the general political life of the East.

Inevitably, however, despite their valor, the Armenians had to succumb to numerical force, and so after the above wars we see their country included in the 13th Satrapy of the Persian Empire, together with the districts of the Ligves and the Carduch, whilst the mountains of the Lesser Caucasus not yet settled by the Armenians but inhabited by the Saspires and the Alarodii were placed in the 18th Satrapy along with the Macrones and the Moschi of Lazistan, and the Matienes of Central Kurdistan and Aberzaidjan. It would seem that at this period the Armenians had not yet reached the middle valley of the Araxes, that they owned, it is true, the provinces of Van and Erzerum, but their main center was rather towards the Euphrates, at the modern site of the town of Erzindjian, on the road leading from Cappadocia to Ararat. In this connection, however, we can only surmise.

The peoples of the 18th Satrapy, hardly yet subdued by the Persians and hostile to the Armenians, encircled the latter on the north and east in a vast semi-circle, whereas towards the east and south-east the royal army kept watch on the great stronghold.

The power of the Achaemenean empire, like that later of the Parthians and the Sassanids, rested on the feudal system, a conception

COIN OF THE ACHAEMENEAN
SATRAP PHARNABAZUS

of government which the Iranians took from Assyria, Chaldaea and Elam, and which corresponded moreover to the traditions of the Aryas formerly divided into clans on the steppes. The kings of the various nations, when they were not themselves satraps of their country, rendered obedience to governors of the Persian race appointed by the Court. But in most cases the local rulers reigned in actual fact over their people. The King of Kings demanded loyalty to his cause, a more or less heavy tribute, and contingents of troops assessed by himself. This system was applied by the vassals and by the heads of districts and even of villages.

My statements are supported by an abundance of proofs; one of these proofs is of particular interest because it deals with the government of Armenia under the Achaemenids.

Herodotus who had visited only the great Powers, and who endeavored especially to explain the causes and effects of the wars of the Medes, was necessarily very terse as regards the peoples subject to the Great King. But Xenophon (1), whose journey had quite another purpose, was much more copious than the Father of History in his remarks on the peoples through whose territory he crossed with his soldiers, and he has left us very detailed information about Armenia. His narrative is of the utmost value for our knowledge of the Armenians about 400 B.C.

He says: "When the army had all crossed the river Centrites (2) "about noon, and had ranged themselves in order, they proceeded for "another five leagues over large plains and gently sloping hills; for there "were no villages near the river, because of the proximity of the hostile "Carducii (Kurds) (3). The village, however, at which they stopped "was of considerable size, and contained a palace for the satrap; upon "most of the houses there were towers, and provisions were in great "plenty. Thence they proceeded, two days' journey, a distance of ten "leagues, until they passed round the sources of the river Tigris. (4).

---

(1) Anabasis, book IV, ch. 2 & 3.
(2) The Bohtan-tchai.
(3) In the Armenian Taurus (Djoudi-dagh).
(4) Rather the Bitlis-tchai.

"Thence they advanced three days' journey, fifteen leagues, to the "small river Teleboas (5), a stream of much beauty and with many vil- "lages on its banks. Here begins Western Armenia, the deputy-governor "of which was Tiribazus, an intimate friend of the king of Persia, who held "the king's stirrup when he mounted his horse. He rode up to the army "with a few horsemen and asked through an interpreter to speak with the "commanders .. He offered to let the army pass and to allow the soldiers "to take such provisions as they required, provided no damage should "be done as they passed through, which was granted. Thence they "proceeded, three days' march, fifteen leagues through a large plain. "Tiribazus followed them with his troops, keeping at a distance of about "ten stadia, till they arrived at palace buildings, with several villages "around stored with abundance of provision While they were encamped, "there fell in the night a great quantity of snow and in the morning it "was thought advisable to take up quarters in the neighboring villages ..
· Here they found all kinds of provisions in abundance, cattle, corn, dried "grapes, vegetables of all sorts, and fragrant old wines . . . (The Greeks) "lighted fires and anointed themselves with oils of sesamum, turpentine, "and bitter almonds, of which there was plenty around, with hog's lard, "and ointments made of all kinds of drugs .. They despatched in the night "Democrates of Temenos with a detachment of men to the hills where "fires had been seen .. He brought back a prisoner who had a Persian "bow and quiver, and a short battle-ax such as the Amazons have . . .
"(It was learned that Tiribazus) with his own troops of the province and "some mercenaries from the Chalybes and Taochians was prepared to "attack the Greeks at the foot of the mountains ... It was therefore re- "solved to seize the passes . The enemy were put to rout, some were "killed, and twenty horses were taken as was also the tent of Tiribazus; "in the latter were couches with silver feet and drinking-cups . . . . Thence "they proceeded three days' journey through a desert tract of country, to "the river Euphrates (1) which they passed not far from its source . . . "They advanced in snow five or six feet deep, many of the baggage slaves "and beasts of burden perished in it along with thirty soldiers "

The army suffered severely from the cold on these high plateaus and lost many men, so they spread out into the villages The Athenian Polycrates with his followers found in the village allotted to him "the

---

(5) Probably the Qara-sou, a river of Mouch, tributary of the eastern Euphrates.
(1) The Arsanias.

"head-man with all the villagers, together with seventeen colts that were
"being bred as a tribute for the king The head-man's daughter, who had
"been married but nine days, was there, but her husband had gone out to
"hunt hares Their houses were underground, the entrance like the mouth
"of a well, the people descended by ladders, but there were other passages
"dug into them for the cattle. In the houses were sheep, cows, goats, and
"fowls, also wheat, barley, vegetables, and beer to drink, which last was
"very strong, unless one mixed water with it, and apparently pleasant
"to those accustomed to it It was drunk with a reed from the vessels; many
"reeds of different kinds, with no knots, lay in the beer, whereon also floated
"the barley. Xenophon made the chief man of the village sup with him
"and told him to have no fear, that they would cause him no vexation if
"he would but lead the army safely to the border. This the chief promised
"and to regale Xenophon showed him where the wine was hidden. The
"soldiers spent the night in the midst of great abundance, setting a guard
"over the chief and keeping his children under their eye. The following
"day Xenophon took the head-man and went with him to Cheirisophus,
"and wherever he passed he found the soldiers feasting. The latter made
"him dismount and sit down to eat with them, serving him veal, lamb,
"pork, together with fowl and bread of wheat and barley. To drink to
"anyone's health, however, it was necessary to go to the cask and drink
"stooping down, like an animal at the trough . . . When they came to
"Cheirisophus, they found them all feasting, with wreaths on their
"heads made of dried grass in lieu of flowers, and being served by boys
"in their native costumes to whom they had to make signs for every-
"thing as to mutes .. . (The chief man when questioned) said they were
"in Armenia, and that the neighboring country was that of the Chalybes,
"and told them in what direction the road lay."

After ten days' march, the Greeks reached the banks of the Phasis (Araxes) (1), and entered the land of the Taochii (Kars), crossed the valley of the Harpasos (Jorokh), the country of the Saspires, and the mountains of the Chalybes (Lazistan), finally arriving at Trebizond

Xenophon states that Tiribazus, on instructions from his king, Tigranes, and following orders he had received from Susa, had intended

---

(1) Xenophon is mistaken in speaking of the Phasis, a river of Mingrelia.

attacking the Ten Thousand on their way through the Armenian territory; whereas his own account shows that actually the Greeks seized Tiribazus' camp without any provocation on the latter's part and merely because of the statement of one prisoner. This attack seems all the less justifiable when one considers that the Armenian governor had taken no precautions to protect his tent; the hospitality that Xenophon's soldiers subsequently received in Armenia and which they seem to have abused, shows that the inhabitants were well disposed towards them, and not hostile.

ALEXANDRIAN CONQUEST

Armenia thus was enjoying very considerable freedom under the Achaemenids when there came the defeat of Darius Codomannus, first at Issus and then at Arbela. The conquests of Alexander the Great caused indeed the greatest revolution that ever changed the face of the Asiatic world. The beneficent civilization of the Hellenes spread as far as India, extinguishing for centuries the obsolete principles of the old Eastern empires, bringing to the various peoples nobler conceptions regarding everything. It was the triumph of civilization over barbarism, and this ascendancy of the Hellenic spirit prevailed in Asia for six hundred years, until the accession of the Sassanids to the Persian throne brought about a return to the old Iranian culture.

TETRADRACHMA OF ALEXANDER THE GREAT

The defeat of the Achaemenean monarchy by the Macedonian king had, as regards Armenia, the only political result of exchanging Persian for Greek authority, but finding in this new status greater civil and religious freedom, the Armenians forsook Mazdeism that they had accepted only under compulsion and returned to the gods of their forefathers. They adopted progress with enthusiasm and under their Greek rulers' influence made great strides.

ALEXANDER'S SUCCESSORS

We have extremely little light concerning the events that took place in this part of Western Asia from the time of Alexander's death until the period of Mithidrates the Great, king of Pontus. We know, however, through Armenian chronologists (1), that in the year 324 B.C. the Greeks had sent into Armenia a governor named Phraataphernes or Neoptolemaeus; that in 322 the latter was replaced by Orontes (Hrant or Ervand) who ruled from 322 to 301; that in 301 (?) the country was governed by Ardoates or Artavazt; and that after a series of rulers whose names are unknown, with the exception of Arsames who struck coins (2) in the year 82 of the Seleucidan era (230 B.C.), Artabazanes or Artavaz (239-220 ?) ruled over Armenia and was succeeded by Orontes II (?) (220-215 ?).

ERVAND I 322-301 B.C.

ERVAND II 220-215 ?

This Orontes (Ervand) just mentioned is credited by Armenian tradition with having founded the city of Erivan. With their southern border constantly threatened first by the Persians and then by the Greeks, and finding their northern enemies far less formidable than those on the south, the Armenians entrenched themselves more and more strongly in the districts north of the Araxes. Ani, already fortified, contained holy places venerated by the people, and Erivan was founded in the plain commanding on one side the chief passages of the Araxes and on the other the gorges communicating from the Araxes valley to that of the river Cyrus.

TETRADRACHMA OF SELEUCUS I, NICATOR

Moses of Khoren has left us a curious description of the new city of Erivan:

"I love to speak of the splendid city of Yervandakert built by king "Ervand, who laid it out delightfully. In its center he built magnificent

---

(1) K. J. BASMADJIAN, *op. laud.*
(2) E. BABELON, *Numis. des rois de Syrie, d'Armenie, et de Commagene,* Paris, 1890.

"edifices radiating as from the pupil of the eye, around the dwellings are "gardens and pastures encircling like the eye's orbit, numerous vineyards "are like a rich and gracious fringe of eye-lashes, the ground to the north " in a handsome arch is indeed comparable to the lofty eye-brows of lovely "damsels, on the south the smooth surface of the meadows remind one "of attractive tender cheeks. the river opens as a mouth between the "two banks that are its lips And this lovely scenery seems to look up- "ward to the eminence whereon stands the monarch's palace. (1)"

The Armenians long considered the succession of princes just mentioned to be the first period of their kingdom, but this was a grievous mistake for it robbed them of their oldest claim to royalty. Before the Achaemenean period, during the reign of Cyrus, Armenia is known to have been governed by its own kings. We do not know the names of the sovereigns of Armenia during the two centuries following Haik's conquest, any more than we do those of the tributary kings under the Achaemenids; only the record of one Tigranes, the contemporary of Xenophon, has been preserved, but we do know nevertheless that these dynasties existed. Therefore, to pass them over unmentioned would be stripping Armenian history of its opening pages. (2).

In any case, after the dynasty that was contemporary with the first Seleucids in Syria, the native chronologers place a period of Greek domination lasting from 215 (?) to 190 B C., to the defeat of Antiochus the Great by the Romans at Magnesia Armenia then became free, and split into two kingdoms, Greater Armenia, on the east of the Euphrates, and Lesser Armenia bounded on the east by that same river

---

(1) MOSES OF KHOREN, II, 42, transl. A. TCHOBANIAN, *Le Peuple armenian son passe. sa culture son avenir*, p 37, Paris, 1913.

(2) Moses of Khoren, and the Armenian historians who drew from his writings, give a list of 36 names of the Haikian patriarchs and make this succession last 1480 years. thus allowing about 41 years to each reign This estimate of duration is inadmissible. Moreover, from 870 to 330 B.C, seventeen are supposed to have reigned, which would give 31 years apiece, which figure we cannot accept either. But if we take the only certain date in this legendary chronology, viz 330 B.C, and reduce to a probable ratio the different reigns, we see that the list of kings corresponds to the time of the Achaemenean monarchy. and that the series of patriarchs can very well be included in the two or three centuries taken up by the nation's advance from Cappadocia to the Ararat country and by their occupation of the new homeland In this case, the successions listed by Armenian traditions would correspond to actuality, the only mistake being the chronological estimates. These estimates are, moreover, of comparatively late compilation, they date from the time that Christian authors endeavored to make Armenian history tally with the Biblical record.

At this same period, about 180 B.C. a prince of the name of Sames, probably driven from Armenia by the Parthian invasion and believed to have been the son of Antiochis, a concubine of Antiochus IV, who married the Armenian king Xerxes, (1) declared himself independent at Samosata, on the Euphrates, and founded the kingdom of Commagene, the destiny

TETRADRACHMA OF ANTIOCHUS THE GREAT

of which was so closely linked to that of Armenia Minor. The empire of the Seleucids was at that time disintegrating into a multitude of small states.

ARTAXIAS CA. 160 B.C. The first king of Greater Armenia was Artaxias or Artashes I, a former general of Antiochus III. This king founded the city of Artaxata on the Araxes, at the foot of Qara-bagh, and made it his capital. The shapeless ruins of this city are still to be seen near the village of Khorvirâh, about nineteen miles to the south of Erivan.

During the early days of the reign of Artaxias, Armenia enjoyed independence; but about 165 or 159 B.C. it was attacked by Antiochus IV Epiphanes, and fell once more under Seleucidan control. In this fight for the independence of his kingdom Artaxias was defeated by Antiochus Epiphanes and lost his life. We do not know how long the new period lasted, but Justin informs us that at the beginning of the first century B.C. a king of Armenia named Ortoadistes was fighting against the king of Pontus. This Armenian

COIN OF SAMES, KING OF COMMAGENE

---

(1) Cf. E. BABELON, *Les Rois de Syrie, d'Armenie et de Commagene*, 1890, p. CCVIII sq.

— 81 —

ruler would appear to be the predecessor of one of the greatest among the sovereigns of Armenia, viz. Tigranes II, who gained such brilliant distinction by his alliances with Mithidrates and his wars with the Romans.

We know through Strabo that the reign of Artaxias was an era of conquests for Armenia. This king, by forming a powerful monarchy upheld by Roman statecraft, became a menace to the kings of Syria, and we may be certain that Antiochus Epiphanes only attacked him to be rid of a dangerous neighbor. With the Parthians pressing them on the east, and Roman power ever on the increase, the Seleucids for the safety of their dominions had to stifle this kingdom in its early stages as it was growing daily stronger and becoming a greater challenge.

ZARIADRAS Whilst Artaxias was reconstructing the kingdom of Greater Armenia, Zariadras, likewise a former general of Antiochus the Great, was founding Lesser Armenia, a State which continued to be ruled by his descendants until the time of Mithidrates.

The names of these two rulers, Artaxias (in Armenian Artashes) and Zariadras (Zareh) are Persian, and we cannot therefore know whether they were Armenians or Iranians. On the one hand, the Achaemeneans had spread their princes around over all the provinces of their vast empire, as viceroys, and these satraps fretting under the Greek overlordship, were inclined to assert their freedom, on the other hand, the Armenians had often adopted Iranian names through the Persian influence; consequently the nationality of these two kings remains uncertain. In any case, they relied on the Armenian element to shake off the yoke of the Seleucids. According to Cicero, Antiochus after his defeat was ordered by the conqueror to make the Taurus the boundary of his dominions, and this stipulation was a great help in furthering the independence of the princes governing in his name in both Armenias.

These kingdoms were then the only really civilized countries of the Transcaucasian region. Their inhabitants were intelligent and industrious, wide-awake, and thoroughly permeated with Hellenic influence. They had adopted the Greek language for their writings, and since the Macedonian conquest had become quite familiar with the use of money. The gold darics and the silver shekels of the Achaemenids and the coins

---

(1) We have no Armenian coins of the Achaemenian period, whereas during that same period, in Phoenicia and Cappadocia, the satraps of the Great King struck silver money with their own names inscribed in Aramaean characters

minted by the satraps (1), which had had little currency in the northern countries, were succeeded by Macedonian money, and that of the Seleucids, also by the coins struck by the Greek colonies on the Black Sea. The drachmas of the Parthians, just then appearing, were to be for several centuries the main medium of trade.

NUMISMATIC RECORDS Moses of Khoren states that Artaxias struck money bearing his effigy, which is extremely probable. But no coin of this ruler has been preserved. Moreover, the sequence of Armenian coins discovered to date is very incomplete, and the interpretation of the inscriptions they bear is often dubious. According to collections available, these numismatic records start with the second half of the first century of the Seleucidan era, and the only rulers whose coins we have are: Charaspes, period unknown, Arsames (ca. 230 B.C.) (1) Abdissares (ca. 200 B.C.) and Xerxes (ca. 170 B.C.) (2), none of which names appear in the Armenian lists; then Tigranes II, Artavazd II, Tigranes III, Tigranes IV, Tigranes V. and his sister Erato. Finally we have the head of Artaxias, the son of Polemon, which is found on the back of some of the coins struck by Germanicus (3).

COIN OF CHARASPES

In the absence of Armenian objects of art or craftsmanship, and of structural remains contemporaneous with the Greek period, (4) the study of the types and inscriptions of what coins we have assures us that Armenia soon became one of the centers of Hellenism in the East. In vain had the Persians tried to assimilate the Armenians, and to impose on them their oriental customs and beliefs;

COIN OF ARSAMES

---

(1) POLYAENUS, IV, 17, mentions an Armenian prince who showed himself a friend of Antiochus Hierax (who died 227 B.C.).
(2) POLYBIUS, *Excerpta*, VIII, 25. This ruler was contemporary with Antiochus IV, Epiphanes (175-164 B.C.).
(3) Cf. E. BABELON, *op. laud.*
(4) A very fine female head discovered at Satala in Armenia has been ascribed to a statue of the goddess Anahit, but we have no supporting proof.

— 83 —

Iranian culture did not meet the aspirations of this people, whereas Greek civilization in line with the traditions of the Aryans of Europe found in Armenia a favorable soil for development.

Such is the history of the beginnings of the Armenian nation. These annals, hitherto little known, are such as to inspire with pride this people who, holding an outpost of Indo-European civilization amidst Asiatic powers, never failed to uphold firmly the Aryan standard. In heathen times the Armenians maintained for centuries Greek culture, and as Christians they became the great champions of our faith and western civilization; consequently their rôle in history has always been a famous one, ever since the conquest of Asia by the Macedonians. But before Alexander the Great even, when the Hellenic peoples were themselves struggling individually, Armenia was a powerful State with which the mighty sovereigns of Asia had to reckon. This is the part of Armenian history that is least known, although it is the most interesting, for the whole life of the Armenian people, up to our times, is but the consequence of those early pages, and the reason that the Armenians for twenty centuries have shown such energy, such valor, and such attachment to their national spirit, is that "noblesse oblige." (1)

COIN OF ABDISSARES

COIN OF XERXES

---

(1) The leading facts contained in this chapter were published in *le Mercure de France*, (Sept.-Oct., 1916) vol. CXVII.

PORTRAIT OF KING TIGRANES II, THE GREAT
(From a tetradrachma in the British Museum)

CHAPTER III

Reign of Tigranes II, the Great.—Lucullus and Pompey in Armenia.—The Country Divided by the Romans.—The Last Kings of the Dynasty of Artaxias

Until the beginning of the first century B.C., the Armenians had encountered on the battle-field only Asiatic peoples, who, though admittedly powerful, were lacking in the organization and discipline that are an army's chief strength. Themselves accustomed to Eastern principles which neither the Greek influence nor the conquest by Alexander had succeeded in uprooting, and governed according to the feudal system like the Persians, they raised troops through the medium of noblemen who remained at the head of their contingents, and whose obedience to the royal power was not always what it should have been for the nation's welfare. But among the Parthians, the rulers of Pontus, all the petty kings of Asia Minor, and even among the Seleucids themselves, administrative and military inexperience was the same as in Armenia. Consequently the Armenian people were able to hold their own, often very successfully, against any of their neighbors seeking to encroach on them.

From the time of Tigranes the Great, however, the opposing elements took on new aspects due to the appearance of the Roman legions. Pitted against equal numbers, the Asiatics' resistance became mythical. The great Republic, relying on its generals and diplomats and on its military strength, used the latter, alternately with its political shrewdness, to get possession of the natural stronghold of Armenia commanding Western Asia and constituting a bridgehead against Media, Syria, and Pontus. As soon as opportunity occurred, therefore, the Roman generals lost no time in taking the very opposite course from that pursued formerly by the Achaemenids, even still by the Parthians, and resumed later by Sassanids, Arabs, and Turks. The possession of Armenia was to be fought over for centuries, and the Armenians were to be subjected to all kinds of influences which often were disastrous when they became divided in purpose. Some of their feudal nobility favored the Persians, others the Romans, and many of them too often, alas! forgot the paramount interests of their king and nation.

ARTAVAZD II CA. 112 B.C.

During the reign of Artavazd II (1), about 112 B.C., his neighbor, Mithidrates V. the Great, king of Pontus, extended by conquest the borders of his dominions. Recognizing all the danger his kingdom would incur one day from the proximity of the newly acquired possessions of Rome, this ruler conceived the idea of founding a vast empire that could hold its own against the Roman generals. The blood of the Achaemenids flowing in his veins inspired him with the thought of recovering for Asia Minor its erstwhile splendor and power, but his idea was a Hellenized

TETRADRACHMA OF MITHIDRATES THE GREAT
(Numismatic Collection, Paris. Drawn by M. J. Emonts)

---

(1) or Artoadistus (123-94 B.C.).

— 86 —

Asia, combining not only the old traditions of the East but also the Greek culture now threatened with ruin by the West. With profound political foresight, he saw the schism that would eventuate later between Rome and Byzantium, between the West and the East. Within seven years, Mithridates had added to his dominions Colchis (2), the Black Sea coast (3), the Tauric Chersonese (4), and a part of Armenia (5) When, however, he sought to expand to the east of the Euphrates, he was stopped in that direction by the valor of the Armenians, and the peoples of the Caucasus leagued together to preserve their homelands. To the east, Mithridates' kingdom never went beyond the pass of Souram (1). and the inhabitants of the valleys of the Cyrus and Araxes, and those of the plateau of Erzerum, preserved their independence. These countries were split up into a large number of petty kingdoms, principalities, and minor domains, whose warlike lords brooked no authority but their own good pleasure. In Transcaucasia and in the mountains, there were gathered a number of still very uncivilized tribes who were ever at war with their neighbors including the Armenians, and only the power of Rome was able to subdue them eventually, even nominally.

TIGRANES II THE GREAT, 94-54 B.C. Such was the situation politically in the north of western Asia, when Tigranes II, called the Great (94-54 B.C.) (2) ascended the throne of Armenia. With him began the most glorious military period in the country's history.

Still a young man, Tigranes had once been a hostage in Persian hands, and it was the Parthian king Mithridates II who caused him to be given the crown. The King of Kings, moreover, exacted in payment sixty-six valleys of Artavazd II's dominions.

---

(2) The basin of the river Phasis.

(3) Afkhasia, Lazistan, Trebizond, as far as Amisus.

(4) The Crimea.

(5) Lesser Armenia, on the west of the Euphrates.

(1) Between the valleys of the Phasis and the Cyrus.

(2) E. Babelon, *Les Rois de Syrie, d'Armenie et de Commagene*, p. 213 (numismatics), calls this prince, Tigranes I and states that he reigned from 215 to 256 of the Selencidan era (97-56 B C.).

DRACHMA OF THE PARTHIAN KING MITHIDRATES II

The definite history of Armenia may be said to begin with the new king, for the statements of native Christian writers, often so questionable unfortunately, can henceforth be verified by the many writings left us by Greek and Latin authors. As for the annals of heathen Armenia, which no doubt once existed either in Greek or in Pehlevi, they have not been preserved to us.

The king of Pontus, Mithidrates, realizing that he would never be able to subdue the Armenians and that Tigranes would be a very dangerous neighbor in his way, unless he could have him as an ally, did all he could to draw Tigranes into his war against Rome. Tigranes, to whom the Pontine kingdom relinquished the whole of the south of Asia Minor, thought this alliance would assure to his dominions a status enabling him to treat as an equal both with the Romans and the Persian Arsacids. He therefore decided to espouse the aims and share the dangers of Mithidrates.

The young king, who already owned vast territories, began by conquering Sophene, then turning his army against the Parthians, he recovered from Persia the districts he had been obliged to give up on his accession. Finally, taking advantage of a palace revolution at Ctesiphon and of the assassination of Mithidrates II by Orodes I, Tigranes—who had had time to establish his power and whose ambition was unlimited—remembering the humiliations he had known at the Parthian court, arrogated to himself the title of King of Kings (1). This title had been borne by the sovereigns of Iran from the time of the Achaemenids. Tigranes thus followed the example set by the Seleucids, and showed that he was contemplating great conquests. He had allied himself by marriage with the family of the shrewd king of Pontus, the sworn enemy of the Romans. Consequently he did not hesitate to attack the rulers under the protection of Rome, and about

TETRADRACHMA OF THE PARTHIAN KING ORODES I

---

(1) Basileus Basileôn, *Vide* coins of Mithidrates II & Orodes I.

91 B.C. he invaded Cappadocia which he considered, probably from tradition, as belonging to the Armenian patrimony. Driving out Ariobarzanus, whom Sulla had just placed on the throne of this region, he put in his stead Ariarathes, possibly the son of his ally Mithridates. The king of Pontus undoubtedly joined in this expedition, for Cappadocia had hardly been conquered before Ariarathes set out to attack the legions then in Attica. The young prince died, however, on the way, and Mithridates vanquished by Sulla was compelled by the treaty of Dardanus to relinquish his claims to Asia Minor and Cappadocia. The former king of the latter province, Ariobarzanus, returned to his throne.

GOLD COIN OF SULLA

MITHIDRATES V. CONQUERED BY SULLA

Tigranes, however, taking warning from the repulses suffered by his ally, deemed it wiser not to pursue his aims on lands protected by Rome and turned to his other frontiers. Within a few years he had subdued Gordyene (2), Median Atropatenes (3), Adiabenes (4), the region of Nisibis (5), and finally the kingdom of Edessa, or Osrhoene, over which he appointed an Arab family, of which Abgar and Manou were later members. His ambitions, however, were not yet satisfied, for then, throwing caution to the winds as regards the Romans, he again took arms against the West. After subduing Sophene for the second time, he ravaged Cappadocia where he captured very many slaves and rich booty and marched on Cilicia and Syria.

During these campaigns Tigranes had encountered no opposition from the Romans. It seemed to him that their generals were afraid to come to blows with a monarch whose dominions had grown to such an extent in a few years. On his way to Antioch, the king of Armenia stopped awhile in his province of the Tigris to draw up the plans and supervise the building of the great city of Tigranocerta which he had decided to found south of the river. The prisoners taken in Cappadocia, Cilicia, and Syria, were engaged in this work when suddenly, after the king had left for Antioch, Lucullus appeared at the head of the Roman legions.

---

(2) Northern Kurdistan.
(3) Azerbaidjan.
(4) Mosul.
(5) Nisibin (Antioch of Mygdonia)

This was the first time that the Armenians had come face to face with the Roman army, for hitherto the Senate had spared the king of Armenia. As a matter of fact, although the ambitions of the king of Pontus ran counter to Rome's political aims in Asia, it was not so, at least for the time being, as regards Armenia. This kingdom, standing between the Parthian dominions and those of the Republic, and being itself hostile to the Persians, was of considerable service by its very existence, and the Armenians besides were the only intermediaries for the trade of the Mediterranean with Central Asia now that relations were broken between Rome and Ctesiphon. However, Tigranes' expeditions into Cappadocia, Cilicia, and Syria, all under the Senate's protection, had aroused in Italy both annoyance and anxiety. It was known that although he had not taken part in the last aggression of Mithidrates V, Tigranes was nevertheless the ally of his father-in-law and brother-in-law, the king of Pontus. An actual coalition of the two kings might become very dangerous, should as was probable these two powerful States join up with the Arsacids of Persia to drive out the legions from Asia. A firm hand was therefore necessary in dealing with the Armenians, whose king must be made to understand that he had to respect the territories under Roman protection and keep to his own frontiers of the Tigris and the Armenian Taurus.

The Senate hesitated to undertake a war against a ruler who seemed to them like another Mithidrates, and were wondering whether the results of any such campaign would be commensurate with the risks to the Republic and the enormous expense it would entail, when Antiochus and his brother, the heirs of the Seleucids who had been driven from Asia, appealed to the Conscript Fathers for the restitution of their dominions. Thereupon Lucullus, more farsighted than the Senators, lost no time in espousing the cause of Alexander's successors ousted from their heritage.

LUCULLUS His late success at Cabira, near the source of the river Halys, over the king of Pontus urged him on, moreover, to proceed with his plans, and without awaiting orders from Italy he haughtily summoned Tigranes to deliver up to him Mithidrates. The latter upon the loss of his army had fled to the Armenian court, after first slaying at Pharnacia his two sisters and his wives to save them from slavery.

Tigranes was at Antioch when Appius Clodius, sent to him by Lucullus, presented himself. Upon the king's refusal to hand over his guest and relative, the Roman general hastened to the Euphrates at the head of twelve thousand veterans and three thousand horsemen, and crossing Sophene marched against the city of Tigranocerta.

Thus threatened, the king of Armenia left Syria and repaired to the mountains separating the sources of the Euphrates from those of the Tigris, after having the messenger hanged en route who had brought him the news of Lucullus' advance. From the center of his dominions he was summoning to arms his many subjects and vassals when he learned that the Roman vanguard, after routing the troops of his lieutenant Mithrobarzanus, was besieging Tigranocerta.

The city resisted bravely, and Mankeos in command of the garrison used all the means of defense at his disposal. The besiegers' engines of war were consumed in rivers of burning naphtha, and the Roman soldiers riddled with arrows were compelled to keep far away from the walls, when Tigranes emerging from the mountains with twenty thousand men advanced to raise the blockade, expecting an easy mastery of Lucullus' small army. The Roman general, however, allowed his adversary no time; leaving five thousand men before the city, he went forward against Tigranes with ten thousand only, and boldly crossed the river separating him from the enemy.

BATTLE OF TIGRANOCERTA Taxile, one of Mithidrates' lieutenants, who was with the Armenian army, wisely advised the king to avoid an all-out battle, to surround Lucullus and harass him unceasingly, till he succumbed from hunger. But Tigranes measuring his great number of men with the comparatively few of the enemy, disdained Taxile's advice, although the latter was counseling him out of experience of Roman prowess learned at personal cost. The king's heedlessness even went so far as to omit occupying two hillocks commanding the ground where his thousands of horsemen were massed. Noticing this omission, Lucullus despatched two cohorts to occupy these small eminences, and as soon as these were secured he let loose his cavalry and attacked that of the Armenians on their flank. Once the battle was on and Tigranes' horsemen were facing the Romans, the legionaries rushing down from the hills charged them in reverse. Attacked on both sides at once, the pick of the Armenian cavalry consisting of the king's body-guard was thrown back on the infantry. The latter had not had time to get into battle array, and thus the whole army was thrown into disorder and giving ground took to flight pursued by the victors. Tigranes owed his life only to his swift steed, and the Romans, carrying the day at the end of a short encounter, picked up his royal head-dress and diadem on the battle-field.

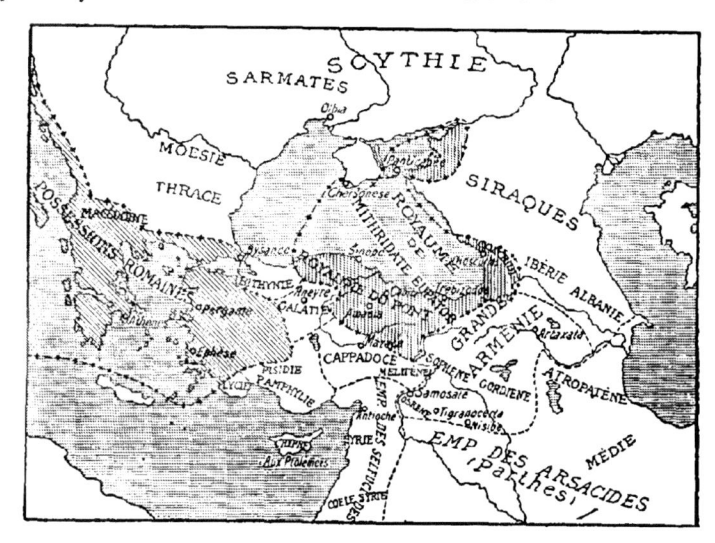

KINGDOMS OF PONTUS AND ARMENIA DURING THE WARS WITH THE ROMANS

At Tigranocerta, Mankeos tried to maintain the garrison's courage following this sudden overwhelming disaster, but the countless Greek prisoners within the walls opened its gates to the Romans. Lucullus found in the city's granaries 20 million medimni of corn (1) and in the treasury 8,000 talents of gold (2), an enormous sum for the time, which enabled him to defray all the cost of the war and to pay each soldier a bonus of one hundred denarii (3).

This battle liberated from Armenian rule all the middle valley of the Tigris and the provinces south of that river taken by Tigranes a short time before from the Parthians and Syrians. Lucullus kept the territory and went on to invade Commagene, the throne of which country he gave to Prince Antiochus Theos. He then took the city of Samosata, passed

---

(1) about 27½ million bushels.
(2) 9 million dollars.
(3) $22.60.

triumphantly through Syria, Phoenicia, Cilicia, Galatia, and Sophene, and re-established the kingdom of the Seleucids.

This was a terrible blow for Tigranes, but the king of Pontus soon restored his courage. While the battle of Tigranocerta was on, Mithidrates was already on the way to his ally's aid with ten thousand Armenians. He arrived too late to prevent Lucullus' victory but he did come in time to save the Armenians from still greater defeat. Tigranes thenceforth was discredited with the Romans, and it was to the interest of the king of Pontus that the war should go on, for if the king of Armenia were to make terms with the victors, the cause of Pontus was irretrievably lost. Consequently Mithidrates used all his influence and all his persuasive powers with his son-in-law and brother-in-law to induce him to continue fighting and to entrust him (Mithidrates) with the generalship. He was then sixty years old and his age and experience with the enemy's tactics and strategy were a guaranty of the success of their allied arms.

COIN OF ANTIOCHUS THEOS, KING OF COMMAGENE

The two kings sent ambassadors to all the rulers of Asia asking them to arise against the common enemy, against the desecrator of their gods, for Lucullus had no scruples in letting his troops sack their most revered temples. Had he not just pillaged the famous holy place of Anahit?

Most of the rulers responded to the appeal of Mithidrates and Tigranes. The king of the Parthians, Phraat III, however, declined all the proposals made to him, even though he was offered the recovery of Mesopotamia and Adiabene that had been taken from him. The Persian king then possibly had his hands full on his eastern borders, or perhaps he was not unwilling to see the downfall of Tigranes who had caused the Arsacids of Iran so many grievances. We have too little knowledge of Persia's annals to be able to discern the reasons for his refusal (1).

A new army was speedily raised, and the two kings, recognizing that Asiatic troops were unable to remain in line against the legions, decided to use the tactics of the Parthians, i.e. to harass the enemy unceasingly without ever joining battle. The great amount of cavalry at the two allies' disposal, practically half their army, enabled them to give the enemy

---

(1) All the historical records of Persia were destroyed by order of the caliphs when the country was invaded by the Arabs.

no respite. Nothing could be more fatal for Lucullus whose prestige was waning every day in Rome, and who was sure to be recalled at the slightest failure. This general's pride and luxurious and aristocratic tastes, had raised him up many enemies in Italy, and those jealous of him accused him of premeditated slowness in waging the war. It was claimed, and justifiably so, that the proconsul was much more concerned with winning treasures than battles. Moreover the Roman army, tired of ceaseless fighting, of iron discipline, and of long and wearisome marches, and sharing very little in the plunder with which their chief was enriching himself so shamefully, were murmuring and threatening to revolt. Lucullus must at all costs carry off a striking victory to raise his soldiers' morale and silence the dissatisfaction in Rome.

TETRADRACHMA OF THE PARTHIAN KING PHRAAT III

After staying some time (68 B.C.) at Tigranocerta, Lucullus left there about midsummer and crossed the Sindjar mountains, the Tigris valley, and the Armenian Taurus, and passing by the eastern side of lake Van entered Greater Armenia and the Arsanias valley. After routing the Armenian cavalry, he crossed the latter river and was about to besiege Artaxata when he was caught by the severe winter which sets in so early on these high tablelands. His soldiers mutinied, and, in these lands so ill-known to the Romans both as regards the problem of supplies and the natural difficulties, Lucullus was afraid of endangering his army. He therefore withdrew into southern Armenia to winter at Nisibis, which important town he took by assault under cover of a dark and stormy night. This withdrawal though caused by the inclement weather was nevertheless made much of by his enemies in Italy.

LUCULLUS RECALLED Upon hearing that Lucullus had gone north, the Armenians had returned to Tigranocerta. The city had been left with only a small garrison under the general's lieutenant Fannius, and the latter unable to man the ramparts had evacuated it and taken refuge in a detached fort where Tigranes was besieging him. Lucullus, despite his promise to his soldiers to return them to Italy, left Nisibis to extricate his lieutenant, but that is as far as his offensive went. Bad news reached him both from northern Asia and from Italy. Mithridates had just wiped out the army corps of Triarius at Ziela (Zillah) not far from the river Iris, and reconquered his kingdom of Pontus, whilst the Senate yielding to the clamors of the demagogues and financiers whose exorbitant dealings Lucullus had interfered with or diverted to his own profit, had recalled the commander of the campaign in the East together with his troops, and were sending in their place a fresh army under Pompey. Lucullus was at Talaura when the orders of the Conscript Fathers reached him. He continued on his way in a memorable retreat through very difficult country, whilst Mithridates, delivered from all anxiety and assisted by a large army brought him by Tigranes, set about reestablishing himself.

Lucullus came back from the East after a barren but none the less notable campaign, laden with enormous treasures as his only triumph. Pompey on the other hand, more fortunate, found on his arrival in Asia his enemies divided. Tigranes, who was of a naturally cruel disposition, embittered by his ill-fortune, had slain two of his own sons, and Tigranes the Younger, the grandson of the king of Pontus by his mother Cleopatra, incited either by fear or ambition, joined the new Roman general and took up arms against his father. Finally by a clever stroke of diplomacy the Parthian king of Iran, Phraat III, allied himself with Rome and for his help was promised his old provinces of Mesopotamia extended to the Euphrates. The contingents of the King of Kings raised Pompey's army to fifty thousand men, whereas Mithridates had only thirty thousand infantry and three thousand horsemen.

CN. POMPEIUS The first encounter of the two opponents took place on the left bank of the river Lycus (Iechil-Irmak), near the future site of the city of Nicopolis, and the Roman success due to a surprise attack was disastrous for the enemy.

Pompey had occupied the heights overlooking the mountain passes through which the Pontine army had to come, and Mithridates ill-informed by his scouts had unsuspectingly halted by the gorge to rest in the heat of the day. The legionaries seized the opportunity to fall suddenly on their enemy's broken ranks and carry out a frightful massacre. The king fled with a handful of officers and one of his wives who had fought by his side, and reached the Euphrates, where he was rejoined by the remnants of his army. Thence he proceeded to Armenia hoping to find shelter and assistance from his son-in-law. Tigranes, however, had been obliged himself to flee into the mountains to escape from his son and the Parthian king Phraat III then besieging Artaxata, and consequently could give his ally no help. Shortly afterwards, however, Tigranes learned of the withdrawal of the Persian king and drove out the body of enemy troops left in his capital, putting to flight his own son's contingents.

Despite these minor successes, the king of Armenia felt the weight of Rome's power, and seeing himself doomed unless he could free his throne from the wrath of the Senate, sent peace terms to Pompey. He promised to forsake Mithidrates and even offered one hundred talents (1) reward to whomsoever should deliver up his former ally. He arrested his father-in-law's envoys and delivered them to the victorious general who, halting his pursuit of Mithidrates fleeing towards the Phasis, Afkhasia, and Crimea, crossed the Araxes and pitched his camp within sight of Artaxata. Pompey certainly was not refusing to negotiate with Tigranes, but he meant to impose his own terms on Armenia in order to keep it in obedience to Rome and to make the country a rampart for the legions against the Parthians with whom Rome's alliance, running counter to the Senate's general Eastern policy, could not last long.

Recognizing all resistance as useless and fearing the intrigues of his son, Tigranes accepted the hard terms of the conqueror. The old king, discarding his purple mantle and wearing only his head-band and royal diadem, rode to the Roman camp and, handing the victors his steed and his sword, was led before the proconsul to whom he delivered his tiara and diadem and did obeisance.

Satisfied with this complete submission, Pompey raised the king kindly, returned him his royal insignia, and treated him as a monarch. The terms Tigranes had to accept, however, were very hard. He surrendered to the Romans Syria and Phoenicia, Cilicia and Cappadocia, Sophene and Gordyene, abandoned all future claims to those provinces, and was to pay the victors an indemnity of six thousand talents (2).

With Armenia thus vanquished and reduced as it were to a Roman protectorate, and Mithidrates in flight and stripped of his dominions, Pompey had no further reasons for any alliance with the Parthians. On flimsy pretexts, he proceeded against Phraat and seized Gordyene and

(1) $108.000
(2) About $6,500,000.

northern Mesopotamia, which he gave to Tigranes in order to prevent any reconciliation of the Armenians and the Persians. On the north, the Iberians and the Albanians having attacked the Romans during the winter of 66-65 B.C. the proconsul threw the Albanians back to the north bank of the Cyrus and drove into the mountains the Iberian king, Artoces. Finally he carved out for Deiotarus, a former tetrarch of the Galatian tribe of the Tolostobogii, a new kingdom of Armenia Minor, comprising Pontic Armenia as far as the borders of Colchis and the territory of Tigranes, the eastern half of the kingdom of Pontus with the cities of Pharnacia and Trapezus (Trebizond). The former possessions of Deiotarus were included in this new State, namely, Galatia and the provinces between Amisus and the mouths of the river Halys.

Pompey's expedition left Asia consequently in a very favorable situation politically for Rome. On the north, Armenia Major and Armenia Minor, both protectorates of the Republic, were a standing threat to the Arsacids of Iran, and enabled the legions to take the offensive against the Persians as soon as circumstances were favorable. It would have been premature to exact harder terms and make Roman provinces of these countries, for the Senate's policy had a much longer range and foresaw the day when, with the conquest of the Parthians, Rome's power should extend over the whole of both the Tigris and Euphrates basins, over the lands to the north of the Araxes, and over the Persian Arabistan or Khouzistan of our times. These ambitions included not only an immense expansion of Rome's Asiatic provinces, but also and above all, possession of the silk caravan routes through Syria and the Persian Gulf. Two thousand years after these events, a large empire also dreamed of world dominion and to satisfy that same ambition let loose the most frightful war, aimed at seizing this great Eastern highway.

On his departure from Asia, Pompey left Armenia not only conquered but humiliated. Tigranes the Younger, in chains, was sent to Rome for the victor's triumph. As for the Arsacids of Persia, they were just as much wounded in pride; driven from Gordyene, and stripped of that province and of northern Mesopotamia in favor of the old king Tigranes, they could dream only of a resumption of arms to get back their lost territory.

By crushing Mithidrates and Tigranes, the Romans had put an end to Macedonian civilization in Asia, for nothing remained of all the States born of Alexander's conquests but mere ruins, petty kings quite unable of sustaining the Hellenic name. The two great kings of Pontus and Armenia were the last who could ever have revived in their lands the splendid civilization of Greece.

TETRADRACHMA OF KING TIGRANES II OF ARMENIA
(on reverse, the Fortuna of Antioch)

Among the finest treasures of Greek numismatics in Asia we must give first place to the splendid tetradrachmas of Mithidrates and Tigranes, two rulers of cultured tastes whose active reigns earned them the title of "Great." No coin of the Syrian Seleucids, nor of the Egyptian Ptolemies, can be compared with the superb portraits of the kings of Pontus and Armenia. The misfortune that befell these two thrones arose from both monarchs daring to stand up to the power of Rome. Had Tigranes and Mithidrates lived in other times, they would have founded great empires, for their political ideas were vast in scope. They both do honor to Greek culture not only in the courage they showed in giving battle to the greatest generals of ancient times, but also in their breadth of view and perspicacity.

Like Alexander, Tigranes founded cities. At his command Tigranocerta rose as in a dream in the south of his kingdom, while in the new capital of Armenia Athenian actors arrived as soon as the theatre was built to play the masterpieces of Greek literature. Greek sculptors were summoned to adorn the city, and just as Mithidrates gathered art treasures at Panticapaeum, (in the Crimea), so did Tigranes cause to be brought to him in his dominions the divinities of ancient Greece. At the royal court all the dignitaries of the kingdom, like all the princes there present, spoke and wrote in the language of Demosthenes, and Artavazd, the king's own son, composed Greek tragedies and discourses of which we still read Plutarch's praises. Thus Tigranes, engrossed as he was with war and vast political schemes, devoted nevertheless his few leisure hours to cultural pleasures. Both at the Pontine court and the Armenian court there was as much mental refinement as at Rome, at Athens, or at Alexandria, the court of the sumptuous Cleopatra.

Fortune was not kind to Tigranes; vanquished by an enemy before whom all the world's rulers had to bow, he had to humble himself, and historians have not always been just to this monarch because of his lack of good fortune. Had he gained the day over Lucullus and Pompey, he would have been lauded to the skies by the ancient writers, and by modern writers in turn.

BRONZE COIN OF TIGRANES II

Tigranes, however, had shown himself a very great ruler, an able warrior, and had not Mithridates drawn him away into ambitions out of proportion to his people's resources, his statesmanship would have been profound. Greater foresight would have enabled this king to found a lasting empire. He had unfortunately Asiatic ideas concerning the creation and government of a State, one success led him to want yet another, and his Oriental views included no other reasons for the possession of power. Inevitably Armenia had to become one day an agent of Rome against the Parthians, but her rulers could have chosen to be the Republic's ally and not its servant.

With the Romans, friendship first and then protection were the forerunners of annexation. But Armenia's position and military strength would have constrained Rome to treat her with consideration, had her kings not alternated in alliances with both the great rival powers, the Republic and the Persians, and if her provincial governors had not been most of the time at enmity among themselves, divided by contrary interests. The Iranian Arsacids and the Romans both had numerous agents working for them in the Armenian dominions, and their influence on the inhabitants, on the ruling classes, and on the monarchs themselves, was pernicious. Tigranes II's superior intelligence and the blood the Armenian people so bravely shed deserved a better reward than the bitter fruit of servitude. Thus crumbled in dust the hopes of two men of genius who at one time seemed raised up by destiny to revive Greek culture in the Eastern world.

The Parthians had just taken up arms once more and were threatening not only Armenia but the Roman possessions in Asia. Rome therefore had to prepare for war.

MARCUS CRASSUS

The Senate selected for the expedition the member of the triumvirate (Caesar, Pompey, and Marcus Crassus) the least fitted for the task. Marcus Crassus, an old man notorious for his ambition, his incompetence, and his sordid avarice, was appointed over the Roman army. He left the Eternal City during the autumn, 54 B.C., sailed from Brundisium with seven legions, disembarked at Dyrrachium, and crossing Epirus, Macedonia, and Thrace by the Via Ignatia, reached Asia Minor by the Hellespont, and proceeded to the Euphrates. On M. Crassus' arrival at the frontier of Armenia, Tigranes' son, Artavazd, whom his father had made co-regnant ever since the battle of Tigranocerta, had been reigning alone since the previous year, the probable date of the old king's death.

ARTAVAZD III
56-34 B.C.

In Persia, Phraat III had prepared an immense expedition against the Armenians, and he would undoubtedly have taken back his former provinces had he been able to carry out his plans, but he had just been slain by his sons Mithidrates and Orodes. After committing this odious crime, the two brothers were fighting one another for the throne of the King of Kings. Mithidrates feeling his side was the weaker had appealed for help to Gabinius, the proconsul of Syria, when he was defeated by an army under the Surena or grand vizier of his brother. He was captured and put to death in his brother's presence at Babylon.

COIN OF THE PARTHIAN MITHIDRATES III

Rid of his rival by this fresh murder, and no longer embarrassed by a civil war, Orodes resumed the execution of his father's plans, and his forces started out against the king of Armenia. Crassus who, after occupying Nicephorium (Rakkah) beyond the Euphrates, was back in Syria, crossed the river again with 40,000 men, uncertain as to which road he should take to advance against Orodes. Artavazd, arriving with 6,000 horsemen, advised the general to go forward through Armenia where his army would have no difficulties and run no danger. Crassus however chose the southern route across the desert. Abgar III, king of Osrhoene, who occupied Edessa and Carrhae, was an ally of the Romans, and the triumvir expected that the great Greek cities of the Euphrates and the Tigris would rise against the Persians and render him much assistance. Abgar encouraged these hopes in Crassus' mind and urged him to take the southern road. Fear lest the Parthian king should carry away the treasures of Ctesiphon into the interior of the empire also weighed much in the greedy general's decision, for mindful of the riches that Lucullus brought back with him from Asia, he thought he saw his own chance of making a tremendous fortune.

Crassus crossed the Euphrates at Zeugma (Biredjik) with seven legions, 43,000 men. On arriving there his lieutenant Cassius advised him to follow the river bank and have a flotilla of boats laden with supplies and material follow alongside on the water, (the method later adopted by the Emperor Julian), so as to strike his enemies a big blow by appearing before their capital cities of Seleucia on the right bank of the Tigris and Ctesiphon on its left. But, lured by the plan of the king of Osrhoene, Crassus marched directly on Carrhae across the desert of eastern Mesopotomia. By way of Tigranocerta and Nisibis the Roman army was to reach the Tigris and going down that river's bank via Hatra reach Seleucia, remaining protected in the direction of Persia. This campaign plan was much less favorable than that of having the legions follow the Euphrates, for it necessitated transporting the war material and supplies on camels, and the enormous supply caravans hindered and delayed the army's advance. Crassus in command for the first time in these arid lands did not realize properly the natural difficulties. He went forward confidently, therefore, but when a few days later the legions reached the Balissos river (the Nahr-Belik), they saw in the distance a detachment of enemy cavalry. Abgar and his Arabs set off in pursuit of the latter, but these men of Osrhoene did not come back. The following day, the Roman army weary and thirsty was six miles south of Carrhae (Harran), a little to the north of Ichnae, when the Parthian squadrons appeared with their standards of gold-embroidered silk. The Grand Vizier was in personal command, and near him was seen the traitor Abgar with his Arabs.

Publius Crassus, the son of the Roman general, commanding a corps of Gauls, was afraid lest he be surrounded; he rushed on the enemy, but the latter going backward drew him away from the main body of his army. Then the Persian heavy cavalry charged down on him from all sides, with their long spears and their steel scale-armor covering man and steed, and the Gauls, obliged to form a ring, were submerged on this shelterless plain under a deluge of arrows. Publius Crassus was wounded, and seeing his six thousand men massacred, ordered his attendants to kill him

A few hours after this first disaster, the host of Parthian bowmen under the protection of mailed lancers were busy destroying two-thirds of Crassus' army. The remnants of the seven legions took refuge first of all in the city of Carrhae, but proceeded during the night to withdraw to the Armenian mountains, led by Caius Cassius. The Parthians, however, did not mean to lose their hold and, harrassing unremittingly the Roman army, forced Crassus to sue for terms. Once they had drawn him into a trap, they slaughtered him and his escorting officers.

Ten thousand Roman soldiers fell into the enemy's hands and were sent to the Persian army of Margiana. Caius Cassius painfully regained Syria, bringing back eight or nine thousand men, all that were left of the splendid army of 43,000 soldiers that had left Italy. The grand vizier sent the Roman general's head to his master Orodes, who was then invading Armenia. Artavazd III (56-34 B.C.) was on the throne of the latter country.

This ruler, the son and heir of Tigranes the Great, was loyal during the early part of his reign to his father's commitments towards the Romans, and he supplied Crassus at the opening of the campaign with a corps of 6,000 men. Whether he forsook the Roman general upon the latter's refusal to pass through Armenia, or whether he was getting ready to come to his assistance, we cannot say. However, the invasion of his kingdom by the Parthians seems to have been his chief reason for withdrawing to his own land. Crassus' disaster prompted him to make peace, and he therefore came to terms with the Persians. To seal the new alliance he gave his sister in marriage to Prince Pacorus, Orodes' favorite son

The news of the great victory won by the Surena reached the Persian court during the celebration of this marriage, and a Greek company of players were giving Euripides' "Bacchantes" before the two assembled royal courts, both sovereigns and their courtiers being well versed in

Greek literature and enthusiastically fond of Greek plays. Artavazd, as we have seen, had himself written tragedies, speeches, and narratives in that language, and his writings were still extant in the first century of our era.

COIN OF KING ARTAVAZD III OF ARMENIA

The player who took the part of Agavē seized the head of Crassus in the place of that of Pentheus, and in a burst of bacchantic frenzy, grasped it by its hair and held it aloft, declaiming the famous lines: "From the mountains, lo! we bring to the palace our new-slain quarry fair. Blessed chase!" We can be sure that the applause of the Armenians amid that of the Parthians could hardly have been genuine, for Artavazd undoubtedly understood that the Romans, his allies of yesterday, would make him responsible for their misfortune.

The Partho-Armenian army invaded Syria, but Cassius in Antioch resisted him successfully, and with the help of fresh contingents that had been sent him posthaste, the former lieutenant of Crassus even managed to drive Pacorus from Coelo-Syria. Six years later (45 B.C.) Orodes taking advantage of the neglect in which Rome seemed to be leaving her Eastern affairs, again sent Pacorus into Syria to give armed assistance to the republican Cecilius Bassus who had risen against Caesar.

At this period, Armenia's history becomes so closely mixed with world politics that it is impossible to speak of the Armenians and their doings without seeing the latter as resulting from the actions of the great empires. Their so-called autonomy becomes purely nominal and their kings become mere lieutenants of Persian or Roman generals as the case may be.

DRACHMA OF THE PARTHIAN PRINCE PACORUS I

Caesar was thinking of avenging the indignity suffered by Rome in the disaster and murder of Crassus, of recapturing from the Parthians at Ctesiphon the standards that had been taken and of punishing Pacorus for his new attempts on Syria, when the dictator's days were cut short by the assassin's dagger. The confusion that prevailed in the Republic upon the death of the great leader left Asia unprotected and allowed the Persians and Armenians to advance into Syria and Phoenicia, and even into Palestine, these provinces now being at liberty due to the flight of their governor Decidius Saxa. Quintus Labienus, the son of Titus Labienus, Caesar's enemy, who had gone over to the Persian side, was back in Syria with the army of Pacorus. Thus the civil war in Rome brought the Parthians unexpected aid. Orodes had himself schooled in Roman methods of war and the tactical formation of armies, and was becoming every day a more formidable adversary.

Despite these disturbing signs, good fortune still attended the Eternal City. Antony, his quarrels with Octavius having subsided, was able to send Ventidius Bassus to Asia Minor. Labienus was beaten and fled to Cilicia where he was taken and put to death, and the skillful Ventidius, in possession of the gorges of the river Amanus, defeated the Parthian general Pharnapates. Pacorus after being compelled to return to the other side of the Euphrates likewise suffered defeat at Gindara, to the north-east of Antioch, where he was killed [1]. Meanwhile, Publius Canidius Crassus vanquished in battle the Armenians together with Pharnabazus, the king of the Iberians, and Zober, prince of Albania, who had joined with the Parthians against Rome. The sovereignty of the Republic thus extended from the deserts of Syria to the shores of the Caspian Sea.

Tired, however, of these seemingly interminable wars, Rome determined to strike a decisive blow, and her opportunity for such action was greatly enhanced by events taking place at the Persian court.

TETRADRACHMA OF THE ARSACID KING OF PERSIA PHRAAT IV

The death of Pacorus and the loss of the Syrian provinces threw the Arsacid king Orodes into despair. He had just appointed his son, Phraat IV, as his successor, when the latter in his impatience to don the diadem of the King of Kings, caused the assassination of his father, his own brothers and eldest son, and all the nobles who showed loyalty to the slain king. These crimes impelled many of the Persian nobility and satraps to flee their country and take refuge with the Romans. Menoeses, one of the highest among the chief Iranian lords, was one of the refugees. Thus the strife in Persia had enabled Rome to take Armenia again under her wing.

MARK ANTONY

The quarrels in Rome seemed stilled for the present, and no longer worried in that direction, Mark Antony with the support of his colleague

---

[1] June 9th, 38 B.C.

and brother-in-law Octavius, set out for the East at the head of 70,000 infantry, 40,000 auxiliaries and 10,000 Spaniards. Armenia supplied the triumvir with a contingent of 6,000 horsemen. The Roman army consisted accordingly of 126,000 fighting men. Their general, reverting to Caesar's plans, and relying on his numerical strength, hoped to recapture at Ctesiphon or Ecbatana the standards lost by Crassus.

Their cruel defeats had taught the Romans finally that the plains of Mesopotamia were too unsafe for any expeditionary force. The triumvir proposed, therefore, to make Armenia his bridgehead and strike through Media to the heart of Iran. But though dauntless in action, he did not have those qualities of caution and foresight, of dominion over himself and his passions, needed to succeed in great undertakings. After wasting in idleness several months of the favorable season, he set out for the Euphrates, accompanied by Cleopatra. Then, impatient to return to his life of pleasure with the Egyptian queen, who had left him when he reached the river, he did not take the time to winter in Armenia. Anxious to finish as soon as possible with the Persians, he crossed the Armenian mountains and entered the plains of Atropatenes. In this too rapid advance, the Roman general was so unwise as to leave in his rear his caravan of besieging engines, and this train of heavy equipment was suddenly attacked by Artavazd, the son of Ariobarzanus, king of Atropatenes, and by Menoeses who had made peace with the Parthians; both of the legions who were in charge of these engines of war under the command of Oppius were overwhelmed by the Persians.

DENARIUS OF MARK ANTONY AND CLEOPATRA "ARMENIA DEVICTA"

On account of this loss Antony was unable to take Phraaspa, one of the strongholds of Atropatenes inhabited by the Sagartii (modern Gherrous), and he was abandoned by the king of Armenia who returned to his kingdom with his six thousand horsemen. The Roman general did not begin his retreat until later, much too late even. He withdrew eventually by way of Gazaka (1), the shore of lake Mateanas (2), and

---
(1) *Chahr-e-viran* (Kurdistan of Moukri).
(2) Lake Urumiah.

the mountains south of the Araxes. But in this march of three hundred Roman miles across dry and barren lands, no less than 24,000 of his legionaries perished from fatigue, cold, and hunger, or else under the arrows of 40,000 Parthian horsemen who, notwithstanding Phraat's promises, harassed the retreating army unceasingly.

Far from acknowledging his own lack of caution, Antony accused Artavazd, the king of Armenia, of being responsible for his disaster, by withdrawing and taking back his cavalry. Nevertheless, so anxious was he to get back to the queen of Egypt that he refused to winter in the Ararat territory and, postponing his vengeance against Artavazd, he pushed on to Antioch in Syria, losing another 8,000 men on the way from sickness and cold.

Amid the shameful feasts he gave at Antioch, however, Antony did not forget his grievances. In vain did he try to induce Artavazd to come to him. In the following spring (34 B.C.) the triumvir returned to Armenia and succeeded through Q. Dellius in persuading the king that he should accept an interview with Antony for the sake of keeping his throne. Hardly did the unhappy prince arrive in Roman hands than in defiance of plighted faith he was placed in chains and paraded as a captive through his own dominions where he was forced to throw open his strongholds and to bring forth their treasures. Antony kept him to adorn his triumph in chains along with his wife and sons, and to walk captive through the streets of Alexandria. Consequently, although vanquished by the Parthians and with his army destroyed, the triumvir did score a triumph nevertheless, his only captives, however, were his former allies.

Antony dreamed of restoring in the East an Alexandrian empire, able to hold its own with that which the Roman State was about to become. He knew the ambitious schemes of Octavius and was preparing to carve out for himself his share of the Republic's provinces. As for king Artavazd of Armenia, he was ousted to make room for the son of Antony and Cleopatra, named Alexander, and also to reward the king of Atropatenes. The latter who bore also the name of Artavazd was the only ruler who had suffered from the Roman incursion into Persia, his suzerain. Phraat, reaped all the advantages of that campaign

**ALEXANDER
SON OF ANTONY
& CLEOPATRA
34-31 B.C.**

The king of Atropatene gave his daughter, Iotapē, in marriage to the new king of Armenia, Alexander, and delivered to Antony the standards taken from Statilius, receiving for himself Symbacia, an Armenian province once a part of Media. The kingdom of Armenia Major fell to Alexander, while Polemon, the husband of Pythodoris, Antony's nephew, who had furthered the intrigues of the king of Atropatenes against the Armenian king, was placed on the throne of Lesser Armenia or Armenia Minor.

**COIN OF KING
TIGRANES II
OF ARMENIA**

But these political arrangements, turning rival peoples into allies and giving nations kings against their will, met with stiff resistance among the inhabitants. The Armenians refused to obey Alexander and set up, in opposition to Antony's son, the son of their own captive king, or Artaxes II (1). The latter, beset by the troops of Rome and the satrap of Atropatenes, was obliged to take refuge with the Parthians at the court of Phraat IV. Finally, taking advantage of the fact that Antony had been compelled to withdraw his legions from Armenia to maintain his struggle against Augustus, the Persian king invaded both Atropatene and Armenia, and gave the latter crown to the national claimant.

**ARTAXES II
30-20 B.C.**

Thinking that the civil war in Rome would last a long time, Phraat IV of Persia and Artaxes II of Armenia were planning to take from the Romans their possessions west of the Euphrates, when a claimant to the throne of Iran, Tiridates II, rose up against the Arsacid monarch, proclaimed himself Great King in Ctesiphon, and forced his adversary to flee for safety to the eastern Scythians (2). Armenia was thus left

---

(1) Archam of the Armenians.
(2) In the Transcaspian territory.

alone to carry out the above ambitions, and feeling herself too weak, she refrained. Meanwhile, Cleopatra having beheaded her prisoner, Artavazd, the son of that unhappy monarch took his revenge by slaying all the Romans within his dominions.

In the meantime, however, the battle of Actium resulted in giving Octavius the supreme power, and he, tired of the unceasing conflicts either because of Armenia or about Armenia, decided to place all the regions on the east of the Euphrates, north of the Tigris, and above the Araxes, under Roman protection. Thus the territories of the Iberians and the Albanians, i.e. all the peoples south of the Great Caucasus chain, were included for the first time. This plan meant a downright check to the power of Persia and Octavius would stop at nothing to carry out his intention. Bribed by Roman gold, the Armenians rebelled against Artaxes II, put him to death, and Tiberius Claudius Nero, then 22 years old, came and crowned as king of Armenia the younger brother of Artaxes, Tigranes III. Armenia then was given up to anarchy. Tigranes III was carried off apparently by sickness, but more probably by poison. Tigranes IV demanded investiture by the Romans, while two other claimants to the throne made their appearance, namely Erovaz (?) and Artavazd IV.

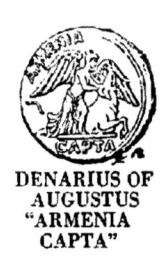

DENARIUS OF AUGUSTUS "ARMENIA CAPTA"

COIN OF TIGRANES III KING OF ARMENIA

LAST SUCCESSORS OF ARTAXIAS

TIGRANES III AND IV 20 B.C. TO A.D. 1

This period of Armenian history is very obscure. The Persians and Romans fought long for influence in the country. Finally, in the first year of our era, Phraat, who had recovered the throne of Iran, relinquished all claims to the kingdom of Armenia, and left his brothers as hostages with the Romans.

But, as we have seen in the foregoing pages,

the word of a ruler was of little value in those days. Each one, whether Roman or Persian, spoke according to his momentary interest. Crimes and treacheries followed one another unceasingly and the Armenian question remained ever the chief concern of the two great rival States, both pursuing their own aims regarding general policy in the East (1).

COIN OF TIGRANES IV KING OF ARMENIA, WITH HIS SISTER ERATO

---

(1) For the facts related in this chapter, consult: PLINY, *Nat. Hist.*; PLUTARCH, *Lucullus, Pompey*; FAUSTUS, TACITUS, *Annals*; STRABO, APPIAN, DION CASSIUS and MOMMSEN, *Rom. Gesch.*; HUBSCHMANN, *Die Altarmen. Ortsn.*; Fr. TOURNEBISE, *Histoire politique et religieuse de l'Armenie*.

* * *
* *
*

CHAPTER IV

THE FOREIGN DYNASTY (A.D. 2-53). — THE ARSACIDS OF ARMENIA (A.D. 53-429) — TIRIDATES II THE GREAT (A D. 217-238). — CONVERSION OF ARMENIA TO CHRISTIANITY — SAINT GREGORY THE ILLUMINATOR

The succession of rulers named by the historians of Armenia "the Foreign Dynasty" coincides with the period when the Armenians, though nominally independent, were subjected in turn to Roman and Persian influence. Divided by their powerful neighbors' policies, they wavered according to circumstances towards the one or the other of these temporary overlords, too weak to assert their national independence. The armies of the Caesars, like those of the King of Kings, imposed for a while their wills on the Armenian court, and the crown was given to the partisans of Rome or those of Persia as the exigencies of the day demanded This was followed by peaceful periods when the Persians and Romans, too busy elsewhere, left Armenia alone and enabled her to throw off the yoke. Even then, however, she remained in a state of indecision as to her course of action.

DRACHMA OF ONONES OR VONONES AS KING OF PERSIA

IMITATION OF DENARIUS of AUGUSTUS (1) STRUCK IN TRANSCAUCASIA

ARIOBARZANUS A.D 2

But national life was still vigorous in Armenia; her army furnished contingents sometimes to the Persians, sometimes to the Romans. The feudal lords maintained very considerable independence, and thought continued to develop along the traditional

---

(1) Obv. Laureate head of Augustus, right: CAESAR. AUGUSTUS. DIVI. F. PATER PATRIAE. Rev. Caius and Lucius standing each with spear and shield, C L CAESARES AUGUSTI F COS. DESIGN. PRINC IUVENT. Field: Augur's ladle and staff. Silver.

lines of the great Tigranes. The little we know of this ill-defined period shows that notwithstanding the constant wars inflicted on the country the people were progressing both under foreign influence and by their own energy. As we have seen, letters and arts flourished at the Armenian court under Tigranes. We know that this progress did not lapse under Artaxias' dynasty, for the moment that the Armenians acquired a few centuries later the art of writing they had lacked, there sprang forth a language of considerable refinement which originated surely from an oral culture. In the same way, many centuries earlier, the Greeks had acquired a taste for literature long before they knew the alphabet, and owned their intellectual development to a number of other Aryan nations who were still illliterate. Moreover, in Rome the Armenians were far from being looked on as barbarians; their rulers were received with great respect, and in the Eternal City writers spoke highly of the sumptuous life of these lordly Easterners.

Under Persian and Roman influence in turn, there arose in Armenia, despite the country's burning desire to regain independence, a period of kings who occupied the throne without belonging to the nation. The first of these rulers was a Persian of the name of Ariobarzanus who reigned about A.D. 2. He was already king of Media and Atropatenes when at Augustus' orders he was made king of Armenia by Caius Caesar. This king was succeeded by his son Artavazd V (A.D. 2-11). A Jewish king, Tigranes V (A.D. 11-14) then ascended the throne, but as this foreign monarch did not govern to the Armenians' liking, the nationalists recalled Erato, the sister of Tigranes IV, who resumed her reign (A.D. 14-15). She was succeeded by Vonones, a Parthian (A.D. 16-17) (1). Then Zeno, the son of Polemon and Pythodoris, to whom Antony had formerly given the kingdom of Pontus, was sent and

COIN OF AUGUSTUS AND ARTAVAZD V

ARTAVAZD V
2-11

TIGRANES V
11-14

ERATO 14-15

VENONES
15-17

---

(1) About A.D. 16 Vonones or Onones, son of Phraat, king of Persia, was a hostage at Rome when, after the murder of Orodes II, the Parthians asked Augustus to appoint a son of Phraat as successor. He was appointed, but, vanquished by Artaban, a rival for the throne, he had to flee to Armenia where he was named king. Abandoned however by Tiberius who had succeeded Augustus, he was driven from Armenia by the Parthians and took refuge in Syria where the Romans had him slain. (Cf. TACITUS, *Annals* II, 2, 4, 68).

ARTASHES III
18-31

ARCHAK I
34-35

enthroned by Germanicus to rule over Armenia as Artashes III. For sixteen years (A.D. 18-34) the latter governed the dominions under Western vassalage. But the Persians regaining the ascendancy, in the place of the Romans the Arsacids appointed one of their number, Arsaces or Archak I (A.D. 34-35) as king of Armenia.

In this period, at the beginning of the Christian era, (A.D. 8), is recorded the accession to the throne of Osrhoene of a branch of the royal family of Armenia. Presumably the Arabian princes who had succeeded Osrhoes (137-132 B.C.) had feudal connection with Armenia. In any case, Moses of Khoren and Vartan both inform us that Abgar V. Uchama, the "Apkar" of the Armenians, a grandson of Artashes and consequently a descendant of Tigranes the Great, left Medzpin and transferred his capital to Edessa, and that his descendants ruled over Osrhoene until the time of Gordian III, when about A.D. 240 that emperor dispossessed Abgar XI of his kingdom and made it a Roman province. This expansion of Armenian influence into Syria played an important part in Eastern political life, but we have insufficient information on this point, and what we have is vague and often contradictory.

COIN OF ABGAR XI OF OSRHOENE AND GORDIAN III

MITHIDRATES
35-37 & 47-51

Fresh wars resulted in the Armenian throne passing to the hands of the Iberians in the person of Mithidrates (A.D. 35-37 and 47-51) who drove out the Arsacid ruler. He was succeeded by his nephew Rhadamistus (A.D. 51-53) the son of Phraasmanes I, king of Georgia, who murdered him in a dastardly statagem. Tacitus (1) has given us the account of this crime in terms depicting vividly the infamous customs of those disturbed times.

RHADAMISTUS
51-53

Rhadamistus arrived at his uncle's court, allegedly fleeing from the unjust severities of his father and stepmother. He craved hospitality of the Armenians, and was received with open arms.

---

(1) *Annals* XII, 44-52.

He was not long in making friends among the nobles of the country, and taking advantage of his uncle's good nature he ere long formed a powerful party. When the time was ripe, he sent word to the king of Iberia, who suddenly invaded Armenia and put his son on the throne. Mithidrates, taken by surprise and betrayed by most of his feudatories, took refuge in the stronghold of Gornea (Garni), the ruins of which town are still to be seen at the foot of the mountains near Erivan. It was then held by a Roman garrison, for Armenia was at that time a vassal State of the Empire, and the king relied on the legions to protect him. But the prefect of the fort, Coelius Pollio, seduced by gifts from the Iberians, planned to deliver up his guest, and while apparently negotiating with Phraasmanes, urged the king to accept a meeting proposed him by Rhadamistus. Mithidrates, however, was not without misgivings. Being a Georgian, he knew he had everything to fear from his nephew's treachery. But as the Romans threatened to abandon him, he at last yielded. The meeting was arranged near a sacred wood at the foot of the mountain where the friendship of the two princes was according to custom to be sealed by a sacrifice to the gods.

The Iberian custom on such occasions was to join the two right hands, tie both thumbs together, and prick them so that blood flowed from each. The rivals then each raised the other's bleeding thumb to his lips and swore the oath, rendering the mutual promise more sacredly binding.

When about to go through this ceremony, Mithidrates was seized and pinioned. Rhadamistus had sworn not to kill his uncle by the sword or by poison, and so he had him suffocated under cushions, while the victim's wife, Rhadamistus' sister, was strangled and her children slaughtered.

These heinous crimes, though committed by barbarians, were a shameful record for the Roman authorities who bore all the responsibility. Nevertheless the governor of Cappadocia, Julius Paelignus, Coelius Pollio's superior, recognized the new king of Armenia. The Iberian gifts had done their work even to the halls of Caesarea. But the Emperor's representative in Syria, Numidius Quadratus, was rightly disturbed as to the public reaction to the misdeed of Coelius Pollio, and was considering punishing him. His council, however, were of a different opinion.

DENARIUS OF GERMANICUS with, reverse, THE CROWNING OF ARTAXIAS

Of what consequence was it, anyhow, that the throne of Armenia should be filled by the uncle or the nephew, or that the barbarians should kill one another; did not their quarrels serve Rome's purpose? The Persians had very little influence over Iberia where Rome was all-powerful; was it not better to let a Georgian dynasty settle in all the districts of Armenia bordering the Parthians? After the death of Phraasmanes, Rhadamistus would unite the two kingdoms and thus form a state strong enough to hold the Parthians in check.

COIN OF ANTIOCHUS IV EPIPHANES, WITH IOTAPE

Rome, moreover, missed no opportunity to strengthen its power by means of the small nations. Antiochus IV. Epiphanes (A.D. 38-72) king of Commagene, had helped Corbulo in his Eastern campaign, and Nero to reward him for his assistance took advantage of disturbances in Armenia to add a part of that country to his dominions.

This episode in one of the most troubled periods in Armenia's history gives an idea of the frightful upheavals this unhappy kingdom underwent. Not only did they suffer from Roman and Persian treachery, and that of their northern neighbors, but they were divided among themselves by the rivalries and greed of their feudal lords . Anarchy was rampant. Every day the frontiers of kingdoms were altered, Armenia was separated into upper and lower countries, whole districts were taken away from or added to the domains of the various rulers, and with continual bloodshed and towns and villages aflame, ruin and mourning spread over the land.

COIN OF ANTIOCHUS IV EPIPHANES KING OF COMMAGENE

The Persians, apprehensive of the increasing Roman power, then invaded Armenia intending to dethrone the Georgian usurper and make these mountain people accept a king whom they themselves could rely on. Rhadamistus fled at full speed, with his wife Zenobia behind him on his horse, she being several months pregnant. This Zenobia was the daughter of the uncle he had murdered. Fainting and unable to bear the mad flight, the queen begged him to end her agony. Plunging his dagger into her breast, the son of Phraasmanes threw her into the Araxes and rushed onward, with the Parthian horsemen sent to seize him, close on his heels. Zenobia, however, did not die. Saved by some shepherds, she was delivered to king Tiridates whom the Persians had just raised to the throne and this king received her with all the respect owed to her rank and her misfortunes.

After the Parthians had left, Rhadamistus returned to Armenia and endeavored to obtain the assistance of the feudatories in regaining his crown; but his behavior to the inhabitants was so wicked and his vengeance so cruel that he was driven off by his former subjects and had to flee back to his father.

At this point begins the rule of the dynasty of the Arsacids in Armenia. These rulers occupied the throne of the descendants of Haïk for about four centuries and gave to Armenian history one of its most brilliant pages.

COIN WITH HEAD OF IOTAPE, SISTER AND WIFE OF ANTIOCHUS IV EPIPHANES

**TIRIDATES I
53-100**

The first sovereign of this dynasty was Tiridates I (A.D. 53-59 and 66-100), the brother of Vologeses, king of Persia. His accession meant Armenia's entry into the wide feudal system of the Arsacids, at the head of which political set-up stood the Iranian overlord who bore the title of King of Kings. Next to him ranked the Arsacids of Armenia; thirdly, those of Bactriana; and the fourth place was that of the Arsacid rulers of the northern Caucasus reigning over the Massagetes. The king of Persia, as suzerain, was alone entitled to mint money and have his head appear on coins.

Rome viewed with misgivings the occupancy of the Armenian throne by the brother of the king of Persia. For a ruler hostile to the Empire to be thus raised to power augured the early downfall of Roman influence in those regions so important politically to the Imperial State. Nero entrusted Corbulo with the task of driving out the Arsacid king and putting on the throne Tigranes VI (A.D. 60-62), the nephew of the last king of that name, and grandson of Archelaos, king of Cappadocia. This protégé of Rome died, however, after reigning two years, and Vologeses induced Corbulo to agree to his brother receiving the Emperor's investiture in Rome. Tiridates went accordingly to be crowned by Nero. But this step meant no humiliation for the Armenian king. He had hardly crossed into Roman territory when he was received as a sovereign and welcomed in every city with signal honors. Tiridates was accompanied by all the chief lords of the kingdom and by the Queen and her children, also by an escort of three thousand horsemen, in short all the splendor of Eastern pomp. Tacitus, Pliny, Dion Cassius, have all given us accounts of the visit of the king of Armenia to Italy. He entered the city of Nicopolis on a chariot to greet the Emperor who was there at the time, but the coronation took place further on at Rome

CORBULO

**TIGRANES VI
60-62**

SILVER COIN OF EMPEROR LUCIUS VERUS SHOWING. CAPTIVE ARMENIA, AND BRONZE COIN SHOWING HIM GIVING ARMENIA A KING. (1)

COIN OF EMPEROR ANTONIUS PIUS SHOWING HIM CROWNING THE KING OF ARMENIA

---

(1) Obv. L. VERUS. AUG. ARMENICUS. Laureate head of L. Verus on right. Rev. T.R.P. IIII. IMP. II. COS. II REX. ARMEN. DAT. SC.

where the Senate had voted the arrangement of sumptuous feasts. Nero seated on a throne placed the royal crown on Tiridates' head, the latter kneeling. Once he was back in his dominions, he restored the city of Artaxata which he renamed Neronia, and took back, with the help of the legions, from the Albanians the land those people had seized from Armenia during the disturbances of the Foreign Dynasty.

EXEDARES 100-113 Exedares (A.D. 100-113), Tiridates' successor, added Lower Armenia to his domains, surrendering it later to the Romans. Lesser Armenia had already become a province of the Empire, after having passed from the

COINS OF EMPEROR TRAJAN, COMMEMORATING HIS CAMPAIGNS IN ARMENIA

TETRADRACHMA OF VOLOGESES I, ARSACID KING OF PERSIA

hands of Polemon, King of Pontus, to those of Archelaos, king of Cappadocia, and then to Cotys, king of the Cimmerian Bosporus, (Crimea)—her last rulers being Aristobulus under Nero and Tigranes under Vespasian. Thus the limits of the Roman Empire gradually moved forward from the banks of the Euphrates to those of the Tigris, and as the Arsacid dynasty of Armenia seemed more loyal to their suzerain power than they were to their kinsmen, the kings of Persia, Rome had every reason to support them (1).

Parthamasiris (A.D. 113-114), Parthamas-

---

(1) The title ARMENICUS in the inscriptions on coins, is given to Marcus Aurelius and Lucius Verus. That of PARTICUS is given to Trajan, Hadrian, Marcus Aurelius, Lucius Verus, Septimius Severus, Caracalla, and Carus. These titles cease before the time of Constantine I, and are never found on Byzantine coins although long used in Imperial rescripts. Justinian I calls himself Allemanicus, Gothicus, Germanicus, Franciscus, Alamicus, Vandalicus, etc.

FIRST ARSACIDS OF ARMENIA 113-238

TIRIDATES II (CHOSROES I) KING OF ARMENIA 217-238

pates (116-117), Vologeses (Vagharch) (117-140), Sohemus (140-162, 163-178), Pacorus (162-163), Sanatruces (178-216), Vologeses II (Vagharch II) (217-238), all these rulers of the Arsacid line followed one another on the throne of Armenia. Constantly at strife with their Persian kinsmen as well as with their Roman suzerains, these kings dealt very tactfully with their powerful neighbors, always acting so as to prevent any setback having irretrievable consequences. These rivalries, however, caused the greatest calamities to fall on Armenia during the reigns of the first Arsacid kings. Finally, Tiridates II. also called Chosroes I the Great (A.D. 217-238) ascended the throne, and from his time began the great development of the Armenian people, later destined by the adoption of Christianity to join forever with Western civilization and break away from Eastern culture.

ADVENT OF THE SASSANIDS IN PERSIA, A.D. 226

A great revolution had just transformed Iran. Artakchater (Artaxerxes), the son of Papek, of the lineage of Sassan, prince of the province of Persis, had overthrown the Arsacid monarchy, and ascended the throne of the King of Kings. Descended from the Mazdean high-priests

**STATUE OF TIRIDATES
KING OF ARMENIA**
(Marble, Louvre Museum)

of Fars, he announced his intention of restoring to his new empire the religion of their ancestors and of expelling the Greco-Parthian deities along with Greek influence. But, although he had vanquished Artaban, the new Great King had not yet conquered all the Arsacid princes, and the Parthians of Armenia were among those who refused to accept him as their suzerain

Agathangelus has left us, in Greek and Armenian, (1) a history of Tiridates II, and his account of the first contacts of the Mazdean-Persians and the still heathen Armenians, although highly colored, shows vividly the new state of things brought about by the revival of the Zoroastrian worship and by the accession of the son of Papek.

"When the kingdom of the Par-
"thians was nearing its downfall
"Ardashir, the son of Sassan, satrap
"of the province of Sdahr [Istakhar],
"killed Artaban, the son of Vologeses,
"and seized his throne. Then he
"drew to his side the Persian armies
"who forsook and shook off with

---

(1) Transl. V. LANGLOIS, *Coll. Hist. arméniens*, vol I, 1881, p. 114 sq.

"contempt the Parthian rule, and with one accord
"Ardashir, son of Sassan, was chosen to be their king.
"Chosroes [Tiridates II], the king of the Armenians,
"learned of Artaban's death. Chosroes held second
"rank in the Persian [Arsacid] monarchy. Although
"he had the news early, he made no preparations to
"fight. He returned to his country extremely sad, not
"having been able to foresee these events or put them
"right.

"But early the following year (227) Chosroes,
"king of Armenia, raised an army. He gathered the
"armies of the Aghouank [Albania], and the Georgians,
"opened the Gate of the Alans [the gorges of Dariall]
"(1) and called forth the Huns to attack the frontiers
"of Persia. He ravaged the lands of Assyria, as far as
"the gates of Ctesiphon; he sacked and put to fire and
"sword the populous cities and flourishing towns and
"ruined the country, leaving it uninhabited. He sought
"to destroy everything; he leveled cities to their foun-
"dations and sought to change the laws of the Persian
"monarchy. He had sworn to avenge his race de-
"spoiled of their kingdom. Relying on his large number of soldiers and
"expecting much from their might, he became inflamed with pride, hatred,
"and desire for vengeance. Many valiant cohorts of
"well-armed cavalry from the Aghouans, the Lepins,
"the Gasps (2), and many others from that region,
"flocked to his side to avenge the blood of Artaban.
"He was so distressed that the Persians should have
"forsaken his kinsmen and submitted as vassals to
"the new rule of the Sdahrs [Princes of Istakhar] that
"he sent envoys to those same kinsmen to urge them
"to gather together with the help of the warlike inhab-
"itants and brave soldiers of the Kouschans (3) and
"beyond, also that of their own subjects. But his
"kinsmen, the heads of families and the notables among
"the Parthians did not listen to him, for they had
"already submitted to Ardashir and were content to
"be his subjects rather than those of their compatriot
"and relative."

DRACHMA OF ARTAXERXES I, SON OF PAPEK, FIRST OF THE SASSANID KINGS OF PERSIA (rev. the Fire Altar)

COIN OF THE LAST OF THE ARSACID KINGS OF PERSIA ARTABAN V

(Footnotes on p. 121)

The Mazdean regression, which the satrap rulers of Persis had long been preparing in the people's thought had been well received throughout the Empire. Only the grandees of the Arsacid stock had attempted any resistance against the new King of Kings Yielding, however, to armed strength, and feeling that the people looked with favor on the old Persian religion being restored, and that theirs was a lost cause, they accepted the new state of things Armenia alone held out.

"Meanwhile Chosroes [Tiridates II] gathered his host of soldiers "and of auxiliaries that had arrived from all sides to fight for him. When "the king of the Persians saw this host rushing so "furiously at him, he moved forward to meet it de-"ploying every unit at his command. But, unable to "stem the enemy, he began to flee. He was pursued ' and the whole Persian army routed. Their slain were "scattered over all the highways and fields, while those "who escaped the sword were dispersed in all direc-"tions"

THE ZOROASTRIAN FIRE TEMPLE (from the reverse of a tetradrachma of the princes of Persis)

Were we in possession of the chronicles of the Sassanid kings, unfortunately systematically destroyed by the Arabs, we should certainly find that the first encounters between Artaxerxes and the Armenian Arsacid were less glorious for the Armenians than Agathangelus relates There was, no doubt whatever, a coalition of the northern peoples against the new regime, for what little we know of the Sassanid history shows these kings as engaged in constant struggles with the nations of Transcaucasia and the Oxus, but if the Persian forces did suffer a few reverses in the early days of this dynasty, they could certainly have been only minor battles.

Agathangelus concludes his narrative (1) after the manner of the Assyrian kings, enumerating the booty taken by Tiridates in this alleged devastating expedition into Persian territory:

"The king of the Armenians after this sanguinary exploit returned

---
(Footnotes p 120)
(1) In Persian Der-i-Alan, gate of the Alans (Cf. PLINY, VI, 11; PROCOPIUS, De Bello Goth, IV, 1).
(2) Nomads of northern Armenia and Georgia, Caucasian mountaineers
(3) Peoples of the Transcaspian territory, probably Sogdians and Bactrians. (CF. SAINT MARTIN Mem sur l'Arménie, vol. II, p 436-437).

(Footnote this page)
(1) AGATHANGELUS, ch I. transl. LANGLOIS, Hist Arm., vol I, p. 117 See also, for this campaign, MOSES OF KHOREN, II, 71-73; and UKHTHANNES OF EDESSA, both of them doubtless influenced by Agathangelus' narrative.

"joyously to Armenia, to the city of Vagharchapat [Etchmiadzin] in the "province of Ararat, having gained the day and taken much plunder He "ordered messengers sent out and letters to be written in various places, "for thanksgivings to the gods to be celebrated in the temples of the Seven "Altars [district of Phaidagaran.] He ordained that in the Arsacid tra-"ditional sites consecrated to the national worship, there be presents of "white bulls and goats, also of gold and silver vestments with brilliant "fringes, also silk cloths adorned with wreaths and festoons, golden crowns, "silver ornaments, magnificent silver and gold vases set with precious "stones, splendid garments and superb decorations. To all this he added "besides a fifth part of all the booty he had taken, and munificent awards "to the priests The soldiers also who had accompanied him were gen-"erously rewarded before they were disbanded."

Western writers (1) throw quite another light on the above events. Artaxerxes, hailed on the 28th of April A.D. 227 as King of Kings and the restorer of the religion and language of the Persians, and calling himself: "The Mazdean, offspring of the gods, King of Kings of Iran and Aniran" (2), revived the Achaemenean claims over all Asia, and summoned the Roman Empire to return to him the old-time provinces of Darius. Alexander Severus sent immediately a large army which was joined by the Armenians and the peoples of the North The center marched on Mesopotamia, the right wing on Chaldea, and the left wing on Armenia and Atropatenes. But the center was stopped by the main body of the Persian army commanded by the king himself, the left wing had to withdraw from Media and return to Armenia, while Artaxerxes would have driven the Romans from Mesopotamia had he been able to keep his troops on a war footing. Abandoned, however, by his troops who clamored to be disbanded, he had to withdraw to his own dominions without obtaining decisive results Armenia remained under Roman suzerainty, and Alexander Severus was the hero, on the Forum, of imaginary victories.

The restoration of a national monarchy in Persia was, from the standpoint of Eastern statesmanship, a highly important occurrence, for the Sassanid rulers never genuinely gave up their claims to the countries formerly included in the Achaemenean dominions. The new dynasty by

---

(1) Cf ZONARAS, XII, 18; HERODIAN, VI, 5, 7; Amm. MARCELL, XXIII, 5, 7, 17. etc

(2) Inscription on his coins· Mazdiasn baghi artahchatr Malkân Malka Irân ou Anirân minoutchetri men yezdân

making the religious question its basis of support had by its very accession restored order in Persia, where affairs had fallen into utter confusion under the last Arsacid kings.

But a development of even greater importance was taking place in the world. While Ahura-Mazda was reasserting his ancient rights over Iran, the religion of Christ was spreading throughout the Roman Empire. To the opposing state interests of the two Empires there would within a few years be added the most implacable opposition of all, that arising from contrary religious convictions.

Prior to the restoration of Mazdeism, while Persia was under the Arsacids, religious quarrels were unknown between Iranians, Armenians, and Romans. The gods of the Parthians, along with those of Armavir, Artaxata, Ani (Gamakh), were all accepted by Roman tolerance. Moreover, impregnated with Greek lore, the Eastern religions had innumerable common ties with that of the West, and the clever assimilations practised by the Romans obviated any danger of religious conflict with the various nations connected with the Empire. This structure so laboriously built up during the centuries was soon to crumble: a new era was opening, and men were reverting to the times when a national god was the nation's standard. Assyria had ruled Asia in the name of Assur; henceforth the religion of Christ was to enter into combat, first against Mazdeism, and then against Islam, to continue until our day. The religious tolerance born of Alexander the Great's conquests and of Roman shrewdness, lasted only five and a half centuries.

Shortly after Christ's crucifixion, the Christian faith made its appearance in Armenia, of that we may be sure. The apostles Thaddeus, Bartholomew, and Jude, who preached the gospel in the Ararat regions, were according to legend put to death by Sanatruces (Sanadruk), then reigning over Adiabene and a part of Armenia.

SAINT GREGORY (from a 10th century miniature)

The Armenians, as we know, then had no written language; consequently no contemporaneous documents of the first three centuries have been handed down to us, and we have very little information concerning the progress of Christianity in this land before its official conversion. However, the religious persecutions said to have been carried out by the kings of Persia and Armenia show the Christians to have been already in considerable numbers at the accession to the throne of Tiridates III (A.D. 250). During his reign the Christian religion was adopted, —thirteen years before it triumphed in the West, i.e. before the date of Constantine's victory at the Milvian Bridge. Only one hundred years later did Theodosius issue his decrees against paganism. Armenia consequently was, according to its historians, the first of any people to adopt Christianity officially (1).

The great evangelist of Armenia was Saint Gregory Loussavoritch, i.e The Illuminator, also called by the chroniclers Grigor Partev (Gregory the Parthian).

Gregory was born A.D 257, of royal Arsacid descent. His father, Prince Anak, while out hunting caused the death of Tiridates II, a crime instigated by the king of Persia who was irked by the latter's power and authority as an ally of the Romans. Tiridates II on his death-bed ordered the extermination of Anak and all his family, a command which was carried out Gregory alone escaped and was taken to Caesarea in Cappadocia, where his foster-brother, a Christian, received him and brought him up in the Christian faith His place of refuge and the facts of his birth were not unknown, however, for on reaching his majority he married the daughter of an Armenian prince, also a Christian Two children were born to them, after which the couple separated to enter monastic life, and Gregory went to Armenia where he hoped to make amends for his father's crime by converting his native land.

TIRIDATES III 250-330, & ST. GREGORY

After the death of Tiridates II, the Persians seized Armenia (238-250), but with the help of the Romans Tiridates III ascended the throne. This ruler had been brought up in Rome, was of an enlightened mind and well versed in the Western languages and literature, and properly understood the duties of a king. According to legend he was of Herculean strength. "His breath," wrote Agathangelus, "burst river-dikes and stopped the raging of waters." He frequently proved his valor and mettle as a soldier. At the beginning of his reign, however, he had the same feelings as his tutors in Rome regarding the Christians, who at that time despite the very wide spread of their religion were still considered as disturbers of the social order. A fervent worshiper of the gods, he was at first extremely

---

(1) This assertion made by all the Armenian historians is not corroborated by the statements of the Greeks and Latins, with the exception of Eusebius. Several modern authors conclude that Armenia became Christian at the same time as the Roman Empire.

opposed to the new faith, and to put an end to Gregory's preaching and his daily increase of converts, he had the evangelist seized and kept him twelve or fourteen years in a dungeon of the citadel at Artaxata where he was most cruelly treated

Meanwhile, say the chroniclers, the king fell ill, and appealed not only to the most renowned physicians of the day but also to his ancestral deities. Receiving no help, he had Gregory brought out of prison, and was healed by him. Moved by gratitude and touched by the unshakable faith of the martyr, Tiridates accepted Christianity along with his whole court, and made his erstwhile prisoner his minister.

CONVERSION OF ARMENIA TO CHRISTIANITY

Gregory, who was still only a monk, then proceeded to Caesarea in Cappadocia where the Exarch Leontius ordained him both priest and bishop He thereupon returned to Armenia, baptized the king, and began his official evangelization of the country.

Armenia's conversion to Christianity was not without difficulties in the way, for the heathen priests were both enormously rich and very powerful. They had from time immemorial reaped profit from every fortunate circumstance attending the kings of Armenia, and although their temples had often been ravaged by war, they owned huge treasures and vast lands on which the peasants, their serfs, were turned into their soldiers when necessary.

Gregory, with Tiridates' support, converted peacefully many districts where the people were ready for the change. In others, however, the bishop accompanied by the chief satraps and a body of troops traveled over the country sacking the pagan sanctuaries, breaking their idols, and slaying without pity any priests offering armed opposition. According to Zenobius of Glak (1), resistance was extremely violent in the district of Taron among others, also in the territory of Palounik. In the large town of Kisané a regular battle occurred between the priests' army and that of Gregory. The victorious bishop "ordered the idol of Kisané to be thrown "down, it was made of brass and twelve cubits high. When those who re-"ceived the command entered into the temple, the ministers of the holy "place seeing them coming rushed at them and attacked them, crying, "'Let us die rather than let Great Kisané be destroyed.' The soldiers sur-

---

(1) *Hist. du district de Daron.* Transl V LANGLOIS, p. 350.

"rounded the priests and killed six of them." After which "the soldiers "overturned the Gates of Death Thereupon the demons raised their "voices, crying: 'Though you drive us hence, there will be no rest for "those who would dwell here.' It seems incredible! Like the city gates "through which pour hosts of soldiers, this place was the Demons' Gate, "their number was as great at Kisané as in the depths of the abyss." Unfortunately the prophecy of the devils of Kisané seems to have come true, for Armenia has never yet found rest

Although Gregory's campaign was intended to convert the people and overthrow paganism, yet the satraps were not disdainful of the riches piled up in the temples

Zenobius continues: "Next day a pagan priest was brought to the "prince of Siunia (1), they [the Christians] pressed him to tell where the "treasures were hidden and disclose the door leading to the underground "chamber. He refused and died on the gallows under torture. They "were consequently unable to discover the treasures."

As regards the lands belonging to the pagan sanctuaries, the new churches were the beneficiaries "After laying the foundation of the church and placing relics thereon, St. Gregory erected a wooden cross at its entrance, on the spot formerly occupied by the idol Kisané, and appointed as church administrators Antony and Gronites. He made Epiphanes the Superior of the monastery, and gave him forty-three monks, also granting him twelve villages to supply the monastery's needs."

The Armenian writer goes on to enumerate the villages distributed to the new clergy; altogether they amount to 12,298 houses, and are able to furnish 5,470 horsemen and 3,807 infantry, a small army of over 9,000 men. The chronicler adds·

"All these villages had been from their inception affected to the idols' "service. The princes confirmed the granting of them to the churches, "and St Gregory arranged accordingly."

"Afterwards", said Korioun (2), "it was decided to fight the bold and "insolent sect of the Borborides. [This sect made its appearance in the "2nd century and denied the last judgment.] Those who would not "yield to the word of truth were given over to terrible punishment, to "imprisonment, chains, and all kinds of torture. If these Godless men "then refused to turn to their own deliverance, they were burned, or else

---

(1) Armenian noble belonging to the bishop's escort.
(2) KORIOUN, *Biogr de Mesrob* Transl. LANGLOIS, *Historiens de l'Armenie*, vol II, p 11.

"incarcerated or driven from the country, after being put to all manner of shame."

FOUNDING OF THE PATRIARCHAL SEE OF ETCHMIADZIN

The king helped Gregory to build the city of Etchmiadzin (i.e. "the place where the Only Son descended") and ancient Vagharchapat became the holy city of the Armenians, the nation's intellectual center An immense group of churches and cloisters built during the centuries, together with edifices in great number, the present-day residences of archbishops, bishops archimandrites, priests, and monks, such is Etchmiadzin, the seat of the Armenian Catholicos. 159 patriarchs in succession have held office, from St. Gregory (A D. 302-305) to Guevorg V (1912). This ecclesiastical dignity can only be compared in Christendom to the papacy, but whereas the successor of St. Peter only mixes incidentally with politics, the Catholicos of Armenia at Etchmiadzin has been forced by circumstances on many occasions to act as a ruler in behalf of his nation long deprived of political rights The consequence has been that his office has become invested with very great powers The seat of the Catholicos has not always, however, remained at Etchmiadzin; it was later transferred to Dovin, to Ani, to Akhtamar, or to Sis, maintaining everywhere its great place in the moral and intellectual life of the nation.

Today the sees of Sis, Jerusalem, and Constantinople recognize, it is true, the primacy of the patriarch of Etchmiadzin, but actually they are autonomous (1).

Having finished his work, Gregory entrusted the patriachate to his son Aristaces who had been his suffragan since the year 318 and had in that capacity been present in 325 at the famous Council of Nicaea, whence emanated the summaries of faith adopted by the Armenians. He then retired to the grotto of Mount Sepouh in Upper Armenia, and died not long after.

The king looked on the conversion of Armenia as a political step. By giving the country a national religion, Tiridates liberated her from

---

(1) The Catholicos of Etchmiadzin alone has the title of "Catholicos and Supreme Patriarch of all the Armenians", being the head of the Armenian Church The patriarch of Jerusalem is a local patriarch, while that of Sis is regional (for Cilicia). The patriarch of Constantinople is the civil and religious head of the Armenians of Constantinople and of all those in Turkey.

Over a year ago (1916), the Turkish government abolished the office of Catholicos at Sis and the patriarchate of Constantinople. and issued a decree naming the Patriarch of Jerusalem as Catholicos of all the Armenians in Turkey, with only a vicar at Constantinople foreign influence, for Rome according to native writers still remained heathen for some years, and Persia had restored the religion of Zoroaster. It meant therefore asserting Armenian nationality and giving Haik's people increased individual character that would foster their racial integrity and thereby their national independence.

Meanwhile Tiridates' conversion to Christianity, together with that of Constantine, caused the Persians anxiety for the future. To forestall the danger they foresaw in an alliance of Christian rulers against Ormuzd-worshiping Iran, their emissaries inveigled a large number of princes and high officials of Armenia into a plot for the restoration of paganism in the lands of Ararat. According to Agathangelus, Tiridates was murdered when out hunting, probably at the instigation of the Persians, but this assassination had no success in restoring the old worship, for the king's death was a cause for national mourning throughout the country.

"The body of Tiridates," says the writer of this king's biography, "was transferred to Thortan, and placed in a silver-mounted coffin "adorned with precious stones, which was drawn by golden-harnessed "mules. Bodies of armed soldiers with standards escorted it on both sides, "while ahead of the coffin funeral songs were chanted, and incense was "burned . . . Behind the bier trumpets and harps played dirges to the "accompaniment of voices of weeping women . . ."

The Sassanid government's aim in opposing the Christian religion was, as we see, political. Every time the Persians made a victorious entry into Armenia, their troops were accompanied by Mazdean priests commanded by their King of Kings to implant the Iranian religion in the country, lest if it remained Christian it should become the advance post of Roman power against Persia. Along with the Christians, the remnants of adherents to the ancestral heathen faith of Armenia were also included in the Mazdean persecution.

"Ardashir (Artaxerxes I)," says Moses of Khoren, "widens the "temple functions, and orders the fire of Ormuzd to burn continually on "the altar of Pakaran. As for the statues erected at Armavir by Valarsace "(Vagharchak) to his ancestors, and to the sun and moon, which had been "transferred first to Pakaran and then to Ardashad, Ardashir demolishes "them. Our country is placed under tribute to him by decree, and his "authority imposed everywhere." (1)

These attempts of the Ctesiphon court to bring back Armenia into

---

(1) MOSES OF KHOREN, II, 77. Transl. LANGLOIS, I. 49.

the Persian sphere of influence by converting it to Mazdeism, went on as long as the Sassanid dynasty lasted.

"At a fixed time, the sixth month," says Elisha Vartabed (2), "they "[the Persian satraps and magi] sought to enforce a royal order that in "all places under the dominion of the Great King (3) all church cere-"monies be abolished, the doors of temples of worship be closed and sealed, "the sacred ornaments be delivered to the treasury officers, and that all "psalm-singing be forbidden. The priests were to give no further in-"struction to the people in their homes, and the books of the true prophets "were no longer to be read to them. Men and women dedicated to Christ "and living in monasteries were to change their garb for that of laymen. "Also governors' wives were to be instructed in the doctrine of the Magi, "while the latter were to teach publicly the sons and daughters both of the "nobility and the people. The institution of holy matrimony received of "their fathers according to the tenets of Christianity was to be abolished, "and instead of having one wife only, each man should have several so "that the Armenian nation be increased; also that there be marriages of "fathers and daughters, brothers and sisters, mothers and sons, and grand-"fathers and grand-daughters. No animals were to be killed for food "without being first sacrificed, and no dough must be kneaded without "wearing the phantam (1). Manure must not be used for fuel. Beavers, "foxes, and hares must not be killed. All snakes, lizards, frogs, ants, "and vermin of every sort must be exterminated, while one's hands must "be washed in cow's urine. (2)

Thus new-born Christianity in Armenia was threatened from its cradle both by Mazdeism and the old pagan beliefs that still smouldered. Faustus of Byzantium informs us in fact that more than a century after the Illuminator's death, the worshipers of the Haïkian gods attempted uprisings. One of the revolts took place during the patriarchate of Schahag I of Manazkert (373-

DRACHMA OF THE SASSANID TYPE OF THE GEORGIAN ERISTHAW GOURGEN

---
(2) Transl. LANGLOIS, *Hist. Armen.*, vol. I, p. 99.
(3) Yezdedjerd.
(1) In Zend: peete-dane, a kind of veil used in religious ceremonies.
(2) In order not to defile water.

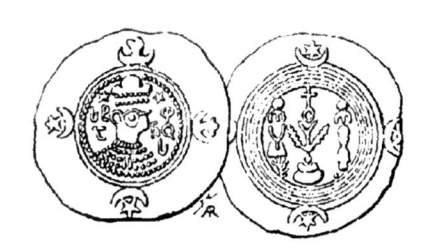

DRACHMA OF THE SASSANID TYPE OF THE GEORGIAN ERISTHAW STEPHANOS I

377); but all such attempts were suppressed.

We are without any archaeological structural remains connected with Armenia during the Sassanid period, but a few rare coins struck by the rulers of Iberia show that in those days Persian influence extended to the foot of the great Caucasian chain, and consequently to Iran's neighbor, Armenia. One of these drachmas minted in the Persian style, bears the monogram of the Eristhaw Gourgen (3) and by the fire-altar shown on the reverse of the coin we have proof that the Iberians likewise were reached by Zoroastrian preaching. On another coin bearing in full the name of the Eristhaw Stephanos I (1), the pyre is replaced by the Christian cross.

THE ARMENIAN CHURCH

"The recognition of Christianity by Tiridates and the investiture of Gregory the Illuminator with the title of Chief Bishop brought the Armenian Church into being without any intervention of the Greek Church such as later occurred in the Slavonic countries when Cyril and Methodius preached there. The founding of the Armenian Church was therefore a national undertaking, and the investiture given Gregory by the Metropolitan of Caesarea had no more significance than a mere act of ordination." (2) This Church, whose dogma at first was that of Rome and Byzantium, separated from Constantinople in the year 491 on account of the Council of Chalcedon (482), for it refused to admit that there were in Jesus Christ a single person and a single nature. Thus there arose a separate church which Orthodox and Catholics alike call the Gregorian Church from the name of its founder, St. Gregory, but which the Armenians name: *Haï Yékéghetzi*, or Armenian Church. This church has produced an abundant sacred literature. In 1166 the patriarch Nerses the Gracious set forth in his *Outline of the Armenian Faith* the ideas of his co-religionists regarding the nature of Christ.

---

(3) Contemporary with Hormisdas (579-589).
(1) Contemporary with Chosroes II (591-628).
(2) K. ASLAN, *Etudes historiques sur le Peuple armenien*, 1909, p. 230.

The divergences between the Armenian and Roman Churches relate to questions of dogma. The Armenians do not accept the Procession of the Holy Ghost, nor do they believe in Purgatory. It is the dogma of Incarnation, however, or rather the belief of two natures and one person in Christ which makes the Catholics consider the Armenians as schismatics, or at least as dissenters. Consequently this Church does not recognize the supremacy of the Pope, and like many other Eastern Christians, distinguishes between the essence and the existence of the Church. It admits the oneness of Christianity like that of its founder Jesus Christ, but maintains that the conditions of its existence vary according to the rites, discipline, and usages of each individual church.

There is every reason to believe that it was to escape both from Papal authority and that of Constantinople that the Armenians entrenched themselves in creeds that could only be discussed or even understood by the nation's intellectual élite. Christianity separated them from the Persians, and they did not wish to come under Latin or Greek domination. We shall see later with what vigor her clergy and nobles rejected proposals for union with Rome or Constantinople when they were made.

I have been compelled to expatiate somewhat on this subject and encroach on the centuries subsequent to St. Gregory's time, in order to show the position held by the Armenian Church in the Christian world. The divergences sprang up by degrees following the Council of Chalcedon, and today the Armenian faith is definitely established as independent of all other Christian churches and as a national Church.

DRACHMA OF THE SASSANID KING SAPOR I

Tiridates III had a very agitated reign. After two years on the throne (250-252), he was driven out by the Persians and for nine years (252-261), Sapor I (240-271) was in military occupation of Armenia. The Armenian king regained his throne (283-294), again lost it (294-298), and finally with Roman help reigned uninterruptedly for thirty-two years (298-330).

The Emperor Valerian's disgraceful capture (Valerian 253-260) had encouraged Sapor, who with Mesopotamia and Armenia at his mercy pro-

ARTAVAZD VI (252-261) ceeded to ravage Cilicia, Syria, and Cappadocia, and to seize Antioch and Caesarea, but he deemed it wise to spare the Armenians and therefore did not deprive them of their liberties. Artavazd VI (252-261), of the Armenian royal house was put on the throne by the Persian army, while Sapor in person marched against Syria. The king of Persia was defeated at the siege of Edessa, and Odenath, king of Palmyra, compelled him to return to his dominions. Odenath had remained faithful to the Emperor Gallienus and been appointed king of Palmyra by the Romans. The Emperor granted him the title of Augustus, and made him his lieutenant in the East. With the help of the legions placed under him, this ruler restored Syria to the Romans, raised the siege of Edessa, and having conquered a part of Armenia, drove out the Persians along with their puppet-king Artavazd VI.

COIN OF VABALATH, SON OF QUEEN ZENOBIA, KING OF PALMYRA EMPEROR

Odenath was assassinated, however, at Emesa (226-267) and Queen Zenobia, less prudent than her husband, claimed in behalf of her son Vabalath the provinces he had conquered, including Syria, Arabia, Cilicia, Cappadocia, and also Armenia which remained under the rule of Palmyra for eleven years (261-272).

Zenobia's ambitions aroused Rome's wrath, and Aurelian destroyed her capital city in the year 273, whereupon Armenia came again under Roman rule. Probus and Carus then restored the kingdom and in 331-339 Chosroes II the Younger occupied the throne. He was succeeded by Tiran (340-350), Archak II (351-367), Pap (369-374), Varazdat (374-378), Archak III (378-389), Vagharchak (378-386) the rival of Archak III, and then Chosroes III (386-392 and 414-415). In this period Armenia, while keeping her kings, was divided (387) between the Persians and Romans.

COIN OF ZENOBIA QUEEN OF PALMYRA

S^T SAHAK I AND S^T MESROP

Vramchapouh (Varahran-Sapor) was on the throne (392-414) when a highly important event took place, the invention of the Armenian alphabet, which gave a great impetus to the nation, increasing its self-consciousness and giving it a literature. Sahak I, called the Great, (387-428 and 432-439) who was then Catholicos of Armenia, had called to assist him as Co-adjutor, Vartabed (Doctor) Mesrop, an apostle, scholar, and man of letters who knew Greek, Persian, and Syriac, besides the speech of his fellow-countrymen. Sahak entrusted him with the task of composing a special alphabet for the Armenian language, so that the Scriptures might be translated therein. Hitherto only the Greek and Syriac versions had been used, and the necessity for the priests to know those two languages and translate them verbally hindered considerably their work of preaching and explaining Holy Writ.

GOLDEN COIN OF THE SASSINID KING OF PERSIA CHOSROES II

INVENTION OF ARMENIAN WRITING

Mesrop utilizing a table of twenty-two letters suggested to him by a priest named Daniel, composed a thirty-six letter alphabet in which each sound of the Armenian language was represented. Later on, at the end of the 12th century, the grammarians added two more characters, so that today there are thirty-eight letters. As is the case with Zend writing, no letter is accented, the different tone-values of the vowels being shown by different characters. Mesrop had the Latin, Greek, Zend, and Indian alphabets to choose from, and did so but added special signs of his own composition while also changing somewhat those he borrowed. He thus created an alphabet adapted to Armenian pronunciation, and this step not only hindered the spread of the language but further separated the Armenian people from their neighbors both on the east and west, and strengthened their national individuality. Georgia also had its own alphabet which though it has some general resemblance to the Armenian is nevertheless altogether different. Moreover the two writings developed in opposite ways, the Georgian characters soon becoming less angular and more flowing, while the Armenian remained square until the modern cursive was adopted.

The inventor of the alphabet himself translated the book of Proverbs and the New Testament, and under his guidance the rest of the Scriptures

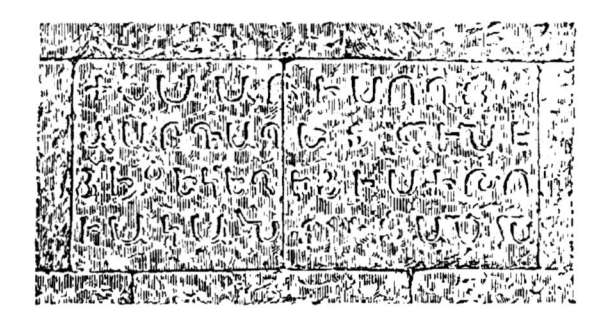

ARMENIAN INSCRIPTION AT ANI (A.D. 622)
(from a photograph by K. J. Basmadjian)

were written in Armenian, young men having been previously sent forth to Edessa, Caesarea, Antioch, Alexandria, and Constantinople, to seek out copies of the sacred writings and especially of the Septuagint version of the Bible, all of which the Persians had systematically destroyed throughout their empire.

Though Armenian literary endeavors were first confined to religious writings, a start had nevertheless been made, and soon there arose a secular literature.

This was a new dawn for Armenia. At the time that her religious freedom was violently threatened by Persian Mazdeism, king Vramchapouh and the patriarch Sahak, both of them foresighted patriots, realized that unless Armenia segregated herself through intellectual development from her powerful neighbors, both her Christianity and her nationality would perish. The king and the patriarch in prompting the discovery of a national alphabet did more than any Maecenas, they saved their whole nation, and the beneficent results of their influence have been manifest down through the centuries to our day. These two men rank among the greatest figures of the Armenian people when one considers the consequences of their work.

LAST ARSACID KINGS OF ARMENIA 416-429

Two rulers, Sapor or Chapouh (416-420) and Artashes IV (423-429) are last on the list of the Arsacid dynasty of Armenia. Thereafter, in the part of the country under Sassanid rule, the kings were replaced by Marzpans or Persian governors, with Armenians occasionally among them. Elsewhere, the provinces under Greek rule were governed in turn by Persians, Armenians, or Byzantines, appointed by the Basileus. In 652 the succession of Marzpans comes to an end, as does that of the Roman prefects in 653. In those years the whole of Armenia fell into the hands of the Moslems, upon the crushing defeats inflicted at Kerbalah and Nehavend on the army of Yezdedjerd IV, the last of the Sassanid rulers.

THE MARZPANS

Nevertheless this era of Marzpans and Byzantine governors lasting two centuries was an honorable one for Armenia, even though the country was no longer self-governed and retained only its language and religion as outward signs of nationality. The Sassanid rulers, who imagined they could overcome the Armenians by converting them to Mazdeism, ordered their governors to stamp out Christianity in their respective provinces, and started persecutions at the same time in Persia proper. Yezdedjerd II (440-457), then on the throne of Iran, issued a decree commanding all Christians in his dominions to embrace the Mazdean religion. This was the signal for a violent revolt in Armenia, the Persians and their Magi were massacred, the fire temples destroyed, and the people flew to arms under Vardan Mamikonian. This brave prince and his small army, however, were overwhelmed near the city of Avarair (455) in Media Minor, Vardan being killed in combat along with thousands of his men.

VARDAN MAMIKONIAN

Vardan Mamikonian through his mother was the grandson of the Patriarch Sahak and one of the most influential noblemen of Armenia, his authority in the nation being enhanced by the esteem and trust in which he was held by the people. Being in command of the Armenian troops and raised to the rank of Stratelat or general by Emperor Theodosius II, he enjoyed considerable repute both at the Persian court and that of Constantinople. He was one of the national delegates who went to plead with Yezdedjerd to rescind his decree against Christianity. His efforts were in vain, however, and only after exhausting all peaceable means did he resort to arms. Forsaken and betrayed, even by one of his own liegemen, Vassak Suni, he was able to raise only a small force. Yet with this handful of men he had the courage to face the Persian cohorts. His death was a severe loss for Armenia, but the battle of Aravaïr saved the nation, for the Iranians never expecting such stout resistance had to stop to make good their losses. Meanwhile grave danger for Persia arose on her eastern borders, and her armies had to rush to the Oxus plains to stop the Huns. Armenia was delivered from the Magi for a while. The memory of Vardan's supreme sacrifice and that of his fellow-soldiers has been so ardently cherished that to the present time the Armenian Church celebrates the anniversary of the battle of Aravaïr and pays tribute to the heroes who fell there.

VAHAN MAMIKONIAN   Under king Peroses (458-488) the persecutions were resumed. Vahan Mamikonian, Vardan's nephew, took command of the Armenian troops, called on the Iberians to help the Christian cause, and carried on the fight. He met with fluctuating success, until Vologeses (488-491), succeeding Peroses who was killed fighting the Hephtalites, deemed it wiser to tolerate Christianity in his dominions and especially in Armenia where the Magi for nearly half a century had kept up a war that had cost the Persian kingdom dear. Thus again the bravery of the Mamikonians had delivered the nation. From then on, till the Arabian invasion, Armenia had self-government under the supreme supervision of the Persian governor, and enjoyed a period of prosperity.

CHAPTER V

The Arab Conquest. — Armenia a Province of the Empire of the Caliphs.

Ever since the Armenians conquered the Ararat country, life had been very hard and uncertain for them the greater part of the time. Nevertheless, although constantly obliged to struggle to maintain their independence, they had been for only brief periods in a state of complete

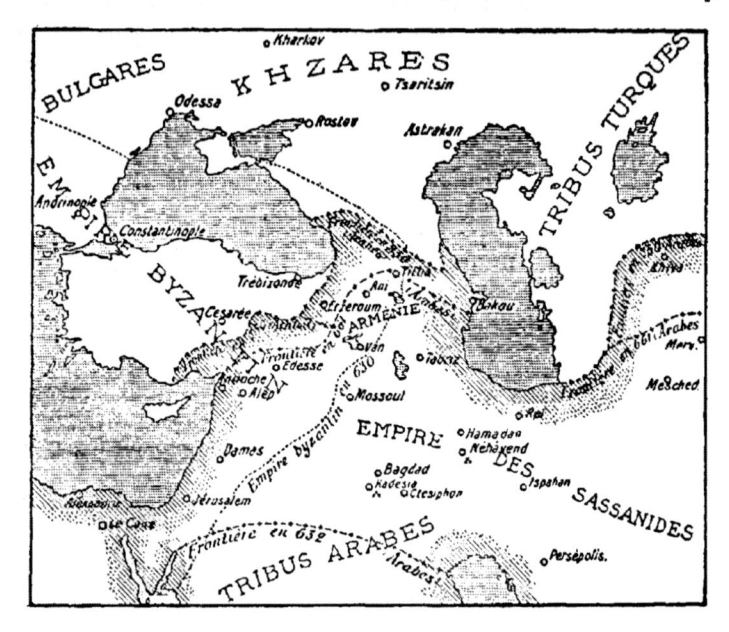

EMPIRE OF THE ARABS

subjugation, for both Persians and Romans had deemed it wiser to leave them practically free under governors who very often were chosen from among their own princes. Consequently the Armenians were able to look on themselves as allies in turn of the Emperor or of the "King of Kings", rather than the subjects of either. But with the entry of the Arabs into the political scene, Armenia's lot takes on a darker hue. The Moslems henceforward considered the Christians of the countries which they conquered as their slaves, and for over a thousand years thereafter used every means and stopped at no manner of persecution to win them over to Islam, while the Armenians clung all the more steadfastly to their religion as the last bulwark of their nationality.

Enslaved by the Arabs, they nevertheless had one splendid burst of freedom towards the end of the 9th century, which lasted nearly two hundred years. From 885 to 1064, they took advantage of the confusion caused by the arrival of the Turks and became their own masters in at least a part of their ancestral domain. The very events, however, which ensured their temporary freedom proved their eventual ruin, for having thrown off the Arab yoke, they were to succumb to that of the Turks and suffer thereunder down to modern times. Armenia's martyrdom began actually in A.D. 645, when the standard of the Prophet appeared in the region of Van.

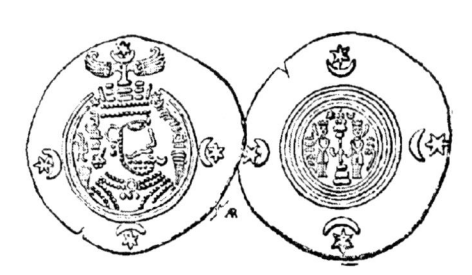

**COIN OF YEZDEDJERD IV
LAST SASSANID KING OF PERSIA**

Mahomet's fanatical Arabian tribes spread like a flood over western Asia. They vanquished Yezdedjerd IV on the plains of Kerbalah, and at Nehavend consummated the ruin of the Sassanid monarchy exhausted both by the attacks of Emperor Heraclius and the disorder that reigned at the Persian court. The Emirs continued their conquests towards India, and the whole East was subdued. On the north and west, however, they found serious obstacles in their way. The Eastern Roman Empire with its tremendous influence and great cultural advantages, although much absorbed on the Danube and in Thrace by the invading barbarians from the north, nevertheless offered the Mahometan invaders resistance that was destined to hold out for centuries. Though in possession of Syria, the Moslem chieftains did not yet dare to attack Asia Minor and march on Constantinople. The eastern provinces of the Empire being more vulnerable, they overran Armenia.

**ARAB CONQUEST
A.D. 639**

About 639, eighteen thousand Arabs led by Abd-er-Rahman invaded the Taron district and Lake Van region from Assyria, and put the country to fire and sword. The Armenians had never before met in battle these penniless and ill-clad warriors, of such unequalled daring and fired with a fanaticism hitherto unknown among the older nations. The Persians and Romans found it to their advantage to show the Armenians some little consideration, for in war they were alternately their subjects or their allies, but the sons of the desert knew no restraints with regard to these infidels sharing the same religion and mode of life as their enemies the Greeks.

Bishop Sebeos (1), the only Armenian historian to give us any account of the Arab conquests which he witnessed, bitterly laments his country's sorrowful fate. On January 6th, 642, the Arabs took the city of Tovin by storm, slaughtered twelve thousand of its inhabitants and carried away thirty-five thousand into slavery.

"Who could tell," wrote the bishop, "all the horrors of the Ishmaelite "invasion setting sea and earth ablaze? The blessed prophet Daniel "foresaw and prophesied these very plagues ... the fourth beast dreadful "and terrible, its teeth of iron and its nails of brass, which devoured, "brake in pieces, and stamped with its feet ... This beast rising from the "south, the Ishmaelite kingdom ... shall be mightier than all kingdoms and "shall devour the whole earth...

COIN OF EMPEROR CONSTANS II

"The following year [643], the Ish-"maelite army entered Atrpatakan (Azer-"baïdjan) and headed in three directions: "one division towards Ararat, another into "the land of the Sephhakan-Gund and the "third into the country of the Aluans. Those "who invaded the Sephhakan-Gund over-"ran that territory, put the people to the "sword, and took booty and prisoners. "They then all marched on Erewan [Erivan] and attacked the fortress, "but unsuccessfully." Constans II (641-668), who was Emperor at Constantinople at the time, indeed sent some troops to Armenia, but they arrived in irregular fashion and the Imperial prefect, Sembat, feeling himself too weak to withstand the Moslem onslaught, forsook the Greek

---

(1) *Histoire d'Héraclius*. Transl. Fr. MACLER. Paris. 1904.

cause and submitted and paid tribute to the Caliph Omar. The latter was shortly thereafter succeeded by Othman I (Nov. 9, 644.)

A.D. 644 "The (Arab) division in the Ararat region invaded the "territory of the Taïans, the Georgians, and the Aluans, "plundering and taking prisoners. They then proceeded to "Nakhtchawan ... but failed to capture the city. They took, however, "the city of Khram, killed the defenders and carried away captive the "women and children."

Nevertheless, the Byzantine court saw the great danger to the Empire if the Arabs were allowed to plant themselves on the Erzerum plateau and threaten the Pontine provinces. Incensed against the Armenians, Constans II determined to regain that province by force of arms, and to compel its inhabitants to embrace the Orthodox religion, hoping thus to have them more closely on his side. He met with no success as regards their religion, but the new prefect Hamazasp who was finding the tribute demanded by the Moslems too heavy, came over to the Emperor. In reprisal the Caliph Othman had 1,775 Armenian hostages slaughtered and was about to take the field against the rebels when he was murdered by his soldiers. His second successor, Mohawiah, the first of the Bagdad Caliphs, followed up his intentions and devastated Armenia, dispossessing Justin II. The latter from his palace summoned the unhappy inhabitants to come back to their allegiance to him. The Armenians replied (1): "How often, under "the government of the Greeks we have had in our worst calamities only "the barest assistance! Frequently, on the contrary, our obedience "has been requited only with insults. To swear fealty to you is but to "court ruin and death. Leave us therefore under our present masters and "under their protection."

COIN OF EMPEROR JUSTIN II

This prudent reply from a people oppressed in turn by both Byzantines and Arabs only exasperated the Basileus. He sent a Greek army

---

(1) JOHN VI, *Catholicos*, chap. XIII.

COIN OF EMPEROR JUSTINIAN II

into Armenia, ravaged the country, carried off what little wealth the Moslems had overlooked, and capturing eight thousand families sent them to distant lands to be sold into slavery.

Meanwhile the Arabs thinking the Armenians were seeking to evade their authority, again overran the Ararat region spreading death and desolation in their wake. They razed a number of cities, destroyed the fortress of Sevan, enslaving its defenders. At the same time the new emperor, Justinian II, stubbornly maintaining the Greek grievance of the Armenians' rejection of the Orthodox creed, caused the Patrician Leontius to devastate Upper Armenia, Iberia, and Albania, countries that had also been obliged to submit to the power of the Caliphs. Thus the Armenians not only had to suffer persecution from the Moslems because they were Christians, but also from the Greeks because of their unpardonable adherence to their national mode of worship.

The Byzantine court at this period displayed the most savage religious intolerance; fierce hatred inflamed the Greeks against those peoples whose creeds did not coincide with theirs, and also spread armed strife among themselves. These passions and the resulting futile wranglings were weakening the Empire, but the Emperors and the people alike were infatuated with the subtleties of casuistry, even while dangerous enemies were bearing down on every frontier.

COIN OF THE OMMIAD CALIPH ABD-EL-MELEK

Greek domination in Armenia, moreover, did not last long. The Basileus after five years of hateful oppression withdrew his legions, and the Ommiad Caliph Abd-el-Melek once more invaded the country. He occupied Tovin and drove out the Roman prefect, appointing as provincial governor Abd-Allah, a cruel ruler who sent the Armenian notables as prisoners to Damascus. The Catholicos Isaac and Prince Sembat were among the captives, but the latter succeeded in making his escape, and was in A.D. 695 again placed over Armenia by the Emperor Leontius who had usurped the Imperial throne.

MOHAMMED-BEN-AKBA, 702 In 702, the Emir Mohammed-ben-Okba who had been named governor of Mesopotamia by Abd-el-Melek was driven out by the legions. Taking advantage, however, of the departure of the Greek army, he regained power and proceeded to establish it further by a reign of terror and nameless cruelties. At Nakhitchevan he shut up the principal Armenians in the church and set fire to the building, burning them alive. And all the while Byzantium was arguing over questions of dogma with the Armenian clergy! Church synods were being convened to discuss whether or not water should be added to the wine in the celebration of the Mass, and whether there should be added to the Sanctus the words: *qui crucifixus es*

Neither was religion the sole concern of the Catholicos. The high clergy went in for politics, and he, just as much carried away as his Byzantine opponents, intruded the spiritual into temporal matters. We see later on Catholicos John VII (1) praising the Patriarch Elias for having denounced to Caliph Abd-el-Melek the queen of the Aghouans and their patriarch Nerses Bakour, as being friends of the Greek emperors and enemies of the Caliphs. He congratulates Elias in having them put in chains on the grounds of their attachment to the Council of Chalcedon! It is true that the Armenian people clung to their religious beliefs and could not see beyond them, but their bishops seized every opportunity to fight their opponents and improve their own position with the Moslem rulers.

The struggle between the Greeks and the Arabs had from the very beginning assumed the religious character which has ever been the main strength of the Mahometans. For centuries and centuries Caliphs and Sultans derived their power therefrom. The fanaticism of these uncivilized men of the desert was accompanied by boundless pride and profound contempt for all who did not share their beliefs. Bishop Sebeos in his history of Heraclius has given us the Armenian translation of a letter which the "King of the Ishmaelites" had the monstrous audacity to write to the "Emperor of the Greeks."

---

(1) Transl SAINT-MARTIN, chap. XIII, p. 88.

"If you desire to live in peace," he wrote, "give up your vain religion "in which you have been reared from childhood. Deny this Jesus and be "converted to the great God whom I serve, the God of our father Abra-"ham. Disband your big armies and send them back home, and I will "make you a great chief in these lands. I will send my Osticans (gover-"nors) into your City; I will gather all its treasures and divide them into "four parts, three for myself and one for you. I will also assign troops "to you, as many as you wish, and will levy on you such tribute as you "can pay. Otherwise, how shall this Jesus whom you call Christ, who "could not save himself from the Jews, ever be able to save you from my "hands?"

The old Roman civilization was thus insulted by a barbarian, an ignorant fanatic, full of pride and greed, who in those few lines expressed the aims of his fellow-religionists.

"The Emperor took the letter," continues Sebeos, "and entered into "the house of God, where he fell on his face and cried 'Look, O Lord, "upon the dishonor which these Ishmaelites cast on Thee. Have com-"passion on us, Lord, as we hope in Thee. Shame their faces, O God, "that they may seek Thy name. May everlasting shame be upon them, "and may they perish in infamy, so that they may know that Thy name "is The Lord, and that Thou alone rulest over all the earth!" He removed his crown, laid off his purple robe, and put on sackcloth; sitting in ashes, he commanded a public fast throughout Constantinople.

The Emperor's attitude was as ingenuous as that of the Moslem, but it was anything but criminal. This passage from the Armenian historian's pen shows how warped on both sides were the concerns of the age. Temporal interests indeed remained the same, but they were hidden behind religious externals over which the masses became fanatical. National honor no longer stirred men's hearts in Constantinople, and something else must arouse them. Even so the Arabs opened an era of fanaticism and dug the fathomless cleavage between the two worlds, of Christian ideals and Moslem aggression.

ASHOT, GOVERNOR, A.D. 744

There were nevertheless sometimes upright men among the Arabs. One such was Merwan, who about 744 softened conditions for the Armenians, and who on becoming

RUINS OF THE CASTLE OF ANI
(Taken from inside the town)

Caliph appointed the Bagratid Ashot as governor of the country. His successors did not, however, follow his example; they loaded the Christians of their Empire with crushing taxes, which led to a revolt of the Armenians. Ashot, although one of themselves, was thrown into prison by his fellow-Armenians, and there blinded. This revolt was quelled in blood.

The Arab governors Soleiman (766), Bekir (769), and Hassan (778) treated the Armenians with incredible harshness and gave the inhabitants over to the cruelties of the soldiery. A fresh revolt arose from these oppressions. Mouschegh the Mamikonian gathered the insurgents around him, and with five thousand men attacked Hassan's troops that were then ravaging the Taron district, and slaughtered them. Under the weight of numbers, however, he fell in combat, and his son Ashot carrying on his father's work drove the Arabs from several provinces, and, on the banks of the Arpa-tchaï in the district of Schirak, fortified the city of Ani that was soon to become the capital of Armenia and the residence of the patriarchs.

ANI, CAPITAL OF ARMENIA

The site of Ani, according to Armenian chronicles, had been inhabited from very ancient times, and its position and remarkable natural defenses made it conspicuously advantageous.

The Ani plateau surrounded by high cliffs is bounded on the south and east by the river Arpa-tchaï, a swift stream coming down from the lake region of the Lesser Caucasus, from the mountains whose northern flanks overlook the city of Alexandropol. On the west another deep valley, that of the Aladja-tchaï (1), bounded the capital city which on the southern side came to an abrupt end by a sharp mountain buttress between the Arpa-tchaï and its tributary, the Aladja-tchaï. Two gorges, whose waters flowed down into each of these two streams, separated the promontory from the neighboring massif, but these two natural ditches were separated at the head of their respective waters by a strip of land about 600 yards wide. There the Armenians concentrated every means of defense, building a double wall with towers commanded by a huge keep overlooking the chief gate of the city. A smaller enclosure was built skirting the edge of the cliffs, while upon a hill at the southern end of this great spur stood the citadel.

The city was about 185 acres in extent.

We do not know of what ancient Ani consisted, how big it was, or whether the city covered the whole plateau. Possibly it comprised only the southern point commanded by the hill of the citadel, and traces of walls and gates still to be seen in the promontory's narrowest part strengthen this supposition. But it is quite certain that the northern ramparts protecting the town were commenced under king Ashot as soon as he had chosen the Ani site as a refuge for his court, because this portion of the enclosure was the most vulnerable, in fact the only one whereby the enemy could attempt an entrance. Sembat II (977-990) finished building these walls.

We have in Europe a good number of towns still surrounded by their medieval fortifications, e.g. Avignon, Aiguesmortes, Carcassonne, in southern France alone, while ruins of this kind are also numerous in the East. Trebizond still has its ramparts built by the Comneni. Military remains are all that is left of Antioch, and on the mountain overlooking Tiflis are to be seen the ruins of the Acropolis of the Georgians. No site, however, is comparable to that of Ani in the deep impression this dead city makes on the traveler. Lost in the middle of a vast solitude, it bears yet the deep wounds it received at its hour of destruction.

---

(1) Dzaghkotza-Tsor, the valley of the gardens.

SKETCH-MAP OF THE SITE OF THE CITY OF ANI

Ani, under the Bagratids, was a large, fine city, with many churches, palaces, and splendid walls built of multicolored volcanic stone often as light as pumice-stone. The cathedral, and the shrines of the apostles, of St Stephen, of St Gregory the Illuminator, and of the Redemption, were the chief religious edifices, but there were an untold number of chapels, so much so that the citizens were accustomed to swear by the Thousand and One Churches of Ani. The ruins of these structures still stand, whereas all private dwellings have disappeared with the city debris No streets, squares, or market places are traceable today, brushwood and brambles cover them all.

This city, whose ruins the traveler visits in these days with deep feelings, was not the work of Ashot alone, but of all the Bagratid rulers who took pleasure in improving their capital, and also of the Armenians of the whole region who gave liberally to it for a couple of centuries (885-1077) Ani personified Armenia that had been so long through deep waters. Former generations had seen Artaxata, Tigranocerta, Dovin, and a number of other flourishing Armenian cities, but these capitals had all fallen one after another, vanishing with only dim memories in their place By raising Ani to the rank of capital city, Ashot gave the Armenians a metropolis, a center, that seemed then destined to remain forever. Within these walls he brought both temporal power and spiritual authority together Ani became the heart of Armenia

The great Hârun-al-Raschid who had just taken up his abode in the palace of Bagdad as Commander of the Faithful, was more humane than his predecessors. The Arab conquests had become well established, and the court of the Caliphs, emerging gradually from the uncouth manners of the earlier soldiers of Islam, had become less harsh and more urbane Unbounded luxury surrounded Omar's successors and encouraged them to leniency

786-818 The Caliph, while keeping Armenia under his authority, and maintaining his Arab governors in the Ararat country ordered his viceroys Yezid II (786-788) and Kouzima (798-818) to treat the Armenians with less severity. These governors however, did not relax their cruelty As Moslem fanatics, they had only hatred and contempt for the Christian peoples at the mercy of their whims, and they did not stop at the most wicked deeds in shedding blood and satisfying their greed In the province of Bagrevand, Yezid's representative, for want of any other pretext for the indulgence of his cruel desires, had one of his own slaves strangled and thrown into a gorge near Etchmiadzin. Then he proceeded to accuse the monks of the crime, to plunder their shrines, and slay forty-two priests.

Fortunately all the Arab governors were not barbarians and the Armenians in their chronicles praise the kindness of some of them, notably that of Haul (818-835) who was sent to Armenia by Caliph Al-Mamoun But there existed terrible rivalries among the Arabs themselves, and a Moslem named Sevada having hatched a plot against Haul, the Armenians made the mistake of espousing the cause of the rival. They were punished, for Sevada's small army was wiped out by the governor of Armenia. Later on, during the revolt of a Persian named Baban or Babek, Bagarat, an Armenian whom Caliph Motassem had placed over the Ararat region, assisted the Arabs in putting down the disorders

Despite this act of loyalty, Caliph Motawakkel appointed a Moslem, Abou-Seth, in Bagarat's stead, followed by the former's son Youssouf, whose oppressions caused the Armenians again to rebel. This was a fresh excuse for putting Armenia to fire and sword. The nobility were wiped out, the people enslaved, towns, villages, churches all disappeared in flames, while any Armenians refusing to embrace Islam were pitilessly slaughtered.

Finally, after a series of Arab governors all more fanatical, greedy, and cruel the one than the other, Caliph Motawakkel-Billah realizing

ASHOT, PRINCE OF PRINCES 859

that his empire would never have Armenia's obedience unless a fair amount of self-government were restored to her, appointed the Bagratid prince Ashot as governor of his own country and gave him the title of "Prince of princes." (859).

The new viceroy did not disappoint either his subjects or the Caliphs. He proved loyal to his overlords, restored the country, and organized the army of which he made his brother Abas commander-in-chief.

"Armenia was beginning to prosper under Ashot's rule, when Iahab, "the son of Sevada, an Arab related to the Bagratids, tried, as did his "father before him, to supplant the governor. But the Commander-in-"chief Abas with a smaller number of troops crushed the rebel forces on "the banks of the Araxes. The battle-field was named the Field of the "Forty, because according to Armenian historians, forty thousand men "overcame eighty thousand who fought for Iahab.

"Delivered from his rival, Ashot devoted his whole energy to the "material and moral welfare of his people. He had new townships built, "to which he attracted many foreigners. Agriculture was encouraged, and "trade assisted by new roads. (1)"

Tired of fighting an energetic people for the possession of a province claimed by the Greek emperors, and already concerned about movements of tribes taking place on the eastern and northern borders of their empire, the Caliphs gradually came round to the plan of creating south of the Caucasus a state they could use as a shield against attacks from the Russian plains, and of thus putting an end to their quarrels with the Byzantine court. In Constantinople, too, Armenia was looked on as lost to the Empire, and it was thought better to keep the legions for the defense of Asia Minor against the ambitious Saracens. Possession of Armenia now that Syria and Mesopotamia were gone had no longer the importance it had when the enemies of Rome were chiefly in Persia. The Emperors and Caliphs undoubtedly came to an agreement, for both courts at the same time granted the title of king to Ashot the Bagratid. Mohammed-Billah sent from Bagdad, Ostican (Governor) Emir Ysa who, in the name of the Caliph his master, came to Ani and solemnly recognized Ashot, delivering to him the crown and royal vestments, whilst the Greek emperor Basil, who was himself an Armenian, also sent the new king the insignia of sovereignty.

After untold misfortunes Armenia, owing to what was happening in the Eastern political world, regained her freedom at last. This revival, due outwardly to the mutual antagonism of the two great empires of the time, was also a result of the Armenian people's own energy, their soldierly virtues, and their unconquerable fidelity to Christianity, for although so often

COIN OF EMPEROR BASIL I

overwhelmed by sheer force and numbers, the nation never once capitulated.

After having conquered and ravaged Armenia, the Arabs had entered the valley of the river Kura and occupied Tiflis, but their forward march was stopped on the north by the Great Caucasus and on the west by the

---

(1) Fr. TOURNEBISE, *op. cit.*, p. 105.

Suram heights. Taiq, Gougarq, and the Phasis river basin remained in Byzantine hands. It was the same with the north of Lesser Armenia and with Lazica where lofty mountain chains protected Trebizond and the Greek possessions along the Black Sea coast. The capital of Georgia became consequently the seat of the Caliph's government in the Armenian province. The harsh treatment of the conquerors caused mass conversions to Islam, the Armenian and Georgian princes setting the example so as to retain their lands. Except in the mountains and inaccessible valleys Christianity disappeared almost everywhere throughout Transcaucasia; churches and convents were in ruins and forsaken, while the minarets of mosques were soon seen in all cities and towns.

Nevertheless those Armenians and Caucasians who had fled before the invaders had withdrawn into the natural strongholds and the mountains adjacent to the river Rion. There they remained in uninterrupted connection with Constantinople, and prepared to counter-attack against their country's oppressors, while at the same time keeping their religious freedom. Their attacks against the Arabs were unceasing and they sometimes carried the day, but the power of the Caliphs was such that despite all their efforts the Christians had to await the weakening of the great Moslem empire before they could recover their southern and eastern provinces.

CASTLE OF KHOCHAB IN KURDISTAN

Going through the mountain regions extending north of the upper Araxes towards Ispir, Kars or Artvin, the traveler every now and then comes across the castles of the Armenian nobles perched like eagle's nests on inaccessible heights, generally fortified on one side only, with sheer cliffs below all the other walls. Thither at the first warning the peasants of the neighboring valleys fled for refuge, taking with them their food supplies and weapons, also their flocks; none but goat-paths led to these retreats, which were capable of months, even years, of resistance against whole armies; and while there echoed in the plain the call of the mullahs to the prayer of the Prophet, churchbells hidden in the clouds rang out the praises of Christ. A strange life, indeed, full of uncertainties, mingled hopes and despair, terror and renewals of courage, and above all, determination not to die, not to deny the faith of their fathers.

After the wars of Heraclius, the Greeks had established Byzantine rule throughout Transcaucasia. The money of Constantinople then circulated in those regions along with the drachmas of the Sassanids, large and very thin silver discs with the head of the King of Kings and the Mazdean pyre.

The Caliphs' governors occupying Tiflis after A.D. 646 and maintaining a strong Arab garrison there, exercised their authority over all the surrounding districts, but until 704 (year 85 of the Hegira) Tiflis had no Moslem mint. In that year Abd-el-Melek had dirhems struck, and money continued to be minted without interruption until A.D. 923, or 311 of the Hegira. At this period there was no national coining of money either in Armenia or Georgia, or in the Aghouank country.

From an economic standpoint, the Arab conquests greatly confused the general situation in the East, but they did give a new scope to trade. Formerly the Roman emperors were almost alone in the minting of gold coins, the Eastern rulers only issuing them in very small amounts. The Arabs put out large quantities of dinars and so compelled Byzantium to increase the fineness and weight of its specie. Moreover, because of the vast extent of their empire, the Moslems were able to extend their trading connections, sea-lanes were opened between the Persian Gulf, the Red Sea and the coasts of India and Africa, of the Malay Archipelago, and China. The Greeks became in a degree dependent on their rivals. The overland routes, interrupted in the north by the thronging tribes of Scythia, shifted in the direction of Iran, Armenia, and Mesopotamia, the routes formerly known to the Phoenicians and still followed by the Semitic Moslems for gaining access to Tibet, central China, and India.

After they had conquered the north of Western Asia, the Arabs made few settlements in those regions, so different in climate and natural features from their own homeland. In Persia, in Transcaucasia, in Armenia, and in the parts of Asia Minor that fell under Moslem rule, the old inhabitants remained in possession of the land but under the yoke of the Arabs, who retained in their hands both the government and the collection of taxes.

The tremendous extent of their empire obliged the Arabs, however, to scatter their strength. They had invaded all the African coast of the Mediterranean, and also Spain, and had carried their arms to the borders of India. They were about to conquer Europe, when they were stopped in the year 732 at Poitiers. The weakening of the Armenian garrisons due to these distant campaigns gave an opportunity for the native princes of that country, from the middle of the 9th century onward, to try to bring about a change, and their efforts succeeded in 885. Moreover, the fear engendered by the Moslem invasion of southern France was to result two centuries later in the great undertaking of the Crusades.

The withdrawal of the Arab army from the Caucasus and Armenia was the signal for the mountain-dwellers to come down from their retreats and recover the lands of their fathers. The Caucasians and Armenians crossed the frontiers of the Caliph's empire, drove out his remaining troops, and with the whole land in revolt founded a number of small kingdoms. Byzantium encouraged these uprisings, and even helped with soldiers and money, thinking that it would be easy to regain the allegiance of the principalities, the rulers of which would not agree together and would each in turn yield obeisance to the Imperial City. At Constantinople there was no thought that the Moslem power would last; it was not realized how vastly the political and military organization of the Arabs differed from that of the various uncivilized races that the Roman world had fought for centuries, the hordes even then pressing along the Danube valley.

CHAPTER VI

Dynasty of the Bagratids (1)

While dealing with Armenia's beginnings, we saw how the historians of the country, who mostly belonged to the clergy, endeavored to link the origin of their nation with Biblical tradition, and how they twisted the old legends to connect the Hebrews with the descendants of Haïk. This propensity related not only to matters of historical fact, but to the genealogies of their ruling families.

ORIGIN OF THE BAGRATIDS According to the native chroniclers, the family of the Bagratids was of Jewish extraction. They claim that the founder of their house, Sembat, was brought captive by King Nebuchadnezzar from Judaea to Armenia and that five centuries later, Vagharchak, the first of the Arsacid kings of Armenia, gave to Bagarat (Pakarat), a descendant of Sembat, the title of "Asped" or Cavalry Commander. Vagharchak supplemented this dignity with that of "Thagatir" which gave the family the honor of crowning the king upon his accession.

This promotion of the Bagratids to the highest State functions hardly tallies with statements by the historians regarding their extraction. Bagarat would seem rather to have been a high nobleman of Armenian stock, perhaps descended from one of Haïk's captains who with him led the nation to the land of Ararat. Vagharchak would certainly not have chosen a foreign prince for the honor of crowning the kings of Armenia, and their own nobles, moreover, so sensitive on this subject, would have claimed this signal distinction for the oldest and noblest of the families descended from Haïk and his companions. In Armenia, as in Georgia and throughout the East, the nobility were too much inclined to give first consideration to their family pride to allow any such slight.

---

(1) Eastern Armenian pronunciation: Bagratid; western: Pagratid.

Besides, even before the Christian era, the Bagratids were lords of Sber in the district of Ispir on the upper Jorokh, and we can presume that they held this domain from their ancestors. In time their possessions grew both by marriage with neighboring princely families and by force of arms. The high Jorokh valley, sheltered by mountains hard to reach, had remained untouched by reverses of fortune, and its rulers had been able to expand their power without arousing cupidity. By degrees the Bagratids had acquired vast lands in the mountain massif of the Lesser Caucasus towards the Araxes and had even pushed into the Ararat country. They owned very large domains in Gougarq and Turuberan. Dariums (Bayazid), Bagaran, Schirakavan, Ani (1), Kars, and Artvin belonged to them, and further south they also possessed Mouch. One of them married the heiress of the kingdom of Georgia, over which his posterity continued to reign. During all the Middle Ages until the end of the 18th century, Karthli was ruled by princes of this family. Some of them, moreover, left highly respected names in this part of Asia. We shall later have occasion to speak of the Bagratid dynasty in connection with the Armenians outside of Armenia. They were consequently very high noblemen, and undoubtedly their fortune and family prestige were the reasons for the patriarch George (870-888) and the other nobles asking both Byzantium and Bagdad that the crown of Armenia should be given to Ashot the Bagratid.

ASHOT I
885-890

The selection of this prince as the new sovereign was certainly a happy one, for Ashot was a wise and just man. also the courts of Constantinople and Bagdad undoubtedly influenced the decisions of the Armenians. Ever since the Arabs seized the country, it was the object of constant strife between the Greeks and the Arabs. Both sides were weary of this state of things, and it was probably by mutual agreement that the two powers decided in favor of Armenia's political rehabilitation. Unfortunately the new king's power was very limited. Notwithstanding the large extent of his family holdings, Ashot had sovereign rule only over the province of Ararat, and, besides, was still under tribute to the Caliphs and saddled with some obligations to the Emperor. However, Armenia regained self-government in the

---

(1) There was another town bearing the name of Ani or Gamakh, situated on the west bank of the Euphrates, in the canton of Daranaghi, Upper Armenia Constantine Porphyrogenetos calls it Kamakha. This stronghold was once celebrated for its temple of Ormuzd, and its burial places of Armenian kings. also on account of the crown treasures being kept there.

north of the Araxes, and both nobles and people seemed pleased with the fact.

Nevertheless, the nobility who had agreed on Ashot's becoming king and who at the instance of the patriarch George had silenced for a while their personal ambitions, did not maintain their submission to the ruler they had themselves chosen. Jealousies that were stilled for a season broke out afresh. Not only did each one seek to be a potentate in his

MAP OF THE ARARAT REGION

own fief, but Ashot had to struggle against several rivals for the crown who sacrificing national interest to their desires, had taken to arms. In the Gougarq region the uprising was the most serious. The king proceeded there at the head of a small army hastily recruited, and hardly had he settled matters in the north of his dominions when his own son-in-law, Gregory Ardzruni, raised the standard of revolt in the province of Vaspurakan. This latter prince, however, who owed allegiance to his king at Ani, rashly attacked also the Moslem chiefs of Khoï and Salmas and was defeated and killed by the Kurds.

With danger averted in that direction, Ashot had to turn against the prince of Kars who was claiming the Armenian crown, and then towards the district of Turuberan. While he was enforcing peace in the interior of the kingdom, his brother Abas scoured the mountains at the source of the Kura river, and then proceeded to punish the rebels at Erzerum. Security reappeared in Armenia as the king's authority was established. But Ashot, constantly threatened by the Moslems of Kurdistan, felt that it would be difficult for him to maintain his realm without effective help from the Greeks; consequently he went to Constantinople where Leo the Philosopher, an Armenian, was then reigning (886-912).

This journey shows that even though Armenia was tributary to the Caliphs, she none the less had ties with the Empire, and that the new king relied on Byzantium to free himself from the Moslems. That, no doubt, was what Ashot intended. The Armenian historians relate that he was magnificently received by the Basileus, and that the sovereigns signed two treaties, one political and the other a trade agreement. We have not the text of these contracts, but if they were signed, it shows that the authority of the Caliphs was remarkably weak in the north of the Moslem empire, and that it consisted only of the annual tribute paid by Armenia.

COIN OF EMPEROR
LEO THE PHILOSOPHER,
(886-912)

The Emirs of Azerbaïdjan and Kurdistan, however, who were under Bagdad's orders, kept unceasing watch on the Christian kingdom and threatened it at every turn, and Ashot sought means of coping with this danger.

During his stay at the Byzantine court, the king of Armenia apparently sent home for troops, and despatched them under the command of Prince Meghrik to help the Greek army then warring with the Bulgarians. From this we may conclude that Emperor Leo undertook to supply Armenia with some legions against the Moslems. Unfortunately Ashot died at Trebizond on his way back. His remains were transferred to the town of Bagaran, the ancient city of idols, on the Arpa-tchaï, not far from Ani.

Although Ashot had been unable to carry out his wise schemes, he had at least had time to pacify the country and compel the obedience of the nobles. He was unable, however, to restore his kingdom from the ruins caused by the Arab conquest. He needed above all positive protection by the Byzantines, and the end of his reign was devoted to bringing about agreements that would assure safety to his throne.

SEMBAT I
890-914

Ashot left a son, named Sembat, and this heir was proclaimed king by the patriarch George II and the nobles. But even while the young prince was receiving his crown, a most dangerous rival rose against him, his own uncle Abas. This commander of the army, the victor of Kars and Erzerum, rallied some of the nobles of Gougarq and marched on Ani to depose his nephew. He listened, however, to the plea of the patriarch, and withdrew to his city of Kars, but kept as prisoner the Bagratid Adernerseh, the Armenian governor of the Georgian territories who had placed the crown on the young king's head.

Without a moment's hesitation, Sembat marched on Kars, and compelled his uncle to deliver up the Bagratid prince and to submit to his authority.

Caliph Mothaded-Billah (892-902) and Emperor Leo repeated the procedure previously adopted for Ashot, and sent Sembat the insignia of kingship. The latter, now assured of peace in his kingdom, pushed back his frontiers as far north as Colchis and the Darial gorges, and to the south-west as far as the city of Karin (Erzerum).

Van and all the southern part of the Armenian territory was then under the direct government of the Arabs, and Afschin, the emir of Azerbaidjan, who had recognized Sembat in the Caliph's name, was suspicious when he saw the young king extending his frontiers southward. The alliance of Ashot and the Emperor, renewed by Sembat, aroused his wrath, and he conceived the plan of bringing Armenia again under the Moslem yoke and having himself placed on the throne at Ani. But Bagdad refused to enter again into strife with the Empire concerning Armenia. No opposition would be offered by the Caliph to the Emir's conquering the country, but there would not be any official encouragement in the way of subsidies or troops.

Moslem forces moving towards Nakhitchevan on the Araxes gave the alert to the Armenian king who made his preparations, but, thinking he might avert war by negotiating, sent the Catholicos George to the Emir with peaceful messages. Afschin expressed his desire for an agreement, but asked that the king should come and talk things over personally with him. This clumsy ruse not succeeding, the disappointed Moslem made the Catholicos his prisoner and hostilities began. The Azerbaïdjan troops advanced to the middle of Armenia, and a battle took place near the village of Dols at the foot of the Alagheuz. The Emir was defeated and fled to his own land with the remnant of his army.

Afschin was humiliated but not disheartened. Learning that the governor of Mesopotamia, Ahmat, had just invaded the District of Taron, and that Sembat had been defeated in the lake Van region, he re-entered Armenia and besieged the city of Kars which had to capitulate. He was thus able to carry away to Dovin as hostages the Queen, the wife of the crown prince Mouschegh, and other Armenian princesses, which obliged the king to consent not only to deliver up his nephew Sembat and his son Ashot, but to give Afschin the daughter of his brother Schapouh in marriage. Although of opposite religion, the Christian rulers often found themselves in those days obliged to send their daughters into the infidels' harems, a humiliation on their part which greatly flattered the Moslems, pleasing their vanity more than anything else. Some centuries later a Comnenus, Emperor of Trebizond, gave his daughter to the Khan of Tartary in the hope of obtaining the latter's assistance against Mahomet II, the conqueror of Constantinople.

Despite the above sacrifices, Sembat could not secure peace for his country. For political reasons he had crowned Prince Adernerseh as king of Georgia, and this appointment to the northern kingdom aroused the jealousy of the Armenian princes, who called on Afschin (898). The emir was getting ready to invade Armenia once more when death overtook him. He was exasperated because his chief eunuch, bribed by Sembat, had restored to him the captive princesses, and he would have taken his revenge by ravaging the kingdom had not fate arrested his ire. His brother and successor, Youssouf, shared his resentment and harbored the same designs, as he took over the rule of Azerbaidjan.

The king of Armenia was accustomed to send the Caliph his yearly tribute through the medium of the Emir of Azerbaidjan. Deeming it improper, however, to continue in this humiliating position towards his sworn enemy and rightly considering that the tribute would be lighter if it were paid direct to Bagdad, Sembat made this offer to the Caliph in writing. The new Caliph Moktafi-Billah (902-908) accepted it, and sent him a gold crown as a token of goodwill.

This change of procedure deprived Youssouf of a large revenue, for his office as middleman was highly remunerative. He was incensed against the king of Armenia, and by gifts and crafty words, he gained the ear of the Caliph who doubled the Armenian annual tribute. Sembat was obliged to increase his levy of taxes on the princes, with the consequence that they in turn revolted. The uprising started in the mountains of the north adjacent to Georgia, and the conspirators planned to bring about the assassination of the king and to give the crown to Prince Adernerseh then dwelling at Tiflis. But Sembat defeated them, captured the ringleaders and blinded them. Adernerseh, however, he spared. (907).

Taking advantage of the disturbances keeping the king away in Gougarq, Youssouf again invaded the Ararat country. Gaghik, one of

VIEW OF THE FORTRESS OF VAN

Sembat's nephews, was on the side of the Moslems. After having raided the Christian territory, Youssouf in the name of Caliph Moktader-Billah (908-932) crowned the Armenian traitor as king of Vaspurakan and enthroned him in the city of Van.

KHATCHIK-GAGHIK, KING OF VASPURAKAN (914-943)

During the last years of Sembat's reign, Armenia became a prey to the Moslems of Azerbaïdjan. In vain did the king endeavor to appease Youssouf. The Catholicos John VI who was sent to the emir with rich gifts was kept prisoner, and Youssouf the following year crossed the Araxes, entered Nakhitchevan, and ravaged Siuniq, the governor of which province, Gregory, a nephew of Sembat, had to surrender. Thereafter invading the district of Schirak, the Moslems seized another of the king's nephews, the commander-in-chief Ashot. Resuming the fight when the winter was over, the enemy reached the province of Nik, east of Erivan. There Sembat tried to withstand the Arabs, but he was defeated in a bloody battle. Gregory, the prince of the Siunians, and Mouschegh, one of the king's sons, were captured by Youssouf in this fight, and shortly afterwards put to death by him. The Catholicos John VI whom the Emir had taken along with him in this campaign was freed on payment of a large ransom, and later consigned to history the misfortunes he had witnessed. He was to describe the atrocities committed by the Azerbaïdjanians in the lands to the east of Dovin and Lake Sevan which they had seized.

The treachery of Gaghik was the chief cause of Armenia's downfall; at Youssouf's instigation he went headlong into a wicked war. The Emir's only aim in sowing dissension among the Armenians was to get them to destroy one another so that he might extend his own dominion over all of Sembat's provinces. The king of Vaspurakan finally realized the full horror of his conduct and the results of his rebellion. He begged Sembat to pardon him and offered him his friendship. It was alas! too late, for the king feeling himself unable to continue the struggle, shut himself up in the fortress of Kapouyt (the Blue Castle) located in the rocky mountains east of the Masis. There the Emir besieged him. After a long siege, Sembat obtained his promise to allow him to leave the fortress with his troops and withdraw to the province of Schirak. Youssouf, however, was afraid that the new alliance between Gaghik and Sembat would result in difficulties for him, and he treacherously seized the king of Ani, and threw him into a dungeon at Dovin, where the unfortunate monarch was subjected to the most degrading treatment.

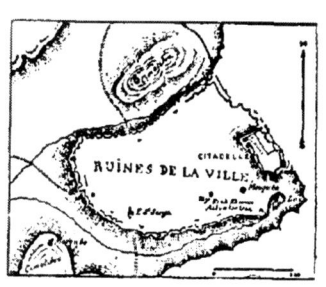

PLAN OF THE FORMER CITY OF MELAZKERT

The king's misfortunes had only begun, however, for his mental suffering was to be followed by martyrdom. Youssouf besieged the fortress of Erendschak, not far from Nakhitchevan in Siuniq, and in order to get the defenders to surrender he had the unhappy king taken in chains before the walls and ordered him to be tortured before their eyes. Sembat, even under torture, proclaimed his Christian faith which the Moslems sought to make him forswear, and faced with his stubbornness, the Emir ordered him put to death. The executioner beheaded him, and his body was taken to Dovin and crucified in the public square.

So perished this unfortunate ruler, the second of the Bagratid dynasty, after a reign of twenty-four years (890-914) during which Armenia was drenched with blood not only from Moslem attacks but also from the internecine warfare of the Armenian princes. The nobles in their pride considered themselves each one a king in his own territory and chafed under the authority of their overlord. This was the great defect of the feudal organization of Armenia, as it was of the same régime in Europe. Internal dissension played the game of their country's enemies; the latter on the contrary were united by their religion and displayed a cohesion that was their strength. Youssouf had some Arabs under him, but the bulk of his army was composed of Kurds, Persians, and Armenians converted to Islam. They all, irrespective of their national extraction or language, marched against the Christians under the Prophet's standard, and any dissensions among the Moslems were never anything more than the results of palace intrigues that had very little repercussion among the masses. The Caliph's authority, although it had greatly diminished, was nevertheless respected generally, and orders from Bagdad were listened to as coming from the head of their religion recognized by all the faithful.

**ASHOT II
914-929**
Ashot II (914-929), Sembat's son, ascended the throne on his father's death, but it was a very tottering throne for, on the one hand, Youssouf had left garrisons in all the chief positions in Armenia, and on the other, many Armenian chiefs refused to submit to the new king of Ani. A part of the people, following the example of their nobles, were engaged in looting. Anarchy reigned in the provinces that Ashot was to reign over.

Notwithstanding these countless difficulties, this new king whom the Armenians surnamed Yergath, (i.e "of iron"), succeeded in driving the Moslems from all the fortresses they had held throughout his dominions. Youssouf, however, aided by the prevailing lawlessness and the dissensions among the nobles, again invaded those provinces which the king could not defend, and sowed desolation in the wake of his army. Encouraged by their master, the soldiers of Islam committed nameless atrocities. The towns and villages that fell into their hands were reduced to ashes; men and women were tied together and cut in pieces; pregnant women were ripped up, and children at the breast crushed, or else thrown from the house-tops, or from cliffs, with other bandits waiting to receive them on their spears below. Thousands of women and maidens were distributed among the soldiers or taken off to be sold as slaves. Youssouf, spurred by ambition as much as by hatred of Christianity, gave the Armenians the choice only of apostasy or death under the most cruel torture. The disaster was tremendous. The peasants fled into the mountains, hid in inaccessible heights or in caverns, abandoning their villages and farms, with the consequence that ere long famine added its ills to those of war.

Armenia would have perished entirely had not Emperor Constantine Porphyrogenetus acceded to the plea of the king and the patriarch John VI, and sent Ashot some military assistance. The latter with this help succeeded in taking a few rebel cities and in driving the Moslems from the plain of Erivan. Among the rebel cities he overcame was the town of Koghp at the junction of the Arpa-tchaï and the Araxes; its inhabitants were severely punished. This town, however, apparently belonged to the commander-in-chief Ashot, son of the uncle of king Schapouh, for this prince looked upon its capture as a personal affront as also the punishment of the inhabitants, and he accordingly took up arms against his suzerain (921-923). Youssouf encouraged him in this revolt and proclaimed him king of Armenia at Dovin. After no less than three reconciliations with his suzerain, due to the offices of the Catholicos John, followed by fresh rebellion, Ashot nevertheless kept his title of king until his death, which occurred twelve years after his final submission (936).

COIN OF EMPEROR CONSTANTINE XI PORPHYROGENETUS

Dovin, not more than a day's march away from Erivan, commanded the Ararat plain and its outlets in the direction of Vaspurakan. By entrusting the rebel prince with this station, Youssouf provided for himself access to the capital of the kingdom of Ani. Moreover the example of rebellion given by a member of the royal family induced a number of other nobles to declare their independence. They were also in hopes of making small kingdoms for themselves, but Ashot II compelled them each in turn to return to their allegiance. Some of these obtained pardon, but others were blinded, by the king's orders.

During this troubled period, not only was Armenia ravaged each year by the Moslems and by the bands of Armenian peasants that infested the country, but the nobles also of Gougarq, Uti, and Artsakh, who had rebelled against the king, called on the Caucasians, the Abkhasians, the Aghouans, large bodies of whom under their respective chiefs overran the country, looting and carrying away the women. Everywhere frightful desolation reigned and in the royal family itself the darkest plots were hatched. Abas, the king's brother, sought

MINIATURE FROM AN ARMENIAN GOSPEL-BOOK, DATED A D. 966
(from a photograph sent by F. Macler.)

— 162 —

Ashot's assassination. When the latter appointed a member of his family as governor somewhere, this relative no sooner reached his new abode than he would proclaim his independence.

The king of Armenia needed indeed an iron will to overcome so many obstacles. In this he succeeded, by dint of courage and skill. At the death of Ashot II, there had been no time for him to restore the cities and towns but Armenia was at least at peace, Youssouf having abandoned his warfare. A period of prosperity seemed about to dawn for the unhappy land

ABAS, 929-953 As Ashot had no sons, the princes on the advice of Gaghik, king of Vaspurakan, offered the throne to Abas, the late king's brother But, under this new sovereign, the revolts which Ashot had suppressed by his vigor, broke out with fresh strength. There was fighting everywhere, even in Persian Armenia, in the districts of Khoi and Salmas, for not only did the nobles refuse obedience to their suzerain, but they were at odds with one another.

Despite these ceaseless disturbances, Abas restored many cities, including Kars which he made his second capital; he built churches and monasteries in the place of those destroyed by the Moslems, and died after reigning twenty-four years (929-953), leaving his kingdom still wasted and a prey to the strife among the nobles

ASHOT III 953-977 Ashot III who succeeded Abas, according to some writers was the son of Ashot II. but as we have seen, that sovereign left no male heir. It is more likely therefore that Ashot III was the son of Abas.

**TOMB OF KING ASHOT III THE CHARITABLE,
AT HORMOS MONASTERY NEAR ANI**

(from a photograph by K. J. Basmadjian)

The change of ruler was a fresh signal for trouble in Armenia. Bands of robbers overran the country and the outlying districts were infested with highwaymen. Nevertheless the new king managed in a few months to enforce peace with the help of a few faithful nobles, and when order was established, he had himself crowned in the cathedral of his capital city of Ani in the presence of the patriarch Ananias, the Catholicos of the Aghouans, and forty bishops. He allowed his brother Mouschegh to assume the royal crown in Kars (962-984). Thus began the splitting-up of Armenia, acquiesced in by the monarch in the belief that the formation of small kingdoms was the only way to keep the allegiance of the turbulent nobles.

THE ARMENIAN KINGDOMS OF THE TENTH CENTURY

ARMENIA DIVIDED INTO SEVEN KINGDOMS

Aboussahl - Hamazasp (958-968) was then reigning over Vaspurakan, but on his death his territory was divided among his three sons, and three kingdoms were thus formed. Ashot-Sahak ruled over most of the country, while his brothers, Gourgen-Khatchik and John Senacherim were kings of Antzevatsik and Rechtunik. As for Siuniq, which comprised the land between the Araxes and the Lake Sevan region, it became independent in 970. Lori, in 982, seceded also from the king of Armenia, and from that time to the middle of the 13th century that city was the royal residence of the third branch of the Bagratids, namely, the Korikians.

In Taïq a new dynasty was founded, but here it was not an Armenian prince who proclaimed his independence, but a Georgian, David Curopalates (983-1001), who, countenanced by the Byzantine Emperor, emerged from Mingrelia where his family had taken refuge at the time of the Arab conquest, and assumed the crown.

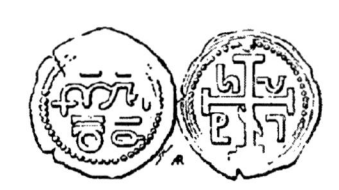

COIN OF DAVID CUROPALATES, KING OF GEORGIA (983-1001)

In this manner, without reckoning the local nobles who had each declared the independence of his district, Armenia was split up among seven kings, almost all at war with one another or with their vassals. The north of the

VIEW OF THE RAMPARTS AND CHIEF GATE OF THE CITY OF ANI
(from a photograph by K. J. Basmadjian)

country was under the influence and nominal authority of Constantinople, while the southern kingdoms paid tribute to the Moslems.

In any case, the more unruly of the ambitious princes having achieved the satisfaction they had longed for, the reign of Ashot III "the Charitable" was fairly peaceful and prosperous. He defeated and slew the Saracen Hamdoun who had revolted against the Caliph and invaded Armenia. This service ingratiated him with Mokti-Billah (945-974). Otherwise, he was satisfied with defending his frontiers, restoring quiet to his realm, and fortifying his chief cities, particularly Ani. But politics in those days were so unstable that after this loyal conduct towards his suzerain the Caliph, Ashot with thirty thousand troops joined the Basileus John Zimisces then threatening the Arabs on the Tigris.

Ashot III was one of the best of his dynasty and his kindness earned him the title of "The Charitable" He was a man of vigorous action in the presence of the enemy or faced with his rebellious nobles, and at the same time of a disposition so charitable that it became proverbial He was

VIEW OF THE CASTLE OF ANI, TAKEN FROM OUTSIDE THE CITY
(from a photograph by K. J. Basmadjian)

of great piety and built very many churches, monasteries, and houses of refuge, and devoted himself to the care of his people. His wife, Queen Khosrovanoisch (daughter of Chosroes) was as devoted and generous as her husband. The convents of Sanain and Aghpat in the territory of Gougarq (1) were founded by this queen.

SEMBAT II
977-989

Ashot III's eldest son, Sembat II (977-989) was crowned in the Cathedral of Ani. At the outset of his reign he had to put down some revolts on the part of the nobles, but these disturbances had no serious results, for the separation of Armenia into seven kingdoms made the country much easier to pacify, as the nobility could not unite against the king's authority

---

(1) Canton of Tseraphor (Tzorognet) 60 miles south of Tiflis

The defense and embellishment of Ani were the king's chief concern. He built the double wall flanked by round towers protecting the city on the north, a work that took eight years. Sembat died just after he had laid the foundations of the magnificent Ani cathedral (989). This superb structure, though partly in ruins today, is still majestic in the purity of its lines and the chasteness of its carvings. He did not long survive his niece whom he had dared to marry contrary to the customs and laws of the Church. As we know, Gregorian Christianity forbade the marriage of near relatives. He was born at a time when the customs of the Mazdeans still left many vestiges, and usage had authorized incestuous marriages among the Persians. The king transgressed the precepts of his religion, and his historians blame him severely, but we may remember that the Catholic church later tolerated such marriages, and the act does not warrant casting a stain on his memory.

In the kingdom of Kars, Mouschegh died (984) leaving the crown to his son Abas (984-1029). Though lazy and frivolous hitherto, he showed himself quite different once on the throne. He was a patron of literature and art, and drew to his capital the most eminent scholars, making a small Athens of his capital.

The kingdom of Vaspurakan, under Ashot-Sahak (968-990), had had a less peaceful time. Abouthelb, chief of Goghten, a land on the right bank of the Araxes, north of Lake Urumiah, had treacherously massacred some of this Armenian ruler's troops and war had ensued. The brother of the king, Gourgen-Katchik (990-1103), brought about the downfall of this State.

**GAGHIK I
989-1020**

At Sembat II's death, his brother Gaghik I (989-1020) received the crown. During his reign the dynasty of the Bagratids of Ani reached its zenith of power. The cathedral was finished, and the little kingdom was covered with churches, chapels, monasteries, and schools. Commerce made strides hitherto unknown. Nakhitchevan, Ani, Ardzen, Bitlis (Baguech), and many other cities became important marts where the products of Persia, Arabia, India, and even China, were exchanged for those of the West.

Despite his lack of political power due to the small size of his kingdom, Gaghik availed himself of this era of peace to turn his subjects actively in the direction of trade, and Armenia became the intermediary between the Orient and the Mediterranean countries. His endeavors were richly rewarded, for the traffic between the provinces of the Empire and the Arab possessions meant huge commissions for the Armenian middleman.

Between the Moslem East and the Christian West ever at war, direct business dealings were impossible; middlemen were necessary, and by reason of their geographical position two nations only could assume this rôle, namely, the Georgians commanding the route from the Caspian to the Black Sea, and the Armenians, living on the plateau above Iran and Mesopotamia. The Kartvelians, however, were indifferent and heedless, unconcerned for the morrow, and wasting their energies on their princes' quarrels or in fighting their mountain neighbors. They had none whatever of the qualities needed to fit them for acting in any economic capacity between the two great centers of world production. The Armenians alone had the capacity to fulfill this mission. They thus brought wealth and prosperity to their country.

VIEW OF THE CATHEDRAL OF ANI
(from a photograph by K. J. Basmadjian)

The chronicler, Aristaces of Lastivert, who lived at the time of the splendor and the downfall of the Bagratid capital, has left us a word-picture of the small kingdom of Ani before the arrival of the Seljuks. These pages are charmingly poetical and naïve, with their truly oriental flavor:

"This country offered the traveler the picture of a radiant and happy

"garden, fertile and verdant, with abounding foliage, and laden with fruit.
"In their seignioral halls with joyful mien sat the princes; clad in
"bright colors, they partook of the springtime floral pattern around them.
"Cheerful words and glad songs alone were to be heard, while the sound
"of flutes, cymbals, and other instruments caressed the soul as with happy
"tidings; the elders sat in the public squares, their hoary heads their crown
"of honor, while the mothers tenderly held their children in their arms
"as doves sheltering their little ones. And how can one depict the loving
"looks and tender passion of the newly wed absorbed in blissful content-
"ment! But let us raise our subject of discourse, and speak of the patriar-
"chal throne and the splendor of the royal presence. Like unto a cloud
"laden with the graces of the Spirit, the Pontiff caused the dew of life to
"fall in showers and water the garden of the Church, whose walls were
"watchfully guarded by those his ministers consecrated by himself. As
"for the King, when he proceeded in the morning from the City, he was as
"the bridegroom issuing from the nuptial chamber, and as the orb of day
"in its ascent draws the eye of every creature below, so he, radiant
"in his shining vestments and pearl-laden crown, constrained all to be-
"hold him and marvel; his white steed in golden harness resplendent in the
"sunshine dazzled all eyes, while the multitude of soldiers marching before
"him in compact array were like waves of the sea following one another
"in succession." (1)

In spite of the wealth of the Ararat country at that time, the Bagratid rulers do not seem to have ever coined any money, for no native coin has yet been found. Having to pay tribute to the Caliphs, the Armenian kings were certainly considered as subject to the Arabs and therefore not entitled to issue their own specie. Further north, in the territories which the Greeks looked upon as belonging to the Empire, there was greater tolerance, and so we have specimens of coins struck by the Georgians. David Curopalates (983-1001) in the Taïk territory,

**COIN OF BAGRAT IV
KING OF GEORGIA
(1026-1072)**

---

(1) Transl. A. TCHOBANIAN.

Bagrat IV (1026-1072), son of Giorgi I, Giorgi II (1072-1089) at Tiflis, have left us their silver and copper pieces struck in the Byzantine style, and the last Armenian king of Albania, Koriké (1046-1082) struck follēs. Both in Georgia and Aghouania, however, this money was insufficient for the needs of trade, and Byzantine and Arab gold pieces were in circulation, as in all Western Asia. For silver coins there were the dirhems issued by the Caliphs, and the old Sassanid and Roman denarii, while as to copper money, all the mints of the Empire put out huge amounts. It is surprising, however, that there were no mints in this region, for Armenia is extremely rich in copper and silver mines.

COIN OF GIORGI II KING OF GEORGIA, (1072-1089)

Though peace had come to Armenia, the same was not true of the surrounding countries. The Caliphs were experiencing unceasing revolts on the part of the emirs, and on the north the people were fighting among themselves, against the Arabs, and against the Georgians. In the west, there was equal misfortune, the Emperor Basil II was threatened by the Bulgarians. The Greek emperors had transferred to Macedonia in the past a large number of Armenian families, and the latter making common cause with the Bulgarians had taken up arms against their former rulers. The chief of the insurgents, named Samuel, was born in Armenia, in the district of Derdchan, east of Erzerum. Momentarily victorious over the Greeks, he laid down his arms on condition that the Basileus give him his sister in marriage, hoping in this manner to forge a claim to the Imperial crown, an ambition flattered by the memory of Leo the Philopher and other Armenians who had worn the purple of the Caesars. But instead of sending him the princess, Basil had Samuel presented with a young slave, who was taken to him by the Metropolitan of Sebaste. In his anger Samuel had the patriarch burned alive. This cruel deed did not remain unpunished, for Basil, "the Slayer of Bulgarians" (Bulgaroctonos), defeated Samuel and executed him.

COIN OF EMPEROR BASIL II

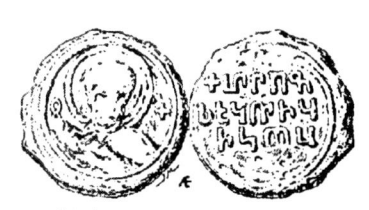

COIN OF KING GORIGE OF ALBANIA (1046-1082)

Gaghik deemed it wise not to meddle with the strife going on in Europe, and besides it would have been difficult to send troops into the West, when the kingdoms adjacent to Armenia were tearing one another asunder.

David whom the Emperor had placed over the land of Taïk took advantage of the death of Pad, emir of the Abahunians, to drive out the Moslems from that territory, and had seized Manazkert. The vanquished enemy called on Mamloun, the emir of Azerbaïdjan, for help, and he with auxiliaries he summoned from Persia won back the districts taken from the Moslems. Whereupon David obtained the assistance of Gorigé I, king of Georgia, and Gaghik, king of Kars, and thus recovered the districts north-east of Lake Van.

Despite his advanced years, David was prevented from enjoying his renown by reason of surrounding jealousy. At the instigation of the nobles of the land of Taïk, the Georgian archbishop Hilarion smothered him, after trying, it is said, to kill him by putting poison in the holy elements reserved for the Eucharist (1).

About the year 1003, the king of Vaspurakan, Gourgen-Khatchik, died and his brother John-Senacherim (990-1006) seized the throne over the heads of the deceased king's children. Gaghik I, his suzerain, who did not dare to oppose this injustice, died nearly twenty years later.

SEMBAT III 1020-1042

Johannes-Sembat, or Sembat III (1020-1042), the eldest son of Gaghik, ascended the throne of Ani, but his corpulency unfitted him for fighting and he had none of the qualities a king needed in Armenia's sorry circumstances. Temperamentally heedless and indolent, he failed to claim the title of Shananshah (or King of kings) borne by his father, with the consequence that the various rulers of Armenia freed themselves from their feudal ties with the overlordship of Ani. His younger brother, Ashot, was enterprising and warlike, and in view of the indifference shown by the new king just crowned by Gorigé, king of Georgia, he claimed the throne for himself and took to arms. Senacherim, king of Vaspurakan, gave him

---

(1) Fr. TOURNEBISE, *op. cit.* according to Matthew of Edessa, I, 22 & 24.— The words on this prince's coins are written in Georgian and not in Armenian

armed assistance and the two allies came to the walls of Ani to give battle. Johannes negotiated through the Catholicos Peter, and Ashot appeared to give way and be satisfied with the title of viceroy for the whole kingdom, on condition he was assured of ascending the throne at Sembat III's death.

This agreement was on the surface only, for Ashot still sought to reign. Taking advantage of his brother's weak character, and being now at the royal court, he formed a powerful party by means of violence and treachery. In the meantime, Gorigé, the king of Georgia captured the king and held him prisoner, and Ashot was on the point of availing himself of the opportunity to usurp the crown. Sembat III ransomed himself, however, by giving up three fortresses to the Georgians, and Ashot, seeing his plan foiled, tried to lure the king into his hands by a ruse, in order that the conspirators might slay him. Prince Apirat, one of the latter, acting from his own motives rather than out of repugnance for the crime, revealed the plot to the king. Ashot in fear of his life fled to the Emperor Basil II, from whom, on the strength of promises we do not know, he obtained help. He went back to Armenia in command of Greek troops and compelled his brother to surrender to him the territories bordering on Georgia and Persia. Of these he made his new kingdom, but it meant a fresh parceling out of Armenia and a considerable reduction in the size of the king of Ani's realm which now consisted only of the territories of Erivan and Ararat.

ARRIVAL OF THE TURKS IN ARMENIA

During this internecine warfare among the Armenians, a terrible storm was darkening the eastern horizon. Barbarous tribes of cruel and fearless character had emerged from the Oxus plains and invaded Khorasan and the north of the Iranian tableland, driving before them the Persians and Kurds and the Arab emirs. None could stand before these swift horsemen and unequalled bowmen, who attacked and retreated with like rapidity. The Seljuk Turks were invading Western Asia and spreading like some overflowing torrent. The Armenian historians called these nomads Scythians or Scythian Tartars, remembering the hordes that fifteen centuries before had likewise overrun Asia from those endless plains beyond the Caucasus and the Caspian and the Bactrian mountains.

The Turks had developed into a nation at the foot of the Altaï mountains, on the steppes still inhabited by the Turcomans, where Jagataï, the early Tartar language, was spoken. Though since converted to Islam, at that time the Turks were neither co-religionists nor allies of the Arabs. On the contrary, they cast greedy eyes both on the rich provinces of the Caliph and those of the Emperor. They were insatiable robbers and unbridled in their thirst for blood. Arab cruelties were nothing compared to those the Turks were to commit.

Even more than Johannes' kingdom, Vaspurakan was then in need of a brave and skilful chief to repel the attacks of the robber hordes issuing from the eastern plains. The Turks had already appeared on the Armenian borders, after making themselves masters of an empire able to measure itself against the power of the Caliphs, but these men of the north were not attracted by the countries of the south. They went forward from east to west along the mountain regions where they found rich pasturage for their herds. It was more than a war, it was total invasion, for the entire tribes followed in the wake of their horsemen, carrying with them all their possessions, their wives and children and old people, along with their booty from the lands they had sacked, ever seeking a new settling ground but unable to reach a new homeland because drawn ever forward by the desire to possess what others owned. The onward wave stopped only in front of Constantinople, stemmed for a time by the might of the Empire.

The first encounters of the newcomers and the Armenians were severe and took place on the borders of Vaspurakan. Shapuh, Senacherim's general, at first put the invaders to flight. This was, however, only a brush with the advance-guard of the Tartar tribes. The bulk of their army was slowly approaching and the king, fearful of having to meet such enemies and aware of his helplessness, gave up his kingdom to Emperor Basil II, keeping only the monasteries with their dependent villages. In exchange, the Basileus gave him the city of Sebaste (Sivas) in Cappadocia with its territory as far as the Euphrates. Sena-

ARMENIAN PRINCIPALITY OF SIVAS

cherim abandoned to the Greeks a principality containing ten cities, twenty-two castles, and four thousand villages, and in 1021 departed to take possession of his new domain taking with him his family and four hundred thousand of his subjects, about a third of the population of his former realm. The remainder of his people, after a short interval of protection against their savage enemy, succumbed to Turkish slavery, never to rise again until the present time.

The new principality of Sivas, in the heart of the Greek empire, seemed destined to have some peace, but its overlords as Orthodox Christians opposed to the Gregorian Armenians could not forget the old sectarian bitterness. The harsh rule of Constantinople bore heavily on the emigrants till the day the Turks in their westward advance seized the country.

The Seljuks were already inside the kingdom of Ani, and in 1021 they reached the fortress of Bedchni on the north of Ararat. There they were repelled by the Armenians under Vasak Bahlavuni, the father of Gregory Magistros, who was killed, however, after his victory. The Emir of Dovin, the Arab Abou-Sewar, fearing for his own safety, allied himself with the Seljuks and fought against the Christians of Armenia. David Anoghin, the chief of Gougarq and Aghouania, with the help of the Abkhasians to whom he had appealed, marched against the enemies of the Cross and defeated them in a frightful massacre, gathering much booty at the same time.

But alas! these were only fleeting and isolated successes. The Armenians supported by small Greek contingents could not stop the ever-increasing stream. Tribe followed tribe; the advance-guards might be stopped for a few months but they were soon reinforced by reserves coming up. The Turks had left large bodies of troops throughout northern Persia and Khorasan, also in the section of Atropatenes where Teheran was later built; but the bulk of the nation continued on their way to the rich provinces of the West. Four and a half centuries still separated them from that ill-fated day for civilization when their conquering descendants crossed the threshold of St. Sophia.

The war was merciless, and both sides indulged in the worst excesses. The barbarity of the Turks incensed the Armenians and the Christians in turn gave no quarter, but the Moslems committed horrors beyond human imagination. A governor named Khoudrik, probably a Kurd, having recaptured from the Greeks and Armenians the town of Berkry on the north-east of Lake Van, had a ditch dug and slaughtered so many Christians that the ditch was filled with blood and he could bathe in it.

Whilst Armenia underwent such suffering, the Byzantines whom

Senacherim had let into the heart of the country, lost no opportunity to compel the obedience of the unfortunate inhabitants. Disembarking at Trebizond, Basil II subdued Abkhasia which had rebelled against him, and secured the province of Taïq which David Curopalates had promised him. Then pretending to believe that Johannes had taken part in the revolt of the king of Abkhasia, he threatened the tiny kingdom of Ani. Caught between Togruhl bey, the terrible Seljuk chief, and the Basileus, Johannes sent the Patriarch Peter (1023) to Basil II to beg for his protection. Feeling lost, he preferred to surrender to the Christians rather than submit to the hateful yoke of the Turks, and he offered to give up to the Greeks after his death the province of Schirak with his capital, Ani itself. This promise, although in writing, remained a dead letter so long as Constantine XI (1025-1028), Basil II's brother, and Michael IV the Paphlagonian (1034-1041) reigned at Constantinople. It was kept, however, in the archives of the Holy Palace giving the Greeks an opportunity of which they availed themselves when the time came, to extend their rule over all the regions as far as the Araxes and beyond. Moreover the little kingdom of Kars, where Gaghik (1029-1064), the son of Abas, then reigned, was likewise coveted by the Byzantines.

COIN OF EMPEROR MICHAEL IV, THE PAPHLAGONIAN

**GAGHIK II
1042-1045**

Johannes-Sembat III and his brother Ashot died almost at the same time, and Ashot's son, Gaghik II, thus inherited both crowns. Emperor Michael Calaphates thereupon claimed the rights conferred on him by Johannes' letter to Basil II, and demanded Schirak and the city of Ani. The Regency council refused to admit a surrender that had been obtained only through fear, and the Emperor sent into Schirak an army supported by Vest-Sarkis, the chief of the Siunians, who hoped to obtain from the Greeks the city of Ani for himself in the place of Gaghik.

The allies were laying siege to the capital when the aged Vahram Bahlavuni defeated and slaughtered them. Then, master of the situation, Vahram took advantage of the dissensions reigning at Constantinople, to have Gaghik II crowned in Ani by the patriarch Peter. This prince was then in his sixteenth year, but in valor he was a worthy king and would undoubtedly have prolonged Armenia's independence had he not been thwarted by treachery.

The danger which seemed averted on the Greek side loomed ever greater on that of the Seljuks. The Turanians were camped on the north of the Araxes on the river Hrastan, the Zenghi-tchaï of the Turks, which flows from the Gheuk-tchaï into the Araxes. Gaghik came out of Ani at the head of his army and lured the enemy into a trap where he defeated them. The Moslems crossing over the Araxes fled to the south-west of Lake Urumiah, towards the Kurdistan of Moukri; then after resting they again took the offensive and invaded Vaspurakan, passing through the mountains of the Kurds who certainly made common cause with them against the Christians. There a leader named Khatchik the Lion with only a handful of men held the enemy in check. The brave soldier fell in the struggle, but his sons arrived with a few thousand men and put the Turks to flight in the districts of Khoï and Salmas.

COIN OF EMPEROR CONSTANTINE XII MONOMACHUS

Hardly had Gaghik II repelled the Moslems than the Greeks again threatened him. Constantine Monomachus (1042-1055) who had just ascended the throne through his marriage with Zoë, claimed Schirak and Ani on the grounds of Johannes' promise. The king refused to listen to the Greek claims, and when they invaded Schirak, they were defeated under the very walls of the capital.

Unable to conquer the kingdom of Ani by arms, the Basileus had recourse to treachery. Byzantine gold subverted a good number of Armenian nobles who gradually got the king to believe that it was to his advantage to accept the Emperor's offers and to go and confer with him at Constantinople about terms of peace.

EXILE OF GAGHIK II Splendidly received at first at the Imperial court, Gaghik soon found himself summoned by the Emperor to relinquish the throne and surrender to the Greeks Schirak and Ani. He refused, and was then threatened with captivity and exile, but to no avail. Then Constantine showed him a letter in which the Armenian nobles affirmed their allegiance to the Empire and offered to deliver to the Emperor the keys of Ani. Betrayed by his own nobles, forsaken by all, and alone in a foreign city, Gaghik gave up his kingdom (1045) and received in exchange the theme of Lycandus, with the towns of Bizou and Golombeghad, near Caesarea, on the border of Cappadocia. He was also given a palace on the Bosphorus and a pension from the Imperial treasury.

The hatred of the Orthodox Greeks for the Gregorians was not assuaged by the annexation of Armenia to the Empire, and the Greeks, to convert the Armenians to their creed, used the same severity as the Arabs and Turks. As a Roman province, Armenia was actually enslaved by the officials sent from the Imperial capital. Heavy taxes loaded down the people, and the extorted gold was used either to pay off the Barbarians or to build churches on the Bosphorus. Byzantium made it its business to get rid by steel or poison of the Armenian nobles who had so much influence with the people, and no noble was sure of living till the morrow

An inscription carved at Ani a few years after the Byzantines seized the city, the text of which was taken down by Brosset, shows its neglected condition at that time It reads "In the name of Almighty God and by "the mercy of the holy Emperor, our Autocrat Constantine Ducas. I, "Bagrat Magistros, Katapan [governor general] of the East, Vkatzi, "decided to confer benefits on this metropolis of Ani. There were ap-"pointed: as Tanouter [Administrator] Mekhitar Hypatos, son of Court; "as Spathara-candidate [Equerry] Grigor, son of Lapatac; also as Spa-"thara-candidate, Sarkis. son of Artabazus. They canceled the taxes "called vetscevor, sailli, camen, and angarion (1) The Katapan, who-"ever he may be, shall give six hundred bushels of seed, and the Tanouters "shall defray from their official purse the cost of the other gifts. As all "supplies have much difficulty in reaching Ani, the wine-merchants of the ' city shall be exempted from paying toll, whether they use carts or "beasts of burden Every inhabitant buying an animal for slaughter is "exempted from paying toll Every porter of the city is exempt for one "half of the cotton (?) Whereas the Qapoudji [overseer of the city gates] "received six gold tahegans and three tram. this is to be reduced by two ".. etc"

His fellow-countrymen's groans reached Gaghik even in exile, and the scornful treatment meted by the Greeks to his former subjects caused him distress He himself had often to bear the insolence of his present masters, and incensed at so much misfortune, the prince vowed to avenge his nation's honor Even in Cappadocia the Greeks lost no opportunity to express their contempt for those Eastern Christians who did not believe in God according to their own ritual The Metropolitan of Caesarea,

---

(1) Vetscevor: one sixth tax Sailli: machine for treading the corn (*tribulum* in Latin); Camen tax on wagons Angarion was the tribute of enforced labor, or corvée.

Mark, who was conspicuous for his ill-will toward the Armenians, took every opportunity to express his scorn for them. This bishop had a very big young dog which he called "Armên", and he also called Armenians "dogs". Gaghik was outraged by this insult, and resolved to punish the impudent prelate. One day he called with a few friends on the bishop who received him with all outwards signs of greatest respect. During the interview Gaghik asked to see the dog, and enquired why he was called Armên. "He is a very handsome dog," answered the Metropolitan, "and so I named him 'the Armenian'."

The king beckoned to his escort, and they thrust Mark and his dog inside a sack, and then struck the dog with a stick so that the animal became wild and bit his master so terribly that the latter died

GAGHIK II MURDERED 1079
Thenceforward Gaghik was hated by the Greeks and they sought every means of getting rid of him. One day as he was walking in the country near the fortress of Cyzistra, west of Caesarea, some Greeks surprised him, carried him inside the fort, and a few days later his bleeding body was hanging from the castle battlements (1079) John and David, his two sons, died shortly after, also Ashot, John's son, all three of them poisoned.

The Greeks did not confine their spite to the royal family of Ani. In 1080, Atom and Abousahl, Senacherim's sons, were killed at Sivas by the Byzantines, along with Gaghik, the son of Abas, the last of the Bagratid kings of Kars, and their lands were annexed to the Imperial realm. Thus the Greeks, more cruel and fanatical than the Arabs themselves, had destroyed entirely within a few years, by treachery and murder, the famous house of the Bagratids, the hope of the Armenian nation. Some collateral branches of the royal stock remained, however, and to this day even the name of the Bagratids is still extant.

These crimes committed by Byzantium were not only wicked but also very unwise, for Armenia as an outpost of Christianity in the East could, had she been made strong by the Emperors, have stemmed for many years the oncoming of the Turks, and been a shield for Constantinople. But at the holy Palace sectarian hatred was the chief thought, and there was no comprehension of the dangers that the Seljuk invasion involved for the Imperial crown. So many previous tribes of barbarians had threatened the Empire that the general thought was indifferent.

The Greeks ruled in western Armenia and shared northern Armenia with the Georgians, whilst the Seljuks held the eastern part of Transcaucasia, and Arab princes occupied the southern provinces. This state

COIN OF THE ORTOKID SULTANS OF MARDIN *in genere*
(Nedjm-ed Din Elpi. 1152-1176)

of things did not last long, however, for the Greeks, blind to the military help they might have had from the Armenians, were unable to maintain in the Ararat region any army that could stand up against the new invaders. Both Byzantines and Caucasians were eventually driven out by Alp-Arslan and his son Melik-Shah (1072-1092), whose dominions soon extended from the Indus to the Caspian Sea and the Bosphorus. From atop the Byzantine towers could then be spied the terrible horsemen of the steppes riding on the Bithynian shore. Emir Sokman, son of Ortok, and his brother Il-Ghazi (the Victorious) founded each an Ortokid dynasty, one at Amidus and the other at Mardin, and Sokman took the title of Shah-Armen, "king of Armenia." (1)

Nevertheless the Turkish conquest of Armenia met with some resistance on the part of the inhabitants, and the Greeks also had still a few legions on the Araxes and on the plateau of Erzerum. From 1048 to 1054 Togruhl bey several times sent out his hordes over the eastern provinces of the Empire. His cousin Kutulmisch and his nephew Hassan were defeated, but his brother Ibrahim laid waste the territory of Vaspurakan, and then proceeding north captured Ardzen, near Erzerum, a city which then had eight hundred churches and enormous wealth. The Turks

(1) According to Miraat-el-iber, Emir Ortok ben Eqsuq was a Turcoman from the city of Schehriman in Transoxiana, and came from there in the year 455 of the Hegira to enter the army of the Seljuk ruler Alp-Aslan. His sons founded the dynasties called the Ortokids.

burned the city after sacking it, and took off 150,000 of the inhabitants of the district into slavery.

Continuing northward, Ibrahim attacked near Ardzen the Greek army of sixty thousand men, who had just seen central Armenia pillaged. The Bulgarian commander of Vaspurakan named Aaron, Prince Libarid of Georgia, and Cramen, the Greek governor of Ani, were in command of this force, and they fought the enemy and made him withdraw. Libarid, however, fell into the hands of the Moslems The Turks were stopped but not defeated, for on withdrawing from the Imperial army, they seized, sacked, and destroyed Kars The ruler of that city, Gaghik-Abas or Koriké (1046-1082), avoided capture only by taking refuge in the famous citadel of Kars, built on an inaccessible rock.

The inroads of the Turks were unceasing. In 1054, Togruhl himself entered the districts of Van and laid them waste. Gaghik-Abas who went out against him was defeated and obliged to flee inside Van, and the Turkish chief then proceeded to besiege Manazkert, a city near the junction of the Tuzlu-tchai and the Araxes. The town was defended by Basil, the son of the Armenian Aboukhab, who was governing it for the Empire. Togruhl failed owing to the garrison's heroic resistance. To avenge his set-back, he plundered the town of Ardzke on the north of Lake Van.

Circumstances, moreover, favored the Seljuks. The death of Constantine Monomachus, and the struggle between Emperor Michael VI and his rival Isaac Comnenus, were then distracting the Byzantine court, and Armenia in fragments, defeated and rulerless, could offer the Turks but slight resistance. Togruhl accordingly devastated western Armenia and Melitene. Lack of supplies for his army compelled him, however, to withdraw, and the Armenians attacked him in the mountain gorges and caused him serious losses. Nevertheless the following summer the Turkish chief took the city of Sivas (Sebaste). (July, 1059). The latter city was sacked, its churches left in ruins, and the majority of the citizens put to the sword. The survivors were carried off into slavery, and the Moslem army left the banks of the river Halys (Kizil-Irmak) with an enormous train of spoil, of carts laden with gold and silver and rich fabrics, for Sivas was then a very important trading center Every year these insatiable robbers repeated their invasions of Armenia, slaughtering mercilessly the inhabitants and sowing desolation in these formerly rich valleys

Togruhl bey died in 1063, and his nephew Alp-Arslan (the brave Lion), who was even more fierce and bloody than his uncle succeeded to the command of the Turkish tribes. He had no sooner taken over than he swooped down on Armenia, subdued the Aghouans and carried desolation throughout the lands of the Lesser Caucasus, laying their towns in ruins. Ani alone shut itself within its gates and resisted with the courage of despair. Bagarat the Armenian, who bore the title of Duke, held the city for the Byzantines, and just when Alp-Arslan had become weary of fruitless attempts to storm it and was about to withdraw, this governor, afraid lest he should have still bigger attacks to meet,

CAPTURE OF ANI BY THE SELJUK 1064

took shelter in the citadel situated as we have seen south of the town. Forsaken by the Greek troops, the inhabitants were already fleeing along the valley of the Arpa-tchai when the Turks scaled the now defenseless ramparts and gained an entry (6 June, 1064). Nameless massacres and devastation ensued, and blood flowed like a river in the streets and squares. Thousands and thousands of people were put to the sword and those who took refuge inside the churches perished in the burning edifices. Any Armenians who appeared to be wealthy were tortured and forced to disclose their treasures.

The Armenian chronicler of the 11th century, Aristaces of Lastivert, wrote "Our cities were devastated, our houses and palaces burned, our "royal halls reduced to ashes Men were cut to pieces in the streets and "women snatched from the homes. Infants were crushed on the pave- "ments and the faces of the young disfigured; maidens were ravished "in the squares and youths killed in the presence of the aged, the hoary "heads of the old men were steeped in blood and their bodies rolled in "the dust"

The looting and killing of the citizens continued for several days, until Alp-Arslan withdrew leaving nothing but ruins. Duke Bagarat and the Greek soldiers had fled under cover of a storm and the Seljuk leader replaced them inside the citadel by a Moslem governor and garrison. Blood-stained and glutted with treasures, Alp-Arslan proceeded from the ravaged city to Nakhitchevan, taking with him an enormous quantity of booty and a multitude of slaves Among the riches stolen from the Bagratid capital was the great silver cross that had crowned the Cathedral dome, this the Turk purposed to lay on the threshold of his mosque in Nakhitchevan so that the true believers should have the satisfaction of trampling on the Christian emblem every time they entered their holy place to praise the glory and might of Allah Ani never arose from its ruins Occupied in turn by the Seljuks (1064-1072), the Kurdish emirs

(1072-1124), the Georgians (1124-1126, 1161-1163), and by the Tartars and Persians, it saw its final days in the 14th century (1) when an earthquake overthrew whatever little remained of its former splendor. The inhabitants migrated into Georgia, the Crimea, Moldavia and Poland.

Ani, the city of a thousand churches, of which I have already described the site, is nothing more today than a ruin-covered wilderness, the abode of wild animals. This very abandonment of the Bagratid capital gives, however, an ineffable charm to the remains of its one-time glory. On this promontory fringed with the deep gorges where its two rivers flow, the dead city stretches out into the mystery-laden air, where the great churches and the ramparts alone survive. Shapeless heaps of rubbish hidden by the brushwood mark the spots where once stood princely dwellings, the streets and squares have vanished, the palaces have crumbled, and yet, amid this tangled mass of bits of walls, are still to be seen imposing sanctuaries, stately in their ordered lines and entrancing in their ornate lace-like carvings and their quaint frescos. The majestic remains of these sacred edifices, the names of which are mostly forgotten today, bear witness to the refined taste both of the kings of Ani and their architects. The double wall defending the city on the north, with its towers, castle, and keep, call forth countless memories linking Armenia with the West. One cannot help but feel intense pity as one walks through these desert places today, pity for the victims of the terrible deeds here committed, of the massacres and sackings so poignantly related by Aristaces. Turkish misgovernment during the ensuing centuries is indeed seen to be Satan's handiwork.

The country around Ani is barren and denuded, with rocks of pink, brown, and yellow-gold lava; the soil is red, and the hills seem still to carry lingering flames of the fires that destroyed the Bagratid city and of the volcanic outbursts that consummated its ruin.

A few remains of Ani's wealth, saved from the pillage, have come down to us. The treasure-room of Etchmiadzin cathedral contains silver crosses, church decorations, objects of worship, and precious manuscripts piously preserved by the priests, whilst other relics that have come to light in recent excavations have been housed in a museum reverently maintained at Ani itself.

About the year 1318 (718 of the Hegira), the first Moslem prince of Ani, Manouchar, the son of Aboul-Sewar, built at the edge of the Arpa-

---

(1) A.D. 1320, or year 769 of the Armenian era.

tchaï cliffs a mosque, the ruins of which are still to be seen. It was a building showing strong Byzantine influence upheld by low squat columns and with semi-circular arches, the edifice was undoubtedly copied partly from the Christian buildings at Ani, particularly the Khoscha-Vank. At the top of the polygonal minaret can be clearly seen, built of bricks in the stone, a Kufic inscription invoking Allah.

Freedom for Greater Armenia was at an end, some of her nobles turned to the Greeks despite their repugnance for the tyranny and treachery of the Byzantine court, others accepted the Seljuk yoke, and some embraced Islam, but the majority of the people did not abandon the land of their forefathers and preserved its traditions and faith, preferring slavery to shame. In the west, a new Armenia was about to rise, and all hope was not lost for the Haïkian nation.

ROLE OF THE ARMENIAN NOBLES

Greater Armenia was over fifteen hundred years old when she sank into political oblivion. As we have seen, she never once ceased her struggle for independence, but her very geographical position between two great empires destined her to fall. From the time of Alexander's conquests and Rome's appearance in Asia, with the constant threats of the Parthians, the Sassanids, and the Arabs on the one side and the legions of Italy and Byzantium on the other, she had no chance against formidable enemies.

Her people, nevertheless, were endowed with energy and warlike qualities; her nobles and kings also showed exemplary bravery, but by the very fact of their origin and of the influence of neighboring States, this aristocracy lacked the necessary community of though to cope with such dangers.

When the children of Haïk conquered the land of Ararat, they were all primitive peoples led by their tribal chieftains or heads of clans, by their Armeno-Phrygian or Brigian nobility. In the process of assimilating the inhabitants of Naïri and Urartu whom they conquered, however, they had to respect the traditions of these latter, whose leaders, having formerly fought the Assyrians, were maintained as nobles in the new community. A comparison of Armenian family names with those of the Urartaean language shows the origin of many of the ruling houses of Armenia. We can be sure that the two aristocracies were not one in sentiment, and that the Armenian stock considered themselves superior, while the Naïri element regretted the time when they were independent.

These basic divergencies were supplemented by additional elements that settled in Armenia during the successive rules of the Achaemenians, the Greeks, the Parthians, the Sassanids, the Romans, the Byzantines, the Arabs, and the Turks. Consequently the nobility of the country became extremely mixed, their interests and trends were varied and often opposed, from all of which causes there arose rivalries, hatreds, and much chafing under the king's authority, with resulting extreme weakness for whole nation.

Even in the days of Darius we see an Armenian betraying his country, and placed by the Persian king in command of an army ordered to subdue Armenia. Throughout subsequent history the nobles continued to put forward selfish claims, their conflicting racial origin showing itself in warring tendencies and interests

No doubt they were valiant, brave even to excess, like their neighbors, the Georgian nobles, but most often they subordinated the interests of the State to their personal ambitions and grudges. The existence of seven small Armenian kingdoms at the time of the Turkish invasion is the best proof of this. Covered with mountains difficult of access and divided by nature into very many regions, Armenia in itself was ill-suited for political unity.

The very same causes have operated to preserve to our own day the numerous peoples of the Greater Caucasus and their mutual independence, likewise the separate tribes of the Kurds who still have each their chieftain and are generally hostile to one another despite their common language and origin. We need not therefore be surprised at the immemorial strife in the land of Ararat, which continued after the conversion to Christianity, although their religion was indeed one unifying link among the different sections of the Armenian people.

Armenia needed a Louis XI or a Richelieu to quell the strife among the nobles and endow royal authority with the power the nation needed in its grave difficulties throughout the centuries; but such great men it did not have Some of the rulers were able, it is true, to tame their feudatories' tempers, but their authority was only fleeting and personal; these provincial chieftains were not subdued, and, as we have seen, Persians, Greeks, and Moslems, all took adroit advantage of their quarrels. Byzantium made a grave mistake in maintaining enmity to the Armenians, and her sectarian policy resulted both in Armenia's downfall and in the Greeks' own final defeat in the East Rome never sought to humiliate Armenia, on the contrary. Instead of a subject people on the southern slopes of the Caucasus, Byzantium needed an allied kingdom extending from the Tigris to the Black Sea and from the Euphrates to the Caspian Sea, able with its ten million inhabitants to put many legions of fighting men into battle, soldiers sworn to drive back the enemies of Christianity. Armenia had such resources at Byzantium's disposal.

An Armenian State so conceived would have meant salvation for the Empire, but at Constantinople, wasted with wranglings over dogma and riven with constant palace revolutions, Roman statesmanship was entirely lost sight of, and instead of strengthening the kings of Ani, the Byzantines did nothing but sow dissension in order to get possession of territories they were never able to hold.

Being more sheltered from the Moslem incursions than their kinsmen on the Araxes, the Bagratids of Georgia kept their throne for six centuries after the fall of Ani. These more fortunate princes had the great Caucasian mountain stronghold to repair to as a last resort whenever they were too hard pressed.

TOMBSTONE OF HAIRAPET, BISHOP OF SIUNIQ

CHAPTER VII (1)

THE BARONY OF NEW ARMENIA (1080-1199)

The Armenian nobles who went with their prince Gaghik II to Constantinople settled for the most part in the new domains of their sovereign, and formed a small court around him. Most of this nobility, more-

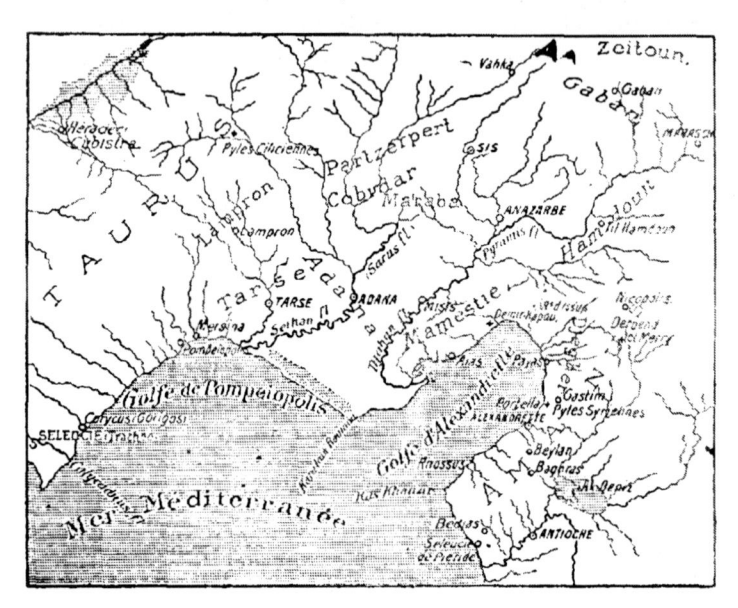

MAP OF CILICIA

---

(1) In Chapters VII and VIII on New Armenia, I have transcribed the names in accordance with local pronunciation which for some letters differs from the eastern Armenian; e.g. *Sempad, Lampron, Gorigos,* etc. instead of *Sembat, Lambron, Korikos,* etc. The letters b, g, d, k, dz, p, and t of the western Armenians are pronounced p. k, t, g. tz, b, d respectively by the eastern Armenians. The latter being the more regular has been adopted as the classical pronunciation.

over, were more or less related to the Bagratid family. One of them was named Rupen, and belonged, some said, to the ancient princely house of the Artzrunis who from time immemorial had figured largely in the court of Greater Armenia. Others claimed that he was a scion of the royal Bagratid line itself.

Writers are not agreed as to Rupen's actual connection with the royal family, but in any case, whether or not his sovereign's kinsman, this nobleman exercised considerable authority over his fellow-countrymen exiled in the country of Zamantia, for immediately upon the murder of the last of the Bagratid kings, he rallied that monarch's former subjects and raised the standard of revolt against the Byzantines.

For centuries the double-dealing, despotism, and oppression of the Greeks had aroused profound hatred for them among the Armenians. Their mutual aversion was increased by the differences between them of language, customs, tradition, and especially religious belief. Nevertheless, since the Ani kingdom's downfall, there were two parties in the Armenian nation: one which out of sheer discouragement decided to yield to the Greeks, and the other which maintained the spirit of the nation and, unable to forget the treachery which led to the Bagratid kingdom becoming an Imperial province, cherished the hope of avenging the infamous murder of their last king. This latter party resolved to withstand the inclination to accept slavery, and to achieve their national independence by force of arms. Besides which, the Byzantine Empire was decrepit and engrossed with religious quarrels and with a number of factions. It was beset on every frontier with imminent danger, and could offer only slight opposition to any provinces in revolt against the tyranny of the dukes, counts, and crowd of officials who had gone out from Byzantium to fatten themselves on the districts for the privilege of governing which they had paid the Imperial treasury. There was no longer any security in the Empire's Asiatic provinces and Rupen's revolt remained unnoticed in its early stages.

RUPEN'S REVOLT, 1080 Under cover of this breakdown of Imperial power, the Armenian prince was able to organize his rebellion, gather around him the sturdiest men of the nation, and rally the malcontents to open war on the Greek government under his standard. Restoring the kingdom of Ani, recently fallen into the hands of the Seljuk Turks, was out of the question, so Rupen looked in the direction of Cilicia where a good many Armenian nobles had already settled under the protection of the Empire.

After having been conquered by the Arabs, Cilicia was again within the Emperor's dominions. Nicephorus Phocas in 964, with a large army, had recaptured from the Moslems the cities of Anazarbus, Rhossus, and Adana, and in a succeeding campaign Tarsus and Mopsuestia. In 966 the Emperor had even extended his conquests as far as Tripoli, Damascus, and Aleppo. These expeditions, like that of John Zimisces in 973, were veritable crusades. Their pretext of seizing the holy places from the infidels did not exclude, on the Emperors' part, a desire to get back the rich Syrian provinces, the loss of which had been severely felt by their Treasury.

COIN OF NICEPHORUS PHOCAS

Southern Asia Minor, however, had suffered grievously from Arab occupation, and was ruined and depopulated. It was essential to rehabilitate those districts and organize them so that they might offer to any new attacks by the Caliphs a strong bastion capable of protecting Constantinople. Many Armenian nobles, fleeing before the Turks, left their lands on the Araxes and Greater Armenian plateau, and took refuge in Greek territory. Byzantium took advantage of this voluntary emigration, and seized the opportunity to build up after a fashion her Syrian marches by peopling the Euphrates banks and the Taurus with these Christians whose military value they had often had occasion to appreciate. One of these Armenian nobles, Nakharar Oschin, had formerly owned the fortress of Mariats-Dchourk (river of the Pines), near Gandzak (Elizabethpol) in Albania. Leaving his country in 1075 he had come to Cilicia where his kinsman Abulkharib Artzuni was already governing Tarsus and Mopsuestia for Emperor Alexis Comnenus. The latter nobleman gave him, as a hereditary fief, the district and town of Lampron (Nimrud-Qal'a) on the Tarsus-tchaï, at the opening of the Cilician Gates of the Taurus, an exceedingly important post for protecting Cappadocia. The

COIN OF JOHN ZIMISCES

Arabs subsequently recaptured Antioch, and Cilicia accordingly again became an Empire outpost.

CILICIA The boundaries of this province of Cilicia are so well set by natural features, and so distinct from the adjacent lands, that one can hardly imagine any other political demarcation than that shown by a relief map of its surface. On the west stand like an immense wall of circumvallation the high chains of Isauria and Cilicia-Trachea, a massif of mountains shaped like a vast triangle, the northern foot of which opens on the plains of Lycaonia. The eastern shore of the Gulf of Satalia forms another side, while the third is the western shore of the Gulf of Pompeïopolis. At the apex of this triangle

CASTLE OF LAMPRON (CILICIA)

is Cape Anamur, *Anemurium promontorium*, the southernmost point of Asia Minor (1). Cilicia's natural situation made it not only of great strategic importance, but also extremely valuable on account of the trade routes leading to it.

---

(1) Ed. DULAURIER. Recueil des Historiens des Croisades. Documents armeniens, vol. I, 1869, p. XVIII

COIN OF ALEXIS I COMNENUS

The valleys of the Seyhoun (Saros) and the Jahan (Pyramus) communicated with Coele-Syria by the so-called Syrian Gates, an opening in the Amanus Mountains between Mts. Guzeldaugh and Akmadagh of the Turks, likewise by the gorge of Alexandretta and the seashore, the Portella of western historians. To the south-east was the city of Issus, the former scene of Alexander the Great's victory over Darius Codomanus and later of the death of Pescenius Niger, vanquished by Septimius Severus. Issus was the crossing place for armies

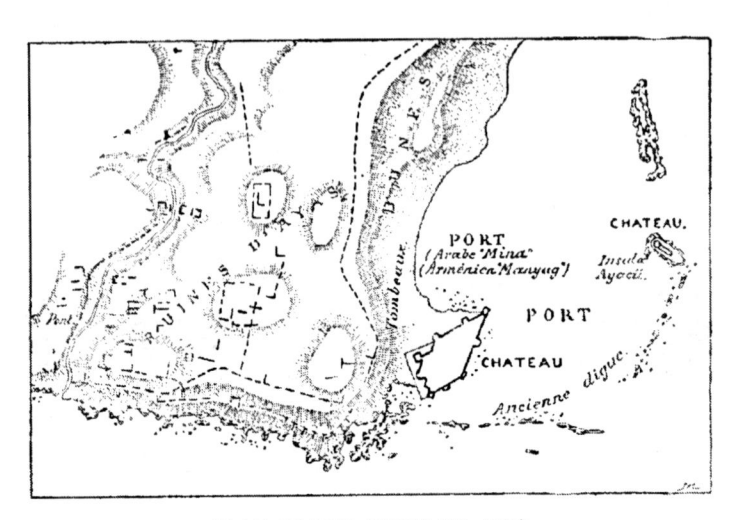

PLAN OF THE RUINS OF AIAS

arriving from the Orontes and going north, or for those from Cappadocia on the march to Antioch.

Aïas on the north shore of the Gulf of Alexandretta was then and continued to be during the Middle Ages a very busy port. It was the head of two very important trade routes, one feeding Cappadocia by way of Lampron and the Cilician Gates, and the other extending via Gamban and Sebaste in Cappadocia to the upper Euphrates and Greater Armenia. Moreover this coast abounded in ports and anchorages. Megarsus, Alaya, Sidē, etc., were safe havens for ships, and these landing places, like Aïas, added greatly to Cilicia's trading facilities with the Syrian coast and the western countries of the Mediterranean.

PLAN OF MEGARSUS

It was therefore the Byzantine policy to man all the passages leading into Cilicia, and to this end the emperors encouraged the formation of small principalities in these regions. The newly arrived nobles received the modest title of Ishkhans, corresponding to that of baron which was later adopted by the Crusaders. In the Taurus and Amanus mountains as also in the plains separating those ramparts, the Ishkhans were already fairly numerous when Rupen started his revolt.

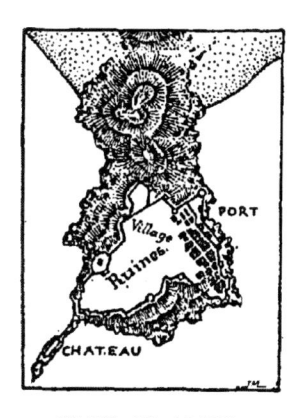

We are unaware of the exact location in Cappadocia of the country of Zamantia, the domain of Gaghik II, but there is every reason to believe that it was north-east of Iconium, for Cyzistra where this last of the Bagratid kings was murdered, was near Caesarea. Rupen therefore set out from the neighborhood of that city. He proceeded first westward to the mountain massif of northern Cilicia, a region that was very difficult to reach but from which he could defy the Greek troops. He seized the fortress of Partzerpert (1), on a tributary of the upper Pyramus (Jahan-tchaï), about a day's march upstream from Sis (2). This last-named stronghold was the cradle of the kingdom of New Armenia.

PLAN OF ALAYA

---
(1) "The Castle above", i.e. on a mountain summit.
(2) Matthew of EDESSA, chap. CLI. Transl. DULAURIER, Paris, 1858, p. 217.

Consequently Rupen did not imitate his fellow-nobles and request the Empire's protection. He declared himself independent, and by so doing obtained at once precedence over the Armenian barons of these mountains, despite the fact that he himself had not acquired right to any title. The historian Hetum writes: "Finally he died in the peace of "the Lord, after living a pious "life, and was buried in the "monastery of Castalon, leaving his son Constantine "(1095-1099) to succeed him." The latter was the first of the Rupenian rulers to bear the title of baron.

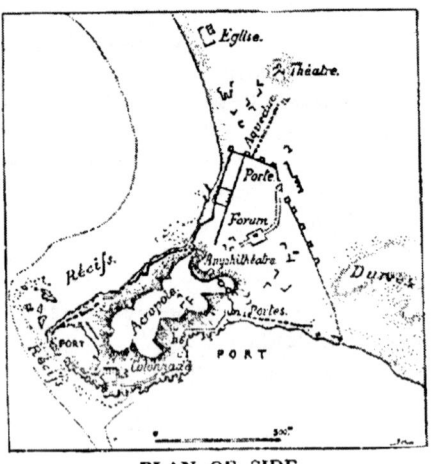

PLAN OF SIDE

It is easy to imagine the utterly forsaken condition at that time of the lovely province of Cilicia, once so rich on account of its fertile land and its commercial activity. Laid waste by the horrors of war, plundered by the Arabs, with most of its people carried into slavery, and again put to fire and sword at the departure of its Moslem masters, the region had become nothing more than a wilderness when the Armenian settlers arrived. The scattered remaining Greeks, Syrians, or Jews were huddled in the ruins of the cities and towns. Only the immediate outskirts of cities and castles were tilled; the rest of the country was abandoned. At the time of the Arab

COIN ASCRIBED TO THE ARMENIAN RULERS OF ASIA MINOR
(National French Collection)

— 193 —

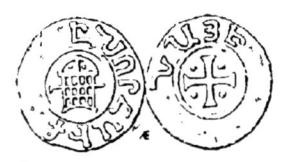

COIN OF AN UNNAMED BARON OF NEW ARMENIA

conquest, a few Greek nobles had taken refuge in the inaccessible heights of the Taurus and Amanus chains and held out there, whilst the pasturages and forests harbored refugees with their flocks. Rupen's successors met, consequently, with but slight resistance from the Greeks, and their fellow-Armenians, who had not yet been many years in the country, appeared on the whole in favor of the formation of the small new State.

CONSTANTINE I & THOROS I, BARONS 1095-1129

Constantine I, Rupen's son, (1095-1129), and his successor Thoros I (1099-1129), carrying on their predecessor's plan, were concerned only with extending their domain at the expense of the Byzantines. Men of violent character, with few scruples as to their means for achieving their ends, these nobles managed by degrees to rally under them all the chiefs of the mountains around Partzerpart. Early in his reign, Constantine obtained possession by stratagem of the fortress of Vahka (Féké) on the upper Sarus, and this placed him a position commanding one of the most frequented roads between Tarsus and Upper Cappadocia.

John Dardel, consigning these narratives to posterity, has the following account of the above feat of arms, or rather of cunning, by which the lords of the mountain secured for themselves the collection of tolls on all merchandise ascending from Aïas to the interior of Asia Minor. The power of the Rupenian rulers had its beginnings, in fact, in this supply of funds.

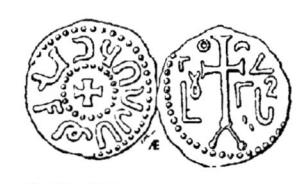

COIN OF BARON THOROS

On one of his usual expeditions, Constantine who had undoubtedly been informed by the Armenian agents whom he maintained among his neighbors "arrived in front of a town [Vahka] where the good folk of 'the country who were 'Armêns', were carrying brambles to close up and 'repair any holes in the walls of the town which had fallen in. Thereupon "Baron Constant and his companions with him took off their armor and "hid it between the brambles, whereof each then made his bundle, which "they carried onto the walls just like the other poor people. And it hap-

— 194 —

"pened to be the day of the Assumption of the Virgin Mary and the very
"hour when the Greeks were at church that the aforesaid Baron Constant
"carried the aforesaid brambles along with their armor onto the walls of
"the said city And when they saw their chance, they put on their armor
' and took the Castle and then went to the church and seized all the Greeks
"who were therein " (1)

ARRIVAL OF THE SECOND CRUSADE The considerable progress the insurgents were making did not fail to cause anxiety in Constantinople, and the Emperor was taking steps to put a stop to the defection in the mountains of Armeno-Cilicia, when the arrival of the Crusaders frustrated his plans Godfrey of Bouillon had passed over into Asia, crossed Cilicia, and following the road of the Sarus, pitched his tents under the walls of Vahka Matthew of Edessa (2) has described for us in detail the route taken by the Latins He writes· ' In the year 546 [25 February "1097 - 24 February 1098] at the time of the two Catholici of Armenia, ' Monsignors Vahram and Basil, and in the reign of Alexis, Emperor of ' the Romans, the host of the Crusaders set out in immense numbers, "they were about 500.000 men Thoros, Seignior of Edessa [for the ' Greeks] was informed thereof by a letter which they sent to him, as also ' by the great Armenian chief Constantine, the son of Rupen who oc- "cupied the Taurus in the region of Gobidar [east of Mopsuestia] and "had taken a good number of provinces Constantine had formerly been "in the army of Kakig [Gaghik] The Franks advanced with much dif- ' ficulty across Bithynia, and crossing Cappadocia in wide-spreading col- "umns they reached the abrupt slopes of the Taurus, their great army "passed through the narrow gorges of that mountain chain into Cilicia, "and arrived at New Troy, that is to say Anazarbus, and thence to the "walls of Antioch "

The Armenians looked on Godfrey as a savior, for had he not just delivered Asia from the Turkish and Arab yoke, contrary to Greek desires? Was he not marching under the banner of the Cross, of a religion that was nearer to the Armenian faith than was Byzantine Orthodoxy Pope Gregory XIII said later "No nation ever came more spontaneously

---

(1) J DARDEL, chap VIII
(2) *Histoire des Croisades Documents armeniens.* vol I p 29 sq

"to the help of the Crusaders than did the Armenians, who supplied them "with men, horses, arms, and food." (1)

The leader of the Crusaders had not failed to acquaint the ruler of the Cilician mountains with the vast plans cherished in Europe concerning Palestine, Syria, and Asia Minor, and with the purpose of the Catholic world to set up in those countries principalities able to withstand all Moslem encroachments on the lands of the Mediterranean. Constantine considered this movement afforded him a unique opportunity to throw off once for all the overlordship of the hated Byzantines and to increase his own power. He supported, therefore, the Crusaders with all his might, and the latter would have fared ill during the siege of Antioch had not the Armenians given them armed assistance and also food supplies.

Matthew of Edessa (2) wrote of the Frankish hosts before Antioch, that "their numbers were so great that famine set in. The Armenian "chiefs in the Taurus, Constantine, son of Rupen, and Pazuni and Oschin, "the second and third of those princes, sent the Frank commanders all "the provisions they needed. The monks of the Black Mountain [Ama-"nus] also supplied them with food, all the faithful vied with one another "in devotion to them in this juncture."

Understanding the important part which New Armenia might take in furthering their aims, the Franks assiduously favored these valuable allies. Constantine received the title of *Comes,* but he is more commonly referred to under that of *Baron* which his dynasty retained. Joscelin, Count of Edessa, married Constantine's daughter, and Baldwin, Godfrey's brother, espoused his niece, the daughter of his brother Thoros (3). In this manner their mutual interests were strengthened by ties of blood, and these Eastern Christians came inside the great feudal organization of the Crusades.

COIN OF TANCRED OF ANTIOCH

---

(1) Papal Bull of 1584 in the *Bull Rom.*—Cf Matthew of Edessa, part II, chap. CLI sq —SEMPAD, *Chron. ad.*, ann. 549.
(2) *Op cit.*, p 33 sq
(3) VAHRAM, *Chron. rim*, V. 197-198.

The Armenians themselves were not long in reaping the benefits of this alliance, for with the help of Tancred, prince of Antioch, Thoros (Theodore, Constantine's son and successor) added considerably to his realm.

In these propitious circumstances, the Armenian baron descended along the Pyramus river into the plain still held at a number of points by the Greeks who had withdrawn before the invading Crusaders into their chief fastnesses. He took from them the famous fortress of Anazarbus, the walls of which originally built by Emperor Justin I had been considerably strengthened by Caliph Harun-al-Raschid, and were thought impregnable. Sis also fell into his hands, and everywhere the king piously founded churches and monasteries and brought in Armenian settlers.

With the help of the Franks of Antioch, Thoros had already seized most of Cilicia and driven out the small Greek garrisons, when the Turkish hordes from central Asia Minor crossed through the Taurus ravines, reached the heart of Cilicia, and expelled the Armenians from Anazarbus. The whole Latin army had gone down into Syria, and the Byzantines had been ousted almost everywhere from the lowland strongholds; consequently the Turks expected to make short work of Armenian resistance. Their aim which they never ceased to cherish until the fall of the Sultans of Iconium, was to gain a footing on the southern shore of Asia Minor. Thoros succeeded with difficulty in hurling back these bands onto the lands of Bazil Kogh, another Armenian noble who reigned at Marasch. There the invaders were defeated and obliged to flee abandoning the booty seized in Cilicia. Two years later after ravaging the south of Melitene they besieged the fortress of Harthan, where they were annihilated. Their chief was captured and taken to Kescoun, his victor's residence, near Marasch in the Araban plain, on a tributary of the Euphrates right bank.

The Turkish hordes, however, could not be held forever in check by the Greeks, nor by the Crusader and Armenian leaders. All lacked sufficient troops to keep the field and safeguard their territory. Each countryside was the scene of ceaseless raids. Generally the towns were able to resist and only the villages suffered the hateful treatment of the Moslem bands. In 1110, Cilicia was nevertheless again overrun by the nomads. The Seljuk Sultan of Iconium, Malek Shah (1107-1116) headed the expedition himself and carried the day in a first encounter, but Thoros was victorious in the ensuing battle. His losses were, however, considerable and a number of the chief nobles fell in the fight. The Sultan withdrew to Kharput, laying everything waste as he went. He laid siege without success to the fortress of Dzowk (1), and then departed carrying with him an immense amount of booty.

LEO I BARON At Thoros I's death, his brother Leo I (1129-1137) succeeded him as the nearest heir to the principality, his nephew Constantine having been poisoned. Upon his accession, Leo followed up his predecessors' aims and descending into the plain took from the Greeks the cities of Mamestia (Missis), Adana, and Tarsus, and pushed on to the Mediterranean seacoast. He needed to possess the coast if he was to establish his power, for through its ports he could maintain profitable connection with Europe, instead of being compelled to resort to the intermediary of the Crusaders, his south-eastern neighbors. The relations of the Franks and the Armenians had become less courteous than formerly. Thoros had to be asked several times before he sent Baldwin his daughter's dowry of 60,000 gold bezants. On one side the Armenians complained of the demands and exactions of the Crusaders, while on the other the Franks accused their allies of being always ready to call on the infidels for help whenever they were in any way dissatisfied.

COIN OF BALDWIN OF EDESSA

COIN OF ALEXIS I. COMNENUS

One of the chief causes of dispute between the Armenians and the Latins of Antioch was the latter's possession of the strongholds of the southern Amanus mountains and the coast adjacent to the Gulf of Alexandretta. The barons claimed these fortresses, but the princes of Antioch asserted that they

---

(1) The "Cybistra" of Strabo (XII, 1); not to be confused with the city in Cappadocia of the same name, situated at the opening of the Cilician Gates.

were theirs by virtue of a treaty made in 1097 bewteen Bohemond and Emperor Alexis I Comnenus. At that date the Armenians had not yet penetrated so far southward, and the Crusaders were then in possession of the fortified places in the middle of the Cilician plain.

By his marriage with Constance, the only daughter of Bohemond II, Raymond of Poitiers had become Prince of Antioch (1136). Shortly before his accession (1135), Leo had seized the fortress of Sarovanticar (1) belonging to the territory of the Crusaders. The Latin nobleman hid his resentment, however, and did not resort to arms on assuming power, but a little later he captured the Armenian baron by stratagem and shut him up in one of his castles.

COIN OF RAYMOND OF POITIERS PRINCE OF ANTIOCH

After two months' captivity, Leo was finally given his freedom, but only on hard terms. He had not only to restore Sarovanticar, but to give up also Mamestia and Adana, and pay 60,000 gold pieces, besides surrendering his son as a hostage. He had to agree likewise to assist the prince against the emperor, John Comnenus.

The unjust and rash seizure of Sarovanticar by Leo I was the first serious quarrel between the Armenians and the Crusaders. It seemed likely to have grave consequences, for the Armenian baron deeming himself entitled to disregard promises extracted by ruse or by force, attacked Raymond, recaptured the territories and cities taken from him, and remained under arms against the Prince of Antioch and his ally Fulk of Anjou, king of Jerusalem. This nascent hostility might have become fatal both for the Armenians and the Franks, for the infidels were only waiting for a favorable moment to swoop down on both belligerents. Joscelin II, Count of Edessa, whose father had married Leo's sister,

COIN OF JOHN II COMNENUS

intervened and brought about an honorable agreement for both sides (1137). An alliance was drawn up against Emperor Jean II Comnenus who was then laying claims to Antioch and Cilicia (2).

During these disputes between the Latins and Armenians over a few towns in Cilicia, war continued with the Turks. Michael the Syrian (3)

---
(1) **On the lower Djihan.**
(2) **SEMPAD**, ann. 585-587.
(3) **Op. cit.** 349.

wrote: "In the year 584 [1135-1136] Baron Stephen, Baron Thoros' "brother, arrived under the walls of Marasch, and his troops effecting an "entrance during the night were received in the homes of those of the in- "habitants who were Christian. This surprise attack was arranged by "a priest of the city with whom Baron Stephen was in collusion. At "dawn his soldiers seized the place and massacred the Turks inside the "walls. Flushed with their victory, they proceeded to insult those who "were inside the citadel and openly dishonored their wives. God in His "wrath therefore did not give the citadel into their hands. They then "set fire to the town and taking away with them the Christians of the "place advanced into the interior."

Also Abulfaradj, relating the same events, adds: "The Turks on "coming back showed some humanity and not only treated peacefully "the Christians that remained but also restored to the Armenian fugitives "that returned their houses, vineyards and fields. But a priest of that "nation whom they suspected of having been in collusion with his com- "patriots was flayed alive. After three days they cut off his tongue, hands, "and feet, and threw him into the flames. The Armenians incensed at "this cruelty put some Turks to death in the "same manner."

Turkish hostility towards the Armenians was moreover paid for in gold by the Byzantine court which, according to Cinnamus (1), maintained as ever its designs on Cilicia and Antioch. John II Comnenus had purposed leaving the throne of Constantinople to his elder son, and wished to give the younger an appanage consisting of Cilicia, Antioch, Attalia, and Cyprus. But Alexis and his younger brother, Andronicus Sebastocrator, both died and the crown fell to Manuel. (2)

COIN OF MANUEL I COMNENUS

CAPTIVITY OF LEO I

Despite the Armenian army's alliance with the princes of Antioch, the Greeks invaded Cilicia, defeated the Crusaders and Leo whose vassals gave him little support, and occupied the whole plain adjacent to Adana and the Gulf of Issus. The baron and his family and

---

(1) I. x.
(2) Ed. DELAURIER, *Histoire des croisades, Documents armeniens*, vol. I, p. 156 note 1.

companions fled into the Taurus mountains. All the Armenians' newly conquered cities and their home centers, Anazarbus and even Vahka, fell to the Emperor. Leo, reduced to the last extremity, had to surrender to the victor with his family, and he was hauled to Constantinople, where he died (1141). The Greeks killed his eldest son, Rupen, after having first blinded him.

THOROS II
1145-1169

From 1137 to 1145 the Byzantines ruled all Cilicia, and the princes of Antioch and counts of Edessa had their hands too full meeting the attacks of the infidels to think about restoring the kingdom of their former allies One of Leo's sons, Thoros, who was a prisoner in Constantinople, was still quite young at the time of his family's disaster, and gave the Byzantine court no apprehension His gracious manners had even won him favor there. When Manuel I Comnenus (1143) succeeded his father as emperor, the young baron felt the time was ripe to throw off the yoke. He fled, disguised as a merchant on a Genoese or Venetian ship, and reached Cyprus, from where he sailed on to Antioch. There Prince Raymond and the monophysite Patriarch Athanasius VIII provided him with the wherewithal to make the attempt he had long contemplated Setting out from Antioch with a small escort he reached the Amanus mountains and soon rallied to his standard the malcontents and outlaws like himself, to the number of several thousand, sufficient to carry off a few initial successes, which brought to his standard all the Armenians in his father's former dominion

Vahram of Edessa, in his rhymed chronicle (1), has left us quite a romantic picture of the young baron and his arrival in the land of his fathers.

"The household of the Imperial palace claim that Thoros stayed "until a Greek princess fell in love with him and gave him treasures which "he took away On reaching the mountains of Cilicia, he met a priest "to whom he confided the secret that he was Leo's son. The priest wel-

---

(1) verses 417-436.

"comed him with joy, and sent him out as a herdsman. The Armenians "remaining in the country dwelt in the mountains, and suffering as they "were from Greek oppression they earnestly longed for the return of their "former rulers. Learning from the priest that their beloved prince had "come back, they at once gathered together and hailed Thoros as their "baron."

Whilst Emperor John Comnenus was subduing Cilicia and approaching Antioch, the Moslems were devastating the districts adjacent to the Crusaders and threatening the Latins. The Byzantines had joined up with the Turks to overthrow the power of the Westerners, destroy the Armenian baronies, and drive the non-Orthodox Christians out of Asia, so fierce was religious hatred in Constantinople. When the Turks, however, entered the territory of Kescoun within the Empire, the Basileus could not stomach the affront and the Byzantine alliance with the nomads came to an end.

Matthew of Edessa, in his chronicle (2) relates the events leading up to the despatch of a Greek army to the province of Marasch:

"In the year 585 [1135-1137], Sultan Mohammed, the son of Amir-"Gazi, the son of Danischmend, arrived with a large army in the region "of Marasch near Kescoun and there set fire to the villages and monas-"teries ... He kept quiet, refrained from attacking the city, and contented "himself with cutting off the waters of the river, pillaging gardens, making "desultory raids and gathering and safely storing the booty he took. The "city's inhabitants, however, who were daily expecting to be attacked, "became so grievously discouraged that one night they abandoned the "outer rampart. Their leaders and priests succeeded in reviving their "courage ... The infidels received no (divine) command to invest and "attack the city, and on the Friday, the day of our Lord's passion, Kescoun "was delivered The enemy burned Garmirvank (the Red Monastery), ""the chapel and the monks' cells, broke the wooden and stone crosses, "and took the iron and brass crosses He demolished the altars ... and "scattered the remains He carried off the door with its wonderful spiral "carvings, along with other objects, and carted them away to his own "country to show them to his concubines and the populace ... Mohammed

---

(2) *Op. cit* vol 1, p. 150.

"beat a sudden retreat when he learned that the Roman Emperor [John
"Comnenus] was hastening to the relief of besieged Kescoun and to the
"assistance of our count Baldwin who had implored him on his knees.
"The Emperor was already nearing Antioch, laying waste the Moslem land
"After deposing our prince Leo, he seized Leo's cities and fortresses, and
"taking him prisoner, carried him off to the Greek lands beyond the sea
"and the extremity of Asia."

Whatever the circumstances of Thoros' return to Cilicia he found his country garrisoned by the Byzantines and his fellow-countrymen subjugated.

The first city he recaptured was said to be Amuda (1), followed by Anazarbus, Adana, Sis, Arewdzpert, Partzerpert. Meanwhile, however, on December 23rd, 1144, Edessa was taken by Eimad-ed-Din Zangui, and the princes of Antioch, fully occupied on their eastern borders, could give no assistance to the young Armenian baron. Only his two brothers, Stepanē and Mleh, who before the fall of Edessa had taken refuge with their cousin Joscelin II, came to his side to share his perils and fortune. The new uprising in Cilicia, meanwhile, caused Emperor Manuel some concern and he sent 12,000 men from Constantinople under his cousin Andronicus Comnenus (1152). This army was defeated by Thoros before the walls of Mamestia which he was besieging.

Humiliated by this defeat and not daring to take further risks, Emperor Manuel resorted to trickery, and by wily procedure induced the Seljuk Sultan of Iconium, Masaoud I (1116-1156), to attack the Armenians in Cilicia.

In those days, and among these Eastern peoples, compositions of this kind were quite customary. The Seljuks were the enemies of the

---

(1) Tumlo-Qalessi. Cf. MICHAEL THE SYRIAN, transl LANGLOIS, p. 307-308.

VIEW OF THE CASTLE OF ANAZARBUS

Greeks, and were planted in the very center of the Empire; they were a threat to the capital itself; they were Moslem and consequently sworn enemies of all Christians, and there was no doubt that the Turks would keep Cilicia if they succeeded in conquering it. Yet none of these considerations, which we today would consider paramount, had any influence with the Greeks. Manuel's only desire was to avenge the disgrace just inflicted on him, and the Moslem Sultan who could but rejoice over the dissensions between the various Christians, invaded Cilicia. Thoros was forced to recognize his suzerainty.

In 1156, however, on some flimsy pretext, Masaoud again sent an army against the Armenians under the command of one of his chiefs named Iakhoub. This general was defeated by the Crusaders and by Thoros' own army. Taken by surprise in the gorges between the Amanus chain and the sea, the Moslems suffered a bloody reverse. The remnants of this expedition withdrew, but proceeded to ravage the districts of Kharput and Marasch. Then resuming the offensive, they laid siege to the castle of Till of Hamdoun, near Sis, at which point the plague broke

COIN OF EIMAD-ED-DIN ZANGUI  **COIN OF ROKN-ED-DIN MASAOUD SULTAN OF ICONIUM**

out in the Turkish ranks and the Armenians were easily victorious over them. In the meantime, Masaoud died, and his son Aseddin Kilidj-Arslan II (1156-1193) made peace with Thoros, who remained in possession of Cilicia and Isauria.

But a new storm was yet about to break over this war-ravaged country. Raynald of Chatillon, who had become the guardian of the young prince Bohemond III, by reason of his marriage with Constance, the widow of Raymond of Poitiers,—according to Michael the Syrian—attacked Thoros on the ground that the Armenian baron had refused to restore to the Templars the castle of Gastim, formerly taken from the knights by the Greeks and recently captured by Thoros. This castle which commanded the gorges of the Portella. between the Amanus chain and the sea, was of the greatest strategic value both for the Armenians and the princes of Antioch. The Byzantines, moreover, frustrated in their attempts to have New Armenia crushed by the Seljuks, were secretly inciting the Crusaders against Thoros.

COIN OF ANDRONICUS I COMNENUS

Matthew's chronicle continues: "Raynald [of Chatillon] had a dispute "with Baron Thoros concerning a fortress [Gastim] which the Greeks "had taken from the brethren [the Templars] and had been seized in turn "by Thoros from the Greeks. Raynald contended: 'The brethren are "fighting for our common Christian cause; restore unto them that which "is theirs.' A battle took place near Isenderun [Alexandretta], and many "perished on both sides. Raynald had to return home feeling disgraced.

"Later on Thoros himself gave up to the brethren the fortresses on the "borders of Antioch, and they promised under oath that they would "help the Armenians whenever they needed succor." (1)

Raynald of Antioch, who had only attacked the Armenians at Byzantium's instigation, felt warranted in asking Emperor Manuel to reimburse him for the expenses of this conflict, but, without repudiating the debt, the Basileus answered the Prince in dilatory language that exasperated him. He therefore determined to take payment himself by some means, and he bethought himself of the island of Cyprus.

The harbors of Cyprus commanded the coasts of Syria and southern Asia Minor, and the island was consequently a most vital position for the Crusaders. Though conquered A.D. 649 by the Arabs, it had since been regained by the Byzantines. Ousting the Greeks from there would secure both the princes of Antioch and the barons of Cilicia against any further Byzantine offensive on Latin shores, and would give them besides a first-class naval base out of reach of the infidels. The Cyprus expedition should not, therefore, be ascribed to mere bad temper on Prince Raynald's part, as most chroniclers of the time picture it, but to a decision that had been long contemplated by the Franks, who were only awaiting a favorable opportunity to undertake the enterprise. On their part the Armenians would not have been at all displeased to be rid of a Greek stronghold facing the shore they so much coveted, and which they had several times already conquered, lost, and reconquered. Circumstances did not allow, however, of the conquest of the island just then, and it was possible only to carry out a quick raid on it, lay it waste, and loot its treasures.

COIN OF RICHARD OF MARASCH

In 1155-1156 the Crusaders' fleet landed on the Cyprus coast a veritable army of Latins and Armenians, and the Greeks who maintained only small numbers of troops on the island were immediately hustled out of their positions. The entire island was overrun by the invaders who behaved with the most frightful cruelty. All possessions were seized by

---

(1) MICHAEL THE SYRIAN. *Histoire des Croisades, Documents armén.*, vol. I, p. 340.

the victors, many of the inhabitants were slaughtered, the Greek women and maidens were the prey of the soldiers, and priests and bishops were massacred. All persons of means were transferred to the continent and only released upon payment of enormous ransom. In short, the Crusaders and Armenians acted towards these Christians exactly as infidels would have done in the circumstance, but it must be remembered that both the Franks and the Armenians had long been weary of Byzantium's treacheries, and their hatred of the Greeks was just as fierce, if not more so, than that of the Moslems.

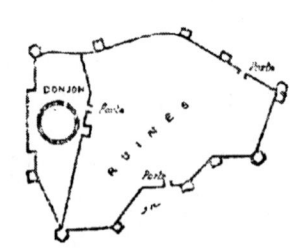

The war, moreover, was not confined to the island. In 1157, Raynald of Antioch, Count Thierry of Flanders, and Thoros laid siege to Cheizar (Caesarea) on the Orontes. Perfect understanding then reigned between the Armenians and the Franks.

CASTLE OF MOUTE (CILICIA)

Manuel Comnenus could not reconcile himself to the ravaging of Cyprus and got ready to avenge himself on the Crusaders and Thoros. He himself with 50,000 men invaded Cilicia in 1158, and Anazarbus, Till of Hamdoun, Tarsus, and the castle of Lamos fell to the Byzantines. Finding it impossible to defend his realm, Thoros withdrew into the Taurus mountains behind the walls of the castle of Dadjeghikhar. Raynald of Antioch and Baldwin III of Jerusalem, Manuel's nephew by his marriage with Theodora, the daughter of the Emperor's brother Isaac, interceded for the Armenian baron, and Manuel feeling that if he did not spare the Franks' protégé he might have all the Crusaders up against him, ratified Thoros' tenure of most of his dominion, but on condition that he recognize him as his suzerain. This feudal tie seems to have been nominal rather than actual, although the new Palatine, of the PanSebastos (The Most August), apparently remained a dutiful liegeman, officially.

COIN OF AMAURY I KING OF JERUSALEM

The fact that Thoros refrained from any further open hostilities against the Greeks did not prevent his brother Stepanë, however, who cared nothing for the Baron's promises, from heading bands of Armenians that laid waste Imperial territory and waged war in the dis-

— 207 —

tricts of Marasch and Cocuse. This prince succumbed to stratagem, for he was invited to a banquet by Andronicus, the governor of Tarsus, and there slain. Thereupon Thoros to avenge his brother ordered the massacre of all Greeks within his borders. War would have broken out afresh between the Armenians and the Byzantines had not Amaury I, king of Jerusalem, intervened. Disheartened by the country's misfortunes, the Armenian baron abdicated.

In 1169 "Thoros, prince of Cilicia, died, shortly after becoming a "monk. He left an infant son whom he named his successor and whose "guardianship he had entrusted to Thomas, the son of his maternal aunt. "Mleh, wroth at being passed over from his brother's succession, repaired "to Nur-ed-Din, and with a body of Turks the latter gave him he invaded "Cilicia. He carried away 16,000 people, boys and girls, men and women, "priests, monks, and bishops, all taken to Aleppo, where he sold them to "the slave-merchants and distributed the money to the Turkish soldiers ".... He put out the eyes, and cut off hands and feet, of bishops and "many notables, besides flaying them, and "their bodies were left a prey for wild "beasts." (1)

COIN OF NUR-ED-DIN MAHMUD

Mleh had already entered the Order of the Knights Templars, but later, after attempting the life of his brother Thoros, he had to flee. He took refuge at the court of the Atabeg of Aleppo, having forsworn his faith. As a Moslem he obtained Nur-ed-Din's assistance and overran the greater part of Cilicia. Faced with such disaster, Rupen's guardian offered the usurper a share of his nephew's barony. Mleh accepted this offer under oath, and then proceeded to grasp the whole power. Thomas the Regent fled to Antioch and placed Rupen in the care of the Patriarch Nerses at Roncla, but soon afterwards the young prince was murdered.

COIN OF EL SALIH-ISMAIL, ZENGUID, ATABEG OF ALEPPO (1173-1181)

---

(1) ABULFARADJ, p. 365 and 370.

**MLEH, BARON
1170-1175**

The reign of Mleh (1170-1175), the renegade and assassin, was but one series of horrors and crimes. Backed by the Atabeg of Aleppo, El Salih-Ismail, he was more than a match not only for the Crusaders, Amaury of Jerusalem and Bohemond III of Antioch, but also for the Byzantines, so much so that Emperor Manuel made a treaty of peace with the usurper, yielding to him New Armenia (1173). Universally hated, the tyrant was at last slain by his own soldiers in the city of Sis (2).

There is nothing so tangled or involved as the history of the East at this period when there were so many rival and conflicting interests. The Greeks alternately incited the Crusader rulers against one another, and the Moslems against the Christians, only to make temporary alliances with their most formidable enemies, and then, changing their tactics, to negotiate with their foes and take up arms against their allies of the day before. Not only at Byzantium were treachery and perjury rampant and all pervading, but throughout the Eastern world, and contact with the Levantines had dulled the sense of honor of even the Latins. The Moslems had no pity whatever for the Christians whom they lumped together in their contempt. About this time the famous Saladin issued a decree in Egypt forbidding any Infidels to ride, whether on horseback or on mules, and commanded Christians to wear continually a belt so that Moslems could at once distinguish them from the true believers (1).

Notwithstanding the constant humiliations the Moslems put upon them, the Byzantines at times treated their rulers with great marks of consideration, showing a pusillanimity that only increased the latter's contempt for them.

COIN OF MICHAEL VII DUCAS (1071-1078)

The Sultan of Iconium "Kilijd-Arslan having learned "that Yakoub-Arslan and the other Emirs were planning to overthrow him "and put his brother in his stead, visited Constantinople where he was re- "ceived sumptuously. He stayed there nearly three months. Twice a "day viands were served him on gold and silver dishes which were left

---

(2) CINNAMUS, VI. 11-12.—MICHAEL THE SYRIAN transl. LANGLOIS, p. 325-326.—ABULFARADJ, *Chron. Syr.*, p. 365.—GUILLAUME OF TYRE., XX. 25-28

(1) MICHAEL THE SYRIAN, op. cit. I, p. 365.

"him as gifts. On one occasion, while dining with the Emperor, the latter "offered him all the table service and decorations, not counting other gifts "at the same time, both to him and the thousand or so Turks of his escort (2)."

The Greeks according to the Arab and Byzantine chroniclers gave magnificent fêtes in the Sultan's honor. "Above a splendidly decorated "platform stood a solid gold throne enhanced with diamonds and jacinths "and other precious stones surrounded by dazzlingly white pearls. An "abundance of lights caused all these jewels to blaze with brightness "On the throne sat in all his majesty the Emperor clothed with a purple "mantle on which were exquisite artistic designs made of pearls and dia- "monds. On his chest, suspended to a gold chain, hung a pink stone as "large as an apple. On either side stood the members of the Senate in "the order of their respective State functions. Kilidj-Arslan on entering "was overwhelmed with so much splendor "and refused at first to be seated despite "the Emperor's insistence; finally he took "a modest seat. During his stay at Manuel's "court he was housed in one of the palaces "in the southern part of Constantinople. All "the pleasures of the Imperial City were of- "fered him, tournaments, amphitheatre "games and contests, and Greek-fire dis- "plays. (1)

COIN OF KILIDJ-ARSIAN II, SULTAN OF ICONIUM

Such was the deference paid by the Imperial Court to the barbarian who from Iconium was threatening all eastern Christendom, who had never ceased harassing the Greek empire as well as Cilicia and the Crusaders, and who in 1148-1149 had taken Marasch, sacked the city and its churches, and in defiance of his plighted word had massacred the Frankish knights, bishops, and priests, and most of the inhabitants, whom he had solemnly sworn to protect (2). What were the Turks to think of these Byzantines who displayed merely their wealth, instead of armies that might hold them in respect? Far from frightening them by his prestige, Manuel only excited their greed. He gave them encouragement not only to fight Cilicia and the Crusaders, but to attack the Greeks

---

(2) ABULFARADJ
(1) Cf CINNAMUS, V. vi.—NICETAS CHONIATES, Manuel Comnenus, chap CVIII.
(2) cf. ABULFARADJ, Chron. Syr, p 343

themselves, even supplying them with the funds with which to turn against both the Franks and himself.

Contemporaneous writers have not recorded the promises the Sultan made to the Emperor, but events speak for themselves.

RUPEN II BARON (1175-1187) Rupen II (1175-1187), the son of Stepane and nephew of Thoros II and Mleh, was chosen by the nobles of New Armenia to succeed his wicked uncle, just when the great Saladin who held all Egypt and part of Syria was preparing to drive the Crusaders into the sea. All the Christian principalities then had the Moslems to meet, Cilicia being threatened by Manuel's whilom guest, Kilidj-Arslan. Feeling unequal to the struggle, the new Armenian ruler in 1180 bought the enemy off. Hardly had the latter withdrawn from his frontier, however, than the Prince of Antioch and Hetum, Seignior of Lampron, at the instigation of Manuel Comnenus, started hostilities against Rupen. The baron, in order to crush Hetum who held the mountain passes and was always so ready to open them to the Greeks, sent his brother Leo to besiege him in his lair. Bohemond III came to his ally's help, and by treachery captured Rupen, only restoring him his freedom at the instance of Hetum whom Leo was seriously threatening inside Lampron. The Armenian Baron had to pay thirty thousand dinars ransom and give up the cities of Adana and Mamestia to the principality of Antioch.

Rupen had married Isabel, the daughter of Humfrey III, prince of Karak and Toron, and was more friendly than hostile to the Crusaders. He was a just and pious ruler and founded a number of religious houses in his realm. Disillusioned by the faithlessness of his times, he abdicated in favor of his brother Leo (1187), became a monk and withdrew to the monastery of Trazargh, where he died after a few months

COIN OF ISAAC ANGELUS

LEO II BARON 1187-1196

Very grave events were then transpiring in the East. On the 2nd of October, 1187, Salah-ed-Din (Saladin) took Jerusalem. Edessa and Acre had been in infidel hands for some time, and Tripoli and Antioch were about to fall. Unless Europe could come to their help, the Crusaders and the Cilicia barony would inevitably disappear in the tempest. The Latin East was doomed unless the western princes raised a new Crusade to meet the storm, retake the Holy Places and set up on the Syrian coast solid States that could hold their own against the Moslem power of Egypt.

COIN OF BOHEMOND III OF ANTIOCH

ARRIVAL OF THE THIRD CRUSADE

The vital necessity of facing this new situation was the prime concern of the European courts and the Pope expended every energy in bringing about a new expedition. The Emperor of Germany, the King of France, and the King of England responded to his call, and Frederick I Barbarossa, took the leadership of the Crusade. On his arrival in Asia, by way of Macedonia, the Emperor crossed the territory of the Baron of Armenia in order to reach Antioch and thence Palestine. Cilicia and the principality on the Orontes had to be his military base, constituting as they did along with Tripoli the sole remnants of the conquests of the first and second Crusades and of the Armenians.

COIN OF SALADIN (SALAH-ED-DIN)

Leo saw in this tremendous expedition against the Moslems an excellent chance to expand his power, add to his prestige, and obtain at the hands of the Western rulers a royal crown in exchange for his baronial coronet. Never dreaming that such a great enterprise could possibly be short-lived, he glimpsed the vision of a Western Asia carved up into Christian States, and it was not his intention to be the vassal of any Latin prince. The future king of New

Armenia looked forward to being an intermediary between the Byzantine Empire and the Syrian principalities. He accordingly lost no time in supplying the Crusaders with provisions, transportation, and guides, and lavished all he could on the Frankish nobles, supplying them with military assistance. This alliance, moreover, strengthened his baronial position in regard to the Greek Emperor. It would enable him, he hoped, to deal one day on equal terms with the Byzantine Court.

By actions as well as promises Leo had won Frederick over to his side, and also gained the good graces of the Pope. The Emperor of Germany had promised him the desired crown. This monarch, however, met his death in the icy waters of the Calycadnus (Gheuk-sou). Thereupon the baron of Armenia looked towards his son Henry VI. However, Leo could not feel satisfied with a grant of kingship from the leader of the Crusade, even though a mighty Emperor. He felt that anything given him by the Frankish rulers might be withdrawn from him one day; therefore he sought to hold his crown from the Pope whose voice had much more weight with Christendom than that of any temporal sovereign, and whose authority would place him and his successors beyond any possibility of dethronement. He accordingly sent an embassy to Celestine III in 1195 to ask the Sovereign Pontiff to give him his blessing and the regal sovereignty of Armenia.

The arrival of the Third Crusade inside Cilicia and the territory of Antioch marked the beginning of a new era for the Armenians, and the

COINS OF JOHN OF BRIENNE AND THE HOLY SEPULCHRE

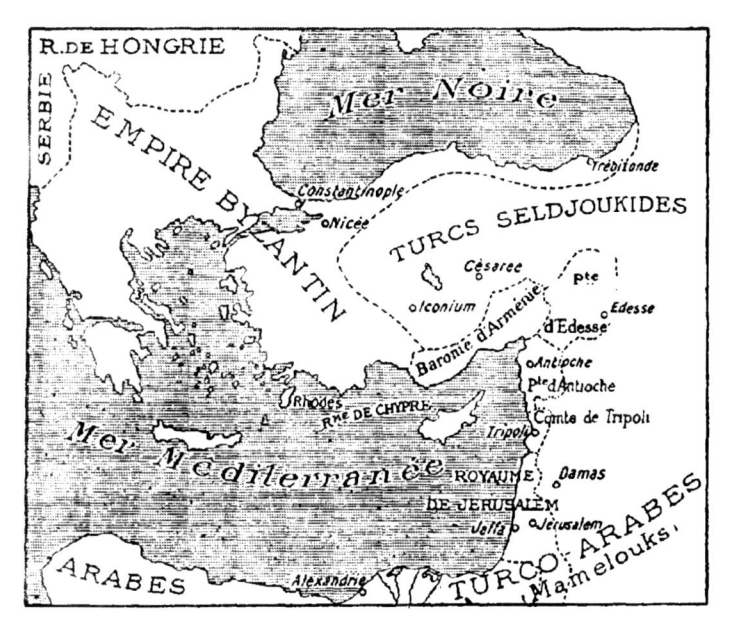

LATIN PRINCIPALITIES OF THE EAST

Moslem bands and the Imperial troops both ceased for a time from raiding Leo's dominion. Both the infidels and Constantinople were watching events, and the Moslems, like the Greeks, were preparing to meet the new exigencies of a situation they could not yet clearly outline but knew to be a coming severe test.

A new Latin kingdom was about to emerge, not at the expense of the infidels, but by stripping the Empire of one of its provinces. In the spring of 1191, King Richard

COIN OF BARON LEO II

of England who had sailed from Sicily with his fleet was compelled by bad weather to put into Cyprus where a prince of the Comneni, named Isaac, had set himself up as independent. This Greek was a tyrant to his subjects and a barbarian towards all strangers. Learning of the shipwreck of an English ship, he rushed to Limassol in the hope of seizing by ruse or force the persons of Berengaria of Navarre, King Richard's betrothed, and her sister-in-law Joan of Sicily, whose vessel had run aground. The ship got clear, however, and rejoined the English fleet. Infuriated at such an outrage, Richard disembarked at Limassol and within a few weeks had possession of the whole island, capturing the despotic Isaac and his family, together with all his treasures. The English king then set sail again for the Holy Land, leaving Guy of Lusignan as the first king of Cyprus. This time the Latins were favored by circumstances. Richard had nothing to fear from the Emperors, who were becoming continually weaker and who ten years later had to seek safety for their crown at Nicaea. Besides, Cyprus was a nest of pirates and spies, and Isaac in his hatred for the Latins had lost no opportunity to injure them in his relations with Saladin and the other Moslem rulers. His downfall could only help the Western cause.

COIN OF ISAAC DUCAS COMNENUS, TYRANT OF CYPRUS

The interference of Latin Christians in Eastern affairs during the two first Crusades, and Frederick's march through the Empire had greatly ruffled the Greeks, and it was a question at Constantinople whether it would not be better to join up with the Saracens and Turks and drive from Asia the flood of Catholics that Western Europe was sending out to conquer the holy places. The Emperors felt that Moslem invasion of their provinces meant only temporary occupation of the Imperial realm, whereas they feared the Crusaders' conquests might be permanent, and the third Crusade headed by an Emperor and two auxiliary kings promised to be much more serious than the preceding ones.

COIN OF GUY OF LUSIGNAN FIRST KING OF CYPRUS

Had the Greeks joined the Crusaders and fought the ambitious Moslem leaders, undoubtedly the Turkish invasion would have been confined to the eastern provinces of what is today Turkey-in-Asia, the Christian kingdoms of Syria and New Armenia would have been maintained and Constantinople would probably have never fallen into the hands of the enemies of Western civilization. But the fanaticism and intolerance of the Orthodox Greeks, the pride of the Emperors, their dynastic and religious hatred, all blinded the Byzantine court and by their intrigues the Greeks not only were heading for ruin but were seriously endangering the civilized world.

Leo had realized that he could no longer pursue the free-lance policy of his predecessors and hold the balance between the Greeks and the Crusaders. His desire for royal rank compelled him to take sides, but his main difficulty lay in the religious beliefs of his people whose ritual separated them both from the Byzantine cult and that of Rome. He must therefore effect a rapprochement with one or the other of these two Churches, if he was to secure a crown and thus establish his nation's independence.

He started simultaneous negotiations with the Papacy and Byzantium. In the latter city, however, the Orthodox clergy showed themselves unyielding. The religious quarrel between the Armenians and the Greeks dated from the early centuries of Christianity. In Greater Armenia they had frequently been very bitter, and both at Constantinople and Sis they remained painful memories. The Armenian people hated the Greeks for their oppression and cruelty, and for their treachery and the intolerance with which they had always met any overtures on the part of the Bagratid rulers. The conversations which were commenced at Leo's bidding had, consequently, but very little chance of success.

The Baron reflected, however, that his interests lay rather in the direction of Byzantium than in that of the Western powers, who after all were at a great distance and whose efforts had just sustained a setback by the entry of Sultan Saladin into the arena. The Greek Empire still enjoyed considerable prestige despite its present dilapidated condition. If he received his crown from the Basileus, he would be linking Armenia's destiny with that of Constantinople, and forging an alliance with what he still looked on as a great power, enabling him perhaps one day to regain Greater Armenia and form a State extending from the Gulf of Alexandretta to the Caspian Sea, capable of blocking any Moslem invasion of Byzantium. There was the Sultanate of Iconium in the centre of Asia Minor, it was true, but the Seljuks once caught between the Greeks and the Armenians must surely fall, and the kingdom of New Armenia would become the bastion of the Orthodox world. This dream was shattered by the failure, easy to foresee, of the negotiations of the bishops sent to Constantinople.

SAINT NERSES (from the Armenian Iconography of 1511)

" 'I am asked,' wrote the Catholicos Nerses to Michael the Syrian (1) " 'to recognize two natures in Jesus Christ and to honor the fourth Council, "to celebrate the birth of Christ on the 25th of December, and the Mass "with leavened bread and water, and not to use the words: God, Holy, "Who wast crucified. On these conditions we are promised [by Emperor "Manuel] great benefactions.' "

Faced with the exactingness of the Byzantine clergy, Leo turned to the West, but in so doing he was following a totally opposite political line for New Armenia's future, one altogether counter to that of a Greek alliance. The Greek emperors in their hostility to the Crusaders behaved so deceitfully to the Westerners that soon the Latins would have to occupy Constantinople itself if they wanted to stop Greek intrigue. By applying to Rome, Leo was espousing the cause of the European rulers, identifying himself with their acts, and casting his lot in with theirs in the East. It was a serious decision, but the baron was ambitious of becoming king, and the Latins flattered his hopes, consequently he pushed on his negotiations with the Pope and the royal Crusaders.

Rome, on the other hand, could hardly fail to derive the greatest satisfaction from seeing a native kingdom formed in the East based on Latin culture and the Latin worship. The new State would give the Crusaders a strong bridgehead and facilitate the growth of the principalities of Syria and Palestine. The latter were envisaged as destined to last forever and to extend by degrees their dominion over all Western Asia, thus protecting Europe from Moslem invasion. Papal sagacity was not deceived, and the western monarchs likewise had no illusions, concerning the fate of the Byzantine Empire They knew it was irretrievably lost, and expected it to be replaced by a Latin State able to safeguard the Bosphorus, keep watch over it, and prevent the Moslems entering Europe from that direction. The conquest of Spain and Sicily by the Saracens, their thrust to the very heart of France, had carried a serious warning to the Catholic Christians, and any support for their arms in the East was welcome. So Leo's ambitions found a favorable response not only from the throne of St Peter but in every European court. It was essential, nevertheless, that Rome should not demand too much in the way of reforming the Armenian ritual, for the people were very attached to their ancient worship and customs and would have great difficulty in giving up their ancestral ways The clergy clung to its pre-

---

(1) *Op. cit.* 1, p 367.

rogatives and some of the nobles looked askance not only at any relinquishment of a religious segregation that had acquired for them national significance, but also on the creation of royal authority to take the place of the former seigniorial tenure which they were sometimes so apt to set at naught.

Leo had received from his maternal uncle Paguran an education that was decidedly more Greek than Armenian, for the nobles of Baberon and Lampron had remained loyal to the Byzantine emperors. This is proved by the fact that Leo, signed his name in Greek followed by his royal title in Armenian. His contact with the Byzantines is also undoubtedly responsible for his being receptive to wide political conceptions and for his ambition of one day wearing the crown. The barons who preceded him, secluded in their mountains and with few contacts except with Frankish nobles and Moslem emirs had hitherto had no aims beyond extending their power and their territory, gathering treasure, and withstanding the encroachments of their dangerous neighbors. Leo saw much further; his desire was for a king's crown so that he might treat on a footing of equality with Byzantine Emperors, Sultans, Caliphs, and European sovereigns.

SIGNATURE OF LEO I
FIRST KING OF NEW ARMENIA

Negotiations dragged on slowly. In 1196 Leo wrote once more to Henry VI, Emperor of Germany. "When Livons [Leo] saw that he "[Henry] was the supreme leader, and that he held no tenure from him, "he sent his envoy to the Emperor Henry in Apulia where he was, with "a message, offering him homage and saying that he wished to hold from "him his land of Armenia; and begged him that he send him the crown "and acknowledge him as a king. The Emperor received the message "with great pleasure, and accepted the homage, promising him that he "would crown him when he crossed the sea." (1)

In addition this aspirant to royal rank communicated his desire to all the nobles of the Crusade, and contrived to get support in all directions. "The Lord of Armenia said to Count Henry [Duke of Champagne

---

(1) GUILLAUME OF TYRE, cont'd. XXVI. 27.

"and King of Jerusalem]: 'I have land enough, cities and castles and "large revenues, sufficient to be a king. As the Prince of Antioch is my "liegeman [feudatory], I beg of you that you crown me."

Meanwhile continuous correspondence went on between Rome and the king, and frequent embassies were sent to the Pope who ordered his legates to examine the question and discuss matters with the high dignitaries of the Armenian Church. Once before, in the middle of the 12th century under Eugene III, the Holy See had studied carefully the possibility of a rapprochement of the Armenian Church and the Papacy, and a letter from Pope Lucius III (1185) addressed to the Catholicos Gregory IV Degha, of which Nerses of Lampron has handed us down a translation, shows how far at that time negotiations had already advanced. The bishop wrote: "In the year 634 of the Armenian era there "arrived Gregory, the bishop of Philippopolis, sent by the Roman Pope "Lucius to our Catholicos Gregory. He brought him the answer to our "Monsignor's [Catholicos'] letter and the book containing the usages or "ritual of the Church, in Latin characters."

Another letter written by Pope Clement III four years later (1189) to Baron Leo, begins thus: "Clement, Bishop, Servant "of the servants of God, to "our well beloved son, the "illustrious Prince of the "Mountains (Leo), greet-"ings and apostolic bless-"ings," and the Pope exhorted the Armenian baron to take part in delivering the holy places.

HANDWRITING OF SAINT NERSES OF LAMPRON ON A GREEK MANUSCRIPT

This exchange of letters with the Pope did not prevent Leo, however, from negotiating at the same time with Constantinople, and from sending the Patriarch Nerses and Baron Paul in 1197 to discuss matters of religion with Alexis Comnenus. Nerses wrote on that occasion to his prince as follows: "After discussing things with "them [the Greeks], we found them ignorant, rude, and materialistic, "as stubborn as Jews unwilling to serve God by the renewal of the Holy "Ghost, only in the oldness of the letter. Our spiritual goodwill was "grievously disheartened and we came away troubled and disappointed "in our pious hope." Leo was motivated, therefore, by political interest and not by any religious convictions. Had he met with more toleration at Byzantium, in all likelihood the Armenians would have adhered to the Greek ritual and the kingdom of New Armenia would have upheld the cause of the Emperors instead of that of the Crusaders.

As early as 1196, some say, while the conversations at Constantinople were still on, Leo received from the Pope, whom he had asked both for a crown and for his people's adoption by the Roman Church, the gift of a gold crown in token that his prayer was granted. The Pope's stipulations for the Armenian Church consisted only of quite acceptable provisos regarding ritual plus the requirement that the Catholicos send an envoy at regular stated intervals to Rome to pay him homage. In this manner New Armenia drew closer to the Catholic Church and widened still further the gulf between itself and the Byzantine Empire.

COIN OF ALEXIS COMNENUS (1195-1203)

Moreover Leo, in spite of the need he had for the Crusaders prior to his coronation, did not always remain on good terms with the Latins. This was particularly the case with the neighboring principality of Antioch, the undetermined boundaries of which were always causing strife. In 1194 he forestalled a plan of Bohemond III seeking to trap and capture him, by himself treacherously seizing that prince and the chief nobles of the court of Antioch, and locking them up in the Castle of Sis. Count Henry of Champagne, the Regent of the kingdom of Jerusalem, intervened and obtained Bohemond's freedom, but the Prince of Antioch had to agree to give back the territory he had formerly taken from Rupen, and a

COIN OF HENRY OF CHAMPAGNE

new alliance was sealed by the marriage of Alice, one of Rupen's daughters, with Raymond III, the eldest son of Bohemond. It was set forth in the agreement that should Alice, Rupen II's daughter, bear a son, he should inherit the throne of Antioch. A male child was born, and Raymond at his death in 1198 made his father swear to keep this promise. Raymond-Rupen,

SEAL OF RAYMOND-RUPEN

the son of Raymond and Alice, was then an infant, and Bohemond III's younger son, the Count of Tripoli, took advantage of his nephew's minority and his father's years, to drive the old prince out of Antioch and seize power. This usurpation to the prejudice of a child under Leo's protection caused the Armenians to rise against the principality of Antioch, so that when Leo received the royal crown, he was openly at war with the usurper.

Feuds of this kind, moreover, were not confined to the East. In France and England, and in all the feudal kingdoms of the West, there was constant strife among the nobility; European political manners were just as brutal as those of Asia.

COIN OF TRIPOLI
WITHOUT RULER'S NAME

CHAPTER VIII

THE KINGDOM OF NEW ARMENIA (1199-1375)

LEO I, KING OF ARMENIA (1196 or 1199 to 1219)

On January 6th, 1199 (?) Cardinal Conrad of Wittelsbach, Archbishop of Mayence, the delegate of Pope Celestine III, presented to Baron Leo II, in the Church of the Holy Wisdom of Christ at Tarsus, the royal crown, and the Catholicos Abirad (1195-1203) crowned and anointed the new monarch who took the name and title of "Leo I, by the grace of the Roman Emperor [Henry VI], King of Armenia." He thus proclaimed himself a feudatory of Western Europe represented by its leader, the Emperor of Germany. A few years after his accession, however, he felt irked by this vassalage, and took the title of "King by the grace of God."

When sending him the crown, the Pope asked the new king to consent to three conditions, all relating to the ritual divergencies between the Armenians and the Latins: First, he was to celebrate Christmas and Saints' days on the same dates as in the Latin Church; secondly, that matins and vespers be said in church, a custom the Armenians had long discontinued, in fact ever since the Ishmaelite (Arab) invasion—these services being observed only when mass was celebrated; and thirdly, the Christmas Eve and Easter fasts were to be broken only with fish and oil. " 'When you have adopted these rites,' " added the Cardinal " 'you need no longer worry about the gifts and dues you have to offer " 'the Emperor and the Pope in homage for your crown. If you refuse, " 'I am commanded to require from you very large sums in gold, silver, " 'and jewels'."

EFFIGY OF LEO I

"Leo called the Catholicos and bishops together and asked them what
"reply he should make to the Latin proposals. They refused to accept
"them, whereupon Leo told them: 'Do not worry. I will satisfy them
" 'just for the present by appearing to give in to them.' Then he said to
"the Roman Archbishop: 'We do accept immediately and unconditionally
" 'the instructions of the great Emperor and of the Sovereign Pontiff.'
"The Archbishop demanded that the promise be ratified under oath by
"twelve bishops, and Leo persuaded a dozen of his prelates to swear ac-
"cordingly." (1)

Leo's words to the Armenian clergy illustrate the policy he followed towards the Latins, a policy continued by his successors. Caught between

COINS OF KING LEO I

the requirements of the Pope whom his paramount interest it was to conciliate and who demanded unity regarding dogma and various disciplinary points, and the tremendous opposition of the Armenian clergy and people, the Cilician sovereigns often were compelled to maneuver. Had they ridden roughshod over national prejudice, they would have come to a tragic end, as did later the Lusignans. (2) On both sides, Latin and Ar-

(1) GUIRAGOS OF KANTZAG.
(2) Cf. DULAURIER, *op.cit.*, vol. I, p. 423. note 1.

menian, there was unyielding intolerance in these matters, and shameful hagglings entered into the discussion of religious convictions. Western fanaticism, aggravated by the Crusades, on the one hand, and Armenian traditions nationally enshrined, on the other, precluded any genuine coming together.

GOLDEN BULLA OF LEO I

Leo's coronation had considerable importance for the Byzantine court, for it meant New Armenia's definite exclusion from the vassalage of the Basileus, and any refusal to acknowledge the new king would have entailed open warfare with the Crusaders and consequently all Western Europe. As usual the Greeks preferred stratagem to force. Alexis III Angelus (1195-1203) copied the Latins by sending him gifts together with a crown, but his presents were accompanied with the following ominous counsel: "Put not upon thy head the crown "the Romans have sent thee, for thou art much "nearer to us than thou art to Rome." Byzantium's entire ensuing policy towards the Armenians is contained in those words.

COIN OF HUGH I OF CYPRUS (1205-1218)

Leo's fondest wishes were realized, and all the rulers of Europe, besides the Basileus and even the Caliph of Bagdad, sent gifts and ambassadors to the new monarch.

The chroniclers are not agreed as to the date of Leo's coronation.

Hetum places the ceremony between July 1197 and January 1198, but according to Latin historians the arrival of the Archbishop of Mayence, the legate of the Holy See, could only have taken place in 1199. Fifteen bishops and thirty-nine Armenian feudatory nobles were present at their sovereign's crowning, as well as a goodly number of knights of the Crusade.

The Frankish crown that he had just placed on his brow made no change in Leo's attitude towards the Latin principality. In 1203 the new king of Armenia again took up arms for the throne of Antioch. Bohemond had died in 1201, and Leo laid claim to it for Rupen-Raymond, the son of Raymond III and Alice. The knights and principal citizens of Antioch had recognized Bohemond IV, Count of Tripoli, the younger son of Bohemond III, as their prince. Repelled by the Templars near Antioch, the king of Armenia had to content himself for the time being with laying siege to their castle.

COIN OF BOHEMOND IV PRINCE OF ANTIOCH

The war between the Armenians and the above Order was waged for several years north of the cape which is called today by the Arabs Ras-el-Khanzir, or The Boar's Promontory. Bohemond IV had entrusted the Knights Templars with the defense of the principality of Antioch, while he himself endeavored to put down two vassals of his own in the earldom of Tripoli, one of whom he was besieging at the castle of Nephin. After many unsuccessful attempts Leo finally captured Antioch through complicity on the part of the Seneschal, Acharie, with the result that in 1216 Peter II of Locedia crowned Raymond-Rupen as Prince of Antioch in the church of St. Peter of that city.

COIN OF RAYMOND-RUPEN PRINCE OF ANTIOCH

Both enemy and ally, in turn, of the Templars and excommunicated by the Pope for refusing to restore to the Knights their cities which he had seized, Leo succeeded in having the pontifical sentence lifted and finally, on August 5th, 1217, in inducing Pope Honorius III to place Rupen-Raymond's family and the principality of Antioch under the protection of the Holy See.

During his warfare with the Count of Tripoli, Leo contrived to ally himself with Theodore Lascaris, the Emperor of Nicaea, by giving him in marriage Philippine, the younger daughter of his brother Rupen. He took steps also to protect himself against the Moslems on his western border, for, beyond the Taurus mountains, the Seljuks who had carved out a kingdom for themselves in the fair provinces of central Asia Minor, still constituted a threat and hoped to reap advantage from Saladin's victories over the Crusaders and from the current dissensions between the Armenians and the Latins. The robber bands of their chief Rustem had even advanced to the walls of Sis, from where Leo drove them away by a bold surprise attack.

COIN OF THEODORE LASCARIS
EMPEROR OF NICAEA

Armenian annals are not at all clear concerning Leo's part in the events that took place at the beginning of the third Crusade. Some accounts picture him in Cyprus attending Guy of Lusignan's marriage with Princess Berengaria of Navarre, others represent him as joining in the siege of Ptolemais (Acre), along with Philippe-Auguste and Richard Coeur-de-Lion, the French and English kings. Latin authorities, however, do not concur with Armenian historians in the statement that Leo was present at the latter memorable siege which lasted two years, although it is certain that some troops from Armenia gave assistance to the Crusaders during that operation.

IMITATIONS BY THE CRUSADERS OF MOSLEM COINS

The King of Armenia was an out-and-out statesman. From the time he first succeeded to the tile of baron (1187) until the close of the 12th century when his unremitting efforts to win a royal crown proved successful, his one concern was setting up his kingdom and putting it on a footing where it could command the respect not only of the neighboring Latin princes but also of the Greeks and Moslems.

COURT OF ARMENIA — Influenced by Byzantine ideas of government, and imbued to an even greater extent with the feudal conceptions of the Western world, the King patterned his court on those of Antioch and Jerusalem. The Assizes of the latter kingdom were authoritative law in Christian Syria and Cilicia; those of Antioch gained the ascendancy, however, and were administered in the new Armenian realm. Latin and French soon became spoken at Leo's court, and were used along with the native language. With regard to the nobles, the new king recalled the misfortunes caused of old in Greater Armenia by the almost unbridled liberty they enjoyed, and tightened up their links with the throne, in line with the feudal customs of the West. The feudatories were given the titles of baron and count; many of the offices of the Bagratid court were abolished, while others received Latin designations such as that of Constable instead of the old title of Sbascalar. On the battle-field the dignitary thus named carried the royal standard. Before his death, Leo created two Regents (bailes, or in Latin bajuli), as had been provided by the Assizes of Jerusalem, one to protect and educate the Crown Princess, the other to administer Crown matters. There was a Marshall to carry the national standard, a Chamberlain (generally the Archbishop of Sis), a Chief Butler (Royal Cup-bearer), and a Grand Messenger, just as at European courts. A few titles of Greek origin, however, continued in use, among them being that of "Proximos" given to the official set over the finances of the realm, and those of Sebastos and Pansebastos (Reverend and Most Reverend).

Leo went a step nearer to the usages of Western chivalry in arrogating for himself upon his accession the right to bestow knighthood on his vassal nobles. In former years, when he was only a baron, this had been the privilege of the Princes of Antioch and he had himself received knighthood at the hands of Bohemond, but on becoming a sovereign, and even a suzerain of the neighboring princes, he claimed sworn allegiance from his feudatories. This right became established, and in 1274 Bohemond VII, the last of the Antioch princes, was knighted by his uncle, King Leo III of Armenia.

Thus the Armenian State, while retaining many of its Eastern characteristics, followed the pattern of the Western courts. Leo's increased royal authority brought him good results, for he was able to bring under his rule the numerous and hitherto unruly Armenian nobles, and to create a stable realm stretching the full extent of ancient Cilicia and protected by the high mountains of the Taurus and Amanus chains where all the passes were in his hands. His dominion comprised, according to the chronicles, sixty-two fortresses (1) the custody of which he was shrewd enough to entrust mostly to European knights including the Templars. He adopted this means of forestalling any inclination to revolt on the part of the native barons, many of whom rather longed for the days when they had entire freedom. He was also in this manner able to frustrate any intriguing by the Byzantines, always so ready to sow dissension among the hated Armenians.

COIN OF KAIKHOSRU I
SULTAN OF ICONIUM
(1204-1210)

ARMENIAN TRADE

While organizing his kingdom and expanding his territory, Leo did not forget to foster his country's development in the economic field. Situated between the kingdoms of the Crusaders, the Moslem dominions, and the Greek Empire, Cilicia was admirably located to serve as a middle ground for trade between the East and the West. The Cilician coasts though possessed of no first-class ports had a certain number of harbors offering quite sufficient shelter for trading vessels to anchor, even if not for galleys of war.

The Armenians were very conversant with Asia and familiar with all the trade routes converging from the Euphrates and the Tigris, Persia and India, towards their country, and knew the great value set by the West on merchan-

COIN OF SULEIMAN-SHAH
SULTAN OF ICONIUM
(1202-1203)

---
(1) MICHAEL THE SYRIAN, op. cit., I. p. 405.

dise from the East. They therefore arranged with the Sultans of Iconium and the Emirs of Aleppo, also the Caliphs of Bagdad, for the traffic to pass through their ports. Ever since the Moslems had gained possession of nearly all Western Asia, caravans proceeded unmolested, from the banks of the Indus to those of the Euphrates. Trade had formerly taken the direction of the Greek provinces of Asia, but the Armenians succeeded in diverting it, owing to their cleverness in negotiating with the Western ship-captains. Under Leo II traders from the West began to flock to Tarsus and Adana, and the small port of Aïas (1) was crowded with European vessels.

Venice and Genoa, the two great trading Republics of the Mediterranean, were the most eager to do business with New Armenia. They had extensive dealing with Byzantium and the Frankish coasts of Syria, but the settling of the Turcomans in central Asia Minor on the one hand and the governments set up by the Crusaders in Palestine and Lebanon, on the other, had caused an alteration in the caravan routes, and the Genoese and Venetian offices on the Bosphorus and in Syria were not doing such excellent business as formerly. The Crusaders were unfitted for trading and the Greeks no longer had the monopoly of the Eastern caravans

Nevertheless, even in Cilicia Western traders met with difficulties because of certain usages prevalent throughout the East. The State maintained its right of preemption on wreckage, also that of escheat, or reversion to the Crown treasury of the estates of foreigners dying within the country. Armenian jurisdiction only was recognized in disputes between Europeans. Business was further complicated by a lot of customhouse vexations. The Genoese and Venetians found all these practices great hindrances in their affairs, but they gradually succeeded in obtaining advantages from which the other traders from Catalonia, Montpellier, Provence, Pisa, Sicily, etc were excluded.

Merchandise was taxed according to the special agreements made between the country of origin and the kingdom of Armenia. The Genoese and Venetians were able to bring in most of their goods duty-free, others paid an *ad valorem* tax of two to four per cent. The caravans arriving from the interior were also subject to customs duty.

In exchange for their products or their sequins the Europeans obtained from the marts of Aïas, Tarsus, or Adana, Eastern wares such as pepper, spices, aromatics, incense, soap, jewels, raw silk, fine Indian and

---
(1) Today: Yumurtalik.

Persian textiles, gold fabrics, and Persian carpets, on all of which precious merchandise the Armenians realized enormous profits while the royal Treasury reaped bountiful customs revenues. Cilicia became a scene of international transit trade comparable to that which twelve centuries before had made Sybaris so opulent.

The Armenians called their king "Leo the Great", or "The Magnificent". Nevertheless, without detracting from this ruler's fine qualities or depreciating the work he accomplished, the historian must refrain from sharing altogether the admiration he was held in by those whom he enriched and whose encomiums regarding him are recorded in the Armenian chronicles. Like most of his contemporaries, he was unscrupulous as to his means for attaining his ends, enlarging his dominions, or making his realm prosperous. He blazed up against any obstacle he found in his path, even against the Church on whom he had called for assistance for so long a time. For no valid reason he repudiated his first wife Isabel, and he put out the eyes of his cousin George, Mleh's illegitimate son. By trickery he got possession of the fortress of Lampron and made Hetum his prisoner at Tarsus on the pretext of marrying Rupen's daughter Philippa to Ochin, Hetum's eldest son. Nevertheless he made some very definite improvements in his realm. He endowed Cilicia with a number of religious and charitable institutions, brought under regulation the slave trade throughout his territory, forbidding the sale of Chritian slaves to infidels, and created hospitals for lepers who were then very numerous in the East. He accomplished much, for he sought every means of making his people prosperous, but unlike Louis XI of France he was unable to master the shortcomings of his day or to bring into final submission the unruly nobles.

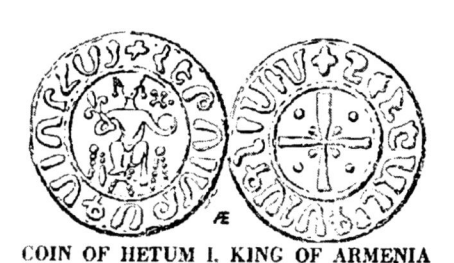

EFFIGY OF HETUM I KING OF ARMENIA

COIN OF HETUM I. KING OF ARMENIA

— 230 —

**ISABEL, QUEEN
1219-1252**

Before his death, Leo had named as his successor Isabel (Zabel), his daughter by his second wife Sybil, the daughter of Amaury of Lusignan, King of Cyprus, and Isabel Plantagenet. In accordance with his expressed wish, the young princess was proclaimed queen under the regency of Adam of Gastim, but this nobleman having been slain by the Ismailians (1), Baron Constantine of the Lampron family was named Regent. Isabel's minority aroused, however, the cupidity of Raymond-Rupen, son of Raymond III of Antioch and Alice, Rupen II's daughter, who entered Cilicia in the hope of seizing the throne. He was defeated and captured by Constantine near Tarsus, and put to death.

Following this quarrel which threatened to upset good relations between the Armenians and the Latins, Constantine was anxious to wipe out all cause for dispute, and therefore brought about the young queen's marriage to Prince Philip, son of Raymond the One-Eyed, Count of Tripoli. This prince made himself very unpopular with the Armenians, seeking to impose western customs on them. Consequently Constantine had him put away in the Castle of Sis where two years later he died of poison. The Regent could not leave the kingdom in the dangerous position of belonging to a queen who was only nominally married. Constantine's treatment of

COINS WITH THE NAMES OF HETUM I, AND OF SULTANS OF ICONIUM

---

(1) The "Assassins".

Prince Philip appears somewhat unscrupulous when it is considered that he had views of his own with regard to his ward whom he wished to marry to his own son Hetum.

Isabel was then in her twelfth year only, and some of the Armenian barons disliked Constantine's plans and were jealous of a Lampron noble, one of themselves, possibly becoming their ruler. They probably condemned, too, the murder of Philip.

HANDWRITING OF HETUM I

These nobles arranged for the young queen to flee for refuge to Seleucia Trachea (1), to the home of some Latin kinsfolk who themselves, perhaps, were not averse to so flattering a connection.

Constantine took arms and laid siege to the fortress which was held by the Knights Hospitalers. Their Grand Master, Bertrand, however, was then at war with the Sultan of Iconium, Ala-ed-Din Kaikobad, and had no desire to take on a fresh quarrel; consequently he surrendered it to the Armenians. The young queen was taken to Tarsus where she had to consent to marrying Prince Hetum, who thus became King of Armenia. On his coins, which are quite numerous, both his effigy and that of Isabel are shown.

HETUM I KING OF ARMENIA 1226-1270

The reign of Hetum (1226-1270) was the longest of all the sovereigns of New Armenia. It began, however, under very unfavorable auspices. The Seljuks of Iconium invaded Cilicia, and their Sultan Kaikobad (1220-1237) compelled the kingdom to do him homage. Hetum was obliged to coin bilingual money with the name of the Moslem overlord and himself.

---

(1) Selefkeh.

At this time, Genghis Khan was proceeding westward from the Ganges and Indus laying everything waste as he advanced. Northern Persia, Greater Armenia, and Georgia (where Rousoudan, a queen notorious for her evil ways, was reigning), had fallen to the might of the terrible conqueror. Hetum and all the Christian and Moslem rulers of Asia Minor joined together and warded off invasion. Genghis Khan withdrew to Kurdistan where he was assassinated in 1231.

HETUM I AND ISABEL

This victory stemmed only for a while the Mongolian wave. Oktai-Khan (1227-1241), Genghis' son and successor, caused his hordes to overrun the countries west of the Caspian Sea, where they spread desolation everywhere, leaving in their wake nothing but ashes, ruins, and heaps of corpses. The suddenness and cruelty of the disaster were unprecedented. In 1235 the Mongols exterminated nearly every inhabitant of Gandzak (Ielisavetpol), and the two following years saw the sacking of Lori, Kayan, Ani, and Kars. About 1242 Karin (Erzerum) shared the same fate. This city was then under the Sultan of Iconium, Gaïath-ed-Din Kaïkhosru II, who had obtained possession of the throne by the murder of his father Kaïkobad. This sultan was completely defeated by the invaders between Erzerum and Erzindjan, and both Caesarea and Sebaste, likewise belonging to the Seljuks, were also laid in ruins.

SEAL OF THE PATRIARCH CONSTANTINE I OF PARTZERPERT

Hetum was appalled by the danger, for the invasion was nearing his borders, and he hastened to surrender to the Mongols. Their Khan, Batchu, demanded

COIN OF ROUSOUDAN, QUEEN OF GEORGIA

— 233 —

that he deliver up to him the mother, wife, and daughter of the Sultan of Iconium who had taken refuge at the court of Sis. Hetum was weak enough to yield to the will of the barbarian, and Kaïkhosru to avenge such an infraction of the laws of hospitality, gave his support to the revolt of the Baron of Lampron, the brother-in-law of the Regent Constantine, and they together invaded Cilicia. Hetum shut himself up in Adana, Constantine and their constable Sempad in Tarsus; but with the help of the Mongols who came to his side the king drove out the Moslems from his realm.

COIN OF KAIKOBAD I SULTAN OF ICONIUM

His alliance with the Khans seemed so valuable and necessary to the king of Armenia that he did not hesitate to go personally to visit Mango, the Mongolian ruler, who dwelt at Karakorum beyond the Gates of Derbend, on the shore of the Caspian Sea, near the mouth of the Volga. There he was received with great honors by the barbarian chieftain, and a treaty of alliance was signed between them, which he put to profit on his return, taking back from the Sultan of Iconium certain districts the latter had captured in his absence.

A strange proceeding, indeed, for this king to leave his Christian court and, crossing the width of Moslem Asia, to act as his own ambassador to a barbarian from the Siberian steppes, a dweller in the heart of hardly known Scythia! Nevertheless, by way of Greater Armenia the Armenians and the Barbarians had linked up, and the heathen horde after laying waste the Ararat region had turned against the Moslems, thereby serving the Christian cause. Hetum looked on them as his natural allies.

COIN OF KAIKHOSRU II SULTAN OF ICONIUM

As one historian writes: "When Mango Can [Khan] had "heard the King of Armenia's petition, he called together his court,

COIN OF MANGO KHAN

"and summoned the king to his pres-
"ence. Then before the assembly he
"spoke thus: 'Because the King of
"Armenia has come ... We do reply,
"King of Armenia, that we will be-
"nignly grant all your prayers. And
"We, in the first place, Who are Lord
"by the grace of God, will be baptized and accept
"the faith, Our Lord Jesus Christ. I will have all
"those of my house baptized; and I will advise the
"others in good faith that they too be baptized, and
"believe the Christian faith. But I will not force
"anyone, for faith and belief do not require force.
"To your second request, we reply that we wish for
"perpetual peace and friendship, we and our people,
"with the Christians ... To the Christian churches
"and to the clergy of whatever sort, religious or
"secular, we will give the privilege of freedom, and
"will not suffer that in any wise they be molested.
"As to the matter of the Holy Land, we would say
"that we would willingly in our own person under-
"take the conquest of the Holy Land, ... But in-
"asmuch as we have too much other business, we
"must give commandment to our prow Alaon [Hou-
"lago-Khan] and he will accomplish this task and deliver holy Jeru-
"salem from the hands of the infidels, and return it to the Christians ...

COIN OF DAVID V, KING OF GEORGIA, AND OF MANGO-KHAN

"and to our brother we will give com-
"mandment that he go and take the
"city of Damascus and that he destroy
"the Caliph, as our mortal enemy . .
(1)"

Hetum was well advised in taking this step, for the mounting storm
was about to strike all Western Asia.
In 1257 the terrible Houlago-Khan advanced to the center of Asia Minor,

COIN OF HOULAGO

---

(1) Hayton (Hetum). "La flore des estoiles de la terre d'Orient". (The flower of the stars of the Orient.) *Histoire des Croisades*, vol. II, p. 167.

overthrew the power of the Sultans of Iconium, and then capturing Bagdad on February 4th, 1258, slew the Caliph Motassem and his two sons. For forty days the slaughter went on in the Arab capital. Everywhere he passed, Houlago had left nothing but ruins: Erzerum, Erzindjan, Sebaste, Caesarea, Iconium, Martyropolis, Aleppo, Damascus, Edessa, Kharan, Amidus, all were laid waste and the inhabitants wiped out. The Christians, however, did not suffer as much as did the Moslems in this appalling work of extermination, due to the intercession on their behalf of Princess Dokouz-Khatoun, and also because Hetum, as an ally of the Mongols, was fighting alongside of them.

COIN OF EMPEROR MICHAEL VIII PALAEOLOGUS (1261-1288)

Houlago was called away by his brother Mango's death, and did not return to Asia Minor. He left innumerable hordes to continue the deadly work of their terrible chieftain, masses of men who were only less dangerous in that they lacked the cohesive purpose of a leader.

COINS OF LEO II

At this juncture Bibars, the Sultan of Egypt, of the Baharit Mamaluke dynasty (1260-1277), entered the scene to take advantage of the upheaval caused by the Mongol invasion, also of the barbarian chief's departure, and determined to destroy the Latin principalities. Favored by the momentary absence of the Tartars, he invaded Cilicia and overwhelmed the army hastily raised to meet him under Hetum's two sons, Leo and Theodore. The latter prince was killed in the fight, and the other carried away prisoner (August 24th, 1266). Adoua, the city of the Templars, Sis, Misis, Adana, Aias, and Tarsus fell to the Mameluke ruler, who destroyed them and slaughtered every single inhabitant. Finally, on May 19th, 1268, Antioch itself was lost to the Crusaders. After massacring the male population, the conqueror distributed the women among his soldiers, the sacking of this city was on an almost unprecedented scale.

Hetum finally obtained terms of peace from the victor but they were very heavy. His son Leo was restored to him in exchange for Schems-ed-Din Sonkor al-aschkar (Red Falcon), Bibars' favorite who had fallen into Houlago's hands at the siege of Aleppo. His eyes opened at last to the vanity of worldly greatness, the king relinquished his crown as soon as his son came back. He abdicated to make way for Leo and withdrew to a monastery where he died October 28th, 1270.

LEO II
KING OF ARMENIA
1270-1289

The new sovereign, sometimes called Leo III by the Armenians, was really only the second king of that name, the first Leo (1129-1137) having been simply a baron, just as Leo II was between 1187 and 1196 (or 1199). Only in the latter reign at the end of the 12th century did Armenia become a kingdom under Leo I, properly speaking. The son of Hetum I was therefore the second *crowned* Leo.

This ruler's reign (1270-1289) was only another series of misfortunes. The king's authority had been much undermined by the disasters under Hetum I, and a number of Armenian nobles preferred to submit to the Egyptian Sultan rather than keep up an unequal struggle against the latter's hosts. Out of sheer fright of the Moslems, these discouraged individuals went so far as to urge the Mamelukes to conquer Cilicia outright. Leo was weak in repressing his traitorous liegemen, and did not go beyond seizing their castles. His clemency only resulted in fanning their spite against the throne.

While the king was doing his best to raise the spirits of his disheartened subjects, suddenly (1273-1275), without the least excuse, Bibars' emirs again invaded the kingdom with a very big army. Misis was captured in a surprise attack, and its people put to the sword. Sis, according to Armenian historians, stood out; according to Makrisi it was sacked. Tarsus fell, the royal palace and Church were burned to the ground, and the State Treasury seized by the Egyptians. Fifteen thousand inhabitants were slain by the yataghan, and ten thousand more carried off into captivity in the land of the Pharaohs. Aïas met with the same fate as the other cities; the whole population, both Frank and Armenian, perished. The disaster was so appalling that it remained a byword both among the horrified Armenians and among the Moslems who withdrew from Cilicia satiated with plunder and gloating over the shedding of so much Christian blood.

COINS OF THE GREEK EMPEROR ANDRONICUS II (1282-1328) THE VIRGIN MARY WITHIN THE WALLS OF CONSTANTINOPLE

Makrisi (1) has left us a terrifying account of the Egyptian invasion of Cilicia. "On the third day of the month Schăban 673 [February 1st, 1275] the Sultan [Bibars] set out "from the Mountain Castle for Syria and entered Damascus, whence he "came out again leading his army and Arab auxiliaries ... The Khăzindar "[Treasurer] and the Emirs in an overland raid took the city of Macica "by surprise and slaughtered all its people. They had brought with them "on mules a quantity of boats taken apart, for the purpose of crossing the "Djeyhan river and the Nahr-Aswab [the Black River], but these were "not needed. The Sultan at the head of his army joined the two Emirs "after crossing the Nahr-Aswab. The army overcame the numerous difficulties encountered on the way and obtained possession of the mountains, "where they gathered an enormous amount of booty in the way of oxen,

---

(1) *Histoire des Sulthans Mamlouks, op. cit.*, vol. I, part 2, p. 123.

"buffaloes, and sheep. The Sultan entered Sis in battle array, and there
"observed the solemn feast. Then he gave the city over to pillage, and
"destroyed the palace of the Takafour [king], its summer-houses, and
"gardens. A detachment which he sent to the gorge of Rûm [Taurus
"Gates] came back with Tartar prisoners including very many women
"and children. The monarch fetched three hundred horses and mules
"from Tarsus. Troops sent to the coast captured a number of ships,
"the crews of which were slain. Other bodies of soldiers raided the
"mountains in all directions and massacred or captured the foe, taking
"quantities of loot. One detachment set out for Aïas and finding that city
"undefended sacked and burned it, killing great numbers. About two
"thousand of its inhabitants had taken refuge in boats which were, how-
"ever, lost out at sea. The amount of plunder was beyond computation."

These terrible events remained graven in the memory of the unhappy Armenians, accustomed though they were for centuries to barbarous enemy treatment. Vahram of Edessa in his rhymed chronicle (1) says: "They [the Egyptians] scoured the mountains and brought down from "the heights both people and cattle. They put to the sword all those "they found in the plain Only those who had found refuge in [natural] "strongholds or who had been able to betake themselves to fortresses "escaped the slaughter. All the rest were taken, none were spared. En- "circling our land they laid the torch to everything. The great city of "Tarsus of such magnificence and renown was laid in ruins. They burned "the Church of St. Sophia and gave the city over to plunder."

Armenian was not crushed entirely, however, the fight was continued relentlessly Leo with the help of the Turcomans succeeded in a few encounters, but Cilicia was then invaded a second time and devastated. Bibars finally died on June 30, 1277; his death meant only a short truce for the Armenians, for in spite of the dissensions at the Cairo court the Egyptians again set out for the north. Mango Timur with fifty thousand Tartars and the aid of twenty-five thousand Caucasians and Armenians met in pitched battle on the plain of Homs (Emesa) the Sultan of Egypt, Malek-Mansur, together with the Sultan of Damascus, Sonkor-Aschkar (October 29th, 1281). The Christians and their allies met with disastrous defeat, and the conquerors pursuing the Armenians entered Cilicia.

---

(1) verses 1261-1274

Through the intervention of the Commander of the Templars of New Armenia, Leo II at last obtained peace with Egypt. A treaty was

SIGNATURE OF LEO II

signed to last ten years, ten months, and ten days; but the terms of the Sultan in Cairo were extremely harsh. Leo was obliged to pay an annual tribute amounting to one million dirhems (1), to release all Moslem merchants who had been taken prisoners and indemnify them for the losses they had sustained, surrender fugitives, and grant the Moslems full freedom to trade, even in slaves whatever their nationality or religion. On his part the Sultan agreed to similar terms, but Moslem prisoners or fugitives were not to be included in the foregoing stipuation.

The remnants of the Latin principalities were likewise in a sorry state at this period, and each of the princes was concerned only with his home protection, whether by arms or, as was more often the case, by composition with the enemy. Ever since Antioch fell to the Moslems, Cilicia had been completely isolated. The above peace, however, although humiliating and grievous for Leo, had its bright side in that it promised eleven years of respite. Famine and plague came on top of Armenia's devastation by war, and yet by wise and prudent government the king succeeded in raising his country once more from ruin. Foreign vessels were again to be seen visiting the port of Aïas, and commerce revived. Numerous writings dating from this reign show how solicitous he was for the education of his people, especially their religious education.

By his wife, Queen Anna, Leo II had eleven children, nine of whom were living at the time of his death.

HETUM II KING OF ARMENIA 1289-1297

Hetum II (1289-1297) ascended the throne at a critical time for Eastern Christendom. The Egyptian Mamelukes who were already in possession of the former Latin principalities of Edessa, Jerusalem, and Antioch, behaved with arrogance towards the last few Frankish domains, as also towards Armenia. Kelaun demanded from Leo the surrender of the strongholds of Marasch and Behesni, in defiance of the treaty made in 1185 with Leo II. Hetum appealed in vain to Pope Nicolas IV and King Philip IV of France; the spirit of the

---

(1) Arab silver coin.

Crusades was dead, so much so that Alfonso III, king of Aragon, Don Jayme, king of Naples, and the Republic of Genoa were all signing commercial treaties with the Sultan, which meant that a portion of Europe accepted the accomplished fact and, in short, disowned the Crusaders. Kelaun continued to conquer, to massacre Christians, and to make slaves of their women and children. Tripoli fell in 1189, followed by Acre (May 15th, 1291). Tyre, Sidon, and Beyrouth shared the same fate. In 1292, Melik-Aschraf-Khalil, Kelaun's son, advanced as far as the Euphrates and laid siege to Romela, the residence of the Armenian Catholicos and a most important stronghold defended by Raymond, Hetum's maternal uncle.

COINS OF HETUM II

The city was taken by storm after thirty-three days' siege, and all the men were put to the sword while the women and children and the Patriarch Stephen went off into captivity. Threatened right in the heart of his realm, Hetum abandoned Behesni, Marasch, and Till of Hamdoun, in order to save his country from utter destruction.

With palace revolutions occurring in Cairo and the plague ravaging Egypt, conditions might have improved for the Latin principalities, had they not become so weak that they were incapable of further effort. Aware that he could expect no help from the Latins, Hetum negotiated with Melik-Adelzein-ed-Dinket bogha who had seized the Mameluke throne, ousting Nascer-Mohammed, and the Moslem ruler gave him back part of the prisoners taken at Romela together with the holy vessels and relics that had been taken with the booty.

SEAL OF BROTHER IAN (HETUM II)

Discouraged by the countless difficulties besetting him at every step, Hetum abdicated in favor of his brother Thoros and withdrew to a monastery, but urged by the Armenian nobles and by Thoros himself to resume the reins of state, he emerged from his retreat. Disputes had arisen among the kinsmen of Genghis-Khan, and the court of Sis followed with anxiety the events transpiring in the reigning family of the Mongols, the only allies to whom the Armenians could look. The new Khan quite willingly renewed the former treaty of alliance with the king of Armenia. On his return to Sis, Hetum was overjoyed to find awaiting him there a Byzantine embassy sent to ask him for the hand of his sister Ritha (Margaret) in marriage to Michael, recently raised to share the Imperial throne. The princess took the name of Xéné (Mary).

LEADEN BULLA OF THOROS

THOROS KING OF ARMENIA, 1293-1295

These alliances with the Mongols and the Greeks and the traditional friendship of the Armenians and the Latins offered Hetum a hope of his country escaping for a while the Egyptian menace. Being anxious to strengthen his ties with the Byzantine court, he proceeded to Constantinople, but his second brother Sempad took advantage of his absence to seize the crown (1296-1298). The usurper captured his two elder brothers at Caesarea and caused Thoros to be strangled, and Hetum to be blinded. Constantine, the prince royal, who had helped his brother Sempad in his seizure of the throne was shocked by these wicked deeds and therefore captured him in turn and held him prisoner, setting Hetum free, and proclaiming himself king (1298-1299).

SEMPAD & CONSTANTINE USURPERS, (1296-1298)

Within a few months Hetum recovered his sight, and the nobles restored to him his crown, in spite of opposition on the part of Constantine and Sempad. The latter were both taken and exiled to Constantinople, where they died.

During Constantine's short reign, Armenia suffered invasion and devas-

COINS OF SEMPAD KING OF ARMENIA

— 242 —

tation once more by the Egyptians, and the enemy captured Tell-Hamdoun and laid seige to Hamous, which held out. The historian Abulfeda, who later became governor of Hamath, tells us that, finding its food supply nearly exhausted, the defenders of the city put outside the walls twelve hundred women and children who were divided among the Moslems, and that he for his share had two maidens and one boy. The usurper obtained peace only by surrendering Hamous and ten other fortified places.

"The Egyptian army consisted of "two divisions, one under Emir Bedred-"din-Bektasch, and the other under Mel-"ik Moudhaffer Takieddin Mahmoud, "Prince of Hama. The former advanced "through the gorge of Bagras towards "the city of Iskanderoun [Alexandretta], "and laid siege to Tell-Hamdoun, whilst "Melik-Moudhaffer went forward on the "side of the Djeihan river. They entered "the gorge of Sis on Thursday, the fourth "day of the month Redjeb [April 17th, "1299]. The Prince of Hama pitched "his camp under the walls of Sis, and "Emir Bektasch took the road to Adana. "There the various detachments of the "Moslem army joined one another after "slaughtering all the inhabitants they "met, collecting all the oxen and buffaloes, and pillaging in all directions. "They then left Adana and returning to Mecica within three days, they "passed through the gorge of Bagras and camped not far from Antioch. "The emirs received, however, orders from Sultan Latchin to attack the "Armenians once more and not to come back without having taken Tell-"Hamdoun. From Roudj [Rugia] the army passed through the gorge of "Bagras again and proceeded towards Sis, whilst Kedjken and Kara-"Anslar advanced against Aïas. The two officers were caught by a sur-"prise attack from the Armenians in ambush, and compelled to beat a "hasty retreat. In the meantime Emir Bektasch advanced against Tell-"Hamdoun which he found abandoned by the Armenians; he entered "and garrisoned the place on the 7th day of the month Ramadhan [June "18th]. At the same time Emir Beiban-Tabakhi, Naïb [deputy-governor]

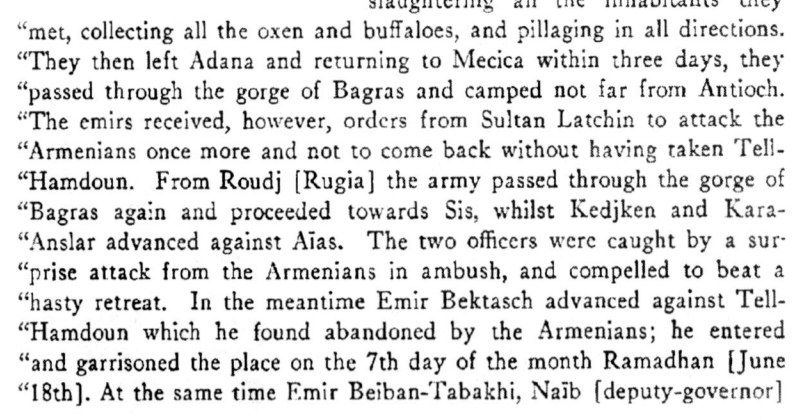

COINS OF CONSTANTINE II OF ARMENIA

"of Aleppo, captured the city of Marasch. The fortress of Nedjimah, con-
"taining a large Armenian population of laborers, countrywomen, and
"their children, surrendered after forty-one days of stubborn resistance
"to the attacks of Emir Bektasch and the Prince of Hama. The Egyp-
"tians captured it in the month Dsulkada [August-September]. The in-
"habitants who had capitulated on terms were allowed to go where they
"wished. Eleven fortified places in Armenian territory likewise fell to
"the conquerors who remained in possession of them until the arrival of

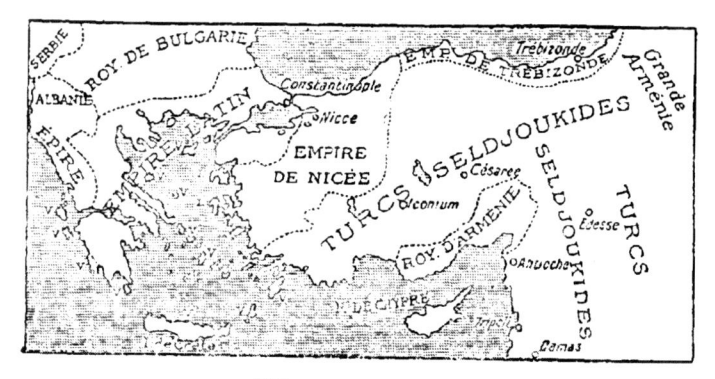

EMPIRE OF NICAEA
(V: Venetian possessions—L: Crusaders' possessions)

"the Tartars. Then the Emir sold all there was of value in them, and
"evacuated the fortresses which were reoccupied by the Armenians (1)."

HETUM'S RETURN TO POWER

Hetum having regained his power, the Mongols now emerged into Syria and supported by the Armenians gained a great victory over the Mamelukes near Homs (22-23 December 1299). The Egyptians were driven from the valley of the Orontes, and Damascus itself fell into the victors' hands. The Armenians restored their former status by the recovery of the territory that had been taken from them. Four years later, however, Egypt's Sultan avenged himself by a crushing defeat of the Allied Mongol and Armenian armies near Damascus (April 20th, 1303). The latter were annihilated, and King Hetum fled for refuge to Khazan at Mossul.

---
(1) MAKRISI. Histoire des Sulthans Mamlouks. transl. Et. QUATREMERE vol. II, part 2, p 60-65.

For a number of years the Mongols had been wavering as to the direction in which they should turn politically. They were still heathen at this time, and with their eye on world events wondered whether to lean toward the Moslems and adopt their religion or toward the Latins and become Christians. The very precarious position into which the Frankish principalities had fallen and Europe's virtual abandonment of them—when considered alongside the great military strength of the Mamelukes—tipped the scales in favor of the Prophet. Had Europe sent a fresh Crusade to the East, the greater part of Asia would have become Christian and the Latins with the aid of the Mongols would have driven Islam back into the Arabian desert. Civilization lost a unique opportunity to crush its hydra-headed foe.

Hetum and Leo, however, continued to be treated as allies by the Khans, and as such to be harassed by the Egyptians whose invasions were becoming ever more frequent and disastrous for Cilicia.

**LEO III
KING OF ARMENIA
1303-1307**

At this date (1305) Hetum finally gave up his crown after first seating on the throne his nephew Leo, the son of Thoros III and Margaret of Lusignan, then only 16 years old. He retained for himself the title of Grand Baron. But the young prince had hardly been crowned when Bilarghu and his Mongols came to the walls of Anazarbus. They were asked inside the city to discuss matters, and once inside they set upon Hetum, Leo III, and a score of Armenian nobles and massacred them. This treacherous crime was reportedly committed at the instigation of other members of the nobility who resented what they considered too close a rapprochement between the elderly king and his young nephew and heir on the one hand, and the Pope and the Catholic ritual on the other. The historian Samuel of Ani (1) voices the discontent among Armenian nationalists caused by the decisions reached at the

COINS OF LEO III OF ARMENIA

---

(1) Histoire des Croisades, Documents armeniens, I, p. 456.

— 245 —

Council of Sis (1307-1308), which seem to show the reasons for the murder of the king and his nobles. He writes: "During the reign of Pope Constantine of Caesarea [1307-1322] the grand Baron Hetum held a Council [at Sis] wherein union with the Church of Rome was effected and the teachings of our Illuminator [St. Gregory] set at nought. It was agreed that Christmas be celebrated on December 25th, and the saints' days on their respective dates, also that water should be used in the chalice in the celebration of Mass."

OCHIN, KING OF ARMENIA 1308-1320

Hetum's fourth brother, Ochin, was informed of the heinous assassination by a messenger from the governor of Anazarbus, and rushing to the spot he drove the Mongols out of Cilicia, pursuing them to the frontier. On his return he had himself crowned in the Cathedral of Tarsus. His religious opinions were not different from those of Hetum, consequently he too met with violent opposition from some of the nobles and the early part of his reign was taken up in subduing their revolts.

COINS OF OCHIN, KING OF ARMENIA

Samuel of Ani writes further (1): "This year 1309-1310 there assembled at Sis, the capital of the kingdom, a large number of monks and clergy, priests and deacons, doctors and bishops, together with many of the people, both men and women, all opposed to the use of water in the chalice at Mass and other changes. King Ochin with the consent of the Patriarch and the chief nobles seized all these people, imprisoned the doctors in the fortress and put to death very many men and women together with some of the clergy and deacons. He then packed the monks onto a vessel, and exiled them to Cyprus, where most of them died."

---

(1) *Op. cit.*, p. 466.

His nephew's murder at the behest of the insurgents and his absolute need of peace within his borders in order to meet the peril from without forced Ochin to take drastic steps against these fanatics who were willing to sacrifice the nation's welfare to their personal feelings and to trivialities relating to church ritual.

COIN OF HENRY II, KING OF CYPRUS

Amaury, Prince of Tyre, had married Isabel, Ochin's sister, whereby the king of Armenia became involved in the affairs of the kingdom of Cyprus, Henry II of Lusignan having been ousted by his brother Amaury and exiled to Cilicia. There Ochin, taking his brother-in-law's part, imprisoned him in the Castle of Lampron. Amaury however was murdered (June 5th, 1310), and at the entreaty of the Pope's legate, Raymond de Pin, Henry II was released and reconciled with Isabel.

The principality of Cyprus was the last remnant of Latin dominion in the East, the king of Armenia's last hope of gaining the ear of Europe; consequently he did everything in his power to retain the friendship of the sovereigns of the island. The Western world, however, was losing interest in the fate of Armenia, and all Ochin could obtain was a grant of thirty thousand sequins sent him by the Pope at Avignon, John XXII (1316-1334). Meanwhile the Moslems continued to ravage Cilicia, and the Armenians continued their struggle to defend their land, sometimes even scoring temporary success, but what could they hope for, isolated as they were now against a sea of enemies!

**LEO IV
KING OF ARMENIA
1320-1342**

Upon Ochin's death (July 20, 1320) his young son Leo IV (1320-1342) ascended the throne. As he was only ten years old, the dying king appointed as Regent Ochin, Count of Gorigos. This nobleman was the brother of Isabel, King Ochin's first wife, and was therefore the new king's uncle. It was accordingly necessary to obtain a special letter (August 10, 1321)

(1) from Pope John XXII to permit the marriage of the youthful sovereign to his cousin Alice, the daughter of the Count. The latter married about the same time Queen Joan, the widow of the Count of Tyre.

The Moslem devastations went on unceasingly; if the Tartars from Iconium were not raiding the country, the Mamelukes in their turn were sowing death and destruction in Cilicia. The Armenian nobles shut themselves up in their castles, and as soon as the storm was over, they resumed their feuds with their neighbors and with their king.

COINS OF LEO IV
KING OF ARMENIA

Once more the Pope interceded and pleaded for Armenia to king Philip V of France (June 22, 1322), likewise to the Mogul Khan of Persia (July 4, 1322). The latter sent twenty thousand Tartars to Leo's assistance. Sultan Malek-en-Nascer thus threatened consented to a peace treaty to last fifteen years in consideration of an annual tribute of fifty thousand gold florins, plus one half of the customs revenues of the port of Aïas and one half of the proceeds of the sale of salt to foreigners. On these terms he withdrew his troops from Armenia.

The western world's concern for Armenia waned, however, more and more. All the Pope's endeavors to start a new Crusade were fruitless. Philip VI of Valois sent ten thousand gold bezants and later on one thousand florins, but the only monarch to make an alliance with Leo III was Hugh IV, king of Cyprus. Leo's territory still suffered from onslaughts by the Moslems notwithstanding the treaty signed by the Sultan.

---

(1) Vatican archives. Reg. Epist. commun. an V. part II. fol. 205, 1326.

Furthermore, the young Armenian king deserved little consideration personally, for he was guilty of crimes of all sorts. On January 26th, 1329, he caused the arrest and death of the Regent Ochin and his brother the Constable Constantine and to curry favor with his most formidable enemies, he sent the head of the former to Malek-en-Nascer and of the latter to the Mogul Khan Abou-Saïd. This double murder was shortly afterwards followed by that of his own wife whom he killed in a fit of anger on the grounds that she had been unfaithful to him. The nineteen year old self-made widower married in 1333 the daughter of Frederick II of Sicily, Constance Eleonora, the widow of Henry II of Cyprus. Finally on August 28th, 1341, Leo himself succumbed to the assassins' daggers, after experiencing fresh defeats by the Mamelukes and swearing on the sacred gospels "that he would have no further relations with the Latins."

LEO IV ADMINISTERING JUSTICE

Leo's life undoubtedly covers him with obloquy, but history should not pass so severe a condemnation on this ruler as it would on a king living in a different environment and under the care of a upright regent. His guardian, Ochin, took over all the royal attributes as soon as the former king died, and proceeded to make himself hated for his inordinate pride and insatiable lust for power. One and all had to cringe to his fancy. He put to death or exiled any who did not bow to his will, and Isabel, king Ochin's sister and the widow of Amaury of Lusignan, was strangled at his orders. Four of Isabel's five children who lived in Armenia were arrested at the same time as their mother; the two eldest, Hugh and Henry, were poisoned, and the two others driven out of Armenia. The cruelties of the Count of Gorigos made him hated by most of the nobles and especially by the king whom as his ward he

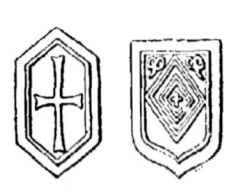

ESCUTCHEONS OF TARSUS

treated most harshly. Leo incensed at his uncle's behavior to him took vengeance, and rid himself of a mentor whose yoke became so intolerable. This first crime dulled his conscience and was the forerunner of further misdeeds.

Jean Dardel writes: (1) "When the aforesaid Baron Ossin had married the Lady Joan of Naples he was so cruel that all who had been hostile to him he caused to be slain or driven from the country. Among others he caused to be murdered by strangling the aforesaid Lady Isabel, the sister of the late King Ochin. Her four children were imprisoned, and two of them put to death, namely Sir Hugh, whom he caused to be poisoned, and Sir Henry. The latter asked for the love of God a little water, whereupon he had him given urine to drink And the other two, namely, Sir John and Sir Bemon at the prayer of some of the nobles he took out of prison and had them put out to sea on a boat so that they should drift wherever they might. These two reached the island of Rhodes and the Knights Hospitalers received them kindly and they remained there three years. Following all of which, the aforesaid Baron Ossin gave his own daughter Aalips [Alix] in marriage to the aforesaid King Leo the Fourth, who was a minor and under his guardianship."

It must be remembered that in all the Latin courts of the East, and unfortunately also in European courts, there reigned at the time considerable lawlessness. Assassination was a usual political weapon, at Byzantium, Cairo, and all the Asiatic cities intrigue, murder, poisoning, were the order of the day. Vengeance was assuaged by horrible massacres, human life counted for naught either with the Christians or the Moslems No one was sure of his life for the morrow, and those who held their own lives so cheap were all the more indifferent to the fate of others.

KING OF ARMENIA, GUY OF LUSIGNAN (CONSTANTINE II) 1342-1344

An important event took place at the death of Leo IV (1342). As this king had no male heir he named as his successor the third son of his sister Isabel, Guy of Lusignan, his nearest kinsman, who at the time of the murder of his mother and brothers had been in safety with the Greeks. Consequently the crown of Cilicia passed from the Armenian princes to a French family of nobles, and the kingdom of Armenia thus became a coun-

---

(1) Chap. XXIII

try under Latin government. In those days when the State was synonymous with the ruler, this was a far-reaching change, for Latin influence would necessarily predominate and national tradition would suffer. For this reason the majority of the Armenian inhabitants remained hostile to the new reigning family. Their clergy and nobility realized that their national identity might disappear, and this would undoubtedly have been the case if the principalities of the Crusaders had been destined to last longer.

Guy was the son of Amaury of Lusignan, Count of Tyre, and of Isabel of Armenia. He was the nephew of Henry II of Cyprus. This prince had been living since 1318 at Constantinople with his aunt Xéné or Mary, the wife of Michael IX Palaeologus (1295-1320) and the mother of Emperor Andronicus (1328-1341). He was Imperial governor of Pheres (Serrhes) in Macedonia, and his first wife was a cousin of John Cantacuzene (1341-1355). Having opposed the usurper of the throne of John V Palaeologus, he was forced to open the gates of Pheres to Michael and retired to Constantinople. In 1342 Guy knew that Leo had chosen him for the Armenian throne, but he was not anxious to accept the honor, knowing as he did the desperate straits the kingdom was in. First of all he refused and asked his brother John, the Constable, Isabel's

COIN OF MICHAEL X PALAEOLOGUS

COIN OF JOHN V PALAEOLOGUS

COIN OF ANDRONICUS III PALAEOLOGUS

other son who lived at Rhodes, to take the crown. Yielding to John's entreaties, he finally set out for Armenia, accompanied by a considerable body-guard.

Disturbed by this change of dynasty and by the intimate connection

COIN OF GUY OF LUSIGNAN
(CONSTANTINE II)

about to exist between Armenia and the kings of Cyprus and the western powers, the Moslems called for payment of the annual dues paid them by Leo. Guy haughtily refused, whereupon war flared up again. The new king who reigned as Constantine II upheld his reputation for valor, and during the two years of his reign (1342-1344), he prevented any Moslem encroachment on his frontiers.

Guy was of the opinion, however, like Hetum and most of his predecessors, that the best policy for the Armenians, if they were to receive from the western world the assistance they so absolutely needed, was to adopt the Roman way of worship. Two ambassadors were sent to Avignon, and the king called together all the chief dignitaries of the Armenian Church to discuss the manner in which the union might be brought about. These negotiations aroused the ire of some of the nobles who were already very vexed by the king's determination not to purchase peace from the Moslems by abandoning territory. The malcontents stirred up a riot in which the king was slain together with three hundred Frankish guardsmen whom Guy had brought with him to Armenia. "Great pity it was "for Christendom, the death of so good a prince, for he was brave and "valorous and very enterprising."

"When the good king Guy de Lissignan reigned in Armenia, he "governed the country with puissance, valiancy, and sovereignty. He "loved and served God with all his heart, and upheld and defended the "common cause with all his power, and the country's freedom did he "most diligently protect, without paying any truce-money whatever to "the infidels. Without respite he withstood his foes and took the field "against them very frequently. And because some Armenians were of "the opinion that he overworked them and too often took them into battle, "a great number of them gathered together and arming themselves pro-"ceeded to the place where their natural liege, Guy, was with his brother "Sir Bemon de Lisegnan, Count of Courch. And without giving them "any warning, they killed them, putting them to death feloniously and "treacherously, falsely and without cause, and with them a very large "number of men-at-arms whom he had brought with his company from the "Western Country to protect the land of Armenia. And those Armenians "also killed a priest belonging to the king's household, while he was "chanting the Mass. All this they did in one day in the city of Adenez [Adana]." (1)

CONSTANTINE III KING OF ARMENIA 1344 1363

The nobles elected Constantine (1344-1363), the eldest son of Baldwin of Neghir, who had died in 1336 in the prison-house of the Emir of Aleppo. For the first time the kingdom of New Armenia chose a ruler outside of the baronial house of Hetum. The new monarch was, however, related to the royal dynasty by his marriage with Mary, the daughter of the Regent Ochin and Joan of Anjou.

The first act of this sovereign was infamous. He confiscated the property of Soldane, the wife of John of Lusignan, and her children Bohemon and Leo, aged five and two years respectively, and shut up the princess and the two little boys on the island of Gorigos where he attempted to kill them by sending them poisoned honey. Failing in this, he ordered the three captives to be drowned. Soldane was warned fortunately and escaped with her two children to Cyprus, where she placed herself under the protection of Hugh IV of Lusignan.

COINS OF CONSTANTINE III OF ARMENIA

Meanwhile negotiations with the Pope continued, and Guy's delegates were still at Avignon when that king was assassinated. Constantine had hardly ascended the throne when at the request of Pope Clement VI's legate, he summoned a new Council at Sis (1345), which assembly discussed the one hundred and seventeen errors imputed to the Armenians and set forth in a Memorandum presented to Benedict XII. Once more, the Armenians agreed to accept all the stipulations of the Holy See.

COIN OF DIEUDONNE OF GOZON

During this time, Armenia

---

(1) Jean DARDEL, chap. XXXIX.

— 253 —

had still to fight against its age-long enemies and once more lost the port of Aïas. Things were becoming more critical every day, but no power in Europe intervened in behalf of the Armenians notwithstanding the repeated entreaties of Pope Clement VI. Through the support of the Grand Master of Rhodes, Dieudonné of Gozon, Aïas was restored to Constantine, but towards the end of the same year, the port was blockaded and captured by the Egyptian fleet, and the Turcomans of Iconium, who were already in possession of Phrygia, marched on Tarsus. At this time the kings of France and England had just signed a two-years' truce, and Philip VI died the same year (1350). Edward III turned a deaf ear to the appeals of the Holy See which, although still involved in the religious problems with the Armenians, continued to assist Constantine with frequent subsidies. While the church discussions dragged on, the distance between Sis and Avignon making them extremely lengthy, Moslem attacks on Armenia went on relentlessly. In 1359 Sultan Al Melek-en-Nascer Hassan's army invaded Cilicia, took Sis, Adana, Tarsus, and all the lowlands, stationed garrisons there and carried off an enormous quantity of booty to Aleppo. On top of this the Moslems of Karaman came and besieged Gorigos (Curco), which was delivered by Peter I of Cyprus.

PETER I. KING OF CYPRUS

The Cypriots thereupon armed a fleet of one hundred and forty-six galleys which was joined by the naval forces of the Knights of Rhodes and those of the Pope. In command of this imposing navy, Peter I of Lusignan captured Satalia and achieved a few other successes, but considering that the Eastern Latins were not numerous enough to be a match for their enemies, he decided to go to Western Europe and ask for reinforcements, and accordingly set sail for Venice. He took with him Bohemon of Lusignan, the son of John and nephew of the late king Guy, whom one Armenian party wanted for their king. It was Peter's intention to have Bohemon crowned by the Pope, but this prince died at Venice at the age of twenty-four. By reason of this death, Peter might have laid claims to the crown of Sis, but the king of Cyprus was concerned with more far-reaching matters; his endeavor was to bring about a new Crusade. John the Good, at the urgent prayer of Urban V took the cross and asked two years in which to get ready, but his death which occurred on April 19th, 1364, frustrated this new venture.

Peter I continued nevertheless with his plans, seeking support and recruits throughout western Europe, and obtaining money with Urban V's assistance.

CONSTANTINE IV KING OF ARMENIA, 1365-1373

In 1363, Constantine III of Armenia died leaving no heir. A party of Armenians wrote to the Pope claiming the crown for Guy's heirs Urban V nominated Leo (1363-1365), a near kinsman of Peter I. During this time, however, the Armenian party who were opposed to the Lusignans, and considered them as usurpers, obtained the election of Constantine IV (1365-1373), the son of Hetum, Chamberlain of Armenia, and nephew of Marshall Baldwin, the father of Constantine III. Peter accepted the *fait accompli*, and Constantine recognized him as his suzerain, with the result that the king of Cyprus thereafter gave assistance to his feudatory and helped Armenia tremendously against the Moslems The Venetians and Genoese, and the Aragonese, remained neutral in these conflicts. They had signed trade treaties with the Sultans of Egypt, and notwithstanding the Pope's threats of excommunication against any Christians dealing with the Moslems, they were only concerned with the success of their business. Anyone but Peter would have lost courage at being abandoned by the very people who had so generously contributed to the success of the first Crusades, but nothing could cool his fervor and on June 27th, 1365, he valiantly set sail from Venice with thirty galleys commanded by French, Italian, German, and English knights Two Byzantine nobles also accompanied them. He sailed to Rhodes, where he formed his small army consisting of ten thousand men and one thousand knights, undoubtedly all of them arrant freebooters Alexandria in Egypt was taken by storm and sacked, but abandoned when the Mamelukes later counter-attacked From Egypt he turned northward and laid waste all the Syrian coast as far as Aïas, where he was withstood by the fortresses, and was unable to obtain Constantine's help in time

> Là li bon roy, que Dieus aye,
> Atendoit le roy d'Ermenie
> Et ses messages li manda,
> Et au partir leur commanda
> Qu'il li deissent qu'il venist,

> Et que convenant li tenist,
> Et venist à tout son effort
> Pour li faire aide et confort,
> Car il est venus comme amis
> Einsi comme il li a promis.
> Quand ce vint au chief des VIII jours,
> Au roy ennuia li séjours,
> Pour ce que le roy d'Ermenie
> Par devers lui ne venoit mie,
> Et pour l'iver qui aprochoit .... (1)

(Translation:

> There the good King, whom God help,
> Awaited the King of Armenia
> And sent to him his messengers
> And commanded them on leaving
> That they tell him that he come,
> And that he keep his agreement,
> And come with all his might
> To give him aid and comfort,
> For he was come as his friend
> As indeed he had promised him.
> When it came to the end of 8 days,
> The King wearied of his waiting
> Because the King of Armenia
> Did not come to help him,
> And because of the approaching winter ...)

The king of Cyprus thereupon returned to the West in search of fresh subsidies and troops, and while he was at Venice an Armenian deputation arrived to offer him the crown. Setting sail for Cyprus on September 28th, 1368, he was intending to cross over into Cilicia and be crowned when he was assassinated on January 16th, 1369, at Nicosia, by some nobles whom, it was said, he had offended by treating them disdainfully. Armenia meanwhile was again the prey of Moslem bands from Egypt, Syria, and Asia Minor.

---

(1) Guillaume de MACHAUT. *La Prise d'Alexandrie.*

The chronicler writes:

"After the death of the king, Constant [Constantine III] the tyrant, "the Armenians chose another king, son of Baron Heyton who was named "Constant [Constantine IV]. They did not elect him king on account "of noble birth but because of wealth, for he was of base-born Cypriot "extraction; and because the kingdom of Armenia was oppressed by the "Infidels, he sent word to the king of Cyprus of whose house he was that "it should please him to receive him in his kingdom freely, him and all "his estate, and that he should do with the kingdom of Armenia entirely "according to his good pleasure. When King Peter heard the petition "of King Constant of Armenia, he coveted the Seigneury thereof for "himself; he kept the aforesaid letters from the Holy Father [giving the "crown to Prince Leo of Lusignan] and did not show or hand them to "the said Sir Leo. But . . . God willed that he be frustrated in his intent "and did not allow him to transfer to Cyprus all the royal wealth of which "he had stripped the kingdom and robbed from the people's possessions, "for the Infidels then occupied the ports [excepting Gorighos]. And also "in the meantime King Peter of Cyprus was slain by his barons and "vassals. Thus it behooved King Constantine to remain in Armenia "against his will."

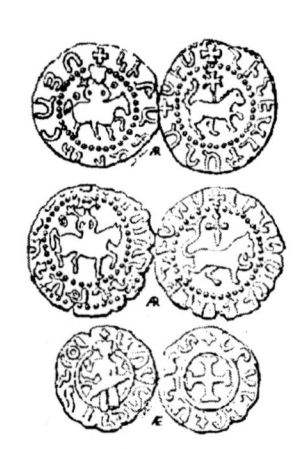

COINS OF CONSTANTINE IV OF ARMENIA

Constantine IV seemed, moreover, to have taken little interest in his kingdom's welfare and to have made no effort to deliver his country from Moslem depredation. The chroniclers figure him as a tyrant, a kind of interloper who abandoned the government to Queen Mary (Miriam), the wife of the late king Constantine III. This princess sent embassies to her uncle Philip of Taranto, the Emperor of Constantinople, and to Pope Gregory XI. The latter stirred up all Europe in his desire to help the Armenians.

Unfortunately the Latin cause in the East was irretrievably ruined by a dispute which broke out among the Christians. The upset occurred on the island of Cyprus between Venetians and Genoese over a question of precedence. The island was laid waste and condemned to pay 40,000 sequins to the Genoese. Finally, on January 12th, 1372, Peter II was crowned King of Cyprus at Nicosia and on the following October 12th, King of Jerusalem at Famagusta.

LEO V OF LUSIGNAN KING OF ARMENIA 1374-1375

Leo, Isabel of Armenia's only surviving grandson, had been brought up in Cyprus. Pope Urban V had suggested as early as 1365 that he should have the Armenian crown, but various schemings had kept him from leaving the Cyprus court. On several occasions after Peter I's death, he refused the throne when offered to him. At last, however, upon the assassination of Constantine IV by his subjects (April 1373), Prince Leo yielded to the entreaties of the barons, the clergy, Queen Mary, and Queen Joan, and accepted the crown. The situation was desperate, and the bells that rang for the new sovereign's coronation sounded in fact the knell of the last Armenian kingdom.

Even before Constantine IV's assassination, the insurgent barons had given the regency to Queen Mary. A letter from Pope Gregory XI (dated February 1st, 1372) to Philip III of Taranto, the titular emperor of Constantinople, bears this out. It reads "Mary, Queen of Armenia, "niece of Philip of Taranto, asks the Pope to come to her assistance against "the Moslems who are greatly endangering her country; she has sent "John, the Bishop of Sis, as her ambassador to the Holy See, and the "latter expresses the desire that the Queen should find a husband among "the Latin nobles able to defend and govern Armenia. The Pope urges "John, Prince of Antioch and Regent of Cyprus, also the Venetians, the "Genoese and the Knights of Rhodes to help the Armenians. He desig- "nates Otto of Brunswick as having all the qualities that would fit him "to become Mary's husband in the present circumstances. (1)"

The Pope's letter was not acted upon. Thereupon Queen Mary despatched to Peter II of Cyprus a knight. Lyon Hamoncy, and two citizens of Sis bearing a letter of which the substance has been preserved for us by Jean Dardel (2)

---

(1) RAYNALDI, ann. 1372, part XXX.
(2) chap. LIII.

"Sire: The Queen of Armenia, the former wife of the autocrat King Constant the First, who today by common assent holds the sovereignty of the kingdom, and our Catholicos, our lord barons and noble knights and all the people hereby do humble obeisance to your Lordship, and inform you that God has wrought His will anent their king Constant, son of Baron Heyton [Hetum], who was no whit their true and natural Sovereign. And now are they without a king, and because their true and natural sovereign is in this land of Cyprus and his name is Lord Lyon of Lisegnan, your cousin the Seneschal of Jerusalem, they do humbly beseech Your Excellency to grant unto him permission to depart from Cyprus and to come and receive the kingdom of Armenia, his true heritage, because we are well aware that he has done homage to you for the fief which he holds in your dominion through his Lady. And should it be that your Lordship were unwilling to permit him so to leave, you must know that the whole country and Christian life of Armenia is perishing and falling to the Infidels, which God forbid as it would be a great calamity and loss for Christendom. Wherefore, Sire, for God's sake and for mercy's sake, do not suffer that this ruin and disaster should happen in your day to Christendom."

COINS OF LEO V OF LUSIGNAN KING OF ARMENIA

But Leo, being Peter II's vassal by reason of his wife's fiefs and obliged to deal prudently with the king of Cyprus as his crown's only support, was unable, immediately upon acceptance, to go to Armenia and take up the reins of government. Peter replied to the Armenian delegates that he could not allow the prince to go until peace with the Genoese had been restored in the island. Leo was therefore obliged to continue with

COIN OF PETER II OF CYPRUS

the campaign against the Italians and to arrange for a provisional government in Armenia consisting of Queen Mary, Phemya, Constantine's sister, Bohemond, Count of Gorigos, and Baron Basil, the son of Baron Thoros. The future king's main anxiety was how to increase the financial resources of the kingdom. This concern is easy to understand in view of the need of raising an army to meet the Moslems, but even Jean Dardel's memoirs which were mostly written at royal dictation rather show that Leo looked to the main chance in his personal affairs.

LEO V AT CYPRUS The delegates returned to Armenia by the port of Gorigos, the only one that had not fallen to the Infidels. They were accompanied by the knight Constant, Leo's equerry, also by Manuel the interpreter, who were both entrusted with the duty of attending to the needs of the royal Treasury. When they arrived outside Sis, they had to cross the lines of Beydemur, governor of Damascus, who was besieging the capital but who withdrew soon after, finding himself unable to take it.

VIEW OF THE CITY AND CASTLE OF GORIGOS

Matters were meanwhile becoming worse for Peter II and Leo in Cyprus. The Genoese succeeded by stratagem in seizing the city of Famagusta, and having got possession of the rest of the island they demanded from the inhabitants the huge sum of 2,560,000 ducats as war indemnity, plus interest at the fantastic rate of 60 per cent, besides the personal levies exacted for their own account by the Italian commanders. Leo was called on to pay the conquerors 36,000 silver bezants, equal to 280 pounds of gold. His silverware, crown, and wardrobe were taken and only restored him on payment of three hundred ducats. In addition, the Genoese admiral, Pietro de Campo Fregoso, the brother of Domenico, the Doge, kept for himself the finest jewel in the royal crown, a ruby, and extracted a promise of 10,000 gold florins to be paid him later. So much for Genoa's obedience to the Pope! Throughout the wars of the Crusaders whether against the Moslems or the Greeks, the Genoese and Venetians had their eye only on profit. Sometimes they gave a little assistance to their Latin brethren, but only as a business policy. Now that the Christian cause was irretrievably lost in the East, they had no further reason to retain the mask.

TOMBSTONE AT NICOSIA

The Cypriots, ground down by the extortions of the Genoese and of their ruler Peter II together with Peter's mother Catherine of Aragon, managed to meet the grievous demands on them, but Leo after surrendering all he had, was obliged to appeal to the Armenian treasury at Sis to help him out of the plight he was in through none of his own seeking. Before leaving, he had yet to give up to Catherine of Aragon his wife's fief with its yearly revenue of 1,000 gold bezants, and also to undertake not to set foot inside the Castle of Gorigos, on the coast of Asia, although it had been ceded to the Armenians by the king of Cyprus. He was to occupy only the castle out at sea on an island some distance from the port. In this precarious situation, stripped by the Genoese and his own Lusignan family of the funds that he most urgently needed, the new king of Armenia landed on the shores of his kingdom on Easter Sunday, April 2nd, 1374. Leo was forced to conceal his resentment both from Cyprus and the Genoese, for they alone could furnish him the means to take the field and seize Tarsus,

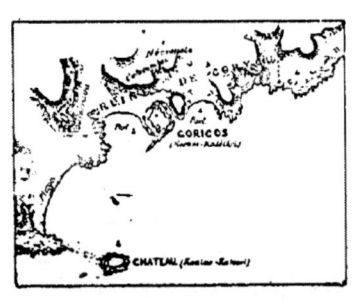

PLAN OF THE PORT OF GORIGOS

which fortress was garrisoned by no more than three hundred Mamelukes. He sold his silverware and his wife's crown to money-lenders, and on receipt of the proceeds the King of Cyprus sent him one hundred soldiers, men-at-arms or cross-bowmen, under the French equerry Sohier Doulcart, a Genoese mercenary. These and a few cross-bowmen and archers whom he recruited at Gorigos made up the small army with which Leo hoped to be a match for the Infidels. The Genoese admiral, even though he had accepted the sums of money sent him, refused to supply the king

VIEW OF THE CASTLE OF GORIGOS

with ships to attack Tarsus by way of the river, "because of the business alliance which the Genoese have with the Saracens." ("pour cause de l'aliance que les Jennevois ont avecques les Sarrasins pour le fait de leurs marchandises.")

The poor young king's difficulties had only just begun. Thinking he could confide his plans to the Commandant at Gorigos who was an Armenian, Leo was treacherously betrayed, for the former notified the Moslem governor of Tarsus and made Peter II and the Genoese believe that Leo was gathering an army in order to cross over to Cyprus and fight for John of Lusignan, Prince of Antioch, against his nephew, the King of Cyprus. Leo had not a moment to lose, for the Genoese galleys would certainly soon arrive to take him prisoner. He sent his mother and wife to the city of Gorigos and he himself left the island where he had remained as he had promised, setting out at midnight with a few men. He landed over seventy-five miles from Gorigos, near the mouth of the Adana river. His knight Doulcart joined him on the following day with twenty-five horsemen and an equal number of cross-bowmen.

Unable to attack Tarsus, Leo decided to go to Sis, the seat of the Council of Regency. To reach the capital he had to cross a region infested with Mamelukes, therefore he needed to move with great speed. The cross-bowmen on foot could not keep up with the horsemen, and so Leo gave them guides and sent them by mountain by-passes.

"And as soon as the heat of the day was past, Sir Leo and his com-
"pany made the sign of the cross and commended themselves to God.
"They mounted the 25 horses, while the 25 arbalesters with two guides
"went on foot. They proceeded until nightfall when the two guides told
"my Lord Leo that he must go forward with speed, for there were many
"dangerous places on their way manned with Turks and Saracens who
"knew of his coming and whom he would have more trouble getting by
"in the daytime than at night. Therefore Sir Leo started to go fast, and
"because he saw that the 25 arbalesters afoot could not follow him, he
"gave them one of the guides to lead them by another way in the moun-
"tains. They went two days and two nights without dismounting, and so

VIEW OF THE CASTLE OF CHAHI-MARAN (CILICIA)

"long and forced was their effort and so great the heat they suffered, that
"two of their company died. Nevertheless, by the grace of God, they
"passed unharmed through the midst of their enemies guarding the passes,
"and they came to within three leagues of the city of Sis. It was not yet
"day, and they dismounted to rest and refresh themselves and their
"horses, for they were sore exhausted. And at day-break, Sir Leo sent

"two messengers on horseback to the city of Sis, to the Queen and citizens, "to acquaint them with his arrival. (1)

Preceded by the Catholicos, prelates, and nobles, a crowd of citizens came out with music and dancing to welcome their king. They were transported with joy, for they had become so utterly discouraged that a number of people were thinking of revolting and killing the members of the Regency, and then surrendering the city to the Infidels.

One hundred and fifty armed men, sent out four days later by the king's orders to the mouth of the river Seihan, brought back his mother and the Queen as far as Anazarbus without encountering the enemy. Unfortunately because of the unwillingness of the people of Gorigos to supply means of transport for the Latins who had accompanied the two princesses to that city, many of them could not leave. The princesses with their suite left Anazarbus about noon and arrived about a league from Sis a little before nightfall.

"When the aforesaid Ladies and their company were one league "away from Sis, they sent word to my Lord Leo who immediately had "the trumpets sound a call to arms, and he armed himself and ordered "his French and Armenian men-at-arms that had remained with him, so "to do. Then went out my Lord Leo and his company to meet the Ladies, "and there followed him all the people in a great procession, each with "a torch in his hand. And when they had met the Ladies, they welcomed "them with great joy and great festivity. And when night fell, they lit "their torches of which there were so many that they extended from one "end of the city to the other, almost one league in length (1)"

After enjoying for a few days his happy arrival, Leo, who was worried over the low estate his unfortunate kingdom had fallen into, and who had long been cherishing thought-out plans for reorganizing it, enquired concerning the state of the Treasury. Besides the royal assets, it was supposed to contain 100,000 ducats which had been previously offered him. Great was his disappointment when he found that the Treasury was empty and that all that was left in it, according to Dardel, was a crown. In vain did they try to explain to him that the Regency had been compelled not only to buy off the Moslems with money but to appease likewise the leaders of factions within the city of Sis itself. The king was not satisfied with these excuses, and on looking over the accounts show-

---

(1) Jean DARDEL, chap LXXII
(1) Jean DARDEL, chap LXXV

ing the disbursements he considered them excessive. Thereupon, acting on the denunciation of the prelates, the barons, and the people, he threw into prison Mariam, the widow of Constantine III and Baron Basil, as responsible for the Regency's extravagances. It was his intention, however, to pardon them generously on the day of his coronation.

CORONATION OF LEO V — Leo wanted to be crowned by a Roman bishop, but this decision caused so much discontent that it was agreed to have a double ceremony, the Latin ritual to be followed by the Armenian. The coronation took place in the church of St. Sophia at Sis on September 14th, 1374. Queen Marguerite of Soissons was crowned with the same ceremonial.

This double coronation was a very serious mistake politically, for the Armenians who were as exclusive as the Byzantines in their religious beliefs, looked on the Catholic ceremony as an insult to the Gregorian ritual, and their discontent took form later in betrayal.

The treasury was empty, the country ruined, the enemy held every province and every city, except Anazarbus and Sis and a few castles around those two places. The army of the young Egyptian Sultan, Melik-el-Ashraf Chaaban, ruled unchallenged in the greater part of Cilicia, and two Turcoman chiefs, Daoudbash and Bukabir (Abu-Bekr) occupied the suburbs of Sis with eleven thousand men under each of them. These barbarians, however, did not show hostility to the Armenians; their clemency went even so far as to supply the capital and the neighboring castles with the food they required. Daoudbash sent presents to Leo on the day he was crowned, and the king of Armenia thinking it would be easy to deal with this intruder, sent him gifts in return accompanied by preliminary steps towards renewing the truce on the old terms. The king was reckoning, however, without his own subjects.

Not only did these tragic days not prevent the malcontents among the Armenians from raising the questions of ritual on the coronation day, but these same people deliberately brought on war by making false reports to Daoudbash. For three months Sis was besieged. The Latin cross-bowmen caused, however, so many losses to the Turcomans who fought without body-armor, that Daoudbash renewed the old agreement by which he undertook to supply Sis with its food requirements in return for tribute payment.

There was living in Cairo at this time an Armenian renegade named

Ashot. This man was a son of Baron Ochin and brother of Constantine III's widow. The Armenian party opposed to the Lusignans, claiming that Ashot had a right to the crown, urged him to come with an Egyptian army and take possession of his dominion.

SIEGE OF SIS The Turcoman chief Bukabir, who was more or less under Cairo's orders, was at Ashot's request given instructions to reduce Sis by hunger, and on the pretence that he had not received the tribute to which he was entitled, he stopped sending in food supplies. At the same time, Leo's enemies were secretly offering to deliver the city to the Infidels. Warned by his spies that the place was about to be attacked the king gathered the population into the fortified upper part of the city, and also into the Castle.

The lower city surrounded by a wall that had not been long erected did not seem likely to offer adequate resistance, whereas the royal palace was protected by a fortified enceinte, proof against any surprise attack and spacious enough to shelter a part of the population. This enceinte took in, besides the palace, various other edifices including the Cathedral Church of St Sophia. Jean Dardel calls this portion of the city "the *bourg*". Strong fortifications stood quite high up on the rock overlooking the city; these constituted the "chastel" of which V. Langlois (1) gives the following brief description: "The Sis-Kalessi is oval-shaped; it has three gates, "three enceintes, and encloses various buildings. On account of the shape "of the rock it is built upon, the castle walls are irregular and unequal in "height. The fortress is flanked by towers and bastions. Owing to the "irregular shape of its structures, the castle is divided into three parts "based on each of the three chief summits of the rock. Empty spaces "separate these different constructions, which are nevertheless intercon-"nected by paths hewn in the rock and skirting the cliffs. The southern "side where stood the keep was more carefully fortified than any other "point of the fortress."

On January 15th, 1375, Bubakir with fifteen thousand men captured the lower part of Sis, which was sacked, but the upper city and the castle remained impregnable.

According to Jean Dardel (2) whose testimony cannot be considered impartial, there then ensued a most abominable piece of treachery. Those

---
(1) *Voyage en Cilicie*, p 384.
(2) Chap. XC.

who had never sincerely accepted the union of the Armenian church with that of Rome and those who hated the Latin house of Lusignan, joined up with all the other malcontents and decided to obtain peace once for all by submitting to the Sultan of Egypt. The Catholicos Paul I (1374-1378) was one of the chief instigators of this frightful betrayal, showing that he preferred the temporal domination of one of Islam's rulers, rather than the spiritual supremacy of the Pope. Seventy-five years later, the same religious intransigence caused the ancient capital of the Greek Emperors to fall likewise into the Infidels' hands.

In answer to the call of the enemies of the Lusignans and the Pope, Emir Seif-ed-Din-Ichq Timur, governor of Aleppo, sent 15,000 men to assist the Turcomans, and on February 24th the Egyptians were seen pouring in under the walls of Sis. Realizing that the upper city could not withstand assault, Leo had it evacuated and set on fire that same night. This act reduced the kingdom of Armenia to the mere Castle of Sis. Even there the traitors were mingled with the defenders.

RUINS OF THE FORTRESS OF SIS

More than thirty thousand of the enemy thronged around the Castle amid the ruins of the city and the "bourg". Leo feeling the final assault to be at hand gathered around him the nobles and clergy, and called on all to swear to be obedient and faithful to the Christian religion and to their sovereign, and he himself swore upon the gospels, held by the Bishop of Hebron, that he would die for Christ. He at the same time solemnly called on the nobles and clergy to denounce and punish the traitors (1).

On the morrow the Moslems began the attack, but the only point

---

(1) Jean DARDEL. Chap. XCII

they could reach on the steep rocky cliffs was the level space in front of the fortress gate. The besieged put up a vigorous resistance; the king himself was shooting with his cross-bow when he was struck by an iron missile which broke his jaw and tore away three of his teeth. Leo withdrew inside the castle to have his injury dressed, while the Saracens who had suffered much loss also returned to their tents. (2)

That same evening Seif-ed-Din sent the Christian monarch a letter informing him: "That the Sultan his Lord had sent him word to let him "[Leo] know that if he consented to surrender the castle and become a "Saracen, he, the Sultan, would make him his Grand Admiral and restore "him his whole country." Leo replied in a worthy manner, that he was determined to die rather than deny his God, and he offered to pay tribute to the Sultan as in the past if the siege were raised and his possessions restored to him (1)

This reply angered the Moslems, and they made several further attempts to take the castle by storm, but without success. (2) Meanwhile, however, the traitors were busy communicating with Seif-ed-Din, telling him of the king's injury and serious condition and informing him that hunger would soon compel the opening of the gates. (3)

Not content with scheming with the enemy, the leaders of the sedition, finding the king adamant to their treacherous counsels, decided to do away with him. The Catholicos, Baron Basil, and King Constantine's widow (who had married the Cyprus knight Matthew Cappe and was herself the sister of the renegade Ashot) incited Cappe, by alluring promises, to commit this deed. This traitor turned against the king some of the soldiers who were from Cyprus, and with them during the night broke into the castle-keep where Leo dwelt. The Armenian guards were massacred to a man. "When the king, who lay so ill on his bed that he was helpless "by reason of the wound from the projectile, heard the assault, he made "an effort and took his coat of mail and armed himself as best he could. "With him in his bed-chamber were two Armenian knights and one Greek "cross-bowman who was the chief engineer and was named Costa de Les- "mirre. When these three heard the attackers breaking down the door of "the king's room with hatchets to get inside and kill the king and them- "selves, the Greek took the king and tied him to a strong rope and let him

---

(2) Jean DARDEL, chap. XCIII
(1) Jean DARDEL, chap XCIV
(2) Id., chap XCV
(3) Id., chap. XCVI

'down by a privy to the second castle, they all three following after "him. (4)

The king took refuge with Queen Mary and found his knight Doulcart, who knew nothing of the plot of the Latin mercenaries. He informed those in the castle of the attempt on his life which he had just escaped, and fearing for the queen and her children imprisoned in the keep, he offered to pardon the insurgents. The latter would not listen, and a fight consequently ensued. Four times the loyal Armenians tried to take the keep and each time they were repelled (5).

SIS TAKEN BY THE MOSLEMS

Meanwhile the rebels were letting the enemy in by means of ropes, and a few Moslems had already joined them when a Jacobite friar who had accompanied the bishop of Hebron to Sis and was then in the keep, fearful of having to embrace Islam, secretly let in a number of Armenians who got possession of the fort.

Thereupon the Catholicos and the other conspirators stirred up the people against the king, and persuaded the Armenians to surrender the castle to the Moslems. They all forsook their sovereign and, breaking down the gates, let the enemy in. Leo, suffering from his injury and stretched on his bed, had with him only his wife and children and the faithful knight Sohier Doulcart. A handful of soldiers alone defended the keep which he still held. But their food was exhausted, and in this terrible position Leo could offer no further resistance. He accepted the decree of Fate, and sent a message to the Moslem leader.

SIS CASTLE CAPITULATES 1357

Following a very courteous exchange of letters, Ishki-Timur sent the king a safe-conduct. He wrote: "We do grant him 'this letter, that he may come down from the Keep and surrender it to 'the mighty Sultan, and then proceed wherever he please. The safe-'conduct is for him, his queen, their children and also for his personal 'belongings and suite, so that he may be respected and honored by all." But the poor king had slight trust in the victor's word. He made his confession, heard mass, and took communion; then hardly able to walk, with his head completely bandaged, he came down from the keep followed by his family. This was April 13th, 1375, less than ten months

---

(4) Jean DARDEL, chap. XCVII.
(5) Jean DARDEL, chap XCIX

after King Leo V of Lusignan had left the island of Cyprus and set foot on Armenian soil.

The Sultan offered to restore him his kingdom provided he embraced Islam. Leo refused with dignity. He was offered one of the castles in Cilicia to live in, but he declined, realizing that within a few years the Moslems would get rid of him. He thought of going to Cyprus, but learning that he would be assassinated on the way, he abandoned the plan, and threw himself on the mercy of Sultan Ashraf of Egypt.

LEO V'S CAPTIVITY After his victory over the Christians, Ishki-Timur entered with pomp into Aleppo, the city *en fête*, with the king and queen of Armenia, their children, Queen Mariam, Sohier Doulcart and his wife, the Countess of Gorigos, the Catholicos Paul I, the Armenian barons and the chief citizens of Sis following behind him. Inside the city the prisoners had to prostrate themselves several times before their conqueror in the presence of the inhabitants. Finally, on May 1st, Leo left Aleppo for Cairo where he arrived on July 9th.

Notwithstanding the promise contained in the safe-conduct delivered in his name, the Sultan refused to allow Leo to go to Europe. He was afraid lest he should start a new Crusade, and he therefore kept him at Cairo, decently treated but closely watched.

The king of Cyprus interceded with the Egyptian ruler for Leo's release, but no consent could be obtained from the councillors of the new young Sultan Melik-Mansur Ali who had ascended the throne after his father Ashraf Chabaan's assassination (March 16th, 1377). Leo wrote to the Pope, to the Emperor of Constantinople, to the king of France, and to other European monarchs, some of them also interceded on his behalf, but none met with any success.

That same year, in July, there arrived at Cairo a number of western pilgrims, nobles, knights, equerries, and others bound for Sinaï and Jerusalem. Among them was a Franciscan monk named Jean Dardel, a native of Etampes, and a Grey Friar of the Province of France. He was asked to say mass for King Leo and had a long talk with him. Leo narrated to him all his woes and confided to him hopes he still cherished, with the result that he induced the friar to remain with him. Dardel thus became not only the king's chaplain but his councillor and ambassador.

DELIVERANCE OF LEO V Bearing the king's ring and letters for the rulers of Europe, Dardel left Cairo on September 11th, 1379, and obtained from the kings of Castille and Aragon the amounts needed to purchase Leo's freedom. The ambassadors sent from Spain to Cairo at last succeeded in getting permission for the prisoner to leave Egypt. On October 7th, 1382, the king of Armenia sailed from Alexandria, accompanied by the friar Jean Dardel whom upon his arrival at Rhodes (October 21st) he made Chancellor of his realm.

Leo V of Lusignan's subsequent life was like that of all exiled monarchs. Nowhere did he find any willingness such as he had hoped for, to help him get back his kingdom. Kings Peter of Aragon and John of Castille treated him generously, and Pope Clement VII of Avignon whom Leo opted for in preference to Urban VI, the pontiff at Rome, awarded him the "Golden Rose", not forgetting Jean Dardel who was given the bishopric of Tortiboli in the province of Benevento. This episcopal see, however, could not be taken over by the Franciscan nominee because Tortiboli was then under Urban VI's control.

The king of Navarre, Charles II, whom Leo visited, lavished gifts on him, and the Count of Foix was also equally generous. With pensions from the kings of France, England, Aragon, and Castille, Leo V withdrew to the castle of St. Ouen generously bestowed on him by Charles VI. He died on November 29th, 1393, in the Palais des Tournelles, Rue St. Antoine, opposite the Hôtel St. Paul, where the kings of France generally lived. His body was interred at the Celestine monastery where it remained until the Revolution, when his remains were scattered to the wind along with those of so many other sovereigns. His tomb, transferred at first to the museum of French Antiquities (Musée des Petits Augustins), was placed, at the Restoration, in the vaults of the royal tombs at St. Denis where it lies today. Around the border of the tombstone runs the epitaph: "Here lieth the very noble "and excellent prince Lyon the Fifth of Lizingue [Lusignan] Latin King "of the Kingdom of Armenia whose soul departed to God on the 29th "day of November in the year of grace 1393. Pray for him." (1)

LEO V'S DEATH AT PARIS 1393

---

(1). 'Cy gist très noble et excellent prince Lyon de Lizingue quint roy latin du royaume d'Arménie qui rendit l'âme à Dieu le XXIXe jour de novembre l'an de grace MCCCXCIII pries pour lui

Jean Dardel died before his master, on December 6th, 1384. The Bishop of Tortiboli was buried in his family burial-ground, the churchyard of St. Basil at Etampes.

It is only through Dardel's chronicle that we know the events of Leo's brief and dramatic reign, and the Etampes monk who wrote as suggested, even as dictated, by the king, judges the Armenians quite severely. If we think, however, of the fate with which the Mamelukes were threatening the last defenders of the Christian kingdom, or the hunger they were enduring inside the Castle of Sis, we can hardly blame the "Armins" so harshly as Dardel. They certainly cannot be exonerated altogether, but considering the desperation they were in they should be remembered charitably.

ESCUTCHEON ON TOMB OF LEO V OF LUSIGNAN

Had there been a chronicler among the defenders of Sis, we should probably have had the events related to us in quite a different manner from that of Dardel's writings, but unfortunately we have no means of judging accurately.

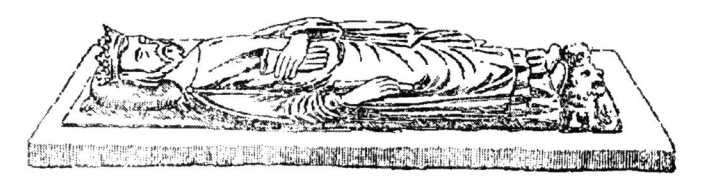

TOMB OF LEO V AT ST. DENIS
(from a drawing given by K. J. Basmadjian)

From the day that Rupen raised his standard of revolt until that of the fall of the Castle of Sis, i.e. during the whole of the three centuries that it lasted, New Armenia had been one perpetual battle-field. Its cities and countryside were laid waste one hundred times by the invading Moslems. The inhabitants were massacred and carried away into slavery, and the Armenians who had seen all the Latin States in the East fall one after the other could only trust in the help of the Almighty. But courage failed them.

Apart from this dejection due to their misfortunes, however, there are some charges that the Armenians cannot be acquitted of. Their political and religious dissensions and the ambitions of the barons contributed to the kingdom's downfall. In the latter part of the 14th century the claimants to the throne were very numerous, and the religious factions maintained all their intolerance of old. Leo V as a Latin Catholic would subscribe to no concession, and the Catholicos, Paul I (Boghos), afraid lest his church should submit completely and irretrievably to the Pope's requirements was on principle hostile to the Lusignan family. All the clergy and a part of the population, also a majority of the nobles, shared the apprehensions and resentment of the Catholicos. Unity in the face of the Moslem enemy was absent among the Armenians, and such was unfortunately the case throughout the Christian world in the East. At Byzantium, hatred for the Latins was even more intense, and only in its dying hours did the Empire look towards western Europe, when it was too late.

Nevertheless, this small kingdom founded by men from far off in the East and Europeanized by contact with the Crusaders wrote a handsome page in the great epic of the Middle Ages. Despite disturbances and wars, amid the greatest perils, the Armenians of Cilicia devoted themselves to literature and art, built churches, monasteries, castles and fortresses, and engaged in commerce. In short, even throughout the horrors of war, this principality showed surprising vitality. Its downfall was caused by the disaster that befell the Crusaders, but whereas the Latins withdrew to their western lands the Armenians had to endure for centuries the yoke of their conquerors. From the time that the Westerners' domains were reduced to the island of Cyprus, discouragement seized the Christians of Asia, and the drama that ended the death-throes of the city of Sis, now that we can view it at a distance of five centuries, deserves censure less severe than that passed by its contemporary, Dardel. Mistakes were made, but if we compare the heroic resistance of the Armenians for two centuries with the supineness with which most Eastern Christians bowed to Islam's yataghan, we cannot but admire this small number of brave people, and find their faults effaced by the courage they manifested up to the last hour, until every hope had faded.

In 1384 Pope Gregory XIII, in his Bull "Ecclesia Romana", does signal justice to the Armenians, and this homage of the sovereign Pontiff should not be forgotten. He wrote: "Among the other merits of the "Armenian nation as regards the Church and Christendom, there is "one that is outstanding and deserves particularly to be remembered, "namely, that when in times past the Christian princes and armies went "forth to recover the Holy Land, no nation, no people came to their aid

"more speedily and with more enthusiasm than the Armenians, giving
"them assistance in men, horses, food supplies, and counsel; with all their
"might and with the greatest bravery and fidelity, they helped the Chris-
"tians in those holy wars."

SEAL AND SIGNATURE OF KING LEO V OF ARMENIA

CHAPTER IX

ARMENIA AFTER ITS LOSS OF INDEPENDENCE

As we have seen, in 1045 Ani and its surrounding kingdom came under the rule of Constantinople, and its last king Gaghik II was assassinated by the Greeks in 1079 during his captivity in Imperial territory; also in 1064 Alp-Arslan finally conquered Greater Armenia, and in 1375 the kingdom of Leo V of Lusignan came to an end (1) From the 11th century until our present day, the inhabitants of Greater Armenia were consequently the Rayahs of the Moslems, as also were those of New Armenia from the beginning of the 14th century. The people living north of the Araxes emerged from under Islam's yoke, however, in 1827 when they fell to the Russian government of the Czar.

Much of the population of these two countries had, for years and years already, fled from their homeland during the terrible wars that have always laid waste the Ararat regions, but the emigration reached its greatest peak in the Middle Ages The horrible deeds of the Arabs, Turks, and Mongols, together with the knowledge that the morrow would be still worse, impelled a large portion of the unhappy inhabitants to seek other lands. A good number of Armenian colonies were founded in the Old World, and later in the New. Consequently, dating from the conquest of Armenia by the Caliphs, this nation's history is divided into two very different branches, that of the enslaved people's struggle for existence, and that of the descendants of Haïk living in foreign countries. Although contemporary, I have thought it wiser to deal with each of these phases separately so as to give a clearer idea of the distinct development of the Armenians in each of these dissimilar environments during this period of history

---

(1) After the death of Leo V the rulers of Cyprus took the title of kings of Armenia. Those who bore this title are: Jacques I, king of Cyprus, 1393-1398; Janus, 1398-1432. Jean II. 1432-1458, Charlotte and Louis of Savoy. 1458 1464; Jacques II, 1464-1473; Jacques III, 1473-1475, Catherine Cornaro 1475-1489.

The Arab conquest, although it marched under the particularly hateful banner of religion and was accompanied with unbelievable violence and cruelty, was mitigated nevertheless by the fact that in the early days of Islam the Mahometans were confronted with the Byzantine Empire, and dealing as they were with Christian inhabitants only, they were obliged to spare the unbelievers to some extent. The speedy triumphs of the followers of the Prophet might after all be only temporary, for the empire of Byzantium had not been overthrown like that of the Persian "King of Kings." The Caliphs behaved, therefore, less harshly to the Christians than to the Mazdeans, for the latter once conquered and subdued had no neighboring State to which they could look for support.

In any case, however, as regards the Christians, all Mohammedans, whether Arab, Turkish, or Persian, followed the lines of policy prescribed for them in the Koran, which they applied with varying degrees of severity, according to circumstances and their own differing characters. They all, throughout the centuries, looked on unbelievers as inferior beings, and their reason for not wiping them out to the last one was that they needed their labor to cultivate the soil and carry out the thousand and one jobs they themselves were too lazy or too proud to undertake.

Within the Byzantine Empire, Christianity had considerably softened the institution of slavery, which in the western world had taken the form of serfdom. Among Eastern peoples, however, barbaric tradition remained in all its rigor, and the conquered fellow-being became his master's absolute property, might making right.

From the very outset of Islam, therefore, the Christian was the Moslem's slave, he was the *rayah* or herd, and even if not always applied absolutely, this primordial law with the Mohammedans remained the basis of the treatment they inflicted for centuries on those unbelievers unfortunate enough to fall into their hands and courageous enough not to deny their faith. If the Christian owned land or property, it was only by tolerance, and his masters could always take his possessions from him, even his children, for their own good pleasure. Their warrant for such cruelty they found in the book of the Prophet, the Koran, "a strange medley of dualism and double-dealing" wherein the two chapters "The Sword" and "War" give fierce orders to slay with the sword or enslave all unbelievers falling into the hands of the Faithful. These two last chapters, dictated by Mahomet when his power was assured, do not tally with the instructions he gave at the beginning of his conquests. Then he wrote. "O unbelievers, if you do not worship what I worship, keep for "yourselves your religion, and I will keep mine for myself." These contradictions permit Moslems to swing as their interest dictates, from tolerance to intolerance,, and whatever their treatment of Christians, to be always obedient to their Master's law.

The Moslems allowed quantities of Greeks, Chaldeans, Armenians, and Copts to keep their religion and language, their religion because of the impossibility of making apostates of them all, and their language in order that the Christian should not mingle with the governing class, and that by his native tongue and customs he should always be conspicuous and despised of the true believer, whom he must work for and serve. This governing class, thus relieved of having to earn their daily bread, could consequently live a parasitical life of ease. This is what occurred in Armenia, Syria, Greece, Egypt, and North Africa as far as Morocco and Spain, throughout the vast Arab empire. It is still the case in Turkish countries, and would be so today in Persia were it not that this country so long decadent has had to bow to the European Powers and not ill-treat the unbelievers dwelling there.

What sufferings and humiliation fell on those unfortunates whom cruel fate threw into the power of such infamous masters! Carrying weapons was forbidden to the "rayahs", whether Christian, Jewish, Mazdean, or Mandaean, to all who did not worship Allah. These people all had to wear special clothing so that they might be recognized on sight, and ordered about or ill-treated. The churches of the worshipers of the prophet Issa (Jesus) with their modest exteriors, without steeples or bells, were constantly the scene of wicked attacks, revolting orgies, and frightful crimes, and the Christian had to remain mute and helpless in presence of the most infamous sacrilege and indignity.

COIN OF GIORGI III OF GEORGIA WITH AL MOKTAFY (1254-1284)

Not satisfied with their own cruelties, the Arabs, Turks, and Persians gave over Christian villages to the most barbaric of all Eastern peoples, the Kurds. We have seen in the preceding pages the behavior of the Emirs of Azerbaïdjan to the Armenians, and if now and then the rulers checked the fury of the Kurdistan bandits, it was only lest they should be unable to levy from a devastated Armenia the enormous taxation they lived on. Never did the Moslem show pity out of kindness or respect for humanity; he was ever motivated by interest alone.

Hatred and contempt for the Christian were so anchored in the Moslem heart that an unbeliever was believed incapable of a good deed, and his duplicity caused him to attribute to Allah any generous act committed by a Christian, who merely was a divinely provided instrument and not entitled to the Mohammedan's gratitude, which must go to the deity of whom he himself was the servant.

TURKISH RULE OF ARMENIA After the downfall of the Bagratid kingdom and the capture of Ani by the Seljuks, Turkish rule extended as far as the foot of the great Caucasian chain, to the countries watered by the Kura and the Araxes. (1) The Armenians, Georgians, Imeritians, and Mingrelians fought unceasingly against the invaders, who being nomads occupied all the pasturages of the lowlands, and whose beys maintained absolute rule in the cities of any size. Sometimes the Basileus of Constantinople sent a few troops, but generally these irregular and insufficient arrivals only resulted in atrocious reprisals as soon as such assistance from the Emperor was out of the way again. Then later came the Mogul invasion which spread terror anew in Transcaucasia and the Ararat country.

THE MONGOLS IN ARMENIA The Mongols started from Central Asia in the middle of the 11th century and crossed the Siberian steppes and the Persian tableland, subduing every tribe they encountered in their onrushing advance. These conquered peoples were mostly themselves of Turkish race, and spoke Jagataï. Their soldiers were constantly added to the Mongol army, with the result that the original element was gradually lost and when the Mongols arrived in Transcaucasia there were hardly any of the original stock left except the chieftains.

In 1206 Genghis-Khan began his conquest of Asia. After vanquishing the tribes of the Turcoman steppe, he destroyed the Moslem dominion of Kharesm on the lower Oxus (about 1217). He then subdued Khorasan, Persia, Irak-Arabi, and northern India, bringing to naught in a few

---

(1) In 1071 the Seljuks advanced as far as the interior of Cappadocia; in 1082 the Ortokids took Jerusalem and in 1092 the Seljuk empire was dismembered

years all the work of the Arabs in those parts. His generals, Subada-Behadur and Chapeh-Nuvian, entered Armenia and Georgia, passed through the pass of Derbend and the Gates of the Alans, and there was founded in southern Russia the empire of Kiphtchak (1223)) which ruled over the former Turkish tribes of the Comans and the Petchenegs.(2) The purely Mongolian armies that had left Central Asia had long ceased to exist, and except for the Mogul court the Mongol language was no longer even used. The name of Tartars subsequently came to include both conquerors and subjects, although they belonged to quite different races.

COIN OF DJELAL-ED-DIN SULTAN OF KHARESM

The first time (1221), the whole basin of the Kura was laid waste despite the valiant struggles of the Georgians and Armenians, assisted by the Moslem emirs of Azerbaïdjan. In 1223 the Tartars were already in the middle of Russia. Then, tired of looting they withdrew to the south to join their monarch Genghis-Khan who was proceeding with a big army from Khorasan towards Armenia. Dovin, Ani, and Gaq, all the region as far as Gandzak, fell into his hands, whilst Djelal-ed-Din, the sultan of Kharesm, who had been driven from his realm and was fleeing from the Mongols, invaded northern Armenia and Georgia. Pursued by the Tartars, this ruler was slain (1231) and his troops absorbed into the Mongol army which camped in every valley. The Georgians retreated into the mountains of the Caucasus and the Armenians into the massifs of Gougarq and the Gheuttchaï. Mango-Khan, Arghoun-Khan, Ghazan-Khan, and the other Mogul

COIN OF DAVID V SOLSAN (Georgia) (1243-1269)   **COIN OF ARGHOUN-KHAN AND DEMETRIUS II OF GEORGIA (1273-1289)**   **COIN OF GHAZAN-KHAN and WAKHTANG III (Georgia) (1301-1307)**

(2) In 1236 they captured Moscow, Vladimir, and Kief, and in 1240 they were in Poland, then in Hungary (1241); in 1242 they were defeated by Frederick II in Illyria.

— 279 —

chiefs reigned over the whole country until in 1387 Timur the Lame (Leng) captured Greater Armenia and founded the second Tartar empire.

The name of Tamerlane remained a frightful one in the memory of the Armenians. This chief overran the land spreading death and destruction everywhere. In Siuniq, Airarat, Vaspurakan, and Turuberan, blood flowed in rivers. At Van all the inhabitants were thrown from the cliffs, and at Sivas the whole population was slaughtered and four thousand soldiers buried alive, while the victors' horsemen trampled the children to death. These horrors went on until Tamerlane died, when Armenia fell a prey first to the Turcoman tribes of the Black Sheep, and then to those of the White Sheep whose chief, Ouzoun-Hassan, proclaimed himself Sultan of Persia in 1468.

The ambition of these barbarian princes was unbridled. Not satisfied with reigning over the whole Iranian tableland and over Transcaucasia and Armenia, Ouzoun-Hassan sought to expand his possessions still further at the expense of Mahomet II (1440-1481), the conqueror

COIN OF BAGRAT V, KING OF GEORGIA (1360-1395)

COIN OF GIORGI VIII KING OF GEORGIA (1452-1469)

of Constantinople and Trebizond. It was to his cost, for he was defeated, and had to give up Armenia (1473) which thus fell for the first time into Ottoman hands.

Just as in ancient times, this unhappy country again became the battlefield of rival empires. Forty-one years later, in 1514, the founder and first king of the Sefevis dynasty in Persia, Shah Ismaïl I (1501-1523) marched against the Turks, but he was defeated on the plain of Chaldiran by Sultan Selim I (1512-1520), the latter seizing all western and southern Armenia as far as Lake Urumiah. Suleīman I (1520-1566) likewise took eastern Armenia from the Persians, and

GEORGIAN COIN (UNCERTAIN) (14th Century)

Murad III (1573-1595) obliged Abbas I (1585-1628) to surrender to him by treaty not only the whole of Armenia, but also Georgia and a part of Azerbaïdjan including its capital, Tabriz. (1585) (1)

PERSIAN RULE Turkish government inaugurated for Armenia a régime of unbearable oppression and extortion for the inhabitants, the leaders of whom, preferring Persian rule to that of the Osmanlis, sent a deputation to Shah Abbas I begging him to intervene and resume possession of the Ararat regions.

Although they had become Mohammedans, the Persians nevertheless belonged to an ancient race which for centuries had headed Eastern civilization. The precepts of Zoroaster had softened their manners and given them ideas of justice that were unknown to Mongol, Turcoman, or Turk. They were therefore more tolerant to the Christians than the Ottomans.

Shah Abbas seized the opportunity offered him to avenge himself of the defeats inflicted on Persia by the Turks since the days of Mahomet II. He invaded Azerbaïdjan with a large army, seized the province of Ararat, and was pushing on his conquests when Sultan Ahmed I (1603-1617) who had just ascended the throne sent against him General Sinan Pasha Djighalé-Zadé. Abbas did not feel he was a match for his opponent, and had to abandon Armenia, but in his retreat he left a wilderness behind him, so as to abandon to the Turks only a worthless country and took away colonies of industrious people to settle within his own dominions. Towns, villages, churches, monasteries, all were burned and reduced to ruins, and the whole population deported to Persia. These orders were carried out with inconceivable cruelty. Those inhabitants who refused to leave their ancestral homes were beaten and often killed. Finally endless caravans left for the direction of the Araxes, where the guards forced the exiles to swim across the river. Many of the unfortunates were drowned in the rapid stream.

The deportees then proceeded across Azerbaïdjan and Kurdistan to Isfahan, where the king founded (1605), under the name of *New Julfa*, a suburb of his capital which is still inhabited solely by Christian Armenians. Shah Abbas showed himself well disposed towards the exiles, and any ill-treatment the poor people suffered during their migration was

---

(1) Cf. KEVORK ASLAN, *L'Arménie et les Arméniens*, 1914, chap VI & VII — K. J. BASMIDJIAN *Histoire moderne des Arméniens*, p 18 sq.

certainly not authorized by him, for as soon as Julfa-Isfahan was founded, he proclaimed freedom of religion throughout his dominions. He often attended religious ceremonies on Christian holidays, and always punished severely any of his subjects who insulted or molestd the Christians. Unfortunately the successors of this generous ruler did not maintain his policy of tolerance, and under the influence of the Moslem clergy who were almost all Arabs, they emulated the Turks in their cruelty to the Armenians

During this time war continued between the Persians and the Ottomans for the possession of the northern provinces, with varying results Finally (1620) the Turks had to relinquish all eastern Armenia including Etchmiadzin to the Shah The Sultan had his hands too full with the wars in Europe to be able to maintain his claims to eastern regions where it was so difficult to collect the taxes.

Shah Abbas adopted a wise and far-sighted policy in his new provinces, the government of which he entrusted to Armenian nobles who under the title of Meliks enjoyed considerable independence and as his administrators served him faithfully. Under Abbas' successors, however, oppression and violence began again, and the Armenians considered the possibility of throwing off the Moslem tyranny.

THE ARMENIANS APPEAL TO EUROPE. ORI

In 1678 the Catholicos Hakob IV secretly called together at Etchmiadzin the chief Armenian nobles, a dozen at most, and proposed to them that they accept the supremacy of the Pope and appeal to the western Powers to obtain autonomy for Armenia. They would in fact revert to the negotiations undertaken of old by the kings of New Armenia.

Following this secret meeting, a delegation set out The Catholicos was to go first to Rome, but he died on the way at Constantinople, and the discouraged delegates made a halt. One young man alone, aged 19, named Ori, departed hoping to succeed by himself in the difficult mission. He reached France by way of Venice, enrolled in the army of Louis XIV, and was captured by the English On his liberation he went to Germany where he obtained assistance from Prince Johann-Wilhelm of the Palatinate to whom he promised the Armenian crown

Ori returned to his country (1699) to prepare the revolution that was to win independence. The new Catholicos Nahapet I (1696-1705), however, was opposed to the union of the Armenian church with that of Rome, and so was the Patriarch of the Aghouans, Simeon IV (1675-1701). The nobles chose therefore the Superior of the Monastery of St. James, Minas Tigranian, who left together with Ori, bearing a letter addressed to Pope Innocent XII (1691-1700).

After visiting the Holy Father, Ori and Minas went to see Prince Johann-Wilhelm, who sent them to Emperor Leopold I (1658-1705) The latter realized, however, that he could do nothing for Armenia without the help of Russia, and advised the delegates to apply to Peter the Great. The Czar promised them his assistance and at the same time sent a mission to Armenia. The Catholicos Nahapet I had died, and his successor Essai (1702-1728) was willing to accept the Pope. All that was necessary was for Russia to act, but time dragged on. Ori returned to Vienna went to Dusseldorf, and then in 1706 we find him again in Russia where Peter the Great entrusted him with a mission to the Shah. The Persians, finally informed of what was going on in Armenia, treated him very politely but refused to listen to him, and he withdrew to Astrakhan where he died (1711).

PETER THE GREAT AND CATHERINE Peter the Great in 1722 despatched an expedition against Persia, and seized Derbend. The troops also besieged Chemakhi. The Armenians were convinced that their hopes were about to be realized, when the Czar called back his army, signed a peace with the Persians, and the following year gave up Georgia and Qara-bagh to the Turks, advising the Armenians to emigrate to the territory of his Empire.

Abandoned by Russia, the Meliks resorted to force. The whole Qara-bagh district rose up under David-Beg who had for several years already been holding out in the mountains. The insurgents met with some success, but upon the Turkish army intervening, David came to terms with Shah Thamaz (1722-1732). Qara-bagh being recently restored to Persia, the Shah made him governor of that province.

David died, and the Armenians quarreled as to his successor. The Turks seized the opportunity to reconquer Qara-bagh. Mekhithar, David's lieutenant, was assassinated by his fellow-countrymen (1730), putting an end to the Meliks' endeavors to restore independence to Armenia.

This odyssey of Ori through Europe and Persia, these religious disputes, and struggles of a handful of men against armies of great powers, also Peter the Great's forsaking of the Armenians after his splendid promises, all remind us of the vain hopes of Greater Armenia in the Middle Ages, and of the New Armenia of the Rupen and Lusignan dynasties. The names are no longer those of the 13th century, but the steps taken and the resultant events are no different.

Russia took no further interest for the time in the mountains of the Lesser Caucasus, and the Turks therefore seized the opportunity to declare war on the Shah of Persia for their possession. Erivan and Nakhitchevan were taken by the Ottomans, whose army marched on to Tabriz. The rivalry going on between Prince Ashraf and Thamaz II was helpful to the enemy, and Ashraf ratified the Sultan's occupation of his newly seized territory. The prince was, however, defeated by his rival, and captured and beheaded. Thereupon the war started afresh, but the Shah lost the battle to the Turks near Hamadan and was obliged to sign a peace treaty giving up the provinces of Tiflis, Erivan, and Chemakhi, and accepting the Araxes river as his boundry.

This grievous treaty resulted in the overthrow of Thamaz who was dethroned by his general, Nadir, (1732) to make way for one of his children, Abbas III. Nadir was thus able to take over the government, and resume the fight with Turkey. A great battle took place on the banks of the Arpa-tchaï, and the victorious general recovered the Transcaucasian provinces surrendered by Thamaz.

The Turcoman Nadir then usurped the throne outright and proclaimed himself Shah of Persia (1736-1747). He made it his first business to grant the Armenians, who had helped him into power, the freedom they had formerly enjoyed under Abbas I. War with the Ottomans still went on in Armenia, however, and in 1743 Nadir Shah invaded Turkish territory as far as Kars. There he had to retreat, and a battle with the Sultan's army ensued below Erivan. He won the day, but it was Armenia again that was the unhappy battlefield. Ruins were heaped on ruins, the countryside became a wilderness, and the people weary of so much

COINS OF EREKLE II, KING OF GEORGIA

suffering and ceaseless danger gradually left their homeland to seek in other countries the liberty denied them on their ancestral soil.

Notwithstanding their misfortunes, the yearning for freedom was not stamped out among them; demands for independence went up from the Armenian colonies abroad, and advances were made to Ereklé II, King of Georgia (1737-1797) with a view to forming an all-inclusive State of Transcaucasia. To further this end, however the Meliks needed the support of Russia, then ruled by Catherine the Great.

War broke out between Russia and Persia in 1768, and it suited the policy of the Empress to stir up a revolt of the Christians in the Shah's northern provinces. Catherine encouraged the idea of Armenian independence, and Grigoriy Alexandrovitch Potemkine, an ardent friend of that country, had even agreed to accept the crown of the new kingdom to be. Heartened by these favorable beginnings, the Armenians under the leadership of a few of their nobles and of the Catholici of Etchmiadzin and the Aghouans, were preparing for a general uprising when Ibrahim-Khan, the Persian governor of the Transcaucasian regions, had the conspirators arrested. The Catholicos of Gandzassar, Hovhannes X, died of poison in prison (1786) while the other Armenian chiefs were kept in chains.

A dispute which broke out between the two Persian governors Ibrahim and Djavad-Khan, concerning the Armenians under the latter's protection, brought about a war between these Tartar chiefs, causing further bloodshed in Eastern Armenia. Ever since the seizure of the Persian crown by the Turcoman Khadjars, unhappy Iran had been torn by rivalry and anarchy, and was rapidly verging on ruin. Throughout the provinces it was one series of revolts, and the eunuch Agha Mohammed-Khan availed himself of the upheaval to seize the throne for himself (1794-1797). Upon Ibrahim-Khan's refusal to acknowledge him as Shah, the new monarch invaded the Qara-bagh (1796), captured Choucha where he put the inhabitants to the sword, and punished with terrible severity the Armenians who had actively taken the side of the Tartars against him. The Russians intervened, however, and within a few weeks drove the Persians beyond the Araxes. Derbend, Baku, Couba, Gandzak, Chemakhi, and Choucha remained in their hands and have belonged to the Czar's em-

CONQUEST OF UPPER ARMENIA BY RUSSIA

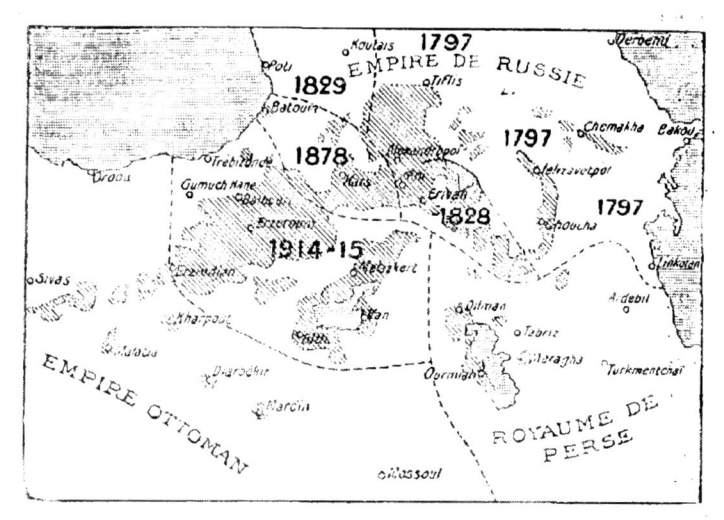

RUSSIA'S ADVANCES INTO ARMENIA (1797-1916)

pire ever since. (1797). The Qara-bagh district did not gain independence, it is true, but it was thereafter administered by Christian governors and forever rescued from Moslem persecution.

By the treaty of Ghulistan, signed in 1813 between Persia and Russia, the Czar was given all Transcaucasia, and the Shah relinquished all claim to the Khanates of Qara-bagh, Gandzak, Shaki, Shirvan, Derbend, and Baku, likewise to Daghestan, Talysh, Georgia, Imeritia, Guria, Mingrelia, and Abkhasia to most of which regions Persia had no right anyhow, King Ereklé of Georgia having bestowed on the Czar his sovereign rights.

Nevertheless Abbas-Mirza, the eldest son of Shah Fath-Ali, secretly arranged for an uprising of all the Moslems of Transcaucasia, and in 1826, when he thought the time was ripe, he invaded with a large army the provinces that had been surrendered by the treaty of Ghulistan. The Russians thereupon despatched a number of armed forces to Caucasia, and cal-

RUSSIAN COIN OF GEORGIA

— 286 —

ling on the Christians received the help of the Georgians and Armenians under General Madatoff, an Armenian of Qara-bagh.

Abbas-Mirba's army was easily driven off and the city of Tabriz in Azerbaïdjan surrendered unconditionally to the "mules of the Russian army." By the treaty of Turkmen-tchaï 1828, Persia gave up the Khanates of Erivan and Nakhitchevan, their sole remaining possessions on the left bank of the Araxes. This resulted in delivering from Moslem rule the "Rome of the Armenians," Etchmiadzin, the residence of the Catholicos Nerses of Ashharac who as the leader of his Armenians had given the Russians his support. There was some question then of forming an autonomous "Russian Armenian province" under the Czar's suzerainty, but this plan was abandoned by Paskievitch, the viceroy of the Caucasus.

The war with the Persians was hardly over when Russia was obliged to take the field against the Turks. Fighting took place mostly in Mingrelia and the north-west provinces of Armenia.

Ever since the Turks occupied the southern and western parts of Armenia, the Ottoman yoke had weighed so heavily on the Christians of those regions and any inclination to revolt had been so pitilessly repressed, that the Armenians bowed their necks and suffered outrageous persecution in utter helplessness. With their lives and property under constant threat from their terrible neighbors, the Kurdish tribesmen hardly acknowledging the Sultan's rule,—crushed by the heavy taxation of the Ottoman officials, and watched with relentless cruelty—these unfortunate people had no means of concerted action towards relieving their woes. The Russian armies' entry into battle aroused in those mountains indescribable enthusiasm, of which the Czar's generals skillfully availed themselves and rallied the Christians against their enemies. Paskievitch commanding the army of the East seized Kars, Akhalkalakh, Akhaltsikhé, Bayazid, Diadine, Alashkert, Hassan-Qal'a, Erzerum, Khinis, and Baïburt. Almost all of Armenia was conquered, and all that remained to the Turks were Van, Bitlis, Mouch, and Erzindjan, that is, the south and west of the Erzerum plateau. In Europe also the Russian armies were equally victorious and were threatening Constantinople. The Western Powers, however, opposed the subordination of the Ottoman Empire, and by the treaty of Adrianople (1829) Russia was allowed to keep only the provinces of Anapa, Potki, Akhalkalaki and Akhaltsikhé, and had to restore to Turkey the greater part of her Eastern conquests.

TREATY OF ADRIANOPLE

The Armenians were cruelly disappointed. They had generously compromised themselves on Russia's behalf, and now were thrown back again into their former servitude to masters who would certainly not forgive their devotion to the Russians. They emigrated in a body to Alexandropol, Akhalkalaki, and Akhaltsikhé. Ninety thousand people forsook the villages restored to the Turks; forty thousand had left the Persian provinces a few years before. Pitiful indeed was the lamentable exodus of destitute families, more than one half of whom died on the way of fatigue, exhaustion, and hunger. The Russian government, moreover, did not manifest much charity for these poor people. With the civilization they inherited from the Byzantines, the Russians absorbed the religious aversions of their teachers, and as Orthodox Christians they despised very much the Gregorian Armenians. The Greeks' dislike for all who did not believe as they did was passed on with its violent fanaticism to the eastern Slavs.

War did not start again with Turkey in Armenia until 1877, for at the time of the Crimean struggle all the fighting took place in Europe, and Transcaucasia remained entirely outside of that conflict. The treaty of San Stefano signed in 1878 at the gates of Constantinople gave to Russia Batum, Adjara, Artvin, Olti, Ardahan, Kars, Ani, and Kaghzian, but the Czar's troops once again handed back to the Sultan the cities of Erzerum and Bayazid to the despair of the Armenian generals, Prince Madatoff, Ter-Ghoukassoff, and H. Alkhazoff, who had been hoping to save their fellow-countrymen at last from the Turkish yoke.

Realizing that they were condemned to remain Ottoman subjects, the Armenians of Turkey had for years petitioned the Sublime Porte for reforms in their behalf. The Sultan did not refuse pointblank, but he nevertheless saw to it that there should be no improvement in the lot of the Christians within his dominions. In 1841 a Council had been created, composed of twenty-seven members chosen from modest Armenian middle classes. This Council had to function outside of the Patriarch's jurisdiction, which had been over the affairs of the community ever since the nation lost its independence. Such a step only resulted in confusion for the Armenians. In 1875 they sought to induce the Sultan to give his approval to a national Armenian Constitution "in contradiction of the very principles of the Turkish Government," but ' a State cannot exist within another State," especially in Turkey. In 1860 a new attempt was made, but disagreement occurred among the Armenians involved, and the Ottoman Government took advantage of the dissensions to intervene and dissolve the commissions. This resulted in 1862 in disturbances, and finally in 1863 to satisfy the Armenian people the Sultan ratified a constitution which to the present time has vested the management of affairs with the Patriarchate, and the statutes of which are incorporated in the Compendium of Laws (Destour) of the Ottoman Empire. It was a first step in the right direction, but the Porte continued none the less to treat the Armenians as slaves; to have granted them *bona fidē* freedom would have incited all the other Christians to set forth their claims, and would have deprived the Moslems of their supremacy, the very basis of the Sultan's Empire.

"Mahometan rulers from the very beginning have always avoided "any footing of equality with Christianity. Their appeal is to the sword, "not to reason. Fearful of equality, they have always disarmed the "Christians, and denied them equal rights, any right whatever, one might "say, before the law. Every time that the Christians, even helpless as "they were, showed any disproportionate excess of population above "that of the Moslems, or any undue superiority in education or well-being, "the Moslem rulers repeated the policy of the Pharaohs with the enslaved "Israelites and cut down their numbers by the methods they employed "in Bulgaria in 1876 and at Sassoun in Armenia in 1894, followed by "crushing and crippling taxation levied on the survivors. (1)"

"After the massacres of the Greeks in Constantinople in 1821 and "on the island of Chios in 1822, Europe demanded from Mahmoud II "[1808-1839] a formal promise of reforms in Turkey. To avoid European "intervention, Abdul-Medjid [1839-1861], Mahmoud's son, proclaimed "on his accession, by a decree known in history as Hatti-Sherif of Gulhané, "the required reformatory measures (Tanzimat). But their solemn "proclamation remained a dead letter! In 1843 a Christian of Constan-"tinople, named Hovakim, who had four years previously become a Mos-"lem, sought to return to the religion of his birth The unfortunate man "was hanged notwithstanding the intervention and protests of Lord Can-"ning, the British Ambassador.

"In 1845 the first massacres began in Lebanon Europe managed "to extract from the Sultan a fresh promise of reforms, and the Hatti-"Humayoun was promulgated in 1856 confirming the previous ones of "1839. Events only showed the Porte's insincerity about applying any "reforms, for in 1858 there were new massacres at Jeddah and also in

---

(1) COLL. MALCOLM, *L'Arménie devant l'Europe*, p 44, Paris 1897.

"Syria and the Lebanon In 1860 during the reign of Abdul-Aziz (1861-1876) there occurred the events of Zeitoun (2)"

ZEITOUN "The Armenians of Zeitoun (3) form a confederation very much in the same position to the Turks as the Montenegrins Sheltered among inaccessible mountains, they "have always lived beyond the Sultan's authority. They have never been "conquered and ask only that the Ottoman Government respect their "independence, even if only on the grounds of their political ownership of "their lands (4)"

At that time the Turks had still utter contempt for their Armenian rayahs, and had no notion that one day the nation might become a nuisance to the Government They considered moreover that a constitution without any teeth to it would never be anything more than a harmless toy, "a square wheel" as one of the Porte's statesmen called it at the time But to the Armenian people, clinging to this figment of liberty it was a means of advancement, a basis for national recovery. One of the most active promoters of this movement was Kricor Odian, a counsellor of Midhat Pasha, who tried to induce his chief to give constitutional government to the whole Ottoman Empire It was a vain dream on Odian's part to believe Turkey capable of any sincere movement for reform. Midhat followed his counsellor's advice, however, at least on paper, so as to prevent European intervention in the crisis of 1877. Meanwhile the Armenian colonies throughout Turkey spread rapidly; schools were opened in every city, and the French and Americans were helping them forward in the various large centers of the empire, so that the Armenian question was assuming more importance every day.

"In some mountain regions forming natural strongholds, such as "Eastern Armenia, Qara-bagh, or Sunik, and in western Armenia, the "Sassoun, Hadjin, and especially the Zeitoun districts, the Armenians had "continued to carry arms and constituted semi-autonomous clusters of "population. The long and glorious epic of Zeitoun is well known. This "little Armenian Montenegro, perched on the heights of the Cilician Tau-"rus, rose up in arms under its four barons more than thirty times in "its history, and always successfully resisted the Turkish troops sent to

---

(2) K. J BASMADJIAN. *op. laud.,* p 93 sq
(3) Cf. ANATOLIO LATINO, *Gli Armeni e Zeitun* (2 vol.) AGASSI, ZEITOUN Transl. TCHOBANIAN
(4) Victor LANGLOIS, *Les Arméniens de la Turquie et les massacres du Taurus.* p. 4, Paris, 1863.

"besiege it. In 1867 Sultan Abdul-Aziz decided to send an army of "150,000 men to destroy Zeitoun with its mere 20,000 inhabitants.(1)" Abdul-Aziz was then a guest at the Tuileries, and Napoleon III persuaded the Sultan to countermand the expedition. Fear of the Armenians, added to their hatred for the Christians, was gaining ground continually in the minds of the Turks, and even the friendly intervention of a ruler who had saved the Ottoman Empire in 1854-55, was a deep humiliation for the Court on the Bosphorus. The interference with Turkey's internal affairs, and the interest of Napoleon III in the fate of contemptible rayahs, caused the Sublime Porte to apprehend the day when the western world might say to Mahomet II's successor: "In humanity's name, you are no 'longer master in your own house." Was not the French Syrian expedition of 1864 a warning?

Europe was stirred by the Christians' forthcoming lot under the Turks, and far from succeeding in appeasing Constantinople's anger by its remonstrances, it only added to it. The Turks were not only afraid of their serfs escaping out of their hands, but they feared also the intervention of the Powers. Throughout the Empire harsher treatment than ever was inflicted on the unbelievers. Two provinces, Bosnia and Herzegovina, revolted in 1875 and 1876, and in December of the latter year Lord Salisbury presented the Imperial Government with a Memorandum relating to Armenia which subsequently became the basis of The Armenian Question. The Russo-Turkish war was about to break out, and as a precaution against events that threatened to turn out ill for the Ottomans and in order to draw to his side the Christians on his Asiatic frontiers with Russia, the Sultan encouraged the Armenians to ask for a measure of home-rule in the provinces they lived in, retaining his suzerainty of those vilayets, (November 1877). The Porte seemed agreeable to this concession but the arrival of the British fleet removed the fears of the Turkish court and the Sultan reconsidered the proposition which after all had been only dictated by fear.

TREATY OF SAN STEFANO — At the time of the treaty of San Stefano (July 10th, 1878), the Russian plenipotentiaries presented a Note concerning Armenia which had been drawn up at the request of the Armenians themselves. The Turkish

---

(1) A. TCHOBANIAN, *op. laud*, p. 23

representatives rejected this request and in the final draft of Art. 16 (1) of the Treaty, the formula "administrative autonomy" was replaced by the words "reforms and improvements". Armenia was to be occupied by Russian troops to guarantee the latter, but at the Berlin Congress the Sultan succeeded in having this guarantee clause omitted.(2) The Armenians then, at the Ottoman Government's instigation, asked the Congress for Administrative Autonomy, whereupon the German diplomats in connivance with the Sultan arranged for the non-consideration of the request. Not only was all hope lost for the Armenians, but their desires they had expressed so frankly and openly, at the suggestion of the Porte itself, created deep resentment among the Turks.

CONGRESS OF BERLIN In the treaty of San Stefano, Russia was of course serving her own interests, but those interests did conform to justice and humanity and to the aspirations of the Christian peoples under Turkish rule. The Czar's delegates signed a notably fine historical document, a step towards the dismemberment of the Moslem empire which had shamed the face of Europe for so many hundred years. It settled the Eastern question to the Czar's advantage. But Great Britain, following a Turcophile policy, and the Dual Monarchy (Austria-Hungary) which since its defeat at Sadowa had adopted a new Eastern policy, were both displeased at the idea of the Czar's supremacy in the Balkans, and imposed on Russia the Congress of Berlin, where Prince Bismarck, the dominant figure, who had little use for the Eastern question, made his own general political views paramount. As a consequence of the Treaty of Berlin, Russia lost the fruits of her victory, and paved the way for the Franco-Russian alliance, while throwing Austria into the arms of Germany and removing the barrier just put up by the Czar in the Balkans.

---

(1) Art. 16 of the Treaty of San Stefano proposed by Russia:
Inasmuch as the evacuation by the Russian troops of the territories they occupy in Armenia that are to be restored to Turkey might give rise to conflicts and complications harmful to the good relations of the two countries, the Sublime Porte undertakes to carry out with further delay, the administrative autonomy required by local needs in the provinces inhabited by Armenians and to guarantee their safety from the Kurds and Circassians.

(2) Passage from the decisions of the Berlin Congress substituted for the text proposed by Russia:
The Sublime Porte undertakes to carry out without further delay the improvements and reforms required by local needs in the provinces inhabited by the Armenians, and to guarantee their safety from the Kurds and Circassians. The Sublime Porte will periodically acquaint the supervising Powers with the steps taken to this end.

All the powers undertook to control the reforms that were to be made in the Turkish Empire in connection with the Christian inhabitants, and in this manner the Armenian question ceased to be an internal matter, and became international. This internationalism could only make the control illusive, and that is just what happened.

CYPRUS AGREEMENT
On June 4th, 1878, a secret pact, called the Cyprus Agreement (1) because thereby Great Britain was given this island by the Sultan, enabled England to make use of her right of supervising the reforms to check Russian influence in Western Asia At that time the two powers, the Lion and the Two-headed Eagle, were watching each other jealously on all the frontiers of Turkey, Persia, and Afghanistan, from the Black Sea shores to the Pamir Mountains.

This plan included not only the Armenians but also all other Christians in the Empire. Germany and Austria, concealing their false play beneath a mask of generosity, brought about its failure by proposing in its stead to divide the six Armenian vilayets and that of Trebizond into two sectors each headed by a European inspector appointed by the Ottoman government from a list of five candidates submitted by the Powers. Six months before the beginning of the Great War, on February 8th, 1914, the Sublime Porte finally signed an undertaking along these lines, at the very same time that Germany, Austria, Bulgaria, and the Turks were preparing to mobilize, and that Kaiser Wilhelm urgently needed Turkey's help A diplomatic farce indeed, unfortunately one to be followed by dramas still more frightful than those preceding it.

---

(1) The single article of this agreement is as follows:

In the event of Batum, Ardahan, and Kars, or any one of those places being retained by Russia and if any attempt should be made at any time by Russia to seize any other portion of the territories of H.I M the Sultan in Asia as determined by the final peace treaty, Gt Britain undertakes to join His Imperial Majesty in defending such territories by force of arms,

In consideration of which, H I M the Sultan promises Great Britain to introduce the necessary reforms (to be determined later by the two powers) relating to the proper administration and the protection of the Christian and other subjects of the Sublime Porte inhabiting the territories in question; and in order to enable Britain to fulfill this undertaking H I M the Sultan further consents to the occupation and administration of the island of Cyprus by Great Britain.

M. Emile Doumergue, in *Foi et Vie* (1), gives a very clear idea of what Turkey's notions of reform were at the beginning of the 19th century. He writes: "Under Sultan Mahmoud II (1809-1839) Turkey seemed "about to enter on an era of reform. Abdul-Hamid I (1774-1789) — not "to be confused with Abdul-Hamid II, The Great Assassin — had re-"ceived from Algiers a very beautiful and intelligent slave whom he "raised to the rank of favorite. She was reported to be a Frenchwoman, "Aimée Dubac de Rivery, who had been captured by the pirates. Her son, Mahmoud II, was the first reformer. On June 17th, 1826, he de-"stroyed the Janizaries, and on November 3rd, 1839, his son Abdul-Med-"jid (1839-1861) promulgated the Scheriff-Hati of Gulhané, promising "all his subjects, of whatever religion, their lives and honor, security of "property, just taxes, and reformatory laws. But the French blood in "their veins was not sufficient to carry these Sultans beyond mere prom-"ises." Their undertakings remained a dead letter, and equally so, later, was the Hatti-Medjid Humayoun of February 18th, 1856, in which Sultan Medjid again promised his subject peoples every blessing. We merely quote for the record these sallies of benevolent hypocrisy.

The stipulations of the Cyprus Agreement and the Treaty of Berlin itself regarding the protection of Christians in Turkey were not fulfilled in the least, and the position of the rayahs, the Armenians especially, deteriorated further to such an extent that the situation in the Armenian provinces became most alarming. In 1880 the six Powers delivered a collective Note to the Sublime Porte demanding the fulfillment of the promised reforms. The Note recapitulated the latter, but the Porte did not even answer it, and owing to European indifference the persecution of the Armenians continued. Everywhere in Armenia they were deprived of their land and in their despair they attempted several uprisings. Then there occurred the events at Sassoun (1894) which the Sublime Porte repressed by massacres. These atrocities aroused indignation in Europe, and Great Britain, France, and Russia called on Turkey to carry out the reforms in the Armenian provinces which she had undertaken under Art. 61 of the Treaty of Berlin. The three Powers even drew up in 1895 a Memorandum and Draft of these reforms. The Porte accepted the latter with a few alterations, but instead of carrying them out ordered

---

(1) Issue of April 1-16, 1916

the general massacres that drenched all Armenia in blood (1895-1896) and which for horror surpassed anything history had yet recorded.(1)

At the time of the Balkan war of 1912, the Catholicos George V appointed a delegation headed by Boghos Pasha Nubar, the son of Nubar Pasha, Egypt's eminent minister, to present the Armenian claims to the London Conference. The Armenians asked to remain Turkish, but called for the performance of the administrative reforms so often promised. So many other international matters, however, crowded the agenda that the Armenians could not get a hearing at that Conference. The efforts of the Catholicos, of the Patriarch of Constantinople, and of the national delegation under Boghos Pasha Nubar had, nevertheless, at least one theoretical result: Russia took the initiative of suggesting to the Powers a plan of reform by which the six Armenian vilayets should be united into one Ottoman province administered by a Christian, and if possible, European governor, under the supervision of the protecting Powers

Such, in its main lines, is the diplomatic history of these famous reforms which were supposed to protect the lives of the unfortunate Christians of the Turkish Empire The Powers could never agree, especially in the more recent period, because they were divided in purpose, and both Abdul-Hamid II and the Young Turks after him knew how to turn European divisions to their advantage. The Central Powers stood by, moreover, practically telling Turkey. "Do nothing for people who are not our "clients," the word 'client' taking on its ancient Roman meaning.

In their hearts the Turks believed neither what they said nor what they wrote, they were determined to make no concessions, except on paper which they treated as bits of rag long before Herr von Bethmann-Hollweg adopted that cynical expression As good Moslems they were apprehensive when they saw any sense of right coming to the fore among their rayahs, or the European Powers showing interest in the despicable Christians whose lives they had been weak enough to spare. Ah! had Mahomet II followed the example of Philip II of Spain and organized a Moslem inquisition for three centuries in his dominions, then there would have been no unbelievers in the realm of the Grand Seignior, and the Turk would really have his house to himself, and the European Powers would have no reason to interfere with his private business

But could not the oversight, the great mistake of the Conqueror of Constantinople, be repaired? Methodical massacres of the nuisances were

---

(1) Marcel LEART, La Question arménienne à la lumière des documents.

all that was necessary, and one had only to say the word, as every good Turkish Moslem was always ready to exterminate the unbelievers.

Such were Sultan Abdul-Hamid II's conclusions when he saw the Armenians and the Syrians asking for reforms and the ambassadors of the Great Powers audaciously meddling with the lot of his slaves. Had he handled the Christian problem in cavalier fashion, however, Abdul-Hamid might have provoked England, France, Italy, and Russia beyond mere diplomatic protests; he needed effective support and he found it in the German Emperor, his self-seeking friend who for the last few years was turning Turkey into a German colony. A European war might result, but what of that! The military strength of the Triple Alliance was surely invincible! Besides, the treaty of San Stefano clearly set forth Russia's ideas, and if Turkey did not act with energy, it would see the six vilayets of Armenians proclaiming their independence and Lebanon following suit, with the Arabs perhaps refusing to pay taxes any longer. Greece, Serbia, and Bulgaria had already escaped, and their example was pernicious, for freedom of one people encourages it in the neighbor, and the Empire of Mahomet II was in danger of dismemberment.

THE CAUSES OF THE MASSACRES It could never occur to the Turk that the Empire of true believers might be transformed into a Federal State. The suggestion of any such political organization would be humiliating and against the commandments of the Prophet, unworthy indeed of servants of Allah, whereas extermination was recommended by the chapters *Sword* and *War* in the Koran, and took on the aspect of a holy task. Encouraged by Wilhelm II's attitude and by the great Kaiser's official expressions of goodwill towards all Mohammedans, Abdul-Hamid decided on massacres.

According to a high Turkish official, "the Government's premedit-"ated plan was to punish the Armenians. The Sultan was infuriated "because of having been forced to grant them better treatment, and so, "after signing the reform plan, he gave orders to destroy the Armenians "in order to show his power." At the very same time Abdul-Hamid wrote (September 30th, 1895) to Lord Salisbury: "When I enforce these "reforms, I will take the document containing them and see to it per-"sonally that each article is carried out. This is my firm decision, to "which I pledge my word of honor." This future tense in its vagueness epitomizes the whole Turkish diplomacy, which M. Rolin-Jacquemynes, the eminent Belgian jurist, defines as follows "The fine art of hiding "the actual barbarity of the facts and of the intended crime by specious "externals; a bland audacity in making promises that the promiser has "no wish whatever or even the ability to keep, in short a pseudo-fatherly "and unctuous tone of voice calculated to create the belief that unjust "prejudice or wicked slander are behind the accusations." What could Christians possibly expect from such masters? What could they hope for from a divided Europe, a Europe paralyzed by the tremendous armaments of the Central Powers and under the constant threat of a war that would set the whole eastern hemisphere ablaze?

In 1914 the majority of the Armenian nation were under the heel of the Turks and had to endure the extortions of the officials from Constantinople. Those were not the only dangers, however, that the Christians were exposed to. Their neighbors were the Kurds and the Lazis, cruel and greedy robber tribes who constantly threatened to raid them. Deprived of all arms, they could offer no real resistance, but they managed to come to terms with the Kurds and paid the most unruly tribes regular sums. Until the Sublime Porte gave the signal for massacres, the Kurds were satisfied to receive the money and the Armenians to save their lives in this manner. Of late, moreover, the Christians had received arms secretly from the Caucasian revolutionaries who urged them to resist, and the Kurds did not always return from their raids without sometimes heavy losses.

What was the attitude of the Armenians during all their centuries of suffering? It was one of dignity and heroism. Of dignity, because the people in spite of their overwhelming misfortunes, clung steadfastly to their faith, their language, their customs, and their national traditions; of heroism, because Armenia did not stop at just shedding tears, but on many occasions, when their deepest feelings were hurt, her people took to arms and poured out their blood, in the revolt of their very spirit

During the centuries that followed Armenia's loss of independence, her sons and daughters, though stripped of all political entity, preserved their patriotism, their traditions, and their national life under the guidance of outstanding fellow-countrymen and of their religious leaders, who managed their public affairs and maintained and developed their institutions.

ARMENIAN NOBILITY IN THE 20TH CENTURY

Most of the nobility emigrated to the western world after the fall of Ani, and this emigration was repeated following the destruction of the kingdom of Cilicia, but there still remained in the country some families descended from royal and princely houses. There are even to the present day some with the names of Artzruni, Mamikonian, Servantzdiantz, Camsaracan, etc. The heads of these families were conspicuous for their solicitude in safeguarding the people, helping them in their endeavors to rise both intellectually and economically, and in keeping alive both their patriotism and their fidelity to religious and national tradition. There were also leading families of more recent origin, who have honorably played the same part in modern times, families founded by brave men who in the 17th and 18th centuries took up again the struggle against the Moslem oppressors and formed the honor roll of valiant leaders in the Qara-bagh region, men who bequeathed to their descendants, along with their title of *melik* still used by these families, traditions of patriotism and devotion to their people's welfare. Some of these meliks, moreover, were descended themselves from princely families of renown. There were also families of note, dating back to the centuries of servitude, founded by men of initiative and talent, including diplomats, architects, merchants, and soldiers, who acquired positions of authority in Turkey, Persia, or in Russia by their own merits and industry, and who used their influence and wealth in their country's behalf. Their posterity have inherited names to be proud of, and their present representatives glory in maintaining the luster of such names by works of beneficence and generous patriotism.

These chiefs, or notables, called "meliks" in Caucasia, and "amiras" or "tchelebis" in Turkey—even though gaining high and merited recognition in service abroad, whether Mogul, Persian, Turkish, or Russian, and no matter what their foreign status—never forgot their duty to their people, and devoted their position and fortune to alleviating the wretchedness of the Armenians, and mitigating their threatened persecutions, besides establishing for them various religious, educational, and charitable institutions.

Among the ancient aristocratic families still existing may be mentioned that of the Arghoutian-Erkainabazouks (Argoutinsky-Dolgoroukoff) who are descended from the "braves" of the time of the Armeno-Georgian rulers of Ani, under Queen Tamara; this family has had numerous eminent men, such as Bishop Arghoutian of the 18th century, one of the noblest patriots of modern times. Also the Abro family, whose ancestors were Pagratids and who, emigrating to Erzerum on the fall of Ani, and settling in various parts of Turkey, have given their nation several public educational leaders, have built churches and endowed many national institutions. To this family belonged Abro-Tchelebi, the favorite of the famous Vizier Keuprulu, who was the leading Armenian of note and one of their chief benefactors about the middle of the 17th century.

A family of more recent ancestry, but one that has played an eminent rôle and become a much-respected name is that of the Dadians, who were for a long time in charge of the Imperial Ottoman Powder-factory. They were illustrious patrons of arts and letters, the best known of them being Ohannes bey Dadian. Another family is that of the Balians, who became a dynasty of talented architects whom the Sultans entrusted with the building of their palaces and mosques during the 18th and 19th centuries. The most renowned of them was Nicohos bey Balian, who built the Palace of Tcheraghan and that of Dolmabahtché. Then again, the Duz family, the heads of the Imperial Ottoman Mint, who greatly promoted literature and art among the Armenians. Also in Russia, the Lazareffs who founded the Armenian Institute that bears their name in Moscow, and which has subsequently become a School of Oriental languages, etc.

We need to mention likewise the many successful self-made men who, even if they do not head family-trees, have left names that are revered today for their generosity and innumerable services to their fellow-countrymen, e.g. Artin amira Kazaz, the favorite of Sultan Mahmoud II, who built the Yedi-Coulé Hospital, the Patriarchal edifice, and the Armenian School at Koumpakou, Raphael and Moorat, Armenians of India, who bequeathed to the Mekhitarist Congregation large sums of money to found an Armenian college in Venice; Sanassarian, an Armenian of Russia who founded a college bearing his name at Erzerum, Izmirlian who created a prize for the publication of philological works, and others (1). Some of these eminent men were themselves active in the intellectual life of their nation and became well-known writers or scholars, such as Yeremia Tchelebi Keumurdjian who in the 17th century brought out at Constantinople a large series of historical works, poems, essays, and translations, Kakaria Markar Khodjentz Amira, a native of Erivan, who published at Constantinople, at the end of the

---

(1) Cf *Treatise on Distinguished Armenians, from 1400 to 1900*, by H. K. MRMRIAN (in Armenian) Constantinople, 1910.

18th century, a number of translations and edited works of ancient authors, besides composing "The Romance of the Rose and the Nightingale;" and Yakoub Pasha Artin, Egyptian Minister and Member of the Institute of France

All these distinguished Armenians, in short, carried on the task of the former "Nakharars" or "Ichkhans", they protected and guided the people during the centuries of servitude. "Ichkhans" moreover was the name the people actually gave to them, meaning "prince" or "director". Since the adoption of a constitutional regime by the Armenians in 1860, the title of "ichkhan" was dropped, however, because the chiefs or leaders of the people are no longer from any caste of rich or influential men nor persons of noble descent, but individuals of personal merit chosen by the people.

The clergy has stood in the same position to the people as have these men of distinction, and even more so. The Catholici of Etchmiadzin, the Patriarchs of Constantinople, Akhtamar, Sis, and Jerusalem, the "aratchnort" or Metropolitans, have been the real leaders of the Armenians. The Catholicos of Etchmiadzin who by the will of the people occupies the throne founded by St. Gregory the Illuminator, and who embodies not only their religious feelings but also their sentiment of patriotism, had precedence over the Patriarchs with their sees in Cilicia, Akhtamar, the land of the Aghouans, Jerusalem, and Constantinople. These six prelates, all of them distinguished men, have been at the head of Armenian affairs ever since the nation lost its independence.

THE PATRIARCHS The roll of Catholici of Etchmiadzin, inaugurated in A.D. 302 by Grigor I the Illuminator has been maintained without a break to the present day. Geuvorg V, the present Patriarch, was elected in 1912, the one hundred and fifty-ninth in succession. The Patriarchate of the Aghouans began in the same year A.D. 302 with a patriarch whose name is not known but who was consecrated by Grigor I, and that roll terminated with Sarkis II (1794-1815) after a series, with a few interruptions, of ninety-five archbishops.

The patriarchate of Akhtamar, founded in 1113 by David I, has only 48 names and has been vacant since 1895; whilst that of Jerusalem commencing in 637 with Abraham I went on until Harouthioun Vehapetian (1885-1910)

Although the Armenians were very numerous in Constantinople in Byzantine times, they had no patriarchate in that city, nor anywhere else in the Greek provinces, the Orthodox Greeks would not have tolerated it. This accounts for the fact that the Patriarchate of Jerusalem dates from the time of the Arab conquest of Syria, and that of Constantinople only from 1461. In that year Hovakim of Brusa (1461-1478) became the first patriarch, eight years after the fall of Byzantium to Mahomet II. The roll of his successors has been maintained until the present day, and the seventy-eighth prelate to occupy this important See is the present Zavene Eghiaïan, elected in 1913.

Cilicia's patriarchs also started quite late. Karapet I (1446-1477) was the first Cilician Catholicos, and today his forty-third Successor, Sahak II (1902), holds the office. Consequently there should be at present five Armenian patriarchates instead of six, that of the Aghouans having become extinct. But recent events have upset the organization of the Church. Sahak who became Catholicos of Jerusalem in 1916 resides at Damascus, and the patriarchate of Constantinople has been abolished by the Ottoman government.

Although the Catholicos of Etchmiadzin has the traditional pre-eminence as the successor of Gregory the Illuminator, the most important of the above prelates has been indisputably the Patriarch of Constantinople, representing as he has done the interests of the largest number of Armenians and being able, from his contacts with the Turkish government and the ambassadors of the Powers, to uphold more energetically than any of the others the cause of his fellow-countrymen. The part played politically by Hovakim and his successors has weighed much in the fortunes of the Armenian people, whereas that of the Catholicos of Etchmiadzin, a willing exile in the Armenian mountains where he is isolated from all centers of important diplomatic deliberations, has been, ever since the fall of Ani, religious rather than political. Nevertheless, at the end of the 18th century and the beginning of the 19th, some of the patriarchs there, among them Nerses of Aschharac, rendered great services to their people by the help they gave to Russia then at war with the Moslems. Since the Balkan war the patriarch of Etchmiadzin has taken over the interests of Armenia, and it is he who appointed the Armenian national delegation representing him today in Europe.

Furthermore, the Armenian people have not remained entirely homogeneous in their religious beliefs, and although the great majority are Gregorians (1), there are among them a number of Catholic communities,

---

(1) The Armenians say: "Armenian rite", the term "Gregorian" being used only by Europeans.

and also Protestant, due to American missionary work. Moreover, under the pressure of Mohammedan masters and unspeakable persecution, many Armenians have been converted to Islam, thereby forfeiting both their faith and their nationality. Some of these newly-made Moslems or their children have sometimes played an important part in Mohammedan countries. We need only mention the Grand Vizier of Shah Nassr-ed-Din, Emin-es-Sultan, later Sadr-Azam, who was the most noted statesman of modern Persia.

In any case, apart from the Armenian Moslems who no longer belong to the nation, those of Armenian speech who have been faithful to their respective creeds have maintained unadulterated their nationality and traditions. They all recognize the Catholicos as the shepherd of their flock, as the standard-bearer of the entire nation. The Patriarch's authority, however, and his influence abroad, were inadequate to regain for the Armenians their lost motherland; the most they could do was to obtain from time to time a few improvements in the lot of the unhappy inhabitants.

As a matter of fact, the Armenians did not base any expectation of deliverance solely on divine intervention or on that coming from abroad; they knew that to obtain their freedom they must merit it by striving for it, hence their ceaseless uprisings both in Greater Armenia and in Cilicia. These were unfortunately only local movements, and ended always in the crushing of the insurgents and the laying waste of their country.

After the Crimean War, Turkey owed so much to the Allies that she was unable to refuse to accede to their wishes, accordingly, on the representations of Britain and France, the position of the Christians was improved, especially in the cities where the Consuls could see what went on. Distant provinces, however, were hardly reached at all by these momentary benefits.

At Constantinople and Smyrna, both of which were watched by Europe, there developed from then on, under the indifferent eyes of the Turks, a great Armenian intellectual movement. Springing up under the influence of Italian, English, and especially French writers, Armenian literature produced some remarkable works. Its pages were, however, vibrant with the most passionate love of freedom and exalted patriotism, and called on the Armenian people to remember their past and prepare for the struggle to free their homeland from the barbarian yoke.

"From the warm ashes of our ancient heroes
May there arise heirs worthy of them,
To give a new life to our people,"

sang the poet Bechiktachelian in his "Nocturne."

The Turk opened his eyes and began to look less disdainfully on the Armenian upsurge. He awoke from the sluggishness produced by his conception of himself as an undisputed and indisputable master, to realize that the Armenians were playing a large part in his government and finances. He was indignant at hearing his rayahs speak of emancipation, and felt humiliated that he had need of their services.

During the twenty-five years that followed the war of 1870, Turkey seemed to ponder the Armenian question and listened, but without giving any heed, to the remonstrances of the European powers. Abdul-Hamid who ascended the throne in 1876 had seen the beginning of his reign disturbed by the war with Russia, and the Young Turk party caused him keen anxiety.

THE YOUNG TURKS   This Young Turk party was nothing new, for it had come into being in 1840 with the avowed purpose of reforming decrepit Turkey by adopting western methods of government. Such a program could not fail to find a sympathetic ear in France, the nursery of the Young Turks as also of all the Christian nations under the Sultan's rule. The Armenians espoused at once with fervor, and even supplemented with their counsel, the new ideas of these liberally minded Moslem patriots who sought to deliver their country from the hands of Abdul-Hamid, but little known were the changes that had taken place in these revolutionaries when in 1876 they replaced Abdul-Aziz, too submissive to the Russians, by Murad V, and then the incompetent Murad by Abdul-Hamid.

The new Sultan who was quite aware of the ideas of those who put him in power, and knew them to be Moslem nationalists proved more Pan-Islamic than the Young Turks themselves. Nevertheless, throughout his reign, he fought them continually, at first by indirect methods and later openly, nor did he forgive the Armenians for making common cause with those who were one day to drive him from his throne. He reckoned that not only would violence towards the Armenians put an end to all European proneness to meddle with the affairs of his Empire, but also that exterminating the Christians would bring his subjects back to the ancient traditions of their race and make them drop the liberal notions that the Young Turk party was spreading around to hide its real purposes. This throned assassin was an astute politician, a great Statesman according to Oriental fashions, and having made his decision, he had the orders given out for the massacres.

THE MASSACRES

This was the end of the year 1895. Officers were sent out from Yıldız-Kiosk, and executions in the provinces marked the passage of the Imperial messengers.

To describe the atrocities then committed would require the publication of a large volume. A passage from the work of Pastor Lepsius (1) is sufficient to give an idea of the unexpected woes that suddenly fell on the Armenians:

"In the village of Hoh, in the Kharput district, the Christians were "gathered together inside a mosque. Eighty young men were chosen "from among them and led outside the village to be slaughtered. Hundreds "of Armenians were tortured because they refused to sign addresses to "the Sultan accusing their relatives and neighbors of high treason. One "of them refusing to swear to a statement which would have delivered "the honest people of his village to the executioner, was ordered by the "judges to be tortured. All night long this lasted, first he was bastinadoed "on the soles of his feet in a room adjoining which were the womenfolk "of his family. They tied him up, flogged him, tore out his beard hair "by hair, burned his flesh with red-hot iron, and still he refused to swear "as was demanded of him.

"I am a Christian, he said, I cannot stain my soul with innocent "blood ... In the name of divine mercy, finish me."

It was important for Abdul-Hamid to have documents in hand to show that the Armenians were revolutionaries, so as to justify his acts to the representatives of France, Britain, and the United States, and to legitimize these heinous crimes by passing them off as acts of justice dictated by reasons of State.

In 1890 the Sultan, already preparing to exterminate the Armenians, had the genial idea to arm the Kurds on the borders of Armenia and give them the name of Hamidian Cavalry. He let loose, as can be well imagined, these bandits against the Christians, and then encouraged by the hesitant attitude of the ambassadors, in 1894 he ordered

---

(1) L'Arménie et l'Europe, (French transl.) p 58, Lausanne, 1896.

a trial massacre at Sassoun, an experiment which lasted three weeks. The regular army itself was ordered to do the killing

"In one place, three to four hundred women, and in another two "hundred, after being delivered up to the soldiers, were despatched by "the sword or the bayonet

"In another place, about sixty women and girls were shut up for "several days in a small church, delivered to the soldiers, and then finally "slaughtered, a river of blood flowed from the church door. Elsewhere, "on a mountain, some thousands of fugitives held out for ten days or so, "but in vain. A woman ran out on a high rock and cried: "Sisters, you "must choose either fall into the hands of these Turks or else follow "me", and holding in her arms her one-year old child, she cast herself "down Her companions followed her, and the Sultan decorated the offi- "cer in command of the murderers, and sent a silver banner to the Kurdish "chieftains. (1)"

From 1894 to 1896 more than 200,000 Armenians were put to death, 100,000 were made Moslems by force, and more than 100,000 women and girls were ravished and sent into harems. Armenia being devastated, there was no harvest, and the remainder of the inhabitants suffered a terrible famine. Fleeing to the mountains and hiding in inaccessible spots, the peasants watched their homes sacked and burned, thousands of their villages being reduced to ashes.

From Europe there went up a tremendous cry of indignation as the groanings of the victims reached the ears of the western world, but no power dared to intervene with the energy that was called for, to have despatched an expeditionary force to the Turkish coasts would have brought about a European war, and so they all held off.

There was a paroxysm of indignation among Armenians abroad, who sent up their protests in Paris, London, Rome, Geneva, and Washington. Some Armenians inside Turkey joined up with some young men from the United States, and in their desperation decided to give vent to their anger and help their fellow-countrymen by a feat of arms likely to entail Europe's intervention. In the summer of 1896 they seized the Ottoman Bank at Galata and held out against the Turkish police and soldiers.

Alas! this attempt to reach Europe's ears by overt act failed, and in his anger the Sultan ordered the massacres to go on with even greater

---

(1) *Foi et Vie*, April 1 16, 1916, p 111, according to Pastor Lepsius.

cruelty. In the very city of Constantinople under the eyes of the ambassadors, ten thousand Armenians were vilely slaughtered.

In 1909, however, the horizon seemed to brighten for the unhappy people. The Ottoman army was won over to the cause of the Young Turks and besieged the Sultan in his palace, although nine months previously he had accepted the Constitution. Abdul-Hamid was forcibly removed from Yildiz-Kiosk and imprisoned at Salonica. All Europe rejoiced, even though the punishment was far too mild for the murderous Sultan, and the Armenians looked forward to an end to all their woes, for had they not collaborated with the Young Turks and given ample proof of their loyalty to the Turkish liberal party? The Armenian section of the population, that had so largely contributed to the success of this revolution, had every right to reap the reward of its sacrifices.

What was thought to be the dawn of liberty caused a frenzy of joy throughout Turkey; Moslems, Christians, and Jews gave way to the most sincere expressions of mutual friendship. Priests and Ulemas embraced one another in the streets to the enthusiastic cries of the crowd. Europe gave its support to the liberal movement, and sent able men to guide the steps of the newly formed Committee of "Union and Progress" that was now in the saddle. Funds from Europe also poured in to help the Committee carry out its plans for a modernized Turkey.

Alas, once more! The Young Turks answered the loyal declarations of the Armenians, even before Abdul-Hamid was off his throne, by the Adana massacres which opened a series of the most frightful crimes ever recorded by history.

The Armenians had been only tools in the hands of power-seeking bandits, who as soon as they had seized the reins and felt themselves strong, had no further reason to conceal their hatred of aliens, and their Pan-Islamism. Possessing none of the slyness and diplomacy of the Sultan they had just overthrown, these imperious revolutionaries were determined to continue the bloody work of Abdul-Hamid and exterminate all the non-Moslems of the Empire, and if they had any reform in mind, it was that of abolishing all European interference in their affairs and calling an end to the Capitulations. "We are Moslems", said one high Young Turk official, "and we can have nothing in common with unbelievers. The Empire of Islam is our heritage, it will be vast enough to enable us to break off all contact with Christians." And he added: "We shall live in peace with every one on our side."

It was not, however, Pan-Islamism properly speaking that was at the back of the heads of the Young Turks, but Pan-Turkism, a sort of Moslem nationalism even more exclusive than Abdul-Hamid's doctrine, for it considered the Turkish race alone capable of any progress, and superior therefore to Arabs, Persians, Egyptians, and Indians These latter people it deemed incapable of advancement, they were mere subjects of infidels The supreme power for the 300 millions of Mahometans in the world it vested in the Committee of "Union and Progress", and purposed driving from their country or exterminating every unbeliever living in the immense Moslem territories In short, a new edition of Mahomet's system for the benefit of a gang mad with lust for power, for self-indulgence, and pelf,—Imperialism in its most degraded form

Naturally the Armenians when they were allied with the Young Turks during the days they kept up 'a common struggle' had a totally different idea of Turkey's regeneration, and their straightforward and loyal liberalism was quite the opposite of the Pan-Turks' plan once they had seized the government These opposite views of the Armenians were Armenia's death-warrant, and to be consistent the Young Turks included all the unbelievers of the Empire in their planned purge.

The two masters of Turkey after 1913 were Talaat bey and Enver Pasha, two adventurers of obscure birth, for Talaat bey in 1908 was merely a copy-clerk in the Constantinople Post-Office, and Enver bey was a captain-adjutant at Salonica The former outlined the acts of terrorism to be applied in the pursuance of their internal policy, the latter represented the party's armed strength. Talaat bey relied on the Turks, and Enver bey on the Germans Talaat bey ordered the massacres, Enver bey carried them out. As for the new Sultan, Abdul-Hamid's successor, his name must not even be mentioned, for he does not reign. The Young Turks created an imaginary documentary file, and announced its existence without ever showing it,—relative to the crimes of which they accused the Armenians, who they said were guilty of sedition and treason. Then, on the strength of this suppositional indictment, they began to carry out the death sentence uttered by Talaat bey

With the exception of those at Constantinople, the massacres under Abdul-Hamid had been carried out unsystematically The Sultan left details to be looked after by his delegates. Talaat bey went one better, however, under the guidance of Enver who had lived a long time in Berlin, and perhaps also of advisers even more versed in European administrative ways, he turned the massacres into a State service

On account of the war that had just been declared on the Entente Powers, all the young Christians of the Empire were called to the colors, but they were not sent to the front. They were divided into sections of several hundreds each, and used for the building and upkeep of roads; then, when they had finished this work, a large number were executed.

The towns and villages with only old people, women, and children left in them, and incapable of any defense, were occupied by the troops. Most of the men and male children were slain, and the remainder were ordered to gather into columns of 1,000 to 2,000 each, to go off into exile. These formalities were accompanied by summonses to adopt the Moslem religion, also by every kind of violence on the part of the soldiers. The property of the evicted inhabitants was distributed or sold to Moslems for next to nothing.

The columns started out, accompanied by soldiers and by Kurdish horsemen who, on the way, indulged in every conceivable brutality, killing as fancy took them, and selling the women as slaves in the small towns and villages they passed through.

Even these sales were conducted methodically. In each town the women and young girls were lined up in front of the Konak (government building) and offered to purchasers, on the following day the remainder of the column resumed the march. Many of the unfortunates exhausted by fatigue and hunger fell by the wayside; most of these rose no more, a spear or bayonet-thrust put an end to their sufferings.

Many of these columns were entirely massacred, especially at a place called Kemagh-Boghaz on the Euphrates below Erzindjan. Others, their ranks greatly thinned, reached Mesopotamia, where most of them gradually died off in the bleak desert climate, homeless and starving. (1)

A German woman-traveler relates that in one of these camps of suffering, composed of people from Zeitoun, one woman said to her: "Why don't they kill us outright? In the daytime we have no water, "our children are howling from thirst, in the night there come the Arabs, "stealing our bedding and clothes, they have carried off our young girls, "and raped our women. If we are unable to walk, the gendarmes beat "us. A number of women have drowned themselves in the river to "escape being outraged, some of them even with their infants."

Talaat bey reckoned on these sufferings to finish off the remnants of the columns of deportees.

To give a better realization, however, of all the horror of these mass

---
(1) *Foi et Vie*, op. cit p 150

executions and pillaging, allow me to add to the above report a few authentic documents covering each phase of these frightful dramas. They may all be summed up in four acts, viz. the execution of the young men, the massacres, the caravan, the desert.

A witness stated. "One day we met a number of workmen. 'They "are going to kill them all off' our traveling companion (a gendarme) "said to me. From the top of a hill our driver pointed out to me with "his whip about four hundred workmen whom they had lined up on the "edge of a sloping piece of ground. We know what happened In another "place, while the gendarmes shot, Turkish workmen finished off the "victims with knives and stones. (2)"

These were the Armenian conscripts which Talaat was having exterminated, while the towns and villages were being sacked.

"The thousand or so Armenian houses in a populous town are "emptied of their furniture and all they contained, one after another, "by the police who are followed by a crowd of Turkish women and children "like a flock of vultures This mob snatch everything they can lay their "hands on and take away, and when the police bring anything valuable "out of a house there is a terrific struggle for it That sort of thing I "see every day with my own eyes It will surely take several weeks "to empty all the houses and stores of the Armenians. (1)"

But the Turks were not satisfied with taking property. Reverting to their old ancestral customs, they treated the unhappy Christians as slaves. "The children and young girls were carried away and sold, two "young girls at four francs apiece At Constantinople, the market is "glutted, young girls are going at a few francs apiece"

"One Turk with his friends sets up as a brothel-owner. The officers "took the women and then passed them on to their soldiers In the "places where the caravan camped overnight, the soldiers and inhabitants "of the neighboring villages were let loose on them in the evening, women "were rented out to them for the night. (2)"

In one town in Armenia, a Danish hospital-nurse was one night awakened by shooting, and realizing that numbers were being shot down before the departure of the caravan, she wrote "I felt really relieved "to think that those victims were at last beyond human cruelty Fortunate "are those who are killed! (3)"

---

(2) *Quelques Documents* (Geneva). narrative of the Danish nurses.
(1) A J. TOYNBEE, The Murder of a Nation, London, 1915, p. 34
(2) Foi et Vie, *op cit*, p. 116.
(3) *Ibid.*

Fortunate victims, indeed! for the lot of the survivors, those whom death did not take, was frightful. The caravan decimated by hunger, exhaustion, and the cruelty of their guards, had to go on and on Sometimes the cries of women and children fill the air. Strength fails, hideous hunger adds its scourge The unfortunates devour straw, grass, whenever they can "I looked at them," said one witness, "and wild animals "could not have been worse, they rushed on the guards carrying food, "and the guards struck them with clubs, hard enough sometimes to kill "them It was difficult to realize that these were human beings"

While the caravan plods along a road strewn with the corpses from the preceding convoy, sometimes through reeking air, the local mob, conscious that here they can prey at will, follow along like a pack of wolves, biting and tearing. The mob kill and steal

When they pass near the river, mothers throw their children in the water and themselves after them. Or else the gendarmes throw in all the children under twelve or fifteen, and any who can swim, they shoot in the water

Even at the end of the seemingly interminable march, their martyrdom is not over for the unhappy survivors, for the desert climate is terrible for these people accustomed to mountain air Among them are to be seen some who from what remains of their clothing appear to have been men of position, educated women speaking European languages, chiefly English and French, people who have known the intellectual and material well-being of civilization!

"Most of the time, the caravans do not go far; shooting, bayonet "thrusts, hunger, and fatigue thin out the ranks as they proceed. All "the most hideous passions of the human beast are vented on the wretched "herd, which melts and disappears If a few débris do reach Mesopotamia, "they are left there without shelter or food, in desert or marshy lands, "the heat and dampness make short work of the poor creatures accustomed "to keen and wholesome mountain air. Any attempt at forming a colony "is out of the question without supplies, resources, tools, assistance, or "able men The remnants of the Armenian caravans die away from "fever and misery. (1)"

"Of the between 2,000 and 3,000 peasants of Upper Armenia brought "to Aleppo," said a German professor in the school of that city, "there "remain forty or fifty skeletons With distorted features, they succumb to

---

(1) René PINON La Suppression des Arméniens p. 29-30, Paris, 1916.

"blows, to hunger, and thirst. Europeans are forbidden to give bread
"to the starving creatures. Forty or fifty phantoms are heaped together
"in one court, they are the demented ones, they no longer know how to
"eat. When offered bread they refused it unconcernedly. They merely
"groan as they await death. Every day over a hundred corpses are taken
"out of Aleppo. Young girls, women, children, almost naked on the
"ground, lie between the dying and coffins already prepared, and breathe
"their last feeble sighs."

In every province of Armenia the massacres were terrible, but those that took place at Mouch surpassed in barbarity the atrocities in any other town. A witness of this awful drama stated: "Day broke, it "was the 2nd of July, 1915, a day of suffering and calamity a day of terror "for the unhappy Armenians. Early in the morning, Kurds and regular "soldiers overran the town shouting, and entered the Armenian quarters "They began by killing those who were still there since the departure "of thirteen hundred people who had gone off in caravan the day before "and been wiped out. Most of the inhabitants, no longer doubting the "fate that awaited them, had gathered in the houses in the center of "the town, where they seemed a little safer. There, families were grouped "together forty, fifty, even a hundred persons huddled together in nar-"row rooms, with doors and windows and all entrances barricaded.

"Soon howls of approaching men drew nearer, the band of madmen "invaded the streets, shooting as they came, and armed with hatchets "they attacked the doors which flew in splinters. Then followed an in-"describable slaughter. Cries of terror and agony were mingled with "the noise of hatchet-blows and with the calls urging on the murderers "The streets ran with blood, and bodies were piling up in front of the "houses, while the Turks continued to shout 'Vour! Vour! (strike! "strike!) The Kurds yelled and howled for blood, as these wild beasts "went from house to house swinging their blood-covered hatchets.

"The unhappy Armenians, crazed with fear, pressed against one "another, were crushed and suffocated. The cries and shrieks of the "women were heard, as children were trampled to death by those who "strove to save them.

"A young woman handed one of the executioners her child she was "holding in her arms. 'Take him,' she begged, 'I give him to you, only "do not kill him." The soldier seized the child, threw it down and cut "off its head with one stroke, then turning to the unhappy mother, with "one more blow with his axe he cleaved her skull.

"A few more minutes, and sinister silence replaced the cries and "moans and dying groans. Only a heap of ripped-up corpses, of shape-"less and bleeding human débris, remained.

"On several sides clouds of smoke are whirling skyward from burn-"ing houses crowded with Armenians perishing in the flames. From one "house some one escapes and rushes towards the river, but he is caught "by the soldiers, who drench him with petroleum and watch him burn "with fiendish glee. Further on are bursts of laughter at the sight of "a six-year old child convulsed with agony from a bayonet-thrust, also "hapless women with bowels ripped open by the Kurds who have torn "out their unborn children. There again, soldiers fight for the possession "of a young girl, the burly winner carrying her off to rape and slaughter."

At nightfall the survivors flee in a body to the river with the hope of getting across into open country, but they are caught between two fires from the Turks, and those who rush into the water are mostly drowned. The town is on fire, and the guns still roar as they drop their shells on the Armenian quarter.

No human language is strong or colorful enough to depict such horrors, or to express the moral and physical sufferings of these innocent martyred people up to the moment of their release in death. Any survivors, hopeless wrecks from the frightful massacres wherein they have seen all their loved ones perish, are sent into concentration camps where torture and degradation worse than death await them.

When Mahomet II took Constantinople by storm, fifty thousand Greeks were put to the sword by the barbarians before their Sultan ordered the slaughter to cease. Europe was then seized with horror, but what must be our feelings today as we look back on the agony of the Armenian nation, an agony that lasted so many years, twenty-two long years in fact (1894-1916), and its toll of over a million victims!

Nevertheless the Armenian nation is neither extinguished nor reduced to a rôle of supplicant. Its national spirit burns more fiercely than ever, for the crime that has been committed, far from extirpating their courage, has armed it with wrath. They are still quite numerous, moreover, and include large settlements outside of Ottoman territory, while their people inside Turkey are far from having been entirely wiped out.

No Turkish statistics have ever been seriously or conscientiously drawn up. Why indeed should there be any census of the rayah population? Such figures would have been rather unprofitable to the Moslems for they would have shown what a great proportion of Christians there are in the territory ruled by the Sultan. At any rate we can arrive at an approximate estimate within a few hundred thousand, and draw our conclusions therefrom.

POPULATION OF THE OTTOMAN EMPIRE
The Ottoman Empire, with an area of 775,000 square miles, has a population of 26 millions, of whom 9 millions speak Turkish, 10 million Arabic, and 2 million the various Kurdish dialects. The total number of Moslems is therefore 21 millions. The other five millions are Christians (Armenians, Greeks, Syrians, and Chaldeans), Jews, Mandeans, and a few other non-Mohammedans adhering to numerically small religions.

The Turks inhabit all the north of the Empire, chiefly Asia Minor, whilst the regions to the east of the upper and middle Euphrates are peopled by Armenians and Kurds. Intermixture of the different elements of population is unknown in Turkey, and each people is isolated territorially, the Turks having only troops and officials outside of their own geographical sphere.

In some parts of Arabia and Mesopotamia the density of population even including the towns, is less than three inhabitants per sq. mile, whereas in the north of western Asia (Armenia, Lazistan, Anatolia, and central Asia Minor), in Coelesyria, the Arabian Red Sea coast and shores of the Gulf of Oman, the density is one to ten inhabitants. Syria, the southern coast of Asia Minor, and Lower Chaldea, on the other hand, are more thickly populated, containing an average of twenty-five to one hundred persons per square mile.

In the Turkish regions of the empire the population is therefore as dense as in those occupied by the Armenians, but to this Christian population which is comparatively compact in Armenia must be added all the large detached groups of Armenians, both on Ottoman territory and abroad, likewise the considerable numbers living in Russia and Persia. If we take in also the more distant colonies, we shall arrive at the total figure of the Armenian people

THE ARMENIAN POPULATION
According to the statistics of the Patriarchate the number of Turkish Armenians in 1882 was 2,660,000 of whom 1,630,000 occupied the six so-called Armenian vilayets, and 1,030,000 dwelt in

Cilicia and the various cities of Turkey. This was the figure submitted to the Congress of Berlin. But new statistics compiled in 1912, i.e. after the massacres and the emigrations of 1894-1896, likewise supplied by the Patriarchate, give only 1,018,000 for the six vilayets. They show also in the same specific region 660,000 Turks and 424,000 Kurds, both nomads and non-nomads, the whole population being 2,615,000. The Armenians constituted therefore 38.9% of the population, the Turks 25.4% and the Kurds 26.5%.

Judging from the above two estimates of the Patriarchate, we must conclude that the Armenian population in the period 1882-1912, by massacre, emigration, or conversion to Islam, decreased by about 612,000.

It is impossible to know, even roughly, what losses the nation sustained during the massacres ordered after 1912 by the Young Turks, for no figures were ever kept. According to documents we have seen, however, the number of victims were considerably over half a million. Besides which, we know that about a quarter of a million went into Russia, and many became Moslems, with the remainder in the concentration camps of Mesopotamia.

Of the 1,030,000 Armenians who in 1882 lived in parts of the Sultan's dominions other than Armenia proper, many certainly lost their lives, but many also emigrated.

We may reckon at one million the number of Turkish Armenians who for various reasons managed to escape and who will return to their own nation the day it is delivered. Over and above these numbers, we must add the Armenian subjects of the Czar and the Shah, also the large and numerous colonies abroad. All in all, we reach a total of at least three millions of people speaking the Armenian tongue.

The élite of the Armenian community unfortunately were unable to escape. Those surviving live today in Paris, London, Petrograd, Odessa, Tiflis, or Venice, working with unflagging energy for their final goal. They constitute a great asset for the cause of this persecuted people, for such an intelligentsia have means to make themselves heard and to vindicate the rights of their brethren to freedom. Four or five hundred thousand Greeks obtained from Europe their independence in 1829, and three millions of Armenians, by their energy, their sufferings, and the respect we owe their glorious past, deserve that Europe should give them honorable status in the world.

CHAPTER X

ARMENIANS OUTSIDE OF ARMENIA — THE INHABITANTS OF
ARMENIA AND THE ARMENIAN COLONIES

With great empires for their neighbors, and constantly exposed to their influence as also frequently to the imposition of their will, the Armenians were from the beginning of their national history obliged to maintain large colonies of their compatriots in the very centers that were their chief sources of supply and at the same time, unfortunately, their chief sources of anxiety. From the time of Cyrus, after that monarch had established Persian rule over all Asia, the descendants of Haïk undoubtedly had their representatives at the court of the King of Kings, and among the nobles from the land of Ararat there were some who succumbed to the lure of Achaemenian gold and served Persia to the detriment of their own country. It was an Armenian prince, named Dadarses, whom Darius entrusted with putting down the revolt of the northern provinces of his empire while he himself was busy besieging Babylon This single fact, related by Darius himself, shows that there was an Armenian colony around the Shah-en-Shah that enjoyed considerable prestige and the confidence of the sovereign.

The same was certainly the case after the Macedonian conquest of Asia, for towards the end of the fourth century B.C Armenian names appear among the princes entrusted with the government of Armenia by the Seleucid rulers of Syria.

Later on, when Rome extended her power over the remains of Alexander's empire and no longer had the long struggle with the Persian Arsacid monarchs to maintain, there gathered at the same time both at Ctesiphon and in the Eternal City populous and energetic colonies of Armenians who often handled matters concerning their homeland, in behalf either of the Romans or the Persians.

THE ARMENIAN EMPERORS Especially after the Empire was divided between the two sons of Theodosius, the Armenians acquired more and more prestige at the Roman court of the East The nearness of the new capit-

— 315 —

al and the common interests linking the Greeks and the peoples of the Eastern provinces drew numbers of Armenians to the shores of the Bosphorus, and by degrees the latter attained to such importance in the State that finally the Imperial purple fell on their shoulders.

The part played by Armenian princes in the Byzantine empire is so great that we need to record their names, their sequence, and their kinship with one another, without going too deeply, however, into the details of their reigns which belong rather to Byzantine history than to that of Asia proper.

Great numbers of foreigners were included in the population of Constantinople; there were whole legions of them in the army, and some of them filled the highest posts in the Empire. Many of these foreigners ascended the throne, but no nation gave more emperors to Byzantium than did the Armenian people, and it would be overlooking one of the most glorious pages of the history of the descendants of Haik if we did not mention the names of these rulers who for more than three centuries occupied the Imperial throne of the Eastern Empire, i.e. during one third of its existence (395-1453).

The Armenian period of Byzantium certainly added some luster to the Empire of the Caesars, for it includes famous names and deeds of renown connected with the portentous collision that then took place between civilization and the barbarism of the Persians and Arabs. Coming from countries that were more exposed than any to onslaughts of the foes of Christianity, the royal Armenian families once on the Imperial throne used their power for centuries to carry on the fight against the invaders, a fight which unfortunately in their old homeland was so often handicapped both by insufficient resources and geographical exposure.

These emperors were unable, it is true, to escape the quarrels that disturbed their capital, and naturally they had to make allowances for the character of their Greek subjects and take the line of prudence in dealing with domestic matters, but they never forgot the rôle destiny had allotted them as the champions of civilization.

COINS OF MAURICIUS TIBERIUS

MAURICIUS TIBERIUS 582-602

The first Armenian (1) to bear the title of "Basileus" was Mauricius. He was born in 539 at Arabissa in Cappadocia, of a noble Armenian family. Flavius Tiberius Mauricius first became a general and gained great renown in his wars against the Persians. He was received in triumph at Constantinople in 582, and on August 13th of that year he married Constantine, the daughter of Tiberius Constantine (578-582). He was crowned emperor that same year, but contrary to what might have been expected from the conqueror of the Sassanid armies, he was lacking as a ruler both in energy and authority. After reigning twenty years, he was dethroned by Focas who was proclaimed emperor by the army in revolt. Mauricius fled, and his ship being compelled by a storm to put in to land

MAURICIUS TIBERIUS
CONSTANTINE and THEODOSIUS
(with countermark of Heraclius I)

---

(1) For proofs of the Armenian origin of emperors and empresses, and of princes and princesses of Constantinople who were of that nationality, consult: CARABED-DER-SAHAKIAN. *The Armenian Emperors of Byzantium*, 2 vol., Saint-Lazare (Venice) 1905, (in Armenian). (The author of this work of considerable repute lost his life in the Trebizond massacres of the spring of 1915). — LEBEAU, *Historie du Bas-Empire*; — F. W. BUSSELL, *The Roman Empire*. 1910; — G. SCHLUMBERGER, *L'Epopée byzantine*;—K. J. BASMADJIAN, *Histoire moderne du peuple arménien*; — *Corpus Historiae Byzantinae*, vol. IX, p. 136 (Venice, 1729), — for Emperor *Mauricius*; *Theophilactus Simocatta Historiae*. — for *Heraclius I*; *Nicephorus Constantinopolitanus, De rebus post Mauricium Gestis*, p. 50 (ed. Bon); —for *Filepicus Bardanes*; *Cedrenus*, I, p. 43, — for *Leo V*; Niebuhr, *Constantine Porphyrogenetus, Theoph. Continuat.*, p. 212; Luitprand. I, 3 — for *Romanus*; G. SCHLUMBERGER, *Un Empereur Byzantin*, — for *John Zimisces*; *Cedrenus*, vol. II, p. 23 and 26, for *Marina*. wife of Constantine VI. To this list should be added *Artavazd* (Cf. SABATIER, *Monnaies byzantines*, vol. II, p. 40) whose Armenian origin seems, however, doubtful. All the princes and princesses for whom I give no references are children of the emperors whose names are on the following pages.

twenty miles from Constantinople, he was captured and beheaded (November 27, 602), after first seeing four of his sons, Peter, Paul, Justin, and Justinian executed in the same manner. A fifth son, Theodosius, who escaped the massacre was arrested in his flight to Persia and taken to

HERACLIUS I CONSUL   HERACLIUS I EMPEROR

Focas who ordered him to be strangled. Constantine, Mauricius' wife, was shut up in a monastery with her daughter Anastasia, Theoctistē, Cleopatra, Sopatra, and Maria. Three years later Focas had them taken out and put to death. Arab and Persian writers state that Princess Maria escaped being slain and became the wife of the Persian king Chosroes II.

FLAVIUS HERACLIUS I 610-641

HERACLIUS. HERACLIUS CONSTANTINE and EUDOXIA

At the instigation of Priscus, Focas' son-in-law, who stood in fear of his father-in-law's fits of anger, Heraclius, patrician and prefect of Africa, and formerly governor of Armenia in 594, — probably a relative of Mauricius, — sent his son Flavius Heraclius in command of a fleet to Constantinople to avenge the Emperor's murder. On October 6th, 610, Focas was overthrown and Flavius Heraclius I mounted the throne, after having offered it first to Priscus who declined it.

The new emperor married his betrothed Flavia or Fabia, whom he crowned under the name of Eudoxia. This empress died on August 13, 612, leaving a daughter named Epiphania, born July 7,

611, and a son, born May 3, 612, who later became emperor under the name of Heraclius II Constantine and reigned jointly with his half-brother Heracleonas (641).

In 614 Heraclius married his niece Martina, the daughter of his own sister Maria, and there were born to them: Constantine, created Caesar in 616, Flavius and Theodosius; these died all three before their father; Heracleonas, born in 626, Caesar in 630, and Joint Emperor in 638; David, born November 7, 630, created Caesar in 641; also two daughters, Augustina and Martina, and other children whom history does not mention.

Taking personal command of his armies, Heraclius drove out the Persians under Chosroes II (591-628) from Asia Minor, and advanced as far as the Tigris. In 622 he entered Armenia. Following this campaign, however, the Emperor returned to his capital, and allowed himself to be engrossed thereafter with religious controversies, neglecting entirely the military affairs of the Empire. In the meantime the Arabs

HERACLIUS, HERACLIUS CONSTANTINE & HERACLEONAS

HERACLEONAS, DAVID TIBERIUS & CONSTANS II

HERACLIUS, HERACLIUS CONSTANTINE and MARTINA

HERACLIUS CONSTANTINE and HERACLEONAS

went rapidly ahead; Aboubeker seized Damascus (632) and Omar took Jerusalem (638); Mesopotamia, Syria and Palestine were forever lost to the Greeks.

We possess coins of Heraclius alone, both as Consul and as Emperor, of Heraclius and Heraclius Constantine, of Heraclius and Heracleonas, of Heraclius, Eudoxia, and Heraclius

HERACLEONAS alone

— 319 —

CONSTANS II and CONSTANTINE POGONATUS

CONSTANS II (641-668)

CONSTANS II, CONSTANTINE POGONATUS, & TIBERIUS

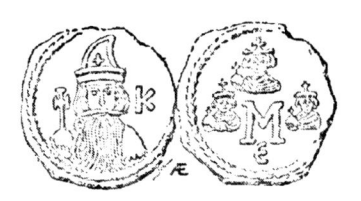

CONSTANS II, HERACLIUS and TIBERIUS

CONSTANTINE IV POGONATUS

CONSTANTINE IV POGONATUS (668-678)

Constantine (610-612), of Heraclius, Heraclius Constantine, and Martina (614-641), of Heraclius and Martina (614-641), of the Emperor with his two sons Heraclius Constantine and Heracleonas (638-641), all of them valuable documentary records of this ruler's family.

According to Nicetas, the Emperor dying at the age of sixty-six decided that his two sons, Heraclius Constantine and Heracleonas, should reign together under Martina's regency. Thus in 641 we have coins of the two princes. But, on June 23rd of that year, Martina poisoned Heraclius Constantine, and her son Heracleonas thereafter reigned alone. He appointed as Caesars to assist him his brother David Tiberius and Constans, the son of Heraclius Constantine.

The reign of Heracleonas was a short one. In September 641 he was deprived of the crown by the Senate. Martina had her tongue cut out, Heracleonas lost his nose, and Flavius Heraclius, better known as Constans II, ascended the Imperial throne. After a reign of no note, he was assassinated (July 15th, 668) in Sicily, leaving three sons, Constantine Pogonatus, Heraclius, and Tiberius.

Constantine IV Pogonatus (the Bearded) ruled with the assistance of his two brothers (668), and in the first year of his reign put down a revolt by an Armenian named Mazizius who had proclaimed himself emperor at Syracuse. This Emperor died on September 14th, 685 after seeing his capital besieged

— 320 —

seven times by the Arabs, between 669 and 678.

JUSTINIAN II (685-695, and 705-711) Justinian II Rhinotmetos (685-695 and 705-711), the son of Constantine Pogonatus and Anastasia, ascended the throne. He was driven from Constantinople and exiled to Kherson, but he regained his throne with the help of the Khazars and the Bulgars, and caused both Leontius (695-698) and Tiberius V Absimarus (698-705) who had usurped the power, to be beheaded.

TIBERIUS IV (705-711) Tiberius IV (705-711), the son of Justinian II, was four years old when his father made him Joint Emperor. But in 711 the people revolted and proclaimed Filepicus Bardanes, who had Justinian II and his son put to death. Thus the dynasty of Heraclius became extinct, after occupying the Imperial throne for one hundred years.

FILEPICUS BARDANES (711-713) Filepicus was of Armenian extraction, a general of Justinian II's army and the son of the Patrician Nicephorus. His reign was brief; on June 3, 713, as the result of a conspiracy and the victory of a faction called the "Greens", the plotters seized him during a repast,

FILEPICUS BARDANES    ARTAVAZDUS and CONSTANTINE V

deposed him, and put out his eyes. In his stead, Artemius Anastasius was proclaimed Emperor.

ARTAVAZDUS (724) Artavazdus was Commander-in-chief of the army in Armenia and had married Anna, the daughter of Emperor Leo III. He proclaimed himself emperor early in 742, but in November of that year he was defeated by his brother-in-law Constantine V. He was deposed

— 321 —

and had his eyes put out, a fate shared by his two sons, Nicephorus who had ruled with him as Associate, and Nicetas.

THE ARMENIAN LEO V (813-820)

On July 19th, 813, Leo V surnamed The Armenian, was raised to the throne by the army which had just defeated the Bulgarians. This prince had married Theodosia, the daughter of the Patrician Arsavir; they had four sons: Sabatius or Sembates (Sempad) who under the name of Constantine VII was appointed Associate ruler of the Empire, Basil, Gregory, and Theodosius. On December 25th, 820, Leo was assassinated, and Michael II the Stammerer seized the power.

LEO V & CONSTANTINE VII

LEO V, THE ARMENIAN

ARTAVAZDUS & NICEPHORUS

MICHAEL III & BASIL I

Associated with the Imperial throne by Michael III surnamed The Drunkard (842-867), Basil (867-886) murdered his colleague and benefactor, and reigned alone. By his second wife Eudoxia he had

BASIL I alone

BASIL I and CONSTANTINE IX

several children, among them Leo the Wise and Alexander. By Maria,

COIN OF EMPEROR LEO THE PHILOSOPHER (886-912)

an Armenian woman whom he repudiated, he had had a son Constantine VIII on whom he bestowed the Imperial title in 868, and who died in 879. Basil died August 29th, 886.

The reign of Leo VI the Wise or The Philosopher (886-912) was without note. He had associated with him on the Imperial throne his brother Alexander, and although he had four wives, he left only one son Constantine X Porphyrogenetus, born in 905. At his death in May 11th, 912, Leo left the throne to his brother, giving him charge of his son.

LEO VI & ALEXANDER

ALEXANDER (912-913)

Alexander was born Nov. 23rd, 871, and reigned from 912 to 913 only. He shared his crown with his brother Leo VI, then with his nephew Constantine X who was aged five only. He died June 4th, 913.

LEO VI and CONSTANTINE X    **ALEXANDER**    **CONSTANTINE and ZOE**    **CONSTANTINE X & ROMANUS I**

PORPHYROGENETUS CONSTANTINE X

Constantine X Porphyrogenetus was named "Augustus" on June 9th, 911. He was then hardly seven years old, being born Sept. 1st, 905. A Council, appointed by Alexander be-

— 323 —

fore his death, ruled therefore with him, and his first act was to call back from exile his mother Zoe Carbonopsinë, with whom he reigned from 913 to 919. In 919 he married Helena the daughter of Romanus Lacapenus, the Commander-in-chief of the Navy. The latter had himself crowned in 920, giving his three sons, Christophorus (920), Stephen and Constantine (928) each the title of Augustus. But in 944, Constantine X consigned Romanus to the island of Protë (where he died in 948), and thereafter ruled alone until the day of his death (Nov. 9th, 959).

CONSTANTINE X and ROMANUS II

Constantine X left a son named Constantine, who according to some historians shortened his father's days by poison (1), also four daughters, Zoë, Theodora, Agatha, and Anna.

ROMANUS I (920-944) Romanus I Lacapenus was the son of Theophylactus Abastactus, and was born in Armenia about the end of the 9th century. Romanus II was the son of Constantine X

ROMANUS I,

ROMANUS II

ROMANUS I CONSTANTINE X & CHRISTOPHORUS

---

(1) CEDRENUS, 337, 20; ZONARAS. XVI, 22.

and Helena, and was twenty years old when he ascended the throne on Nov. 10th, 959. He married Theophanon and had three children by her, Basil whom he made Associate of the Empire April 22nd, 960, Constantine whom he also made associate on April 8th, and a daughter named Anna. Poisoned by his wife, this ruler died March 15th, 963, Theophanon becoming Regent for her sons Basil II and Constantine XI. The

ROMANUS II and BASIL II

JOHN ZIMISCES

Empress married Nicephorus Focas who thus became Emperor (963-969), but she had him assassinated on Dec. 10th, 969, in connivance with John Zimisces, who took advantage of the youth of the two emperors and usurped the crown (969-976). Theophanon was exiled, but the death of John Zimisces on Jan. 11th, 976, restored the throne to the two sons of Romanus II. Basil II died Dec. 15th, 1025 at the age of seventy years, leaving his brother to reign alone.

THEOPHANON

BASIL II and and CONSTANTINE XI

CONSTANTINE XI PORPHYROGENETUS

Constantine XI Porphyrogenetus (1025-1028) had three daughters: Eudoxia, who took the veil, Zoë, and Theodora. Before his death he named as his successor the Patrician Romanus Argyrus, and ordered him to repudiate his wife Helena and marry his daughter Theodora. The latter refused him, however, so he married Theodora's sister, Zoë. The Byzantine throne departed consequently from the descendants of Leo V.

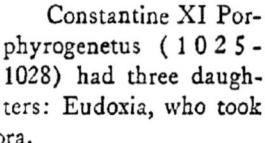

COIN OF JOHN ZIMISCES

COIN OF CONSTANTINE XI

— 325 —

THE ARMENIAN EMPRESSES

The following are the names of Armenian princesses who wore the Imperial crown:

Maria or Marina (788-795), the wife of Flavius Constantine VI; Theodosia (813-820), wife of Leo V; Euphrosinē (823-830), daughter of Constantine VI and Maria, wife of Michael II the Stammerer; Theodora (830-867), wife of Theophilus; Helena (919-961), wife of Constantine X Porphyrogenetus; Theodora (971-976) daughter of Constantine X and sister of Romanus II, wife of John I Zimisces; Zoë, daughter of Constantine IX, who was the wife of Romanus III Argyrus (1028-1034); Theodora (1041-1056) daughter of Constantine XI and Helena, wife of Constantine XII who reigned alone in 1055 and 1056; and Rhita, Xéné or Maria, the sister of Hetum II and daughter of Leo II, the king of New Armenia, who married Michael IX (1).

THEODORA (1041-1056)

THE ARMENIAN OFFICIALS OF THE GREEK EMPIRE

Among the great number of Armenians who played important parts as officials of the Empire, we must give first mention to the eunuch Narses, a general of genius who by crushing the forces of the Goths and Franks restored Rome to Emperor Justinian I. From 542 to 568 he governed the reconquered western portion of the latter's dominions. Also Isaac the Armenian, Exarch of Ravenna, who governed Italy from 625 to 643.

THEODORA and MICHAEL III

Armenian names were innumerable in the army, and the influence of such men of another land was felt not only from the military point of view but also in the various branches of the Government, likewise in science, art, and commerce. It extended even beyond the Empire,

---

(1) Mentioned by PACHYMEROS, vol. II, p. 205, and Niceph. GREG., Hist. Byz. VIII, 11.

and so-called barbarian countries sometimes had Armenians to rule them, e.g. Samuel (of Terdjan) who was king of Bulgaria in the 10th century.

THE BAGRATID DYNASTY OF GEORGIA

The Armenians not only attained a status of eminence in the capital of the Eastern world; their influence spread to the lands bordering on their own homeland. To the southeast their talents for public service had no scope in the face of Parthian and Sassanid hostility, and to the west and southwest Byzantine power was paramount; but in the north, in all the Transcaucasian countries, among the uncivilized nations, the Armenians were recognized for their superior ability. Georgia, the *Modicum Hiberiae regnum* of Tacitus (1) had from remotest times been divided into a great number of Eristhawates or domains of princes, which were in turn split up into lands belonging to the Aznaours or feudatories of the Eristhaws. Sassanid rule did not bring about any alteration, so that there was no political unity whatever among the Georgians, until the Armenian emperor Mauricius placed upon the throne of Iberia the first Bagratid sovereign of the country, Gouaram (575-600). Thereafter Georgia, Aghouania, Mingrelia, and all the small Kartvelian states of the southern slope of the Caucasus were governed by Armenian rulers, and the last of the Georgian kings Ereklé II was still a Bagratid descendant. We will not go into any detailed list of this

NARSES and THEODORA
(Mosaic at Ravenna)

long line of kings, who had to fight, in succession, the Sassanids, the Arabs, the Turks, the Mongols, and the Persians, and whose dynasty at least a score of times was placed in subjection, or even driven from their throne at

---

(1) XII. C. 43.

SARCOPHAGUS OF ISSAC THE ARMENIAN
(Ravenna)

Tiflis or Mtzkhet. In their vicissitudes, they had help either from the Byzantines of Constantinople or from those of Trebizond, and lastly from the Russians, according to the ebb and flow of history.

The kingdom of Georgia has some fine pages in its chronicles showing forth the struggles of the Kartvelians to maintain their national independence. They lacked, however, the high level of intellectual culture found in Armenia. The Georgians like all other Caucasians were Asiatic in their mode of warfare. Their art was taken from the Byzantines and Armenians, and at Tiflis, Mtzkhet, Gori, and the small towns of the Greater Caucasus are to be seen fine examples of Christian Greek architecture, modified of course by local preferences. Their literature, however, with the exception of a few poems and an epic entitled "The Leopard's Skin", is almost wholly of a religious character and of secondary interest only. We must in justice add that among all the Kartvelian peoples, the Georgians alone showed any refinement, — the other Caucasians remaining up to modern times entirely uncivilized. The Georgians undoubtedly owe their cultural superiority as compared to their neighboring kinsmen to the influence of the Byzantines and also of the Armenian dynasty that ruled over them for so many centuries.

THE ARMENIANS IN PERSIA AND CONSTANTINOPLE

Though the Bagratids were called to reign over these Christian people, no such opportunity was offered them in the other countries bordering on Armenia. At the Persian court, as also at that of the Arabs and later the Turks, differences of religion naturally stood between the Armenians and the throne; they filled nevertheless very important governmental positions. This dissemination of those who went out from Armenia into diverse groups was undoubtedly very prejudicial to their own nation's interests, for each group had its partisans in the homeland, and opposing factions stopped at nothing to safeguard their private interests and obtain the adoption of their particular views. They may, it is true, have secured helpful alliances for the Armenians, but such alliances most frequently were burdensome for the people.

One could easily mention a number of Armenians who forswore their religion and achieved eminence in the Moslem States. Saladin, we are told by Alishan, was an Armenian Kurd, if not actually an Armenian. Azam Atabeg, prime minister of Shah Nasr-ed-Din, belonged to an Armenian family, as I have already said. But we need not recall these renegades' names; in renouncing their faith, they joined the enemies of their own nation.

Just as the Byzantines drew Armenians into their service, the Moslem rulers also realized the assistance to be had from these active, intelligent, and industrious people Shah Abbas I founded New Julfa at the gates of his capital. Mahomet II after the taking of Constantinople, desirous of offsetting Greek influence, invited the Armenians of Asia Minor to come and settle by the Golden Horn where there dwelt already a large colony of them. In 1461 Mahomet appointed, as Patriarch over all Armenians in Turkey, Hovakim, the bishop of Brusa, granting him the same privileges as Selim I, the Greek patriarch. After his victory at Chaldiran over the Persians in 1514, the Sultan brought many Armenian craftsmen from Tabriz in order to develop and improve industry within his dominions. In the early days of Ottoman rule there were at Smyrna and all coastal cities of the Black Sea numbers of Armenian artisans who enjoyed the goodwill of the authorities. Not only did the Turks appreciate the services rendered to their government by such good workers, but they were also glad to counterbalance in a degree the Greek Christians who were always a very numerous and turbulent element in their empire.

Political causes for Armenian emigration were by no means the chief reason for the wide dispersion of this nation. They were certainly a large factor in strengthening Armenian business establishments in the great States adjoining their ancestral homeland, and such causes resulted in even more distant migrations; nevertheless only at Constantinople and at Isfahan did Armenian settlements really spring from any political background. The reason for the exodus of so many inhabitants to more benign lands is first and foremost the endless woes of their unhappy country, ever the cause and the scene of bloody warfare.

Attracted by the opportunities for trade offered them within the Roman empire, many Armenians had settled from ancient times in the southern Black Sea ports. Armenian colonies had as early as the reign of Mithridates the Great taken up their abode in Trebizond, Cerasus, Amisus, Sinope, Pontine Heracleum, and many other cities on the Anatolian coast, as also at Phasis in Iberia, and probably on the shores of the Caspian Sea, in Atropatenes, at Rhagae, and along all the great trade routes of the East. Persepolis, Ecbatana, Babylon, and Susa had formerly been the great Oriental commercial centers, but at the beginning of our era their places were taken by Pasagardae, Ctesiphon, Shuster, and Ahwaz, all of them marts for the goods landed in Chaldaea at the ports of Alexandria (of the Shatt-al-Arab) and ancient Teredon (Koweit). These cities traded with the north and naturally had their Armenian agents. Likewise, escaping from the persecution of their bloodthirsty oppressors, many others from the Ararat country fled to northern lands, to the Russian steppes and the Crimea where they remained in business relations with their homeland.

The largest emigration that took place, however, was that following the fall of the Bagratid dynasty. As we have seen, Armenian colonies arrived in Cilicia and Cappadocia when Gaghik II was deported. Still larger numbers went out from the city of Ani and especially from the district of Shirak, and trekked to the Crimea. From that peninsula which was peopled with Tartars, they went westward in two main branches, one of which reached Galicia, Podolia, and Volhynia, and the other Moldavia, whilst still another section of the Ani exiles settled in the city of Astrakhan after crossing the Qara-bagh and the Derbend pass.

THE ARMENIANS IN POLAND
Just recently, a Polish writer, Adolf Novatchinsky (1) has given us an account of the relations formerly existing between the Armenians and the Poles, and the arrival of the emigrants from the East in the Vistula and Dniester regions. He writes:

"Long before the downfall of the Armenian kingdom, which occurred "in 1375, the Armenians made their appearance among us, having been "invited to come by David, the ruler of Galicia.

"The first dismemberment of their country resulted in a heavy emi-"gration; the Armenian exiles, carrying with them a handful of their "native soil wrapped in cloth, scattered into southern Russia, into the "Caucasus, and the land of the Cossacks, and forty thousand of them "reached Poland. From then on, fresh waves of Armenian emigrants at "regular intervals left the Pontine shores for our hospitable Sarmatian "land, and it must be confessed that these guests from such a distance "were found to be the 'salt of the earth', so useful and desirable were "they in their new surroundings. They settled chiefly in the cities, and "in many places became the nucleus of Polish middle-class life. The city

---

(1) In the *Kuryer-Poranny* of Warsaw.

"of Lwow (Lemberg), the most patriotic center in Poland and the scene
"of so many historic upheavals, owes its renown largely to Armenian im-
"migrants Kamenets-Podolsk, the gem among our ancient fortresses,
"got all its celebrity from the Armenians who settled there. In Bukovina
"and all Galicia, the Armenian element plays a leading part in political
"and social life, in industry, and in intellectual activities. Furthermore,
"throughout Poland and its capital, Warsaw, the descendants of the
"former great people on the Araxes have distinguished themselves in
"all walks of life. In the battles of Grunwald and Warna, forbears of
"the Alexandrovics, the Augustinovics, the Abgarovics, the Agopsovics,
"and the Apakanovics took part. Also from the same Armenian stock
"we have later such famous Poles as Malakovski, Missasowicz, Piramo-
"vics, Pernatovics, Yakhovicz, Mrozianovsky, Grigorovicz, Baroutch, Theo-
"dorovicz, etc. . . . "

Through their repeated emigrations, the Armenians in Poland gradually became a colony of two hundred thousand spread over most of the cities and towns. They were welcomed by the Polish kings, and the rulers granted them not only religious freedom but also special political privileges. Casimir III (1333-1370) for instance gave the Armenians of Kamenets-Podolsk in 1344, and those of Lwow in 1356, the right to form a national council entirely composed of Armenians and entitled the "Voït". This council of twelve judges administered Armenian affairs as a wholly independent body. All official acts and minutes were drawn up not only in the Armenian language but also according to Armenian law. From the year 1183 the Armenians of Lwow had a church, built first of all of wood, which was pulled down in 1363 and replaced by a larger edifice. This church became the general residence of the Armenian prelates of Poland and Moldavia. In 1516, by orders of Sigismund I (1507-1548), king of Poland, the Armenians opened, in the middle of a rich and aristocratic quarter of Lwow, their first Law-Court or *Ratouché*. Consequently these new arrivals in Poland were specially looked after and given many privileges. A trouble-maker arose in this peaceful colony, however, in the form of an Armenian priest named Nicol Thorossowitch. This priest, notwithstanding the protests of the Armenians in Poland, had been consecrated as their Bishop by the Assistant Catholicos of Etchmiadzin, Melchisedec I of Garni (1593-1628), and at the instigation of the Jesuits of Lwow he started religious dissension among the Armenians The quarrel took on such proportions that the Armenians openly revolted against Nicol and in 1631 complained to the new Catholicos, Moves III (1629-1632), who sent a special legate to investigate the matter, at the same time writing both to the King of Poland and the Pope asking that aid and protection be given his envoy in the difficult task he had to accomplish. Nicol managed by his scheming to frustrate the intervention of the Catholicos, for this bishop actually proclaimed himself an adherent of the Roman Catholic and Apostolic Church, and with the help of the Jesuits succeeded in confiscating the property and church buildings of the Armenian community. Thereupon, outraged by Nicol's actions, the Armenian inhabitants who numbered over fifty thousand departed from Lwow. Those who did remain, about five thousand of them, gradually yielded to the entreaties and propaganda of Vardan Hovnanian, Nicol's successor, and embraced the Roman Catholic faith (1689) A century later, in 1790, the Armenians of Poland lost all their religious and political privileges, and came under the general law of the land. (1)

Poland was the birth-place of a certain number of Armenian scholars including *Stepanos Rochkian* and *Stepanos of Poland*

So ended this colony of Ani refugees in Poland, a community which foundered on the rock of religious dissension, ever the great scourge of the Armenian people. There remain, nevertheless, many indications today of the Armenian origin of these Poles whose ancestors once came from Asia. They have lost their language, it is true, but they have preserved some of their traditions, they intermarry, have their own church, and for pilgrimages they generally select Lwow where they have their cathedral built long ago on lines recalling their churches of old in ancient Ani. Until comparatively recent years, they had their own archbishop, Monsignor Theodorovicz. The Slavic Poles always designate these families by the name of "Armens"

Of those who emigrated from Lwow in the 17th century, ten thousand or so went to Moldavia, but in 1671 they were forced during the Turco-Polish war to settle in Bukovina and Transylvania. In Bukovina they chose the city of Suczawa and its surrounding district, while in Transylvania they themselves founded two new towns, Erzsebetvaros (Elisabethstadt) and Szamos-ujvar (Armienerstadt) which were by special privilege declared free cities by Charles VI Emperor of Austria (1711-1740). (2)

---

(1) Cf. K J BASMADJIAN, op. cit, p. 71 sq.
(2) Cf. K. J. BASMADJIAN, op. cit, p. 36 sq.

THE ARMENIANS IN WESTERN EUROPE

Three centuries after the fall of Ani, another great exodus took place from the second homeland, new Armenia. Very many Cilicians fled abroad for fear of the Moslems Crowds of them were received in Cyprus, Rhodes, and Crete, also at Smyrna and Constantinople, and all the lands still belonging to the Byzantine Empire. The coming of the Crusaders had familiarized the Armenians, however, with the Latin nations, and they soon began to flow towards Venice, Leghorn, Rome, Milan, Naples, Genoa, and Pisa, Armenian colonies being gradually formed in all these cities. Other emigrants settled in France, at Marseilles where there is still a "Rue des Arméniens", and in Paris where unhappy King Leo had spent his last days.

Egypt, where the last Armenian ruler was kept so long a prisoner, then had a considerable Armenian colony, and notwithstanding the humiliations and countless vexations the Christians were exposed to in that country from the Mamelukes, quite a number of refugees from Cilicia settled there.

Amsterdam also had its Armenian colony, but not of refugees from Ani or Sis. These arrivals were men and women from New Julfa near Isfahan, who had been doing business in India and the Persian Gulf with the Dutch and who eventually came to the Netherlands to settle.(1)

Abbas had a purpose in protecting the Armenians and getting them to settle just outside his capital, for all business with the East was then in the hands of Christians (English, Portuguese, Dutch) with whom the Moslems found it difficult to deal directly; whereas the Persian monarch recognized that the Armenians would be the very middlemen he absolutely needed to bring prosperity to his dominions. With the encouragement of the Persian court, large Armenian colonies were founded in the busiest ports of India, Bombay, Calcutta, and Madras, also in Ceylon.

THE ARMENIANS IN INDIA

Armenian business relations developed far afield, and enterprising merchants among them went still further Eastward, establishing themselves at Singapore, in Batavia, and even in China.

In eastern Asia, as we have seen, there were Armenian colonies at quite an early date. The oldest records we have of the settlements in

---

(1) The carved inscription formerly in the Armenian church of Amsterdam is now at Marseilles in the Borelli Castle museum.

India go back to 1497, when they were already in Calcutta, long before Job Charnoch made it an important commercial metropolis in 1690. Consequently the capital of India owes its beginnings as a business center to the Armenians rather than to Europeans.(2) We have proofs of this in the tombstones discovered in the former Christian burial-grounds of Calcutta dating back earlier than 1690. In 1688 Armenians trading in the Indian ports obtained from the East India Company a charter dated June 22nd, securing them special benefits, and their factories became famous. In 1692 they enlisted in the English army, and fought with it during the 18th and 19th centuries. In India and in the Malayan archipelago, in the Philippines, Siam, Burma, and even in China (Canton and Nankin), they still number today more than twenty thousand.

THE ARMENIANS IN VENICE

Of all these colonies, however, one of the oldest(1) in the Mediterranean and one of the most important, at least intellectually, was that of Venice. It owed its renown to the so-called Mekhitharist Congregation(2) who settled there on the island of Saint-Lazarus and became the leading Armenian cultural center. In 1510, when the art of printing was spreading throughout Europe, the Mekhitharists started the first Armenian printing-press which subsequently rendered incalculable services to their people. A branch establishment at Trieste was followed by still another at Vienna.

THE ARMENIANS IN RUSSIA

The Russian campaigns in Armenia against the Persians and Turks, and the return of the Ottomans to the plateau of Erzerum resulted on numerous occasions in a large emigration of the Armenians under Moslem rule to the Czar's Transcaucasian possessions and to Russia itself. Moscow, Astrakhan, and the Crimea had colonies of them in the 17th century, and in 1708 Peter the Great gave these foreigners special privileges.

---

(2) Cf N. & H BUXTON, Travels and Politics in Armenia, p. 194.

(1) In 1253 Count Marco Ziani offered the Armenians settled in Venice a house that still bears the name of "Armenian House."

(2) From the name of its founder Mekhithar of Sebaste.

RUSSIAN ADMINISTRATION OF THE ARMENIANS

In 1746 the Russian Senate authorized the application of the national Armenian code to the Armenians of Astrakhan. In 1765 Empress Catherine II granted the same privileges to the Armenians of New Nakhitchevan. When, however, General Paskievitch, who sent Archbishop Nerses into exile, came to power, Russian policy towards the Armenians changed, and the privileges granted by Peter the Great and Catherine II were one by one abolished, and replaced by a statute called *Polojenié* (11/23 March, 1836) setting forth the control of the internal affairs of the Armenians in Russia, both religious and national, and placing the Synod of Etchmiadzin under the supervision of the Ministry in Petrograd, which was to be represented in the Synod by a Procurator.

The Armenians are very numerous in Russia; there are about two millions of them, who belong to two distinct groups. One consists of the inhabitants of the Armenian districts conquered from the Persians and the Turks, these were consequently liberated from Moslem rule. The other group is that of the Armenians who have emigrated at various periods and are scattered all over the Russian empire. The part of Armenia that came under Russian rule, from the 18th century until the treaties of Turkmen-Tchai in 1828 and San Stefano in 1878, comprises the former provinces of Gougarq, Uti, Phaidagaran, Artsakh, Siuniq, Airarat, and Taïq, also the colonies of Baku, Tiflis, Batum, Poti, and that of the northern Caucasus.

The Armenians in Russia are divided into six dioceses, governed by bishops whose appointment is subject to the Czar's approval. Each diocese has its *Consistory* presided over by its bishop, and these consistories are responsible to the Synod at Etchmiadzin.

The Armenian dioceses in Russia are at present divided as follows:

I. *Erivan*, comprising the provinces of Erivan and Kars, also the south-west portion of the province of Ielisavetpol, i e the canton of Zanguezur. By the terms of the Polojenié statute, the bishop of the diocese of Erivan is none other than the Catholicos of all Armenians himself.

II. *Tiflis*, or Georgia and Imeritia, with the provinces of Tiflis, Koutais, and the Black Sea, as well as the northern part of the province of Ielisavetpol

III *Choucha*, or Qara-bagh, a diocese consisting of the cantons of Kariaguin, Choucha, Djivanchir, Noukhi, and Areche in the province of Ielisavetpol.

IV. *Chamakhi*, containing the province of Baku and the canton of Daghestan

V. *Astrakhan*, consisting of the province of Astrakhan, the eastern Russian provinces, together with Siberia and Turkestan

VI. *Bessarabia*, comprising the western, northern, and southern provinces of Russia.

THE ARMENIANS IN AMERICA In addition to the colonies in the Old World, at present quite numerous in Paris, London, Rome, Petrograd, and most of the large European and Asiatic cities, we must remember the North American Armenians of whom there are over 100,000 today.

The first Armenians to go to the New World(1) were two experts in silkworm-breeding, who at the invitation of the governor of Virginia, settled in that English colony in 1655. Very few Armenians landed on the shores of America until early in the 19th century.

In 1834 a young man, 16 years old, Khachatour Voskanian came to New York to finish his education. He became a journalist and was active in American literature. Later, Harouthioun Vehapetian arrived for the purpose of continuing his studies there, he became Patriarch, first at Constantinople, and then at Jerusalem.

From 1834 to 1867 there were no more than fifty or sixty Armenians in the United States all told, and in 1870-1871 they numbered only sixty-nine. Then there began, however, the actual emigration caused by Armenia's sufferings during the Russo-Turkish war of 1876-1877. Armenians thereafter went to the New World no longer just to study, but to earn a livelihood and if possible make enough money to go back one day to their native land.

Armenian arrivals in America increased in proportion as the unhappy people's woes overwhelmed them, as is shown by statistics. In 1912, 9350 landed in United States ports, and the following year over 10,000, so that by 1916 their numbers reached at least 100,000.

We find therefore that, omitting the few Armenians who are scattered in South America and Oceania, and taking just the principal settlements, about 300,000 Armenians have left their homeland to live abroad; 100,000 are in the United States, 20,000 in the Far East, 40,000 in Egypt, and 20,000 in Austria-Hungary. These latter are either the remnants of the medieval emigration to Poland, or newcomers in Budapest, Vienna and other large centers. Bulgaria has about 20,000 Armenians who

---

(1) Cf. Edw. EGGLESTONE, *The Beginners of a Nation*, New York, 1875.

came after the fall of Ani or later from Constantinople. The 8000 Armenians in Roumania are emigrants from Poland, as are also those of Bessarabia. Those at Kief have been living there ever since Alexander, the great Prince of that city, called them to his side in 1060 to help him fight the Poles. Most of the Armenian groups in the northern Caucasus date from the Middle Ages, but since the incorporation of part of Armenia in the Czar's territory, Russian Armenians have founded business houses and industries in all the large cities of the Empire.

Cyprus, the isles of the Archipelago, Greece, Italy, and western Europe contain about 8000 Armenians who largely belong to the nation's élite. So that up to 1914 we find the total number of Armenians to be 4,160,000 — of whom 2,380,000 were living under Turkish rule, 1,500,000 under that of the Russian Emperor, and 64,000 in the provinces of Persia and various other foreign settlements. This brings to about 4,500,000 the total number of Armenians in the world, a number which the recent disasters have reduced to an extent we cannot yet accurately calculate. We can reckon, however, that there are at least three millions of Armenians throughout the globe.(1)

This is not the place, in the history of a people, to delve into its possible future. We have seen in the foregoing pages that the Armenian nation has been struggling for two thousand years to preserve its freedom, and that early in this 20th century it has been placed by fate in the most cruel position that could befall a people. Politically speaking Armenia exists only in the past, but from the viewpoint of their nationality, this race has lost none of the vitality, of the initiative, and the aspirations it had in the days of yore. And so she stands today before the tribunal of the world's conscience and claims her century-old rights to liberty and life.

ARCHITECTURAL DESIGN ON THE CHURCH OF SAFAR

---

(1) The population of many of the smaller states of Europe is not above that of the Armenian nation: Denmark has 2,450,000 inhabitants; Servia, 2,625,000; Switzerland 3,325,000, Bulgaria, 3,745,000, etc.

CHAPTER XI

Literature, Science, and Arts among the Armenians

PHARAGIR ARMENIAN WRITING

When the Armenians were in Asia Minor and still belonged to the Phrygian nation, the art of writing was unknown to them, and such was the case among all the Indo-European peoples of those remote times.

ANCIENT ASIATIC WRITING   The only known systems of writing used then were Egyptian hieroglyphic and their derivatives, hieratic and demotic, in the Nile valley, the cuneiform in the southern part of western Asia, and the Phoenician alphabet drawn from the Egyptian hieratic on the Syrian seaboard. The Hittites maintained their hieroglyphic writing and lagged, therefore, behind the

Chaldeans and Egyptians who developed this system into more cursive modes of thought-expression.

Whilst the Armeno-Phrygians were dwelling together in Asia Minor, i.e. in the 9th to the 8th century B.C., the Greeks adopted the use of writing from the Phoenician system. The records reaching us from antiquity would indicate that this progressive step took place in the island of Thera known to have been one of the chief centers of Phoenician culture in Hellenic lands. Herodotus tells us(1)· "The Greeks were first "taught the use of letters as they were employed by the Phoenicians. "Subsequently alterations were made in the values of the different char-"acters and their application." In any case it took several centuries for writing to be established and diffused in Greece, and the Armenians had already left Phrygia for the Ararat regions when the peoples of Asia Minor first realized the importance of the art of writing

The Phrygians also adopted a graphic system taken from the Hellenic alphabet, and the few inscriptions left us of this people are all extremely ancient. The chief ones among them are those on the monumental tombs cut out of the rocks of the ancient Phrygian city of Prymnessus.(2). The largest of these burial-places contained the remains of a king named Midas. These inscriptions were studied by Ch. Lassen(3) who succeeded in ascertaining to what linguistic family Phrygian belonged, and in discovering all the forms of Phrygian declension besides definitely establishing the values of its different characters

We cannot tell whether the Armenians ever knew this system of writing, but from the complete lack of any very ancient stone inscriptions both on the rocks of Armenia itself and in any of the territory they crossed on their way to Ararat, we are impelled to the conclusion that the Phrygian alphabet was born subsequently to the eastward trek of the descendants of Haik.

The cuneiform system would seem to have disappeared from the Ararat regions along with the overthrow of the Urartu kingdom. The spoken language of the Urartaeans certainly must have taken a long time

---

(1) Herodotus. V. 58
(2) Cf TEXIER, Description de l'Asie Mineure, vol. I. pl LVI & LIX, p. 156
(3) *Ueber die Sprachen Klein-Asiens*, in Z. d D. M G, vol X, p. 371-376

to fade out entirely, but it ceased to be in evidence at all politically.

During the Achaemenian period, Aramaic writing, which was a special form of Phoenician, was in current use in the dominions of the Great Kings. This system did not suit the character of Aryan languages, and the Persians when they made use of it wrote in the Semitic language. The Iranian tongue was expressed only by transformed cuneiforms, made into syllables. Neither of these two methods of writing, therefore, could meet the needs of the Armenians.

The conquests of Alexander which made the use of the Greek alphabet widespread, gave the Asiatic Aryans a chance to crystallize their various languages, but the Hellenic characters did not include signs that corresponded to all the sounds of the Persian and Armenian languages, and consequently Greek was used in Persia at the same time as the so-called Persepolitan characters. The latter were derived from the Aramean which under the Sassanids had already developed into the Pehlevi. Bactriana evolved a different mode of writing, while India had a distinct development. both these countries being indebted, however, to characters of Phoenician origin for the basis of their respective graphic systems.

ARMENIAN WRITING There is reason to believe that many centuries after Aramaean writing developed into Persepolitan, Pehlevi, Syriac. and other forms that met the needs of the various Semitic languages, the Armenians adopted a special mode of writing with characters borrowed largely from the Syriac alphabet. the Greek, and others akin to that used at Palmyra. Agathangelus, Faustus, and Lazarus of Pharp seem of this opinion. This alphabet must have remained in a rudimentary state, however, and it was probably inadequate for all the sounds of the Armenian tongue. It may have been used at the time that Christianity was first preached in Armenia, but in any case, if it ever existed its inadequacy soon made it obsolete, and towards the end of the 4th century of our era it was still known only to a few scholars such as Daniel, the Syrian bishop and philosopher. This alphabet was eventually taken and improved on by Mesrop, assisted by the monk Rufin.

ARMENIAN CARVED STONE ERGATHAGIR WRITING
(Department of Medallions in Paris)

As long as the Arsacid dynasty lasted in Persia, Greek was in great vogue throughout western Asia; it was the official language of Iran and the second language of the Roman Empire. It was very useful to those preaching Christianity in Armenia and the Caucasian countries. With the arrival of the Sassanid rulers, however, Greek was forbidden throughout the dominions of the Great King and the Persians did everything possible to drive it out of Armenia, where Syriac took its place for religious books. As a matter of fact the masses of the Armenian people were familiar neither with Greek or Syriac, nor with Pehlevi-Persian. Only in a few border provinces were those languages used as an auxiliary tongue, whilst Armenian alone was understood in the interior.

MESROP It became more than ever necessary, therefore, to follow the general line of progress, and stabilize in writing the Armenian language, giving the people a sacred literature they could understand. Mesrop set to work to meet this need.

His hardest task, certainly, was to analyze the different sounds, for the Armenian tongue was not homogeneous; it varied according to provinces. Mesrop selected one of the dialects, that of the Ararat country, either because he considered it the purest, or because it was spoken by more Armenians than any other, or else again because it was employed at court. In any case, with the help of Greek, Syriac, Iranian-Avestic, and Semitic Pehlevi, he accomplished his work. He gave (as in Zend and sometimes also in Greek) special signs for the various vowel intonations, and he expressed all consonantal sounds whether simple or compound by single characters. This method of alphabet-formation was adopted later, moreover, by the Russians and the other Slavic peoples. The splitting of consonantal sounds would undoubtedly have simplified the

ERGATHAGIR ARMENIAN WRITING OF THE 10TH CENTURY (966)
(Tarkmantchatz Gospel, Constantinople, from document lent by M. F. Macler)

new alphabet by doing without some of the letters, but the scholarly analyst of those days did not use the strict methods we follow today. Mesrop sought to achieve a means of complete phonetic rendition, and he succeeded with remarkable perspicacity.

Some writers, including Vartan, are of the opinion that Daniel's alphabet had 22 characters and that Mesrop adopted only 17 of them, adding first 12 consonants and then 7 vowels of his own. According to Assoghik, on the contrary, Daniel's alphabet contained 29 letters, and Mesrop merely completed it with 7 vowels.

We feel we must reject Assoghig's opinion because it was impossible for Daniel to find in Aramaean, Syriac, or Pehlevi all the consonantal sounds of the Armenian language and practically all the vowels were lacking in those languages. Mesrop, after numerous unsuccessful attempts to employ Daniel's alphabet, took the latter as merely his starting-point

ERGATHAGIR ARMENIAN WRITING OF THE 10TH CENTURY (989)
(Gospel-book at Etchmiadzin, from a document lent by F. Macler)

and applied himself to the study of the Greek system of writing. Influenced by the latter he formed the final Armenian alphabet which like the Hellenic was used from left to right, in contradistinction to Oriental usage. Mesrop adopted for Armenian the Greek method of forming syllables. Accordingly the Mesropian alphabet consists of signs taken from Daniel's letters with some changes probably, filled in beyond question by borrowings from the Greek and some Oriental alphabets in order to express the vowels and consonants missing in Daniel's system, missing because they were not present in the Semitic languages. About this time a similar transformation, and one due to the same causes, took place in Iran where the Zoroastrian clergy taking the Pehlevi writing as their basis created an entirely made-up Zend alphabet. Their aim was to rescue the Avestic writings of the old Aryan language from the obscurity to which they were relegated by the use of Semitic characters.

The blessing of a written language in the Ararat country meant the beginning of a great intellectual upswing for Armenia. Not only could the Scriptures and scriptural commentaries be translated into Armenian, thanks to the new alphabet, but it caused a development of secular literature, and raised the general cultural level. Until then the people had been satisfied with oral traditions just as the Greeks and all Indo-European peoples once were. With a language and a literature all their own, national sentiment took fast hold of both, and it cannot be gainsaid that it is largely due to Mesrop that the Armenian people came through all their centuries of struggle, servitude, and persecution, without losing their nationality.

NOTRAGIR ARMENIAN WRITING
(More recent form)
(Zeitoun 1596)

Mesrop's task was chiefly undertaken with a view to spreading the Christian religion, but a subsidiary purpose was the emancipation of the Armenians from the influence of foreign clergy. The first works in Armenian, consequently, were translations of Greek and Syriac writings all dealing with religious subjects. They included the Bible and the Gospels, the writings of Ephrem the Syrian, the Hexameron of Basil of Caesarea, the homilies of St. John Chrysostom, the Ecclesiastical History of Eusebius, that of the conversion of Edessa, the (apocryphal) correspondence of Christ with Abgar, by the Syrian Laroubna, the Syriac liturgy, that of St. Basil, etc., besides the various writings in Armenian itself such as Mesrop's biography by his disciple Korioun, the 'refutations of sects' by Eznik, the history of Armenia's conversion to Christianity, ascribed to Agathangelus, and the history of Armenia under the Persian Arsacids, ascribed to Faustus of Byzantium. To these must be added the hymns written in Armenian ascribed by tradition to Mesrop and his great collaborator, Catholicos Sahak.

ANCIENT ARMENIAN LITERATURE Before the time of Mesrop, there was certainly no written Armenian literature. Statutes and royal rescripts, along with administrative documents, were written in Greek during the period of Arsacid rule, and in Pehlevi under the Sassanids. The same applies to the historical chronicles or annals compiled during those centuries whether by Armenians or non-Armenians. These latter works have not been preserved to us, and Moses of Khoren alone makes mention of any of their authors. He mentions Mar-Apas-Katina (whom some authorities think might have been Berose), Olympius (Aghioub) of Ani, the high-priest of Ormuzd, who lived in the later half of the second century of our era and wrote a history of his times, Bardesanes and Khorohput, two Iranian annalists. Some contemporary authorities look upon these writers as inventions of Moses of Khoren, but such a view is very questionable

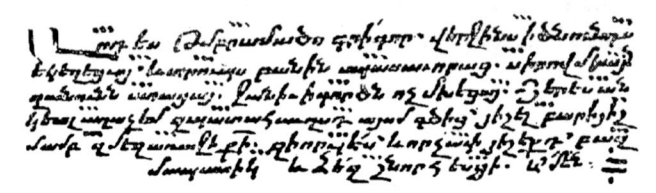

BOLORGIR ARMENIAN WRITING

and hardly tenable, for it is not at all likely that a country that had reached Armenia's state of development would not have recorded its history. We know, moreover, from reliable sources that the Armenian upper classes were quite cultured, and that both at the court and at the residences of the Satraps, living was sumptuous and embellished with all kinds of expressions of art. Among the nobility were literary men of note, such as Artavazd, the son of Tigranes the Great, who wrote tragedies and discourses in Greek and whose works are praised by Plutarch; Vrouyr, of a royal family of satraps, mentioned by Armenian historians as a poet of merit; and Parouyr (Proeresios in Greek), the "prince of orators", who was known for his eloquence in Rome, and to whom his pupil Gregory of Nazianzus refers with great admiration in his writings. Historians tell us that in the Imperial City a monument was raised to Parouyr with the following inscription: "Rome, the Queen of Cities, to the King of Eloquence." What constituted the real Armenian literature of this period, however, were the orally transmitted songs of the bards. All that has come down to us, unfortunately, of this ancient poetry are fragments quoted by Moses of Khoren and Gregory Magistros. We do know, however, from the chroniclers' frequent reference to them, that these songs were not only numerous and diversified, but enjoyed great popularity. Even Christianity, according to Faustus of Byzantium, did not succeed in uprooting them altogether in spite of centuries of effort, for the spirit permeating them reappeared in a new form, in the Middle Ages, among the troubadours.

This ancient poetry was vibrant with epic inspiration. It sang of the gods mighty and serene, of Ormuzd "the founder of humankind", "the father of the Gods and all heroes", "the Architect of the Universe", "the Creator of Heaven and Earth", the "Wise" and the "Valiant One", of Mihr, the invisible Fire, Son of Ormuzd, the essence of universal life, the god of light and heat; of Nana, the goddess of motherhood, the protectress of the family; of Astlik, the goddess of beauty and love, protectress of virgins; of Amanor, the god of the New Year and of hospitality; of Anahit, goddess of fecundity and wisdom, the "temperate and immaculate Lady", the "golden-winged Mother", the protectress of Armenia; of Vahakn, the god of strength, Astlik's lover, who fought with dragons, hunted wild beasts, and who was born in the birth-throes of heaven and earth:

> In travail were both heaven and earth,
> In travail was the crimson sea,
> The small red reed was seized with labor in the sea,
> And from its stem there issued smoke,
> From the small reed's stem there issued flame,
> And athwart the flame there sprang a youth,
> Sprang a fair-haired youth;
> His hair was as of fire,
> His nascent beard of flame,
> And his eyes, they were as suns! (1)

This early Armenian poetry sang of legendary or historic heroes, of Haïk, the "sturdy hero of noble frame, with his curly hair, his keen eye and robust arm, brave and renowned among the Giants" (2); of Aram, the vanquisher of Nioukar, the Median tyrant whom he took pris-

---

(1) Moses of KHOREN, I, chap. xxxi.
(2) ID., chap X & XI.

oner and with his hand nailed through his forehead to the top of the tower of Armavir, Ara the Handsome, who in fidelity to his motherland and his wife Nevarte, refused the hand of the wanton Chamiram (Semiramis) fallen violently in love with him, and who died in combat with the Assyrian queen seeking to possess him by force of arms; King Tigranes who killed the tyrant Ajdahak, king of the Medes; King Artashes II, who overcame all his country's enemies and raised his land to a high level of power and prosperity. It sang of Artavazd, the gloomy and passionate prince-royal who, cursed by his father, good King Atashes, was thrown by the genii from Mt. Ararat into a deep abyss where he forever dwells, doomed to live always, chained to a rock lest "should he emerge, he destroy the world." It sang also of Tork, the Giant symbol of Strength, who crushed rocks in his hands, scratched eagles' wings on stones with his very finger-nails, and who one day caused a crowd of ships to be engulfed in a storm in the Black Sea by throwing therein huge rocks from a hilltop.(1) In all these indistinct legends and traditions we find Assyria, Media, and Persia mingling with Grecian myth and ancient national memories of the descendants of Haïk.

Victor Langlois, in the foreword to his collection of ancient and modern historians of Armenia, devotes some very interesting pages to its popular songs of those remote times. He writes· "These songs chiefly "recall events, mostly heroic and legendary, that took place at quite "different periods, leading to the conclusion that they must have been "composed at various times by rhapsodists whose names are forgotten. "The subject-matter of these songs clearly shows that they did not spring "either from pagan priests, or from poets influenced by the latter, for "recital in religious ceremonies or altar-worship. We must recognize, "on the contrary, that they were composed by national bards with free "access to the ruler's palace and the satrap's court " These minstrels are the ancestors and forerunners of the modern achoughs who in our time still go from village to village and house to house singing their poems.

As regards knowledge of Armenian beginnings, however, the achoughs must bear little comparison with those ancient bards who sang of the struggle to conquer the Armenian land, of the battles waged by the giants, by the companions of the great Haïk. Their ballads are gone forever.

We might lean to the opinion, if we heeded what Moses of Khoren says of the oral poems of old, that they formed a complete epic, like the Shah-Nameh of the Persians. The fragments we have, however, and

---

(1) A TCHOBANIAN, Chants populaires arméniens, Introd , p. lxxv. sq.

the conditions under which the poetry sprang up, point rather to their being detached compositions, love poems, dancing and wedding songs, sacred hymns, and invocations to the gods, reminding one of the Spanish romancero

These epic songs were, moreover, not the only literary output of the Armenians in pagan times; they undoubtedly possessed narratives passed on by word of mouth, recited by their old folk during the long winter evenings to the family seated around the hearth, stories in prose or in verse, recalling for their emulation the deeds of prowess achieved by men of their race, by villages, or by tribes These are lost treasures, unfortunately, forgotten epics whose fables would have been so much valued by us today, but for which Christian historians substituted fictions woven around Bible subjects. The first historical works are so imbued with this superposition of Christian legend that for centuries the early days of the Armenians were represented by fanciful tales mostly based on Hebrew legend, and the effects of this unfortunate deviation are seen too in all writings of medieval Christendom.

The literature peculiar to Christian Armenia owed its inception and main development to the clergy and was naturally governed by the spirit of the new religion. It consisted of Scriptural translations and commentaries, theological writings, liturgical hymns, dissertations, sermons, and numerous historical works wherein the religious element was predominant. Nevertheless, notwithstanding this absorption of thought and the exclusiveness of the clergy, ancient predilections were so deeply rooted among the people that some links were maintained between the ancient heathen poetry and that of the new civilization. There came about in Armenia just as in western Europe a revival of that pre-Christian sentiment, and quite a number of priests (as was the case in France from the 15th century on) let themselves be carried away by secular themes.

As we find it in the most ancient writings preserved to us, whether in the original or in translation, the Armenian language is seen to contain a wealth of poetry and lyric rhythm, and to be permeated with sturdy patriotism. We cannot help concluding that its early writers, in fashioning the national medium of thought that they used so splendidly, must have drawn generously on the ancient Armenian bards. Aided by Greek culture mostly imbibed in the Byzantine centers which they purposely visited, they endowed their native tongue, already well-rounded by their heathen predecessors, with a scholarly and refined finish. All experts who have undertaken a close study of the Armenian language agree in assigning to it a very high place among the most accurate vehicles of human thought. The translation of the Bible, for instance, is looked upon as an outstanding literary monument, and the original work of Eznik, the purest Armenian writer of that period, is the equal of that of any among the most renowned masters of prose.

Although we are not in a position to compare the lost heathen literature of Armenia with that of its early Christian period, we notice nevertheless many flights of ancient national thought in frequent passages of certain historians, as also even in religious hymns. Cannot the same be said, moreover, of the Catholic literature of the west, in our own church hymns, and also in the liturgical words of the Orthodox Church? The breath of Greece and Rome left indelible impressions everywhere that it reached

In an historical work such as this, it is impossible to mention all the writers among such an abundant literature, much less to give any analysis of their respective works. I will limit myself, consequently, to naming just a few of the chief Armenian authors, and beg the reader seeking to enlarge his knowledge of the subject to refer to the special works thereon.(1)

---

(1) The following are some of the books and articles dealing with this subject: Ed. DULAURIER, *Recueil des Historiens des Croisades*, vol. 2, *Les Documents arméniens*. — Etienne ASSOGHIK, *Histoire universelle*, transl of part I. — Victor LANGLOIS, *Collection d'Historiens arméniens*, 2 vols. — BROSSET, *Collection d'Historiens arméniens*, 2 vols. — *Histoire d'Arménie*, by VARTABED ARISTACES of Lastivert, transl by Evariste PRUD' HOMME. — SAINT-MARTIN. *Mémories historiques et géographiques sur l'Arménie* vol. 2 *Histoire des Orpélians*, by Etienne ORPELIAN. — *Prosopopée-Allégorie*, from the *Rose* and the *Nightingale* of Mark-Zacharia CHODJENTZ of Erivan, transl. by Ed LEVAILLANT DE FLORIVAL — Felix NEVE, *L'Arménie chrétienne et sa littérature*. — A TCHOBANIAN, *Poèmes arméniens anciens et modernes; Chants populaires arméniens; Les Trouvères arméniens; L'Armenie, son Histoire, sa Littérature, son rôle en Orient; L'Arménie, son passé, sa culture, son avenir; La France et le Peuple arménien*; Poems: *La Vie et le Rêve; Offrande poétique à la France; La Littérature arménienne ancienne et contemporaine*, 3 articles (*Revue Encyclopédique Larousse*); *Grégoire de NAREK*, (*Mercure de France*); transl of the novel *Djelaleddin*, by RAFFI (*Revue des Revues*). — Frederic MACLER, *Histoire d'Arménie*, of Bishop SEBEOS, *Fables* of MEKHITAR GOCHE, *Contes arméniens, Nouvelles*, by Marie SEVADJIAN *Petite Bibliothèque arménienne*, (a series of volumes containing translations of the works of CHIRVANZADE. Rupen ZARTARIAN, Av. AHARONIAN, BARONIAN, and H. ARAKELIAN) — Minas TCHERAZ, *Nouvelles arméniennes; Poetes arméniens* — Tigrane YERGAT, *Littérature arménienne*, (*Revue des Revues*). *Revue Franco-Etrangère* (issue of May 1916) poems by Daniel VAROUJAN. Adom YARJANIAN, H TOUMANIAN, DJIVANI, etc — Miss Alice Stone BLACKWELL, *Armenian Poems*, Boston — Miss Zabelh BOYAJIAN, *Armenian Poems and Legends*, London — *La Poésie arménienne*, translation of selections published under editorship of Valery BRUSOFF, Moscow — *Anthologie arménienne*, published at Petrograd under editorship of Maxim GORKY.

Most of the large number of historians and chroniclers of the 5th to the 14th centuries furnish us with highly interesting documentation regarding not only Armenia but also adjacent Asiatic peoples and the Byzantine Empire. Some of them, moreover, are authors of considerable note, including a few who are real poets rather than annalists.

The earliest of these writers is undoubtedly *Korioun*, who lived about the middle of the 5th century, and whose *Life of Mesrop* contains very many interesting details concerning Armenia's conversion to Christianity, also concerning the invention of writing. The most noteworthy historians of this period, however, are *Agathangelus* and *Faustus of Byzantium*. It was long thought that the two books ascribed to these authors (believed by some to have been written by Korioun himself) were originally in Greek, but this opinion is no longer held. The *History of Gregory the Illuminator and King Tiridates* by Agathangelus is a fine piece of literature, both for purity of style and language, while Faustus' *Chronicle* is more picturesque and vivid. As historical documents these two works, especially the second, are most valuable. The same may be said of The *History of Taron*, by *Zenobius of Glak*, who lived in the same period. He relates the furious fighting of the pagan priests against the preachers of Christianity and the satraps who accompanied the latter.

One of the leading figures of the same period was *Elisha* to whom we are indebted for the story of the uprising of Christian Armenia against the rule of the Sassanid Persians, worshipers of Ormuzd, including the deeds of valor of Vardan Mamikonian, Armenia's national hero. Elisha is a real epic poet. Then we have *Lazarus of Pharp*, an excellent historian, restrained, chaste, and precise in style. In his *History of Vahan Mamikonian*, (his contemporary), he rehearses the prowess of this valiant prince whose courage and ability raised Armenia from the ruin she was in after the fall of the Arsacid dynasty.

In the 7th century *Sebeos*, another author of note, wrote his *History of Emperor Heraclius*, most valuable for students of that time and extremely useful for Byzantine history. Likewise *Moses of Kalankait* wrote concerning the Aghouan people and events of the same period in Transcaucasia.

Teh Bagratid era is no less prolific in writers than the preceding period of the Graeco-Persian struggles for Armenia. This era includes *John Catholicos* and *Thomas Artzruni*, both of whom relate the events of their day in the kingdom of the Bagratids and that of Vaspurakan; *Stephen Assoghik*, author of a *Universal History*, the second part of which deals with events under the Bagratids; *Ukhthannes*, who wrote a *History of Armenia;* and finally, *Aristaces of Lastivert* who chronicled the disasters culminating in the fall of Ani and the destruction of the Bagratid kingdom. This writer's stirring pages have earned him the title of the "Armenian Jeremiah."

Among the historians of the Armeno-Cilician period, i.e. from the 11th to the 14th century, we must mention *Vahram of Edessa*, secretary of King Leo III (1271-1289), who wrote a rhymed chronicle as a sequel to the historical poem of *St. Nerses the Gracious*, dealing with the Haikian, Arsacid, and Bagratid dynasties of Greater Armenia; *Matthew of Edessa* whose History relates the events of the time of the Emperors Nicephorus Phocas and John Zimisces, *Samuel of Ani*, author of a chronicle summarizing Armenia's history from its very beginning up to his own time; *Stepanos Orbelian* who in his *History of Siuniq* gives us a sketch of the satrapal family of that province; *Vartan Vartabed* and *Kirakos of Gandzak* who both wrote of the Mongol invasions, *Hetum*, Marshall of Armenia and Count of Gorigos, whose *Narrative of the Tartars* and *Chronological Tables* include the period 1076-1308; *Sempad*, Constable of Armenia and brother of King Hetum I who has left us a chronicle that is an epitome of those of *Matthew of Edessa* and *Gregory the Priest* (952-1152) followed by his own compilation until the year 1274, with an anonymous continuation up to A.D. 1335. (We should add that *Samuel of Ani's* work is based first on Eusebius' chronicle which he adapted to the history of Armenia in particular, and that he then carried it on until 1140, after which date an unknown writer continued it until A.D. 1340.)

MOSES OF KHOREN
Among all the historians of Armenia, however, the most famous is indisputably *Moses of Khoren*. This writer was for many years looked on as the Herodotus of Armenia, but his work is much contested today and has lost some of its earlier reputation for reliability. Its value is certainly diminished by his attempt to link up his nation with Biblical traditions, but as we have seen, this is a defect common to most Christian Latin and Greek writers in the early days of Christianity. Moses of Khoren is notable for his pure style and concise language, and his work is especially meritorious for its frequent refusal to voice merely the one-sided sentiments of the new religion and willingness in many cases to transcribe for us pagan traditions and legends; thus we are indebted to him for whole pages of annals, which have been since lost but which he

was able to turn to in the originals. We owe to him what little has been preserved of the ancient songs of the people, along with a large number of documents that open up a wide vision of the centuries prior to Mesrop.

Some authorities consider this historian to have lived in the century following the Arab conquest, while others assign him to the sixth century. In any case his writings constitute a precious record of the thought of ancient Armenia, and are of inestimable documentary and literary value.

LITURGICAL POEMS   Naturally enough, the poetical genius of the Armenian people underwent a change under the influence of Christianity, at least in the subject-matter of their poems. The heathen songs to the gods of yore were replaced by Christian hymns, composing which was a pursuit highly esteemed throughout Christendom St. Mesrop and St. Sahak themselves were, according to tradition, the pioneers of this new vogue which spread rapidly in Armenia. In countless monasteries, in the parish-churches, and bishop's palaces, new hymns were composed daily to the glory of the Lord. These works of which many are still used in the Armenian liturgy were mostly anonymous, and we have to wait till the 7th century for a church poet who has left us any name, viz: *Catholicos Komitas*.

Gregory of Narek, the most noted among these religious poets belongs to the 10th century. His extant works, which are entirely devotional, consist of religious poems, a commentary on the *Song of Songs,* eulogies of the saints, and a prayer-book. All his writings voice fervent Christian sentiment, both original and forceful in style.

The 12th century gave us *St Nerses the Gracious,* whose voluminous works deal with theology, sacred verse, and religious music. Many hymns written by him are still sung in the churches of Armenia. Contemporary with him, *Katchatur of Tarôn* was another distinguished writer of the same category.

Armenian intellectual activity was not restricted, however, to themes of piety. Theologians, moralists, and scholars of all sorts were numerous at all times. *Eznik, John Mandakuni,* perhaps also *David,* surnamed The Invincible, belong to the 5th century. The last-named author was a commentator and translator of Aristotle. In the 8th century *Anania of Shirak* was a successful mathematician, and in the 9th, *John,* called The Philosopher, was in great repute as a moralist and theologian.

Even deep in the Middle Ages, in the 10th and 11th centuries, Greek literature was not neglected, for Prince *Gregory Magistros* translated some of Plato's works along with other Greek authors not yet seen in Armenian, in addition to which he was the author of epistles and poems of considerable merit.

In the 12th century *Nerses of Lampron* was a theologian and moralist of Cilicia, and a renowned orator.

Mekhitar Goche, in the 13th century, the author of much esteemed compendiums, was a well-known jurist, and drew up the Armenian Code *John of Erzenga,* a moralist, theologian, and poet, was also a distinguished grammarian. Constable *Sempad,* already mentioned, wrote in this same period a summary and commentary in demotic Armenian of Mekhitar Goche's Code and that of Byzantium, together with a translation of the *Assizes of Antioch* Alishan used this translation into Armenian to produce a French version of the Assizes, which is most valuable as the original text is now lost. The works of *Sempad,* as also those of the physician *Mekhitar of Her,* are written in demotic Armenian, and are the earliest specimens of works of a serious nature in the language of the people. *Mekhitar of Her* wrote on medicine

The above are the outstanding representatives of Armenian classical literature, but alongside of these learned works of the higher stratum of society, there existed another literature in the language of the people, unrestricted by the austerity of religion and voicing in its native purity the feelings and tastes of the Armenian nation This poetry sprang from the primitive folk-songs which from time immemorial till now have always expressed the impulses of the heart in anonymous verse.

SECULAR POETRY I cannot do better, to depict this form of Armenian poetry, than quote A. Tchobanian's eulogy of it. In several of his works he has revealed to the world the beauty of this literature which hitherto had never been suspected in Europe.

"The poetry of Armenia shows, in its form, some of the characteris-
"tics peculiar to the whole Eastern world It, also, found birth under the
"dazzling sky of ancient Asia But running through this Oriental im-
"press, even through these general features of Eastern culture, Armenian
"poetry along with all other branches of Armenian art makes us con-
"scious of a deep-seated kinship, an innermost connection with the art
"of our western lands.

"There is comparatively more restraint, more clarity, and purity
"of expression, in Armenian art than in the complex and sensuous art

"of most other peoples, especially that of the eastern Moslems." The reason is that the Armenian soul is Aryan and responds to that breath of heaven it received at its birth, for the flame that burns within it is that same flame which gave the Hellenes both Phoebus and the Muses.

"The poetry of the people has blossomed forth in nature's school, "and nature pervades and rules it. Nature is not merely scenery for "these poems, it is a leading figure in them, it is the confidant, the friend, "who suffers and rejoices with man. A deep tenderness inheres in this "poetry and is felt; even pain therein is freed of its sharpness, and be its "sound soft or strong, it is never strident, never hateful.

"These songs are usually composed by achoughs or wandering bards, "but often the people themselves improvise them. The womenfolk share "conspicuously in these compositions, and the finest village songs of "Kobh in Russia Armenia come from the young girls of that loc-"ality. Especially in the town of Eghine in Turkish Armenia, the wo-"men are celebrated for their poetical talent."(1)

Does not this evoke the very same picture as that which we have always conceived of the earliest poetry of the Greeks? Homer singing on his lyre of his ancestors' prowess, maidens playing in grove or meadow, dancing around a trunk-hewn image of Ceres or Eros, chanting to the beneficent deities their ingenuous poems redolent with nature and the joy of living. Thus they sang to the springs and the murmuring brooks, to the flowery pastures and the dark forests, to the rustic courts of good old King Saturn. Armenia has happily preserved this ancestral poetical spirit so fast disappearing from our own countryside.

How can foreign influence stand against such spontaneous expression of a people's soul? Their language is the same as of old except for a few adaptations to present needs; it retains its main purity because it is unconstrained, echoing only the feelings of unpretentious hearts.

This poetry of the people is of all categories, including love-songs, lullabies, childrens' rhymes, playful or satirical couplets, prayers, dirges, dancing and holiday songs, marriage hymns, rhymed tales, historical and national ballads, exiles' laments, and various other songs glorifying nature or harvest, apostrophizing the birds or the seasons or depicting the scenes of daily life.

There are also popular epics of which the finest is undoubtedly that

---

(1) A. TCHOBANIAN, *Le Peuple arménien, son passé, sa culture, son avenir.* Paris, 1913. p. 21 sq.

of *David the Man of Sassoun*, the great athlete who with his herculean strength tamed lions and tigers, killed the tyrant Mesramelik, and delivered his native city from the oppressor's yoke.

ARMENIAN TROUBADOURS The Troubadour poetry of the Middle Ages is essentially one with the nameless folk-songs of the period except that it is more chaste in expression, more scholarly and more personal in its nature.

"The poems of the Armenian troubadours fall into two main cate-
"gories. First, those composed by professional minstrels, which have the
"most character. Their sparse resemblances to Persian poetry are super-
"ficial only; most of the more recent troubadours had some acquaintance
"with Moslem popular poetry and borrowed a few constructions and
"images of thought together with a few forms of prosody, but they re-
"tain their own fundamental individuality. They have, moreover, en-
"riched Moslem folk-song with more than they received from it. Most
"Armenian troubadours likewise composed songs in Turkish, Persian, or
"Kurdish. Some of the most famous singers of popular Turkish and
"Kurdish songs were, and still are, Armenians, who undoubtedly have
"imparted to Moslem poetry something of their national temperament
"and also of their Christian spirit. Among the minstrels of olden time,
"however, we find no trace whatever of imitation of foreign poetry from
"any source, their sole fount of inspiration was the native and instinctive
"poetry of the Armenian folk-song.

"The second category consists of Armenian poems written in the
"language and grace of the troubadour by scholars and authors, many
"of them members of the clergy.

"To this branch belong the greatest number, preserved chiefly in
"the manuscripts we possess. The professional troubadors were un-
"doubtedly the forerunners of these scholarly imitators, but the works
"of the latter being put into writing have come down to us, whereas the
"spontaneous and original poems of the street-singers prior to the 14th
"century have been lost, not having been saved from oblivion by writers
"or copyists.(1)"

Among the troubadours whose names are known to us from translations, the most renowned are: *Ghazar of Sebaste, Keropé, Channes, Saiat-Nova, Djivani*, and—the most original of all— *Nahabed Koutchak*,

---

(1) A TCHOBANIAN, *Les Trouvères arméniens*, Paris, 1906, p. 12 sq

who was born probably in the 15th century and has left us a long series of small poems, mostly quatrains, the majority of them delightful love-songs.

Among the poetically-minded clergy who composed in imitation of the troubadours, we must mention *Constantine of Erzenga, Frik, Hovhannes of Telgouran, Gregory of Akhtamar*, all of whose colorful and refreshing verses exhibit at the same time much altitude of thought and feeling

The above brief summary is ample proof that from the 5th to the 14th century, notwithstanding the terrible struggles in which they were ever involved for their very existence, the Armenians never dropped out of the world's scientific and literary movement. In the monasteries freedom of the mind still found expression even amid the nameless terrors without. The whole world was in great turmoil during those centuries of barbarism, but in the western lands, in Byzantium, and among the Arabs and Persians, there were nevertheless comparatively long periods of calm such as the Armenians never knew. The Armenian people must certainly have been possessed of unusual strength of character for them to have kept their hold on spiritual and cultural subjects in the very center of Western Asia, a veritable furnace throughout the Middle Ages.

MODERN ARMENIAN LITERATURE

Following both the fall of Ani and the departure of the last sovereign of New Armenia into exile, the nation finding itself subjected to the most cruel oppression sent away its sons to settle in many a foreign land, and these expatriates took with them their love for their native tongue and literature. New centers of culture were thus formed, whereas in the enslaved homeland the pursuit of letters was restricted to the monasteries and a few privileged homes. Armenian literature was already abundant, however, and persecution only made the works of the past all the more highly treasured. The Armenians consequently looked up to their writers as being the champions of their national independence. There came about as a result a number of independent literary centers with little or no interconnection, but all working along the same lines, so that their endeavors as a whole never lost their homogeneous character.

Nevertheless the distance from one another of these same centers, and their differing environments, did have considerable influence on their trend of development.

At Moscow and Tiflis, the spirit of Russia oriented the exiles, and the influence of German literature so widespread in the Czar's empire was likewise felt At Constantinople and Smyrna, where there was a higher level of scholarship than in the homeland, the Armenians came into contact with Europeans and maintained greater intellectual independence, and the same was the case at Venice and Vienna and in all the great western centers where the cultured in mind found every opportunity and freedom of thought. At Etchmiadzin and the other monasteries of Armenia the men of letters had to live to themselves and feed mainly on their nation's past, not taking so large a part in the general literary movement In all the above-mentioned foreign centers, the predominant element of literary education was that of French authors.

Gradually the new literature spread everywhere and comprised all branches of expression the theater, the novel, the epic, and the epigram, all appeared in the Armenian tongue Historical, archaeological, philological, philosophical, sociological, and scientific works were added to Armenian bibliography, while the political press also began to promote the aspirations of the nation. All these endeavors under the influence of all manner of teachers, but mainly French, grew rapidly and resulted in literary achievements wherein the spirit of Armenia, albeit in evolution, retained its distinctive character

Owing to the innumerable difficulties the Armenians encountered in striving to keep up with the general advancement of thought of the civilized world, their progress in the various centers was dissimilar Constantinople, Etchmiadzin, Moscow, Tiflis, St. Lazarus at Venice, and the Armenian monastery at Vienna were for many years in the fore of the movement, of these Venice for a considerable time was the leading center. There in the city of the Doges, the Mekhitarists found not only freedom to express their thought in writing, but also hospitable hosts, along with the inexhaustible resources of the western world for men of science and letters. For these reasons, St Lazarus during the 18th century and the first half of the 19th was preeminetnly the intellectual center of the Armenian people.

The teaching at St. Lazarus included the study of the best ancient and modern authors whom the Mekhitarists specialized in translating. It turned out scholars often of the highest merit, men who went out into the world to impart to the various Armenian colonies the spirit and exquisite taste of the Graeco-Latin writers. Many of them became eminent in the literary world and achieved positions of distinction in Armenia's national life.

From the 17th century onward a veritable revival of Armenian literature took place. The first writers of this period, chiefly at Venice, used classical Armenian, whilst those in Russia and Turkey endeavored to raise the spoken tongue to the rank of a literary medium. Their efforts, though at first timid, were crowned with success, among Russian Armenians about the middle of the 19th century, and among those in Turkey some twenty or thirty years later. This movement had been foreseen by Mekhitar, the founder of St. Lazarus, for in his lifetime he composed a tentative grammar of the modern language. The printing-press and the appearance of reviews and periodicals of all kinds was of great assistance in bringing about this change, by making foreign and Armenian works known to the masses and reaching the people instead of merely the scholars. The great questions of national freedom which rightly stirred all Armenians could not be treated in archaic language. At Tiflis, Moscow, Constantinople, all the centers where the minds of the people needed to be reached, classical Armenian was relegated to the rôle of a learned language meant only for the Church and a literary élite.

The works and writings in Armenian from the 17th century to our time are innumerable, and they are of infinite variety as regards subject-matter. I cannot list them, therefore, any more than I could those of classical times. I will just mention the most noted writers in each branch of literature, and am sorry I have not space for even a brief analysis of their respective works.

The name of *Mekhitar*, the founder of the Congregation of St. Lazarus at Venice has remained famous, not only in the Armenian nation but throughout the world. To *Mekhitar*, whose many works were written in classical Armenian, we are indebted for his admirable action in creating this center responsible for a galaxy of scholars and men of letters. Among the pupils of this great school were: *Tchamtchian* and his *History of Armenia*, *Indjidjian* and his archaeological treatises, also his *Geography of Ancient Armenia*, *Aucher*, who wrote theological works and biographies of the Saints; *Arsene Bagratuni*, and *Eduard Hurmuz*, translators of Homer, Virgil, Sophocles, Milton, Racine, Voltaire, Alfieri, and Fenelon's *Telemachus*. Bagratuni wrote a great epic poem on the struggle of Haïk with Bel the Giant, and Hurmuz an imitation of the *Georgics* entitled "The Gardens" This all shows how desirous the St. Lazarus Institute was to associate Armenian thought with the great development of literary progress in the world. *Alıshan*, the natural scientist, geographer, and historian, in 1850 adapted modern scientific methods to the study of Armenia. He was primarily a poet and his works, partly in classical, partly in modern Armenian, earned him merited distinction He was followed by scholars like Father *Basil Sarghissıan* and men of letters such as *Arsene Gasikıan* who continued in demotic Armenian the classical work of Bagratunı, and translated from the great ancient and modern poets, *N. Andrikıan, S. Eremian, Garabed-Der-Sahakıan*—the poet and historian who gave us a history of the Armenian Byzantine emperors, and many others.

At Vienna the Mekhitarists sent out mainly scholars and scientists, but the novelist *Sahak Tornian* was also among them. *Katerdjıan* and *Karakachıan* are historians who were educated there, while another pupil *Aıdnıan* wrote his analytical grammar of modern Armenian, and in his wake *Dachian, Kalemkıar, Menevichan,* and *Akınıan* became renowned philologists and linguists.

In the meanwhile, the Armenians in Russia were also active From the very beginning of the 19th century they were conspicuous in Armenian literature, and this intellectual revival greatly expanded when in 1828 the Czar came into possession of the countries north of the river Araxes and eastern Armenia began to enjoy security. From that time on the Armenians were able to progress freely in the field of intellectual labor.

Katchatour Abovian (1804-1848), a writer of fables and novels, was born at Dorpat. Chiefly under the influence of Armenian national tradition and folklore, he was the first author of that period to write his works in the demotic language. He must be considered as the founder of the new literature among the Russian Armenians, and he raised it to the front rank by his epic and realistic novel, *The Wounds of Armenia,* in which he gives a poignant picture of the sufferings of his fellow-countrymen including himself under the heel of the Moslems, both Persian and Turkish He was followed by *Prochiantz* who wrote a long series of popular novels; then by *Mikael Nalbandıan, Stepanos Nazarıan,* and *Chahazizian,* all of whom by their poems and articles in recently started magazines helped to arouse in the Armenians not only their taste for literature but their patriotic feelings and hopes

The poet *Kamar Katiba,* the novelist *Raffi,* the news commentator and essayist *Gregory Artzruni,* each in turn contributed to this revival, and were in their day among the leaders of Armenian literature in Russia. These writers exercised great influence on the awakening of the whole nation. Their work was carried on by novelists such as *Mouratsan, Chirvanzadé, Léo;* by short story-writers like *Aghaian, Papasian, H. Arakélian*—playrights, including *Soundoukian, Chirvanzadé, Léon Chanth,* —by the lyrical prose-writer *Avetik Aharonian* who depicted the sufferings of Armenia both under the tyrannical Abdul-Hamid and after that bloody despot's downfall—and also by *Hovannes Toumanian,* the best of the epic poets of Russia. Likewise the poets *Hovhannes Hovhanessian, Avetik Issahakian, A. Tsatourian, Vahan Terian,* Madame *Kourghinian,* all of whom produced excellent verse; the historian *Arakel Babakhanian (Leo),* the philologists *Chalatianz, Emine, Patkanian, S. Malkhasian;* the ethnologist *Lalayan; Barkhoudarian* who translated Goethe and Schiller, *Ohannes Khan Massehian* who gave his people a splendid version of Shakespeare's chief masterpieces; scholars such as *Carapet Ter-Mkrtchiantz, Garekin Hovsepian, Galoust Ter-Mkrtchiantz, Mesrop Ter-Movsessiantz; Komitas,* the musician, with others of the Congregation of Etchmiadzin.

In Turkey, the Armenian literary impetus was not long in producing works of note. Constantinople from Byzantine times had a large Armenian colony, and literary light had never been extinguished there, but with few exceptions Armenian literature on the Bosphorus was almost all of it greatly influenced by Latin standards, especially Italian and French. However, there were a few writers who remained purely Armenian, for instance, Monsignor *Khrimian,* an orator, author, and a public-spirited man who ever preached patriotism to his people. He left numerous works both in prose and verse. Also *Servantztdiantz,* the author of folklore stories and word-pictures of Armenian life; *Devkantz,* known for his novel, breathing love of country; in Siberia, *Chahen; Hrand Telgadintsı,*

MGR. KHRIMIAN

and *Zartarian* all of whom depict the lives of their compatriots in impressive language.

The two last-named writers, together with the author *Zohrab* and the poet and essayist *Ardashes Haroutiounian*, were deported to an unknown destination, and it is to be feared that they shared the fate of their distinguished colleague Zohrab who was murdered during the deportations.

The first great Armenian newspaper, *the Ararat Dawn*, appeared in Smyrna in 1840, and from then on newspaper writers acquired considerable prestige in Turkey. *Tchilinguirian, Osganian, Gosdanian,* and *Mamourian* are those chiefly remembered; the last-named translated some of the best works of western literature, and thus made his fellow-countrymen familiar with the literary progress of France, Italy, England and Germany.

Deroyentz, Utudjian, Zoraian, Odian, Missakian, Bechiktachelian, Hekimian, Tersian, and *Adjemian*, several of whom were former students of the Mekhitarists at Venice, acquired a reputation in the press through their articles on varied subjects, and also in the writing of plays and poems. *Bechiktachelian* and *Tersian*, along with their contemporaries *Bedros Tourian* and Archbishop *Khoen Narbey* were the best lyric poets of the period, while *Dzerentz* and Madame *Dussap* were also distinguished novelists.

The satire or epigram was also well represented by *Haroutioun Sevadjian*, its pioneer, and by *Baronian*, another pastmaster of the art.

It would take very long to mention all the Armenian authors who have written of late years on all kinds of subjects, which are today dealt with in Armenian literature in the demotic language, often by men and women of outstanding merit. I will mention just the poets *Setian*, Madame *Sibille, Mezarentz, Tekeian;* the authors *Demirdjibachian, Berberian, Tcheraz, Arpiarian, Tcherakian, Mrmrian, Zohrab, Pachalian, Zarian, Gamsaragan, Tigran Yergat, V. Savadjian, M. Gurdjian, S. Bartevian,* Monsignor *Mouchegh Seropian,* Madame *Marie Sevadjian,* Madame *Zabel Essaian,* Madame *Anais, the* humorist *Yervant Odian,* the scholars *Norayr Puzantatsi,* Monsignor *Ormanian,* Monsignor *Elisha Tourian,* Monsignor *Papken Gulesserian, Karnig Fundukhan, Tinakin, Adjarian, K. H. Basmadjian, Toromanian,* etc. I would recall also *Daniel Varoujan* and *Adom Yarjanian* who were great poets that sang of Armenia's sufferings and struggles. They were deported along with so many of their fellow-countrymen; *it is* feared that they succumbed to Turkish cruelty in the visitation of 1896.

I must mention finally the poet *A. Tchobanian* who is so well known for his writings in French in which he has made us acquainted with literary Armenia and has pleaded so fervently the cause of his nation. He has composed splendid poetry and his extensive Armenian work has earned for him considerable and well-earned renown among his compatriots.

The foregoing pages give an idea of the great impetus that Armenian literature has had for the last hundred years, and show that all branches of human thought are included in its wide cultural development, and that it is still going forward in the pursuit of knowledge that has generally but little appeal for Eastern peoples.

Armenia today is in the same position linguistically as was France in the days of *langue d'oc* and *langue d'oil*. One branch of its language, that in Russia, is based on the dialect of the Ararat region, whereas Turkish Armenian has for its foundation the speech of Lesser Armenia (Armenia Minor) and New Armenia (Cilicia). The latter form is descended from the Armenian of the Middle Ages, whilst the former is more dialectal, more mixed with foreign words and expressions, and its grammar contains more Iranian infiltrations. As for the vocabulary, the Turkish is purer and more classical than the Russian, which on the other hand is more demotic and intermingled with foreign terms. In Turkey, especially in Constantinople, writers have turned to the French language as their standard in giving Armenian its modern polish and form, but in Russia German literature rather has prevailed in that direction.

Before closing this chapter on the Armenian language, it may be helpful to add a few words on versification.

ARMENIAN VERSIFICATION The few fragments of heathen poems and the earliest specimens of religious poetry that have been preserved to us are in blank verse, without metre or rhyme, but nevertheless rhythmical and adapted to song. Such are most of the church hymns, and this mode continued until about the 10th century. Then there began under Arab influence a metrical and rhymed versification that was expressed in a great variety of forms. Verses were of 15, 12, 11, 10, 9, 8, 7 etc. syllables composed of 4, 3, and 2 hemistichs, but in the longest verses the caesuras are always numerous. All the troubadour poetry is metrical and rhymed, just as are modern poems, but the latter amplify their peculiarly national features with a few innovations from European verse-making. Consequently we have extremely varied versification. The blank verse of olden times has been revived in our day by *Arsene Bagratuni* and other poets.

THE SCIENCES As we have seen above, Armenian authors from earliest times have included men of science, and this is once more the case in these modern times of general advance in knowledge among all civilized nations. In our present period a number of Armenian scientists both among their own people and abroad have won distinction either by their achievements or their teaching. Medical publications which appeared as early as the 12th century, are very numerous from the 17th to the 20th century. Among them, I may mention the works of the physician *Amirdovlat* (17th century), the medical dictionary of Dr. *Resten* (end of the 18th century), the writings of *Physica Boghos*, still in MS form, dating from the early 19th century and dealing with physical and chemical science. As for political economy and the exact sciences, they were long taught in the Ottoman schools by such Armenian professors as *Hovsep Youssoufian, Mikael Portoukal Pasha, Hovhannes Sakiz Pasha*, etc. Some Armenian scientists have achieved distinction also in European circles; there are a number of Armenian professors in the universities of Europe and America, and some of these scientists and scholars have made names for themselves by their writings and discoveries.

THE ISLAND OF ST. LAZARUS AT VENICE

PRINTING In this brief review of Armenian intellectual progress, we must not forget the importance of the press and the growth of printing.

It was in the Venetian republic, always so hospitable to the Armenians, that the first book in St. Mesrop's characters was printed in 1513. An Armenian from Cilicia, named Hakob (Jacob, or James) sent out from a Venice printing-house a *Calendar* followed in 1514 by a Missal, an anthology of poetry, and a book on astrology. This was hardly fifty years after the invention of printing, long before Russia and the whole Eastern world adopted this means of disseminating thought, destined to revolutionize the world. About 1565, under the patronage of Catholicos Mikaël, an Armenian press was set up in Constantinople, and from the middle of the 17th century on, increasing quantities of religious books were published at Venice, Marseilles, and Amsterdam. Etchmiadzin and Julfa-by-Isfahan followed the example of the western world and soon Armenian presses were established at Smyrna, in the Caucasus, and at Madras. The Mekhitharist Congregation was founded, as we have seen, at the beginning of the 18th century. Its printing-house was set up from the outset, and when it opened a branch in Vienna it also started presses in Austria. Subsequently all great cities of the world have come to have their printing establishments equipped with Armenian type, and there is hardly a country today where a book in that language could not be turned out.

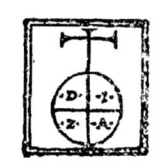

STAMP OF THE ARMENIAN PRINTER HAKOB (1513)

We must remember that the Armenians were not only suffering from religious and literary restrictions; driven from their land by the tyranny of the oppressor, they thirsted for liberty, and printing gave them a means of disseminating their thought, of communicating with their many colonies scattered so far throughout the world, and enabling the various sections of their people to find a common ground for hopes for the future. The reason that the Armenians and the Greeks were the first two peoples of all the near East to start newspapers and reviews is that they both were similarly situated, deprived of their national independence.

NEWSPAPERS AND MAGAZINES REVIEWS

At the beginning of the 18th century, the Armenians in Calcutta, in the enjoyment of the freedom they were given in India, founded the first newspaper ever to appear in their language, viz: *Aztarar* (The Intelligencer). Their example was not followed by the Mekhitharists until the end of that century, when the *Yeghanak Puzantian* (Byzantine Season) was brought out in Venice The same Congregation likewise about the middle of the 19th century started the publication of *Pazmaveb*, a highly esteemed review from both the literary and documentary standpoint, which is still appearing today.

About the same time, the Armenians of the Protestant faith in Constantinople brought out *Chtemaran bidam kidehatz*, a missionary magazine, while at Smyrna the first daily made its appearance, entitled *Archalouis Araradian* (the Dawn of Ararat) Thereafter newspapers multiplied, and every Armenian colony had its local press.

At Constantinople, the great intellectual center for the Armenians, a great number of newspapers and reviews came out, the chief ones among them being· *Masis* (Ararat), which started as a newspaper but later became a review, *Arevelk* (the East), *Hairenik* (the Fatherland), *Puzantion*, *Azatamart*,—among the newspapers; *Iergrakound* (the Globe), *Dzahik* (the Flower), *Vosdan* (the City),—among the reviews.

Meanwhile the Armenians in Russia were also active in the same direction. There appeared at Moscow *Hussissapaïl* (the Northern Dawn), a review which came out about 1850, at Tiflis,-*Krounk Haiots Achkharh*i (the Crane of the Armenian Land), *Ports* (Endeavor), *Mourtch*, (The Hammer), *Gords* (The Work), and the daily newspapers entitled *Mschak* (The Worker), *Ardzagank* (The Echo), *Nordar* (The New Century), and *Horizon*, all of them published at Tiflis; *Arev* (The Sun) published at Baku. There was also an interesting ethnographic review *Azgakragan Handes* and the art periodical *Gheharvest* (Fine Arts)

The newspaper *Haiastan* (Armenia) published at Tiflis since the outbreak of the present war (1914) is the organ of the refugees from Turkey Andranik, the people's heio, is its editor-in-chief.

At Etchmiadzin, the *Ararat* has been published for a good many years. In Turkey,-there appeared about 1860, at the monastery of Varag near Van, *Ardziv Vaspurakani* (the Eagle of Vaspurakan), and at Mouch, *Artsvik Tarono* (The Tarôn Eaglet), both of them monthly reviews.

Among the most important of the periodicals in Armenia centers, we should mention also *Handes Amsorya*, a monthly philological review of high repute published by the Mekhitharists in Vienna.

In England, the headquarters of the Armenian revolutionary Committee founded in London a monthly organ called *Hentchak* (The Handbell), and also in the English capital there has appeared for many years the bilingual French and English review entitled *Armenia*, published by the eminent patriotic writer *Minas Tcheraz*.

A PAGE FROM THE CALENDAR PUBLISHED AT VENICE IN 1513 BY THE ARMENIAN PRINTER HAKOB

Several reviews appearing in Paris must likewise be mentioned: *Massiats Aghavni* (the Ararat Dove), *Anahït*, published by *A. Tchobanian*, and *Banasser* by K. J. Basmadjian; while at Marseilles we have *Armenia*, and at Geneva *Droschak* (The Flag), the organ of the Armenian Revolutionary Federation. In Egypt and in the large centers of the United States there are quite a number of newspapers in Armenian; but we can hardly give a complete statement of the modern Armenian press. The foregoing will at least show how large a place these newspapers and periodicals have in Armenian

ABGAR, THE ARMENIAN PRINTER FROM VENICE,
PRESENTING HIS PSALM-BOOK TO POPE PIUS IV,
(1565)

national life It is obvious, of course, that most of the Armenian literary men and scholars are happy to find organs in which they can publish their writings, and it may be mentioned that for the greater part these authors' works are contained in the reviews and have not yet been published in book form.

Armenian cultural output is not confined, however, to literature All branches of art, music, dancing, architecture, fresco and miniature painting, sculpture, goldsmith's work, in short all the arts and crafts represented in the incomparable treasures of the Middle Ages, are successfully pursued by Armenians today, and in many cases the talent and craftsmanship are maintained and developed in new forms adapted to modern times

MUSIC
"The Armenian people has from all time enjoyed the art "of music, been familiar with it, loved it and practised it. With "or without historical foundation, tradition has it that two thous-"and years ago and more, their ancestors sang of the exploits of their "heroes to the accompaniment of instruments of which we have unfort-"unately but scanty information (1)"

Armenia certainly retains both in its liturgy and its folksongs, many lingering traces of this ancient music, just as in the churches of the western world many a strain from the old heathen times is still in use; but the origin of these remote tunes can no longer be traced because of the late dates of their recordings In any case, the oldest Armenian music to which we are able to assign a definite period is that of the Middle Ages, which was of two very distinct categories, viz the great storehouse of liturgical material, and the numerous folksongs, both of them unisonal The first of these two forms of music is grave and mystical, the second, lively and distinctly peculiar to the Armenian people, although showing sometimes foreign influences, either Persian or Turkish. A learned member of the clergy at Etchmiadzin, Father *Komitas,* who has collected a large number of these melodies and harmonized some of them, was the first to make a competent selection from this great amount of material. *Alexanian,* a talented composer and performer living in Paris, has put

---

(1) F. MACLER, *La Musique en Arménie,* p. 3 Paris, 1917.

these ancient tunes into use and with his profound knowledge of western music has obtained excellent results from them.

Tradition has it that in the 5th century St. Sahak and St. Mesrop wrote the first models of sacred music which the Armenians call by the name of *charakans*. There is no certainty of this, but we do know that those two bishops had successors whose names are definitely recorded and whose compositions have been preserved to modern times. The most famous are *Hohan Mandakuni,* the sister of *Vahan of Golthn* (martyred April 18th, 737), *Stepanos of Sunik, Katchature Vardapet of Tarôn, St. Nerses the Gracious, etc.*

Regarding the troubadours, we have already seen what a large part they played in the literature of the people. They were not only poets, but talented musicians who composed new melodies or else maintained the ancient music by oral transmission. When copying the poems of some of these troubadours, such as those of Koutchak for instance, the copyists were always careful, moreover, to state on their manuscripts that the songs were composed on the "Armenian mode."

These achoughs, or wandering bards, were not satisfied with singing within the confines of enslaved Armenia whose national life they thus helped keep up, but they also went abroad into Turkey proper, into Persia, Georgia, and Kurdistan, where they exhibited their talent to the Moslems, and sang their verses in foreign tongues following the musical modes of the country they were in. Armenian musicians and singers are known to have been in high repute at the courts of the Sultans and the Shahs, also at those of the Georgian kings and the most powerful of the Kurdish chieftains.

Modern Armenian music has kept pace with general development in this field. Composers and performers have become more and more numerous since the early 19th century, and foreign works not only were included in the Armenian repertory, but they added their technical progress to the expanding output of national melodies. Even though adopting the various musical schools and styles prevailing abroad, the Armenians have succeeded in keeping to their own national traditional modes of expression. Very talented composers, such as *Alexanian* already mentioned, have been able, sometimes with national themes for their basis, to create a modern Armenian music combining scientific excellence with an individuality of its own equal to that of the medieval bards. Alexanian, moreover, had for his forerunners in this modern field *Ecmalian, Komitas, Spendiarian, Tigranian, Proff-Kalfaïan,* and *Mirzaïants.*

THE STAGE The strides made in literature and music must necessarily have their counterpart in theatrical progress, and such was the case about the middle of the 19th century. In ancient times the Armenians, along with the Greeks of the Asiatic mainland, were great lovers of the stage. Artavazd, the son of Tigranes, as we have seen, composed tragedies, and the Arsacid court had its theaters, for example the one at Tigranocerta. These plays were only in Greek, however, for no writer ever mentions the use of any native language on the stage in those days.

With the arrival of Christianity, love of the stage disappeared almost everywhere throughout western Asia, and religious ceremonies and popular festivals were the chief features of daily life. Armenia never even had our western mystery plays, and not until modern times did there spring up an Armenian stage, due to the influence of Europe. Constantinople and Tiflis were the scenes of the first attempts in this direction, and the Armenian theaters in those cities blossomed forth on diversified lines; foreign plays were given in Armenian, together with original ones written in the native tongue. Furthermore, a European theater in the Turkish language was inaugurated at about the same time by Armenians also; they either translated western plays or composed entirely new Eastern ones. Both in Armenian and Turkish, the Armenian actors, men and women, achieved distinction through their perfect interpretation along every line. *Adamian,* an Armenian Salvini, made a name for himself by his Shakespearean repertory; *Rechtuni* and *Abelian* were noted for comedy; *Touriantz* was a delightful comedian, and among other talented players were Madame *Hratchia* and Madame *Stranouche.* About the same period *Tchouhadjian,* who had studied his art in Italy, introduced theatrical music, for both the Armenian stage and the Turkish.

ARCHITECTURE & SCULPTURE For indications of taste for sculpture among the Armenians we have only the Christian period to guide us, and even there the specimens we possess do not belong to the early days of con-

— 370 —

version. We have no relics of the transitional times between heathendom and Christendom such as exist at Rome, in Italy and Greece. The Armenian shrines that survived the disasters of war and earthquake date from several centuries later than those built by Gregory the Illuminator

Conflicting influences have always been at work in Armenia Achaemenian styles of architecture, derived from Chaldaean and Assyrian modes, prevailed in western Asia when the Armenians arrived on the political scene, but Alexander the Great's ensuing conquests spread Greek styles everywhere, and these were reverenced by the Seleucids and the Arsacid Parthians. At the time the Armenians were converted to Christianity, the Sassanids ascended the throne of Persia, and they brought great changes in Iranian tastes. It is therefore altogether likely that heathen architecture in Armenia was Hellenic until the end of the third century. The only structural remains of this period of which we have any knowledge, unfortunately, are those of the palace of Tiridates at Garni; and the pictures we possess of it are hardly reliable, for the early Christians destroyed such buildings to their very foundations, and erected their churches on the sites Systematic excavations among the ruins of Artaxata, Tigranocerta, Nisibus, Achtichat, and other large pagan cities of the Armenians, if undertaken, would reveal at least the plans of the vanished structures, but no such research has yet been attempted.

The statues that disappeared with the advent of Christianity were much esteemed in Armenia in pagan times, for historians often tell us of images of deities made of wood, stone, brass, or even gold. According to all our available texts these statues were entirely confined to the gods Apparently, however, Greek and Roman liking for images of high personages penetrated to Armenia along with western influences generally, and their sovereigns came to have their statues similar to those of the great men of Greece or the emperors of Rome The statue of Tiridates we possess was executed in the west and for the west, and is consequently no criterion in this connection

We have seen how predominant Greek literary influence was in Armenia at the time of its conversion to Christianity Rome and the Empire were still heathen, and the churches of the early Christians, both Greek and Latin, were very roughly designed without any of the later beauty of the first cathedral churches In fact they were merely chapels built on pagan lines, adapted to the needs of the new religion and with symbolic paintings on the walls. Persecuted in every direction as they were, the Christians were still obliged to remain hidden and to conduct their worship out of sight both of the crowd and of the Roman officials. These precautions were considerably relaxed, however, in the second century—especially in Syria and the other Asiatic provinces. Prior to Armenia's official conversion, the Christian religion was already prevalent throughout the Roman East, and it had early reached the Ararat country— only it dared not yet come out into the open. Church-building was still out of the question.

The priests who preached the gospel in Armenia brought with them from Syria not only the new religion but also the Syriac liturgy and plans for organizing the new clergy. Undoubtedly they received from their teachers instructions how to lay out their places of worship, and the first churches in the Ararat region were built on Syrian lines.

Zenobius of Glak (1) writes as follows regarding the building of the first Christian edifice at Tarôn at the order of St. Gregory: "When "the soldiers had destroyed the idol "(of Demetri), St. Gregory laid "the foundations for a church. "There being no materials available "locally, he took rough stones, and "having discovered lime in the "heathen temple, he began the "building of a church on the site of "the shrine of Demetri, following "the same measurements."

From these lines we may presume that the first churches in Armenia were built approximately along the same lines as the pagan edifices, but we have no positive documentary evidence regarding either.

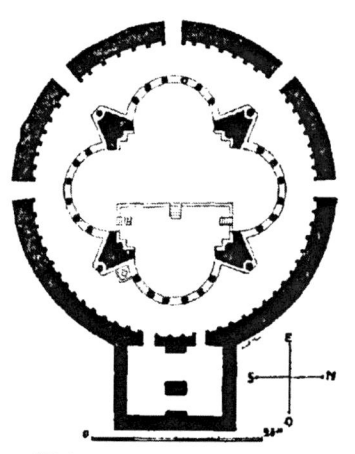

PLAN OF THE CHURCH OF
ST. GREGORY (ZVARTNOTS)
NEAR ETCHMIADZIN

---

(1) Transl. V. Langlois, vol. II, p. 348.

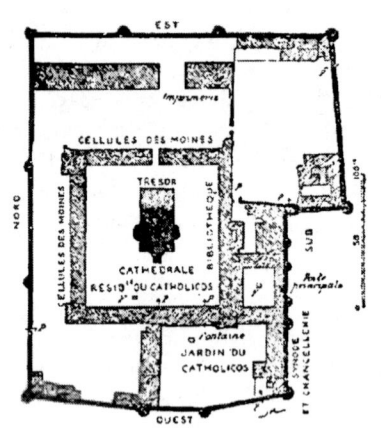

PLAN OF THE PRESENT MONASTERY AT ETCHMIADZIN

Emperor Constantine's conversion, a few years only after that of King Tiridates, was revolutionary in its effects on the world not only from the moral standpoint but also that of architectural development throughout the Empire. Everywhere, in every big city, town, and village, churches sprang up. They were sometimes of the basilica type like St. Sophia or St. Irene at Constantinople, or round or octagonal buildings such as the Church of the Holy Apostles at Byzantium, the rotunda of St. Constance at Rome, the Church of the Ascension on the Mount of Olives at Jerusalem, or the great octagonal Church of Antioch, the oldest example of this style of edifice.(1) The Emperor encouraged the building of religious institutions, and gave liberally from his treasury to the

VIEW OF ETCHMIADZIN CATHEDRAL

---
(1) Cf. Ch DIEHL, Man. d'art byzantin, p. 3.

— 373 —

Christians. The large edifices that were built on his orders and at his expense became architectural patterns throughout the Christian world.

By reason of its geographical location, Armenia at an early date was in a specially conspicuous position. Having considerable intercourse with Syria, Mesopotamia, and Persia, she naturally derived much useful instruction from these countries. On the other hand, her close political relations with Byzantium subjected her to Greek influence. A number of the patriarchs at the head of the Armenian church from the 5th to the 7th century had been brought up in Byzantine territory, and Justinian's architects, moreover, had built quite a few edifices in various districts of Armenia that could be taken for models. From these two contacts, Greece and the East, there arose in the 7th century a style of architecture in Armenia that was interesting and original. This style is comparatively little known as yet, not having been adequately studied. Many unsolved questions confront us regarding it, but those who have examined Armenian constructions are aware that this nation's builders were outstanding craftsmen who, living as they did in an essentially rocky country, brought the art of stone-cutting to an unusually high pitch of excellence. (1)

PLAN OF ETCHMIADZIN CATHEDRAL

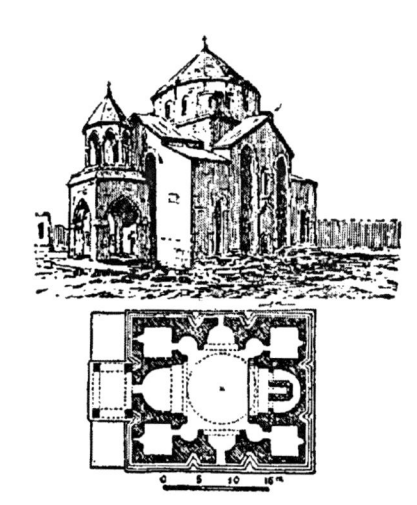

VIEW AND PLAN OF THE CHURCH OF ST. RIPSIME AT VALARSAPAT

The Cathedral of Etchmiadzin built, it is said, in the 5th century and restored in the 7th, is apparently as regards its design one of the

---

(1) Ch. DIEHL, op. laud., p. 315.

MONASTERY OF ST. VARAG AT VAN

CHURCH OF ST. STEPANOS AND MONASTERY OF MAGHARD

oldest churches in Armenia. This design is quite original, being in the general form of a Greek cross with a central cupola. It seems to have been built on the model of Sassanid structures. The Church of St. Ripsimé at Valarapat, dating also from the 7th century, shows the same design, but is roofed in a sixteen-sided cupola of conical shape, used from very remote times in the East. This structural design was copied by the west about the 10th century and probably was the guiding influence in the building of the churches of Mount Athos in Greece.

Likewise in the 7th century, Catholicos Nerses III (640-666) built not far from Etchmiadzin the church of St. Gregory the Illuminator (Zvarnots). This church, now in ruins, is an immense round tower 128 feet in diameter, surmounted by a cupola upheld by four enormous supports. The outline of this edifice is clearly Byzantine, including the capitals which were apparently carved by Greek sculptors. According to Sebeos, the above prelate was "reared from childhood in the land of the Greeks." The plan of the ruins reminds one strikingly of the church of the Holy Apostles at Byzantium.

MONASTERY OF NAREK

"Were the ancient structures of Armenia built along Byzantine architectural patterns, or was it Armenia that taught Byzantium?" is a question asked by M. Ch. Diehl. My opinion is that both suppositions are warranted, for Greek modes of construction apparently underwent alterations at the hands of the Armenians influenced in turn by their neighbors and frequently by their Persian Sassanid rulers. These very changes which were governed by discriminating taste were destined later to furnish architects of the western world with fresh inspiration in their profession.

Long before it came into use in the West, the arch was known to the peoples of Asia. It is found in Egypt dating from the first dynasties, sometimes even with a fair amount of amplification (1). The structures of Nineveh likewise show numerous examples of the cupola. The Sassanids were consequently only carrying on their ancestral tradition in using these modes of architecture. (2) They seem, however, to have added the corner pendentive to join the spring of the cupola with main edifices of square design; (3) and because of using materials of small and uneven size (4) they were led to build raised elliptic arches, with or without framed soffits, (5) from which later sprang the Gothic arch. At the same time they attached much importance to decoration, and according to the ancient custom of their country, they were very fond of polychromy. These

CHURCH OF ST. GEORGE AT ANI

---

(1) e.g. at Dahchur, along with others of the 12th dynasty.

(2) Servistan, Firuzâbâd.

(3) Palace of Chosroes II at Kasr-e-Chirin.

(4) Smooth pebbles. Palaces of Kas-e-Chirin, Haouch-Kouri, Rumichkhan, Chirvan, Derre-i-Chahr, ets. Cf. J. DE MORGAN, *Mission en Perse, Etudes archeologiques.*

(5) In the Sassanid buildings (Kasr-é-Chirin, Haouch-Kouri. Derre-i-Chahr, Chirvan, etc.) there can still be seen on the lower surface of the arches the mark left in the plaster by the wooden support of the soffit.

notions of art superimposed on those of Greece and Rome were largely responsible for the creations of the Byzantine schools, and if architectural taste on the Bosphorus was influenced by the Orient, such must have been even more the case in Armenia which was nearer to the Sassanid Empire and frequently under its rule.

Among none of the peoples of ancient times who reached to high levels of architecture, whether Egypt, Assyria, Chaldea, Greece, or Italy, did the disasters encountered in the course of the centuries ever wipe out all vestiges of their structures; and past grandeurs are evidenced by num-

CHURCH OF AKHTAMAR NEAR VAN

erous and imposing ruins. Unfortunately this is not so in the regions of Armenia, nor in the north of western Asia from the river Halys to the eastern borders of Iran. In the absence of any remains worthy of note, we must incline to the opinion that the different peoples inhabiting those parts did not undertake any very extensive building, and that, notwithstanding the statements of native writers, it was Christianity and Byzantine influence which caused the development of architectural art among the Armenians. The churches built in profusion, as soon as the new religion was established, in every town and village were undoubtedly erected along western lines, even though they included useful borrowings from Persia. History tells us furthermore that the sumptuous sacred edifices built by Constantine in the Holy Land were objects of marvel because of their splendor and originality, and that they were at once adopted as models for Christendom's basilicas. Some writers, however, consider that the Greek-cross type of

LION CARVED ON THE
RAMPARTS OF ANI

church, of which Etchmiadzin cathedral is a very early specimen, formed by adding four semi-circular apses to the square Persian construction, is of purely Armenian origin. We consider this thesis disputable.

CHRIST, THE VIRGIN, and
SAINT GREGORY
(Stone carving at Ani)

The churches of Ani, dating from the Bagratid period, are all likewise very instructive as regards their designs. Most of them are cross-shaped, but others, e.g. the Chapel of St. Gregory, are octagonal with a conical dome over a round tower upheld by columns which in turn are separated by semi-circular recesses.

One chapel, near the citadel of the Bagratid capital, shows a square door with a flat moulding, the ornamentation of which in some respects recalls pagan Greek or possibly Achaemenean times, whereas the eastern façade of the Church of the Apostles, built before 1348, is purely Moslem in style, and the basements of the Castle of Ani are clearly Sassanid both in their ground and structural outlines.

As can be seen, Armenian builders were guided not by any set purpose of copying western models, but by a wish to enrich their structures with both Byzantine and Eastern standards of taste.

ANI TOMBSTONES

When they came under Moslem sway, the Armenians were influenced by the architectural and decorative ideas of their rulers. Thus we see the gate of the palace of Ani surmounted by a semi-circular arch with Moslem ornamentation, whilst the window above this gate is ogival in shape. But these transformations of a structure, which was originally Byzantine and was ruined by the Arabs and the Seljuks, and restored under Manouchar, the son of Abul-Sevar, the first Moslem prince of Ani, were carried out at the time they were rebuilding the city's mosque, itself a western-style construction.

In Armenian churches, the capitals are nearly all of clear Byzantine type, e.g. at Etchmiadzin and at Ani, also at Khoscha Vank where the porch has columns and capitals which would not be out of place in a Roman building of the 3rd or 4th century.

The ornamentation, carved along Byzantine lines, shows nevertheless some peculiarities of detail We must remember that the Sassanid decorators largely used cut-out plaster-work (1) and that the Moguls (2), the Arabs, and the Turks carried forward the Persian tradition. It is easy to understand, therefore, how oriental influence invaded the Armenians' style and altered somewhat their Byzantine patterns.

Even the tombstones with their carvings are Byzantine in conception. They are very numerous in the burial-grounds of Armenia, and but for their inscriptions might easily be taken for Coptic or Syrian funerary steles of the same period

FRESCOES AND ICONS
I must hold to the same opinion as regards both mural paintings and manuscript ornamentation. Byzantine Christian art adopted its wall decoration from the ancient technical processes of Rome and Syria, adapting it to the needs of the new religion. Taken altogether, Byzantine fresco paintings and mosaics are entirely homogeneous, and any variations according to different periods or localities are only minor changes due to temporary or provincial preferences, with slight effect on the primal conception Armenian paintings, like those of Egypt and the Neo-Byzantine mosaics of Russia, all derive from the same decorative methods.

The same is the case with icons, whether Greek. Russian, Georgian, or Armenian, they all show the same motifs, they are all similarly treated and express the same spirit. Any differences among these pictures are due only to varying trends of schools, variations that are always minimized by strict rules of tradition.

MANUSCRIPT ILLUMINATION
The illumination of manuscripts offers more variety because the artists gave freer rein to their imagination and were not above introducing popular scenes into their work, giving the latter a realistic

---

(1) Qal'ai-Hazar-dar at Derre-i-Chahr, Kasr-é-Chirin, etc.
(2) Mosque of Hamadan.

TOMBSTONES

touch with little concern for flagrant anachronisms.

This great latitude in the illumination of manuscripts was general throughout the Middle-Ages, and it is as common in eastern MSS. as in western. It is peculiar to each country and faithfully portrays local tastes. In Armenia, not only were popular scenes and legendary monsters depicted, but also foreign subject-matters, and designs suggested by Persian and Arab illuminators are constantly met with. These latter themselves sometimes originated much farther east, so that Armenian miniature-

DESCENT FROM THE CROSS
(Wooden carving in the Treasure House at Etchmiadzin)

CARVED DOOR AT THE MONASTERY OF SEVAN

painting has quite a special character. But religious subjects are all wrought on Byzantine patterns, just as are our western books of the romanesque period.

The library at Etchmiadzin is very rich in ancient manuscripts, and includes therefore a complete collection of these methods of illuminating. Comparing the various works one can easily follow the development of Armenian style both from within and from outside influences. From the outset there is seen a tendency to copy faithfully the Byzantine, and then gradually imagination creeps into the works and subjects are left to the illuminator's discretion. The growth of this local talent reached its zenith in the time of the Rupenians. As for religious subjects, they became in time more and more hieratic, quite the contrary of what took place in the west where drawings became increasingly realistic and reached their peak of elegance in our incomparable manuscripts of the Renaissance.

This freedom in the choice of details is also seen, but to a much lesser degree, in the carved motifs of church ornamentation. There too, the sculptors have sometimes given free rein to fancy, but they have always maintained the general lines of Byzantine style. We must not, however, forget to mention a very curious and handsome church at Akhtamar, on an island of Lake Van, where the walls are covered with carved relief representations of Christ, the Virgin, the Saints, and also animals and fanciful

THE FALLING ASLEEP OF THE VIRGIN FROM THE ARMENIAN ICONOGRAPHY

MINIATURE PAINTING ON A SISSOUAN MS. DATED 1330

subjects. Looking at these singular carvings, one cannot help thinking of the rock-carved bas-reliefs of the Chaldeans, the Assyrians, and the Hittites. This church, built in Greek-cross shape according to Byzantine rules, dates from the first quarter of the 10th century. Thousand-year

ANIMALS FIGHTING
(Armenian iconography taken from Alishan)

old traditions of ornamentation seem to have been preserved on its walls

There is practically nothing left us of the civil architecture of the Armenians prior to the taking of Ani by the Seljuks. There is every reason to believe, however, that it likewise was Byzantine and Persian in conception. As for military construction the walls of Ani seem to show the same architecture as that used by the Byzantines and the Sassanids, and even all Mediterranean countries at that time The only difference is in the abundant ornamentation and the unusual selection and arrangement of the material used Although they are very massive, the fortifications of Ani are quite elegant and are a handsome spectacle.

There exists unfortunately no successions of coins of Greater Armenia subsequent to the series of entirely Greek-style coins minted contemporaneously by the Syrian Seleucids and the Persian Arsacids This hiatus is much to be regretted, not only on account of the value of numismatics in confirming history, but also because coins would have given accurate information as to the prevalent trends in art of each successive period, from the advent of the Sassanid rulers in Iran down to the downfall of the Bagratid dynasty. Lacking any Armenian coins for the period referred to, we must fall back on those we have of the Georgian rulers who were so often mixed up in the affairs of Armenia and whose territory in the Kurah valley was subjected to almost the same vicissitudes as the northern and eastern provinces of Armenia.

THE VIRGIN
(Miniature painting on a MS. written for King Hetum II)

GEORGIAN COINS

About A D. 575, the Georgian eristhaws, who were fighting the Persians then holding almost all Transcaucasia, coined money similar to that of the last Sassanid kings Hormidas IV, Chosroes II, etc Byzantine influence was considerably on the wane at that time in this part of Asia. Following this comes a break of four centuries in the numismatics of Karthli (Georgia), a break coincident with the Arab conquest, the arrival of the Seljuks, and the wars that convulsed Transcaucasia. David, the ruler of Taïq, late in the 10th century struck a follis of the current Byzantine style, and Bagrat IV (the adversary of the Turk Alp-Arslan), Georgi II (1072-1089), and Koriké (1046-1082?), king of Armenian Albania, all minted similar coins of the Byzantine type. David II, surnamed The Restorer, then struck aspers with obverse stamped similarly to money of the Empire of Trebizond, and reverse reading in Arabic characters: "King of Kings Daoud son of Giorgi: the Sword of the Messiah." Dimitri (1125-1154), however, was obliged to have his coins bear the names of the Arab ruler Al Moktafy and Mahmoud, the Seljuk Sultan of Persia. Giorgi III (1154-1184) who seized from the Turks the cities

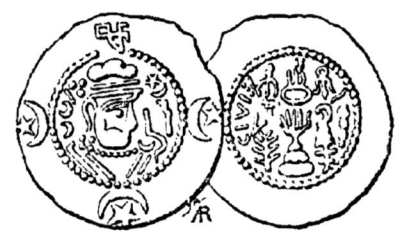

GOURGEN, ERISTHAW OF GEORGIA

of Ani, Etchmiadzin, Dovin, Gandzak, and a large part of Armenia, issued coins of uncommon appearance, as did also his daughter, Queen Thamar, but both these Georgian sovereigns struck practically at the same time other money that was mixed Byzantine and Moslem.

BAGRAT IV, KING OF GEORGIA

Roussoudan (1223-1247), Thamar's daughter, copied Byzantine coinage, and her son David V issued imitations of that of the Comneni of Trebizond. The Mongols had just extended their rule over Georgia and Armenia, however, so that coins of the same David V (1243-1269), of Dimitri II (1273-1289), David VI (1292-1310) and Wakhtang III (1301-1307) all carry, in Mogul or Arabic characters, the names of the Khans their suzerains. Under Bagrat (1360-1395), aspers similar to those of the Comneni reappear, as

GIORGI II, KING OF GEORGIA

they did also under Giorgi VIII (1452-1469). After that, there were no further issues of Georgian coins until the time of Russian occupation.

Such a checkered history, as can be imagined, greatly handicapped and disturbed the progress of art in Transcaucasia. The influences at play were most varied. As Christians, the Georgians and Armenians naturally inclined towards Constantinople and Trebizond, and close relations were maintained with the Empire, but in innumerable ways they were none the less thrown back on themselves.

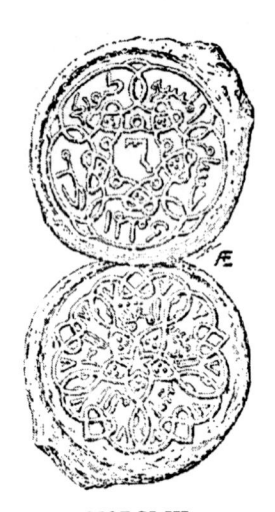

GIORGI III,
KING OF GEORGIA
and AL MOKTAFY

In Cilicia, under the Rupenians and the Lusignans, all the coinage was of Latin character. Latin influence penetrated everywhere, including civil and religious architecture which in New Armenia showed a curious mixture of Byzantine and Gothic. The Rupenian buildings consequently differ considerably from the medieval structures of Greater Armenia.

The well-known architect Toramanian, who has studied Armenia's antiquities for very many years, considers that his country has a national art which he divides into four cycles. The last of these cycles, one of comparative distinction, lasted from the 13th to the 14th century when Armenia was fast disintegrating politically. I cannot adopt his views in this connection, my own opinion being that Armenian art is an offshoot of Byzantine art. It is true that it developed along lines somewhat its own and was subjected to foreign influence, but it always adhered more or less closely to the standards of Constantinople.

Byzantine art, like that of the Greeks and Romans, took on especially in Asia and Africa a very characteristic provincial complexion. The Roman sculptural remains of Egypt are a striking example. These essentially local tastes have been conspicuous in Armenia almost down to the present day. The same is the case with Russia where Byzantine art developed along quite special lines, both in

ROUSSOUDAN, QUEEN OF GEORGIA

RELIQUARY AT ETCHMIADZIN

**CIORCI VIII.
KING OF GEORGIA**

architecture and sculpture, as also in mosaic.

I would be the last to wish to deny the Armenians some originality in their architecture. They adapted Byzantine art to their own preferences, and made skillful use of what they learned from their Persian neighbors, but Armenian art must, I consider, be looked on as a branch of Byzantine, in the same manner as the Coptic, the Rumanian, and the Russian.

INDUSTRIAL ARTS From our knowledge of the goldsmith's work, the weaving of cloth and carpets, embroidery, and other branches of Armenian craftsmanship, this people stands out as proficient in those minor arts, at any rate since the Middle Ages. Today they may be safely said to be almost the only people in the Turkish empire engaged in fine artistic handicrafts.

The libraries and churches of the East all contain triptychs, icons, bookbindings, sacred vessels, reliquaries, church vestments, and tapestries, rugs, and fabrics of Armenian workmanship, and among them all it is easy to pick out those expressing native culture (mostly Byzantine) and those fashioned or woven along Moslem lines, the latter having been wrought presumably for Turkish or Persian patrons.

At Constantinople, Smyrna, Trebizond, Teheran, Hamadan, Tabriz, Erzerum, Erivan, Tiflis and nearly all the northern centers of western Asia, jewelry and goldsmith's work is produced in the "Armenistan", or Armenian quarter, of each city while inside the Armenian homes the womenfolk weave and embroider rugs, carpets, and the like, which go out into the world including European centers where both commercial houses and the general public are under the impression they are Moslem workmanship. The Armenians put their individual native stamp on what they produce for themselves, and, naturally enough, meet the customer's preferences as regards the remainder placed on sale. These industrious people have always shown themselves assiduous and progressive artisans, and we can be sure that numbers of the goldsmiths and engravers who worked for the Byzantine emperors were Armenians.

In the higher sphere of architecture, Armenians likewise have played an important part in the East. It is known that the architect Tiridates, who built so many of the Ani churches, restored the magnificent cupola of St Sophia at Constantinople, which was originally constructed by the Greek architects Anthemius of Tralles and Isidorus of Miletus, and which collapsed during the earthquake that struck the city in A.D. 989. This new cupola, which we still admire, is in the form of an elliptical arch, and, built of light material, is still cited today as an outstanding model, in classes dealing with the stonecutter's art. Tiridates had a large number of emulators in the Byzantine empire.

Furthermore, the Arabs, Turks, and Mongols,—who were incompetent themselves to build the fine structures which we mistakenly ascribe to them and whereon were inscribed in gold the names of their Caliphs, Sultans, or Khans,—entrusted to Christians the task of immortalizing their great men. According to the different countries, Greeks, Syrians, and Armenians were the master-builders throughout western Asia and as far east as India, with the one exception of Persia. In the latter country the Iranian traditional skill handed down from their great architects of old had been preserved.

Love of art has never died out among the Armenians, whether as applied to their own requirements or as exercised in working for their Moslem rulers, and in every branch of it which they have maintained since the Middle Ages they have retained their preeminence of old. Until the 18th century, they clung to their ancient styles of work imposed on them by tradition or necessity. but with the 19th century an era of progress opened up for them, and as the case with their literature and music, they launched out into fresh modes of expression under Europe's influence. Architects, painters, and sculptors, all subscribed to the western schools, received instruction in Art's larger unfoldment, and kept pace with its forward movement.

In the 18th century. *Stepanos of Poland*, an Armenian painter, executed for the monastery of Etchmiadzin some paintings in which the Italian school predominates.

Since the early nineteenth century, a whole generation of workers have striven with success to assimilate European standards in sculpture, painting, engraving. and dancing. *Yervant Osgan*, a talented sculptor, has for many years been the Director of the Ottoman School of Fine Arts at Constantinople, and many Armenian names are to be seen on the roll of our leading European artists, e g *Aivazovsky*, the best Russian marine painter, *Edgar Chahine*, whose paintings and etchings are known to everyone in Paris, *Zakarian* and his still-life productions, *Mahokian* and *Chabanian*, marine artists, landscape-painters such as *Alhasian* of Paris, *Bachindjaghian* and *Thadevossian* of Tiflis, *Terlemesian* of Van, *Surian* of Moscow, and many more, without forgetting the many young pupils of our western Art schools whose future is still ahead of them.

DANCING   Dancing, formerly restricted to folk-dancing, and ever popular throughout the countryside, has acquired social standing and increasing vogue in the *salon* as also on the stage, where recent performances of Mlle. *Armene Ohanian* have been acclaimed by the Paris public, appreciative of her charming and graceful adaptations of the Terpsichorean art.

* * *
* *
*

CHAPTER XII

Events in Armenia subsequent to the fall of the Czar in Russia (1917-1918).

While this book was in the press, grave events in Russia have thrown turmoil into Eastern affairs and once more caused the Armenian people to weep, inflicting on them one of the most frightful crises in history.

Ever mindful of Peter the Great's testament to his successors, the Czars aimed at the possession of Constantinople and the Straits. Finding themselves blocked of late years in their attempts to reach the shores of the Bosphorus via Europe, the Bulgarians and the Rumanians having been freed from Turkish rule and secured national independence, Russian diplomacy was seeking to achieve its purpose by way of Asia, and as a step toward the century-old goal of the Romanoffs, it coveted Turkish Armenia and Anatolia. From 1914 on, Russian armies in Asia strove to that end, in furtherance of which France, England, and Italy gave Petrograd a free hand. Under the conviction that German military power was invincible, the Young Turks confident of Berlin's victory were imprudent enough to declare war on the Entente, a step which threw open the door to the Russian generals and gave the subjugated Christians of Turkey the opportunity to rise and assert their freedom.

But although the Armenians had openly espoused the cause of Germany's enemies, Petrograd did not see eye to eye with Tiflis and Erzerum. Russia did not intend to grant political liberty to Armenia, whose liberal and home-rule notions were in high Czarist circles looked on as dangerous to the Imperial régime and the Romanoff dynasty. Furthermore an independent Armenia would have blocked the road to the Straits via Asia Minor, just as Rumania and Bulgaria by gaining national freedom had closed the way through Thrace. The Armenians were considered, therefore, from the Russian Government's standpoint, as future subjects of the Czar, just as the many other subject peoples of that Empire. This prospect, although not the one nearest to right and justice, had at least the merit of delivering the Armenians from Turkish tyranny, and the Russian rule was looked on as a stepping-stone to further later developments. The progress achieved by their people in the Russian Transcaucasian provinces, despite their relative unpopularity there, encouraged them to look forward self-reliantly to their national future Conscious of their own energy, they felt that the above outlook was only temporary and that changes would occur after the war. Anyone with perspicacity could see that the Russian empire, seriously affected by its agrarian and social difficulties and ill-supported by a decadent government, must inevitably undergo a very severe crisis as the outcome of which the causes of the various nationalities would come to the fore, for they were bound to be upheld by the western democracies. It was felt also on the other hand that the Czar's government, to save itself, would be forced to grant large concessions. In view of all this, Armenia's future despite the uncertainty seemed auspicious

The Russian troops had already seized the majority of the Turkish vilayets of Armenia. Erzerum, Van, Mouch, Erzindjan, Baibourt, and Trebizond had all just been snatched from the infamous Turkish rule, when at the beginning of the year 1917 there ensued the frightful catastrophe of the Russian revolution.

Petrograd's foreign policy thereupon entered on a new phase, that of defeatism. Imperial trends, i e desire for conquest, gave way abruptly to the abandonment of centuries of tradition. Peter the Great's testament was torn up, and at Berlin's orders, the new Government in Germany's pay, forsaking all Russian views concerning Constantinople, gave up any interest in Asia. As a matter of form, it did enunciate the principle of the liberation of oppressed peoples (the guiding principle of the Entente against the Central Powers), but this lip-service, too lofty to maintain the Russian masses, soon gave way to the crass selfishness and greed of the new masters in Petrograd. Their pious utterance remained just words and soon were flagrantly contradicted by the frenzied acts of those who seized power with Germany's aid.

The Russian debacle was not long in assuming incredible proportions; its extent was vividly brought out in the treaty of Brest-Litowsk, where the lawless Soviet government abjectly surrendered to Berlin's imperious orders From then on, amid the most terrible disorders, the various peoples felt abandoned, isolated; each nationality, thrown back on its own resources and home forces, imagined it could save itself from the tempest by proclaiming its independence An ephemeral republic was formed in Transcaucasia composed of Armenians, Georgians, and Tartars, but this political amalgam had no possibility of lasting. The Moslem Tartars had hated the Armenians for centuries, and serious dissensions had recently cropped up between the Moslems and the Georgians. The result was that the Tartars espoused the cause of Islam and took sides with the Turks against their allies of the day before. As for the Georgians, they took part in the defense of Transcaucasia against the Ottomans, but then forsook the Armenians who were left to face the enemy alone.

The Soviet Government, however, though ready for any act of betrayal, thought it might be to its interest to have it believed that it entertained liberal views regarding the freedom of oppressed nations, and therefore on January 13th, 1918, the following Decree was published in Petrograd:

"The Council of Commissaries of the People declares to the Armenian "people that the Government of Workers and Peasants of Russia upholds "the right of the Armenians in Turkish Armenia occupied by Russia to "make free choice of country and even to choose independence. The "Council of Commissaries considers that this right may be realized by "drawing up a list of preliminary guarantees, which are absolutely re- "quisite for a referendum on the part of the Armenian people. The Council "of Commissaries recognizes the following conditions to be partial guar- "antees to this end:

ART. I.—Evacuation of Armenia by the Russian troops and immediate "formation of an army of Armenian militia in order to guarantee the "safety of the lives and property of the inhabitants of Turkish Armenia.

ART. II.—Return to Armenia, without hindrance, of the Armenian "fugitives, as well as of the Armenian emigrants dispersed in different "countries.

ART. III.—Return to Armenia, without hindrance, of the Armen- "ians driven out by force during the war by the Turkish authorities into "the interior of Turkey. The Council of Commissaries will insist on this "condition in the peace negotiations with the Turkish delegates.

ART IV.—An Armenian provisional government will be created in "Turkish Armenia in the form of a Council of Delegates of the Armenian "people, elected on a democratic basis. Stepan Chahoumanian, who has "been appointed provisional Commissary Extraordinary for Cau-

"casian affairs, is entrusted with the task of giving all assistance to the
"inhabitants of Turkish Armenia for carrying out Articles II and III,
"and for the creation of a mixed commission, in order to appoint a date for
"and means of evacuation of the Russian troops in accordance with Art. I
"The geographical frontiers of Turkish Armenia will be determined by the
"representatives of the Armenian people elected according to democratic
"procedure in agreement with the Moslem and other inhabitants of the
"border provinces in dispute, also with Commissary Chahoumanian."

This monstrous document recognized the right of the Armenians to live and govern themselves, but imposed on them an anarchic form of government, i.e. one contrary to the interests of the Armenian nation whose capitalists were one of their chief sources of strength, and it handed over the organization of an incipient State to the will of the ignorant masses. It proclaimed, moreover, the Soviets' intention to withdraw the Russian troops from Turkish Armenia and to abandon that country consequently to the fury of the Ottomans who would not forgive the Armenians for having sided with the Entente armies This was the basest treason, the vilest crime imaginable, and the Bolshevists cynically added that they expected to enter into negotiations with the Turks who had not yet even been consulted regarding the future of the Christian vilayets about to be surrendered to them. The People's Commissaries merely gave a vague promise that they would seek to negotiate.

It meant delivering up Armenia to new massacres, to slavery even more frightful than that endured by the unhappy country for so many centuries. How indeed could the Armenian people struggle to any purpose against the Sultan's armies aided by the Kurdish tribes and led by German officers?

That was but the beginning of Bolshevist infamy, for two months after the above disgraceful decree was issued, the Maximalist government signed (in March 1918) the shameful treaty of Brest-Litowsk giving up Russia to Germany, and Armenia and Transcaucasia to Turkey. Not satisfied with undoing with one stroke of the pen the whole work achieved by the Grand Duke's army in Asia and thus abandoning the Christians of Turkish Armenia to their tormentors, they actually added at the dictation of the German and Turkish plenipotentiaries an even more despicable paragraph, one sacrificing former Russian territories peopled with Christians and throwing the door to the Transcaucasian provinces wide open.

This shameful capitulation reads, Art. IV.:

"Russia will do all in her power to ensure the rapid evacuation of the eastern provinces of Anatolia and their restoration to Turkey. Ardahan, Kars, and Batum will be evacuated without delay by the Russian troops."

The name of Armenia even is no longer mentioned in this enemy-dictated text; instead we read "eastern provinces of Anatolia." It is equivalent to saying that the Armenian people do not exist; they are officially handed over to the hatred of their former rulers. Thus the Bolsheviks denied the most sacred rights of humanity and trampled on their own professed principles.

The blow was a terrible one for the Armenians, for not only were the vilayets to be re-invaded, but the evacuation of Batum, Ardahan, and Kars insisted on by the Turks showed beyond doubt that they expected at least the Ottoman reoccupation of their districts lost in the war of 1878. They even went so far in Constantinople as to say that "the natural boundary of the Ottoman Empire is the Greater Caucasus chain."

Confronted with such a menace, the Armenians resolved to defend their homes to the death, and they therefore armed themselves while the Russian troops were evacuating Ottoman territory and the western districts of Russian Armenia. But of what avail were a handful of brave men against the Turkish armies? The fight began in April. Trebizond fell, as also did Erzindjan despite the desperate resistance put up by five thousand Armenian volunteers defending the latter city; then Erzerum, Mouch, Van, in turn were the scenes of stubborn battles which sometimes ended

THE ISLAND AND MONASTERY OF LAKE SEVAN
(RUSSIAN ARMENIA)

successfully for the Armenians. These local successes did not affect the outcome, however, and gradually the battle turned to the north, to the former Russian provinces.

Batum had just been captured by the Turks from the Georgians, and the victors had besieged Kars, were by-passing that city and laying waste the regions of the Lesser Caucasus, when the Georgians forsook the common Christian cause and started negotiations with the enemy The Armenians themselves had to be satisfied with a tiny portion of their country, in the region of Erivan and Lake Sevan. There they formed a small republic, pending better days. These latter seem to be drawing near, now that Britain has intervened in northern Persia and has gone so far as to seize Baku for the present in her intention of closing the way to India,—and now that great events are occurring in the west Meanwhile, small Armenian forces are still fiercely defending themselves in the mountains against the Tartars, for the struggle is still far from finished.

By occupying Baku, the important Caspian port, Britain secured a most vital point on the transcontinental route to India but her intervention would have meant so much more had she given assistance a few months before to the Armenians, who were then still in considerable numbers The Transcaucasian natural stronghold would have been secured, intercepting communications between Turkey and the eastern Moslems,—Tartar, Turkish, Azerbaidjanian, and Turcoman.

As I have already said, the historian is not entitled to speak of the future Whatever the outcome of this merciless war between the Armenian nation and its oppressors, the memory of this struggle will remain one of the finest pages in the annals of the Haikian people Her steadfastness, courage, and nameless woes have earned Armenia a glorious niche in the record of the World War.

* * *
* *
*

DRAGON
(Armenian Iconography, from Alishan)

APPENDICES

CHRONOLOGY (1)

REMOTEST TIMES

LEGENDARY DATA

Patriarchs.

1. Haïk, 2350 B C
2. Armenak
3. Armaïs
4. Amassia
5. Guegham
6. Harma
7. Aram
8. Ara the Handsome
9. Ara Araïan, or Kardos } 2300-2000 B.C.
10. Anouchavan
11. Paret
12. Arbak
13. Zavan
14. Pharnas
15. Sour
16. Havanak
17. Vachtak
18. Haïkak I } 2000-1870
} 1870-1700
} 1700
19. Ampak
20. Arnak
21. Chavarche
22. Norair
23. Vestam
24. Kar
25. Gorak
26. Hrant
27. Endzak
28. Gueghak
29. Horo
30. Zarmair
31. Pertch
32. Arboun
33. Hoï
34. Houssak
35. Kaïpak
36. Skaïordi } to 1200 B.C.
} 1200-870

Kings.

1. Parouir
2. Hratchia
3. Pharnouas
4. Patchouitch
5. Kornak
6. Phavos
7. Haïkak II
8. Erouand I
9. Tigranes I
10. Vahagn
11. Aravan
12. Nerseh
13. Zareh
14. Armog
15. Bagam
16. Van
17. Vahe } 870 to 330 B.C.

(None of the above dates should be given undue consideration.)

---

(1) We are indebted for this appendix entirely to the fine work by K. J. BASMADJIAN, *Chronologie de l'Histoire de l'Arménie*, published in the *Revue de l'Orient chrétien*, Vol. XIX, 1914. My only contribution to it is the data we have on events prior to the 4th century B C.

HISTORICAL DATA

Earliest times.

Arrival of the Armeno-Phrygians in Thrace	(?)
Crossing of the Bosphorus by the Armeno-Phrygians	ca. 1250 B.C.
Settlement of the Armeno-Phrygians in Phrygia	1000(?)
The Armenians separate from the Phrygians	ca. 800
Occupation of the Ararat region	ca. 600
Median rule (Cyaxares)	ca. 590-559
Achaemenian rule of Persia	ca. 559-330
Macedonian rule (?)	ca. 330-315(?)

FIRST PERIOD OF INDEPENDENCE

1. Phraataphernes or Neoptolemy seizes Armenia, 323 B.C.
2. Orontes I Hrant or Ervand, 322-301.
3. Ardoates or Artavazd, 301. . . . (?)
4. Artabazanes or Artavaz, 239-220 (?).
5. Orontes II, 220 (?)-215 (?).

RULE OF THE SELEUCIDS 215 (?)-190 B.C.

SECOND PERIOD OF INDEPENDENCE

DYNASTY OF ARTAXIAS

1. Artaxias or Artashes I, 190-159 (?) B.C.
2. Artavazd I, 159 (?)-149.
3. Tigranes I, 149-123.
4. Artavazd II or Artoadistus, 123-94.
5. Tigranes II The Great, 94-54.
6. Artavazd III, 56-34.
7. Alexander, 34-31.
8. Artashes II, 30-20.
9. Tigranes III, 20-12.
10. Tigranes IV } 12-5 B.C. and A.D. 2-1.
11. Erato
12. Artavazd IV, 5-2 B.C.

FOREIGN DYNASTY

1. Ariobarzanes, *Median*, A.D. 2.
2. Artavazd V, *Median*, 2-11.
3. Tigranes V, *Jewish*, 11-14.
   Erato (again). 14-15
4. Vonones, (*Parthian*), 16-17.

— 402 —

5. Artashes III or Zeno, *Roman*, 18-34.
6. Arsaces or Archak I, *Parthian*, 34-35.
7. Mithridates, *Georgian*, 35-37 and 47-51.
8. Rhadamistus, *Georgian*, 51-53.

ARMENIAN ARSACIDS

1. Tiridates I, 53-59 and 66-100.
2. Tigranes VI, 60-62.
3. Exedares, 100-113.
4. Parthamasiris, 113-114.
5. Parthamaspates, 116-117.
6. Vologeses or Vagharch I, 117-140.
7. Sohemus, 140-162 and 163-178.
8. Pacorus, 162-163.
9. Sanatruces, 178-216.
10. Vologeses or Vagharch II, 178-217.
11. Tiridates II or Chosroes I the Great, 217-238.
    End of the Parthian Kingdom, 226.
    Rule of the Sassanids, 238-250, 252-261, 272-282 and 294-298.
12. Tiridates III, A D. 250-252, 283-294, and 298-330
13. Artavazd VI, 252-261.
    Palmyrian rule, 261-272.
14. Chosroes II the Younger, 331-339.
15. Tiran, 340-350.
16. Arsaces or Archak II, 351-367.
17 Pap 369-374
18. Varazdat, 374-378.
19. Arsaces or Archak III, 378-386.
20 Vagharchak, 378-386.
21. Chosroes III, 386-392 and 414-415
    Division of Armenia between the Romans and the Sassanids, A.D. 317.
22. Vramchapouh, 392-414.
    Invention of the Armenian alphabet, A.D. 414.
23. Sapor or Chapouh, 416-420 (1)
24. Artashes IV. 423-429

PERSIAN RULE

MARZPANS OR GOVERNORS-GENERAL

1. Vehmihrchapouh, *Persian*, 430-438.
2. Vassak Suni, *Armenian*, 438-451.
   Vardan the Great, died 451 (great battle of Avarair).
3. Atrormizd, *Armeno-Persian* 451 465
4 Atrvechnasp, *Persian*, 465-481.

---

(1) As regards the above lists, consult: F JUSTI, *Iranisches Namenbuch*, Marburg 1895. E. BABELON, *Les Rois de Syrie, d'Arménie et de Commagene*, Paris, 1890; H. ASTURIAN, *Die politischen Beziehungen zwischen Armenien und Rom*, Venice, 1911, J. MARQUART, *Philologus*, Gottingen, 1896; K. J. BASMADJIAN, *The True History of Armenia* (in Armenian), Constantinople, 1914.

5. Sahak Bagratuni, *Armenian*, 481-482.
6. Chapouh Mihranian, *Persian*, 483-484.
7. Andekan, *Persian*, 484-485.
8. Vahan Mamikonian, *Armenian*, 485-505.
9. Vard Mamikonian, *Armenian*, 505-509.
. . . . (?)
10. X. Nikhorakan, *Persian*, 548-552 (?).
11. Vechnasp Bahram, *Persian*, 552-554 (?).
12. Denchapouh, *Persian*, 554-560 (?).
13. Varazdat, *Persian*, 560-564 (?).
14. Suren, *Persian*, 564 (?)-572.
Vardan V Mamikonian, Armenian general, 572-578.
15. Vardan Vechnasp, *Persian*, 572-573.
16. Golon Mihrah, *Persian*, 573.
17. Philippus, Lord of Sunik, *Armenian*, 573-578.
18 Tam Khosrov, *Persian*, 578-580.
19. Varaz Vezur. *Persian*, 580 581.
20 The Great Parthian Generalissimo, *Persian*, 581-588.
21. Frahat, *Persian*, 588.
22. Frartin Datan, *Persian*, 588-590.
23 Vendatakan Nikhorakan, *Persian*, 591-?.
24. Merakbout, *Persian*, 594-598.
25 Yazden, *Persian*, 598-600.
26. Boudmah, *Persian*, 600 (?)-604.
27 Foyiman, *Persian*, A D. 604-608.
28 Ashtat Yeztaiar *Persian*, 608-610.
29. Chahen, *Persian*, 611-612.
30. Chahraianpet, *Persian*, 612-613.
31 Parseanpet Parchenazdat, *Persian*, 613-?.
32 Namgarun Chonazp, *Persian*, 616-619 (?).
33 Chahraplakan, *Persian* 620 624 (?).
34 Tchrotch or Rotch Vehan, *Persian*, 624 (?)-627
35 Varaztirotz Bagratuni, *Armenian*, 628-634.
Fall of the Persian Empire, A D 652.

GOVERNORS-GENERAL OF BYZANTINE ARMENIA

1 John the Patrician, *Armenian*, 591
2 Heraclius, general, *Armenian*, father of Emperor Heraclius I, 594.
3 Suren, general. *Persian* (?), 604
. . . . (?).
4 Mejej Gnuni, general, *Armenian*, 630-635
5 David Saharuni. Curopalatus, *Armenian*, 635-638
The Arabs break into Armenia, A D. 636
6. Theodorus Rechtuni, general and patrician, *Armenian*, 641-646.
7 Thomas *Byzantine* (?). 640-646
8 Varaztirotz Bagratuni. Curopalatus. *Armenian*, 646 646.
9. Sembat Varaztirotzian, Curopalatus, *Armenian*, 646-656 (?).
Theodorus Rechtuni comes back (general), *Armenian*, 646-653
10 Maurianus general *Byzantine*, 653
11 Hamazasp Mamikonian Curopalatus and Patrician. *Armenian*, 658-661.
12 Sembat Bagratuni Sembatian. Curopalatus, *Armenian*, 703-705.

ARAB RULE

OSTIKANS OR GOVERNORS-GENERAL [1]

1. Theodorus Rechtuni, *Armenian*, 654-658.
2. Mouchegh Mamikonian, *Armenian*, 658-660
3. Grigor Mamikonian, *Armenian*, 661-685.

---

[1] To complete the list of Arab governors of Armenia from Armenian sources, we give the following roll of the same period as taken by K. J. BASMADJIAN from Arabic writers such as AL-BELASDORI, TABARI, IBN-KHALDUN, IBN-AL-ATHIR, etc. The numbers in brackets preceded by = refer to the corresponding name on the Armenian list.

1. Abd-er-Rahman, 636 (?)-644.
2. Welid, son of Oqba, 644-?.
3. Hozeifa ? *under Othman*, 644-656.
4. Moghira, son of Choba, ? *under Othman*.
5. Qacim (= 7 ?) son of Rabia or Amr son of Moawiya } *under Othman*
6. El-Oqaili ? *under Othman*.
7. Achath, son of Qais ? *under Ali*, 656-661
8. Habib, son of Maslama, died 663 *under Moawiya I*, 660-680.
9. Abd-Allah (= 6 ?) son of Hatim ?-? *under Moawiya I*.
10. Abd-el-Aziz (= 8) son of Hatim ?-? *under Moawiya I*.
11. Othman, son of Welid, ?-?, *under Abd-el-Melik*, 685-705
12. Mohammed I, son of Merwan, brother of Abd-el-Melik, 692-700 (?) and 704-710 (?), died 719.
13. Abou-Cheikh, son of Abd-Allah, 701-702.
14. Maslama I, brother of Welid, 710-?
15. Adi, son of Adi, or Hatim, son of Noman ?-?, *under Soleiman*, 715-717.
16. Milaq, son of Isafar Behrani, ?-?, *under Yezid II*, 720-724
17. Harith, son of Amr, ?-?, *under Yezid II*.
18. Djerrah, son of Abd-Allah Hakami, 723-725 and 730
19. Maslama II, son of Abd-el-Melik, 725-730.
20. Saïd I el-Harichi (= 9), 730-732
21. Merwan (= 10), 732-744
22. Thabit, 744.
23. Ishaq (= son of Moslim), 744-749.
24. Abou-Djafar el-Mansur, 749-753
25. Yezid I (= 12), son of es-Seyyid Selami, 753-?
26. Hassan (= 14), son of Qahtaba, ?-?, *under Mansur*, 754-775
37. Othman (= 16), son of Omara, ?-?, *under Mohammed el-Mahdi*, 775-785
28. Raouli (= 17), son of Hatim, ?-?, *under Mohammed el-Mahdi*
29. Khozeima (= 18), son of Khazim, ?-?, *under Moussa el-Hadi*, 785-786.
30. Yezid II (= 19), son of Mezyed, ?-?, *under Harun-er-Raschid*, 786-809.
31. Obeid-Allah, son of Mahdi ?-?, *under Harun-er-Raschid*.
32. Fadi son of Yahya, 792-?
33. Saïd II, son of Salim, ?-?, *under Harun-er-Raschid*
34. Mohammed II, son of Yezid, ?-?, *under Mohammed el-Emin?*, 809-813.
35. Khalil, son of Yezid, ?-?, *under Abdallah el-Mamoun*, 813-833
. . . . (?)
36. Haider, son of Kaous, ?-?, *under Mohammed-el-Motecim*, 833-842.
. . . . (?)
under Harun-el-Wathiq, 842-847.
37. Yussuf (= 26), son of Mohammed, 849-856 (?)
38. Bogha, 856 (?)-?

Rule of the Khazars, A.D. 685.
4. Ashot Bagratuni, *Armenian*, 685-688.
5. Sembat Bagratuni Sembatian, 688-703.
Mohammed, Arab general
6. Abd-Allah, *Arab*, 703-705
7. Qacim, *Arab*, 705-706
8. Abd el-Aziz, *Arab*, 706-730.
9. Seth Harachi, *Arab*, 730-732.
10. Meruan, *Arab*, 732-744.
Ashot Bagratuni, Armenian Patrician.
11. Ishaq, *Arab*, 745-750.
Grigor Mamikonian, Armenian general.
Mouchegh Mamikonian, Armenian general.
12. Yezid I, *Arab*, 751-760 (?).
Sahak Bagratuni, Armenian general.
13. Bekr, *Arab*, 760 (?)-761 (?).
14. Hassan, *Arab*, 762 (?)-775.
Sembat Bagratuni, Armenian generalissimo, died 775.
15. Yezid II, *Arab*, 775-780.
16. Othman, *Arab*, 780 (?)-785.
Bagarat Bagratuni, Armenian generalissimo.
17. Roh, *Arab*, 785
18. Khazim, *Arab*, 785-786.
19. Yezid III, *Arab*, 786-787.
20. Abd-el Kebir, *Arab*, 787.
21. Soleiman, *Arab*, 787-790.
22. Yezid IV, *Arab*, 790-795
23. Khozeima, *Arab*, 796-806
24. Hol, *Arab*, 807-847.
Sembat Bagratuni, Armenian generalissimo.
Bagarat Bagratuni, Armenian prince of Taraun.
Ashot Artzruni, Armenian prince of Vaspurakan.
25. Abou-Seth, *Arab*, 847-851.
26. Yussuf, *Arab*, 851.
Bogha, Arab general.
Ashot Bagratuni Sembatian, generalissimo (856) and Armenian "Prince of Princes." [1].

THIRD PERIOD OF INDEPENDENCE

DYNASTY OF THE ARMENIAN BAGRATIDS

1. Ashot I, A.D. 885-890.
2. Sembat I, 890-914.
3. Ashot II, The Iron, 914-929.
Ashot the Usurper, 921.

---

[1] Concerning the Persian rule of Armenia, consult M. PORTOUKAL, *Critique d'Elisé* (in Armenian), Venice, 1903; P. GULESSERIAN, *Etude critique sur Elisé* (in Armenian), Vienna, 1909; SEBEOS, *History of Heraclius* (in Armenian), Constantinople, 1851; J. CATERGIAN, *Universal History* (in Armenian), Vienna, 1852; K. J. BASMADJIAN, *La Vraie Histoire d'Arménie*, Constantinople, 1914 For the period of Arab rule, see: GHEVOND, *History of Armenia* (in Armenian), St. Petersburg, 1887; S. ASSOGHIK, *Universal History* (in Armenian), St. Petersburg, 1885.

4. Abas, 929-953.
5. Ashot III, the Merciful, 953-977.
6. Sembat II, the Conqueror, 977-989.
7. Gaghik I, Shah-en-Shah, 989-1020.
8. Sembat III or John Sembat, 1020-1042
9. Ashot IV, 1020-1042
10. Gaghik II, 1042-1045, (died 1079 at Cyzistra).

Kingdom of Vaspurakan (1)

1. Khatchik - Ghakik, 914-943.
2. Derenik-Ashot, 943-958.
3. Abussahl - Hamazasp, 958-968.
4. Ashot-Sahak, 968-990.
5. Gourgen - Khatchik, 990-1003.
6. John Senecherim, 990-1006, died 1026.
7. *David*, at Sivas, 1027-1037.
8. *Atom*, at Sivas, 1037-1080.
9. *Abussahl*, at Sivas, 1037-1080.

Kingdom of Kars.

1. Mouchegh, 962-984.
2. Abas, 984-1029.
3. Gaghik, 1029-1064, died in Greece 1080.

Kingdom of Armenian Albania (2)

1. David, died 1046.
2. Koriké, or Kuriké, 1046-1082 (?).

FOURTH PERIOD OF INDEPENDENCE

DYNASTY OF THE RUPENIANS (3) IN NEW ARMENIA (CILICA)

1. *Barons.*

1. Rupen I, A D. 1080-1095.
2. Constantine I, 1095-1099.
3. Thoros I, 1099-1129. Leo I, 1129-1137, died 1141 at Constantinople

(1) Cf. Thomas ARTZRUNI, *History* [of the House of the Artzrunis] (in Armenian), Constantinople, 1852; S. ASSOGHIK, *Histoire Universelle*, St. Petersburg, 1885; K. J BASMADJIAN, *The True History of Armenia*, Constantinople, 1914.

(2) Concerning the Bagratids, the kingdom of Kars, and that of Albania, see: M. BROSSET, *Histoire de la Géorgie*, St. Petersburg, 1851; S ASSOGHIK, *Histoire Universelle*, St. Petersburg, 1885; ARISTACES OF LASTIVERT, *History* [of Armenia] (in Armenian), Venice, 1844; and HOVHAN CATHOLICOS, *History* (in Armenian), Jerusalem, 1867.

(3) L. ALISHAN, *Sissouan*, Venice, 1899, E. DULAURIER, *Hist. des Croisades, Documents arméniens*, vol. 1, Paris, 1869; Ch. KOHLER, *Histoire des Croisades, Documents arméniens*, vol. II, Paris, 1906; K. J. BASMADJIAN, *Leo V of Lusigan, last king of Armenia*, (in Armenian), Paris, 1908.

4. Leo I, 1129-1137, died 1141 at Constantinople
   Rule of the Byzantines, 1137-1145.
5. Thoros II, 1145-1169.
6. Meleh, 1170-1175.
7. Rupen II, 1175-1187.
8. Leo II, 1187-1196, then as King Leo I, 1196-1219.

II. Kings.

1. Leo I, 1196-1219.
   Isabel, A D 1219-1252.
2. Philip, 1222-1225.
3. Hetum I, 1226-1270.
4. Leo II, 1270-1289.
5. Hetum II, 1289-1297.
6. Thoros, 1293-1295.
7. Sembat, 1296-1298.
8. Constantine I, 1298-1299.
9. Leo III. 1301-1307.
10. Ochin, 1308-1320
11. Leo IV, 1320-1342.
12. Guy or Constantine II, 1342-1344.
13. Constantine III, 1344-1365.
    Leo the Usurper, 1363-1365.
14. Constantine IV, 1365-1373.
    Mariam, 1373-1374
15. Leo V, 1374-1375, died 1393 at **Paris.**

ECCLESIASTICAL CHRONOLOGY

I CATHOLICI [1]

CATHOLICI OF ETCHMIADZIN

#	Name	Years
1.	Grigor I the Illuminator,	302-325.
2.	Aristaces I the Parthian,	325-333.
3	Verthanes I the Parthian,	333-341.
4	Houcik I the Parthian,	341-347.
5.	Pharene I of Achtichat,	348-352.
6	Nerses I the Great,	353-358.
	—	363-373.
7.	Chahak I of Manazkert,	373-377.
8.	Zavene I of Manazkert,	377-381.
9.	Aspuraces I of Manazkert,	381-386.
10.	Sahak I the Great,	387-428.
	—	432-439.
11.	*Surmak* (Anti-Patriarch)	428-429
	—	437-439.
	—	440-444.
12.	*Berkicho the Syrian* (Anti-Patriarch),	429-432.
13.	*Chemul the Syrian* (Anti-Patriarch),	432-437.
14	Hosvep I of Hoghotzime,	440-452.
15.	Melite of Manazkert,	452-456.
16	Movses I of Manazkert,	456-461.
17.	Gut I of Araheze,	461-478.
18.	Hovhannes I Mandakuni,	478-490.
19.	Babguen I of Othmous,	490 515.
20.	Samuel I of Artzke,	516-526.
21	Mouche I of Adaberk,	526-534
22.	Sahak II of Oughki,	534-539
23	Christaphorus I of Tiraritch,	539-545.
24	Chevond of Erast,	545-548.
25.	Nerses II of Bagrevand	548-557.
26.	Hovhannes II Gabeghian,	557-574.
27	Movses II of Eghivard,	574-604.
28	*Hovhannes of Bagaran* (Anti-Patriarch),	590-611.
	Verthanes the Poet (locum tenens,	604-607.
29.	Abraham I of Aghbathank	607-615.
30.	Komitas I of Aghtsik,	615 628.
31	Christaphorus II Apahuni,	628 630.
32.	Ezr I of Pharajnakert,	630 641
33.	Nerses III the Builder,	641-652.
	—	658-661.
34.	Anastasius I of Akori,	661-667.
35.	Israel I of Othmous,	667-677.
36.	Sahak III of Dzorapor,	677-703.
37.	Eghia I of Artchech,	703 717.
38.	Hovhannes III of Odzun,	712-728.
39.	David I of Aramonk,	728-741.
40.	Tiridates I of Othmous,	741-764.
41.	Tiridates II of Dasnavork,	764-767.
42.	Sion I of Bavonk,	767-775.
43.	Essai I of Eghipatruch,	775-788.
44.	Stephanus I of Dovine,	788-790.
45.	Hovab I of Dovine,	790-791.
46	Soghomon I of Garni,	791-792.
47.	Gueorg I of Ochakan,	792-795.
48.	Hovsep II of Parpi,	795-806.
49.	David II of Kakagh,	806-833.
50	Hovhannes IV of Ova,	833-855.
51	Zacharia I of Dzag.	855-877.
52.	Gueorg II of Garni,	878-898.
53.	Matchtotz I of Eghivard,	898-899.
54	Hovhannes V the Historian,	899-931

---

(1) Mgr. Malachia Ormanian in his work *Eglise Arménienne* (Paris, 1910) gives a list of the first preachers of the gospel in Armenia, viz: St. Thaddeus, martyred at Ardazus about A.D. 50; St. Bartholomew, martyred at Albacus about A.D 68; St. Zakaria, martyred about A D 76; St. Zementos, died about A.D. 81; St. Atirnerseh, martyred about A D. 97; St. Mousché, died about A.D 128; St. Schachen, died about A D. 154; St. Schavarche, died about A D. 175; St. Ghevondios, martyred about A.D. 193; and St. Mehroujan 230-260.

— 409 —

#	Name	Dates
55.	Stephanus II Rechtuni,	931-932.
56	Theodorus I Rechtuni,	932-938.
57	Eghiche I Rechtuni,	938-943.
58.	Anania I of Moks,	943-967.
59.	Vahan I Suni,	967-969.
60.	Stephanus III of Sevan	967-971.
61	Khatchik I Archaruni,	972-992.
62.	Sarguis I of Sevan	992-1019.
63	Petrus I Guetadardz,	1019-1036.
	— —	1038-1054.
64.	*Dioscorus of Sanahin* (Anti-Patriarch)	1036-1037.
65	Khatchik II of Ani, as Coadjutor,	1049-1054.
	alone,	1054-1060.
	(vacancy),	1060-1065.
66	Grigor II or Vahram,	1065-1105.
67.	Gueorg III of Lori, coadjutor,	1069-1072.
68.	*Sarguis of Honi* (Anti-Patriarch),	1076-1077.
69	*Theodorus Alakhocik* (Anti-Patriarch)	1077-1090
70.	Barsegh I of Ani as coajutor,	1081-1105.
	alone,	1105-1113.
71.	*Poghos of Varag* (Anti-Patriarch)	1086-1087.
72.	Grigor III Pahlavuni,	1113-1166
73	*David Thornikian* (Anti-Patriarch),	1114-?
74	Nerses IV the Gracious,	1166-1173.
75.	Grigor IV the Younger,	1173-1193.
76.	Grigor V or Vahram,	1193-1194
77	Grigor VI the Wicked,	1194-1203.
78.	*Barsegh II of Ani* (Anti-Patriarch),	1195-1206
79.	Hovhannes VI of Sis,	1203-1221.
80.	*Anania of Sivas* (Anti-Patriarch),	1204-1206
81	David III of Arkakaghine, coadjutor,	1204-1206.
82	Constantine I of Partzerpert,	1221-1267.
83	Hakob I the Learned,	1267-1286.
84.	Constantine II of Katuk,	1286-1289.
85	Stephanus IV of Rumkale,	1290-1293.
86.	Grigor I of Anavarza,	1293-1307.
87.	Constantine III of Caesarea,	1307-1322.
88	Constantine IV of Lampron,	1322-1326.
89.	Hakob II of Tarsus,	1327-1341.
	— —	1355-1359.
90.	Mekhithar I of Grner,	1341-1355.
91.	Mesrop I of Artaze,	1359-1372.
92.	Constantine V of Sis,	1372-1374.
93.	Poghos I of Sis,	1374-1377.
94.	Theodorus II of Cilicia,	1377-1392.
	(*Vacancy*),	1392-1393.
95.	Karapet I of Keghi	1393-1408.
96.	Hakob III of Sis,	1408-1411.
97.	Grigor VIII of Khandzoghat,	1411-1416
98.	Poghos II of Garni,	1416-1429.
99.	Constantine VI of Vahka,	1429-1439.
100	Grigor IX Mussabegian,	1439-1441.
101	Kirakos I of Virap,	1441-1443.
102.	Grigor X of Makou,	1443-1466.
103.	*Karapet of Tokat*, (Anti-Patriarch),	1446-1447.
104.	Aristaces II as coadjutor,	1448-1466
	alone,	1466-1470.
105.	*Zacharia of Akhtamar* (Anti-Patriarch)	1461-1462
106.	Sarguis II, as *coadjutor*,	1462-1470.
	alone,	1470-1474.
107	*Stephanos of Akhtamar* (Anti Patriarch)	1467-1468.
108	Hovhannes VII, as coadjutor,	1470-1474.
	alone.	1474-1484.
109.	Sarguis III, as *coadjutor*,	1474-1484.
	alone,	1484-1515.
110.	Aristaces III of Etchmiadzin, coadjutor,	1484-1499.
111	Thadeus I of Vagharchapat, coadjutor,	1499-1504
112	Eghiche II of Etchmiadzin, coadjutor,	1505-1515.
113	Hovhannes VIII of Etchmiadzin, coadjutor,	1505-?
114.	Nerses V of Etchmiadzin, coadjutor,	1506-?
115	Zacharia II of Vagharchapat, as *coadjutor*,	1507-1515.
	alone,	1515-1520
116.	Sarguis IV of Georgia, as *coadjutor*,	1515-1520.
	alone	1520-1537.
117	Grigor XI of Byzantium,	1537-1542.
118.	Stephanus V of Salmasd, as *coadjutor*,	1540-1542.
	alone,	1542-1564.
119	Michael I of Sivas, as coadjutor,	1542-1564.
	alone,	1564-1570.
120.	Barsegh III of Etchmiadzin coadjutor,	1549-1567 (?)
121.	Grigor XII of Vagharchapat, coadjutor,	1552-1570.
	alone,	1570-1587.
122.	Aristaces IV of Vagharchapat, coadjutor,	1555-1563 (?)

123.	Stephanus VI of Arindj, coadjutor,	1567-1575.
124.	Thadeus II, coadjutor,	1571-1575
125.	Arakel of Vagharchapat, coadjutor,	1575-1579.
126.	David IV of Vagharchapat, coadjutor,	1579-1587.
	alone,	1587-1629.
127.	Melchidesech I of Garni, coadjutor,	1593-1628.
128.	Avetick, coadjutor,	1602(?)-1620.
129.	Grigor XIII Serapion, coadjutor,	1603-1605
130	Sahak IV of Garni, coadjutor,	1624-1628
131.	Movses III of Tathev,	1629-1632.
132.	Philip I of Albac,	1633-1655.
133.	Habok IV of Julfa,	1655-1680
134.	*Eghiazar I of Aintab* (Anti-Patriarch),	1663-1682
	Eghiazar I of Aintab (the same),	1682-1691.
135.	Nahapet I of Edessa,	1691-1705.
	(*Vacancy*),	1705-1706.
136.	Alexander I of Julfa,	1706-1714.
137.	Astvatzatour I of Hamadan,	1715-1725.
138.	Karapet II of Zeitun,	1726-1729.
139.	Abraham II of Khochab,	1730-1734.
140.	Abraham III of Crete,	1734-1737.
141.	Ghazar I of Djahouk,	1737-1751.
142.	*Hovhannes of Agoulis* (Anti-Patriarch)	1740-1741.
143	Petrus II Kntour (interim catholicos),	1748-1749.
144	Minas I of Eghine,	1751-1753.
145	Alexander II of Constantinople,	1753-1755.
	Sahak of Keghi (not consecrated),	1755-1759
146.	Habok V of Chamakhi,	1759-1763.
147.	Simeon I of Erivan,	1763-1780.
148	Ghoukas I of Erzerum,	1780 1799
	Hovsep Arghouthian, (not consecrated),	1800-1801.
149	David V Ghorganian (usurper),	1801-1804.
150.	Daniel I of Soumari,	1801-1804.
151.	Eprem I of Dzoraguegh,	1809 1831.
152	Hovhannes VIII (IX) of Karbi,	1831-1842.
153	Nerses V (VI) of Achtarak,	1843-1857.
154.	Matheos I Tchouhadjian,	1858-1865.
155.	Gueorg IV Kerestjian,	1866-1882.
	Nerses Varjapetian, (not consecrated),	1884 1884.
156.	Makar I Ter-Petrossian,	1885-1891.
157.	Mkrtitch I Khrimian,	1892-1907.
158.	Matheos II Izmirlian,	1908-1910.
159	Guevorg V, present Catholicos,	1912-

CATHOLICI OF CILICIA

1.	Karapet I of Tokat,	1446 1477
2	Stephanus I of Saradzor,	1478-1488.
3.	Hovhannes I of Antioch,	1488-1515.
4.	Hovhannes II of Telguran,	1515-1525.
5.	Hovhannes III of Kilis,	1525-1539.
6.	Simeon I of Zeitoun,	1539-1545.
7.	Ghazar I of Zeitoun,	1545-1547.
8	Thoros I of Sis,	1548-1553.
9.	Khatchatour I Tchorik,	1553-1560.
10.	Khatchatour II or Khatchik of Zeitoun,	1560-1584.
11.	Azaria of Julfa.	1584-1601.
12.	*Tiratour* (Anti-Patriarch)	1586-1593.
13.	*Hovhannes* —do—	1588-1590
14	Petros I of Karkar,	1602-1609.
15.	Hovhannes IV of Aintab,	1602-1622.
16.	Minas I of Erzerum,	1622-1626.
17.	Simeon II of Sivas,	1626-1636.
18.	Nerses I of Sivas,	1636-1643
19.	Thoros II of Sis,	1643-1658
20	Khitchatour III of Sivas	1658-1673
21.	*David I of Aleppo* (Anti-Patriarch),	1663-1673.
22	Sahak I,	1673-1683.
23	*Azaria II* (Anti-Patriarch),	1683-1688.
24	Grigor I of Adana,	1683-1689.
25	Astvatzatour I of Sassoun,	1691-1694.
26	Matheos I of Caesarea,	1694-1701.
27.	Petros II of Aleppo, coadjutor,	1701-1705.
28	Hovhannes V of Hadjine,	1705-1721.
29.	Grigor II of Caesarea,	1721-1727
30.	Hovhannes VI of Hadjin Ter-Adam,	1727-1734.
31.	Ghoukas I of Sis,	1734-1737.
32.	Michael I of Sis,	1737-1758.
33	Gabriel I of Sis,	1758-1770.
34	Ephrem I of Sis,	1771-1785.
35.	Thoros III of Sis,	1785-1791.
36.	Kirakos I of Sis.	1791-1822.

37. Ephrem II,	1822-1833	
38. Michael II of Sis,	1833-1853.	
39. Kirakos II,	1853-1866.	
40. Kirakos III,	1866-1871(?).	
41. Mkrtitch I Kefsizian,	1871-1894.	
42. *Grigoris Aleatdjian*, (not consecrated),	1895	
43. Sahak II Khabaian,	1902.	

Catholici of Akhtamar

1. David I Thornikian,	1113-?
2. Stephanus I,	?-1276.
3. Stephanus II Sefedinian,	1288-1292.
4. Zacharia I Sefedinian,	1301-1336.
5. Stephanus III Sefedinian,	1336-1346.
6. David II Sefedinian,	1346-1368.
7. Nerses I Polad,	1369-1378.
8. Zacharia II the Martyr,	1378-1393.
9. Nerses II,	1393-1395.
10. David III of Akhtamar,	1395-1433.
11. Zacharia III of Akhtamar,	1434-1464.
12. Stephanus IV Gurdjibeguian,	1464-1487.
13. Nerses III Gurdjibeguian,	1487-1489.
14. Zacharia IV,	1489-1495.
15. Atom I,	1496-1510.
16. Grigoris I of Akhtamar,	1510-1534.
17. Grigoris II the Younger,	1542-1612.
18. Stephanus V,	1612-?
19. Karapet I,	?-1661.
20. Martyros I of Moks,	1652-1663.
21. Hovhannes I,	1669-1683.
22. Thomas I Doghlanbeguian,	1683-1698.
23. Sahak I of Artzke,	1698-1704.
24. Hovhannes II.	1698-1704
25. Hairapet I Verdanessian,	1705-?
26. Grigoris III of Gavach,	1711-?
27. Hovhannes III of Haiotz Dzor,	1720-?
28. Thomas II of Amuk	?-?
29. Ghazar I of Moks,	?-?
30. Grigor IV of Hizan,	?-?
31. Paghtasar I of Bitlis,	1735-1736.
32. Sahak II of Albac,	?-?
33. Hakob I of Amid,	?-1738.
34. Nikoghaios I of Sparkert,	1738-1751.
35. Grigor V,	1751-1762.
36. Thomas III of Akhtamar,	1762-1783.
37. Karapet II of Van,	1783-1787.
38. Markos I of Chatak,	1788-1791.
39. Hovhannes IV of Sparkert,	?-?
40. Theodorus I,	1792-1794.
41. Michael I of Van,	1796-?
42. Karapet III of Chatak,	?-1803.
— —	1814-1816.
43. Khatchatour I the Miracle-worker,	1803-1814.
44. Haruthium I of Taraun,	1816-1823.
45. Hovhannes V of Chatak,	1825-1843.
46. Khatchatour II of Moks,	1844-1851.
47. Petros I Bulbulian,	1859-1864.
48. Khatchatour III Chiroian,	1864-1895.

Vacant from 1895 to the present time.

Catholici of Achouan

1 Ehgiche the Apostle,	died 79
2. X. X. consecrated by Grigor I the Illuminator,	(302-325).
3 Grigoris I the Parthian,	340-342.
4 Matheos I,	342-?
5 Sahak I,	?-?
6. Movses I,	?-?
7. Pani,	?-?
8. Ghazar,	?-?
9. Zacharia I,	?-?
10. David I,	?-399
11 Hovhan I,	400(?)-?
12. Eremia I,	423
13. Chouphaghicho,	500-551(?).
14. Abas,	552-594
15. Viro,	596-630.
16. Zacharia II,	630-645.
17. Hovhan II,	645-670.
18. Ukhtanes,	670-682.
19. Eghiazar,	682-688.
20. Nerses I,	688-700.
21. Simeon I,	700-702.
22. Michael,	702-737.
23. Anastas,	737-741.
24. Hovsep I,	741-758.
25 David II,	758-762.
26. David III,	762-771.
27 Matheos II,	771-773.
28 Movses II,	773-774.
29. Aharon,	774-776.
30. Soghomon I,	776-776.
31. Theodoros,	777-781.
32. Soghomon II,	782-794.
33. Hovhannes III,	794-819.
34. Movses III,	820-820.
35. David IV,	820-848.
36. Hovsep II,	848-873.
37. Samuel,	873-888.

38.	Hovnan,	886-896.	68.	Hovhannes VII,		?-1470.
39.	Simeon II,	896-917	69.	Matheos IV,		1470-?
40.	David V,	917-923	70.	Aristaces I,		?-1478.
41.	Sahak II,	923-941	71.	Nerses IV,		1478-1481.
42	*Gaguik II* (Anti-Patriarch)	941 958	72.	Chmavon I,		1481-?
43.	Hovhannes IV,	941-961.	73.	Thomas,		?-1495.
44.	David VI	961-968.	74.	Arakial,		1495-1511.
45.	David VII,	968-974.	75.	Aristaces II,		1511-1521
46.	Petros I,	974-990.	76.	Sarguis I,		1521-1555
47.	Movses IV,	990-996.	77.	Grigor II,		1556-1573.
48.	Markos I,	996-?	78.	David IX,		1573-1574.
49.	Hovsep III,	1038.	79.	Philippos,	1563(?)-?	
50.	Markos II,	?-1077.	80.	Hovhannes VIII,		?-1586.
51.	Stephanos I,	1077-1103.	81.	Chmavon II		1586-1611.
52.	Hovhannes V,	1103-1130.	82.	Aristaces III,		1588-1593
53.	Stephanos II,	1130-1132.	83	Melchiseth.		1593-1596.
	Vacancy,	1132-1140	84.	Simeon III,		1596-?
54	Grigoris II or Gaghik II,	1140-?	85.	Hovhannes IX,		1633-1634.
55	Bejguene,	?	86	Grigor III		1634 1653
56.	Nerses II,	1171(?).	87.	Petros III,		1653-1675.
57.	Stephanos III,	1155(?)-1195.	88.	*Simeon IV* (Anti-Patriarch),		1675-1701.
58	Hovhannes VI,	1195-1235				
59	Nerses III,	1235-1262	89.	Eremia II,		1676-1700.
60.	Stephanos IV,	1262-1323.	90.	Essai,		1702-1728.
61	Soukias,	1323-?	91	*Nerses V* (Anti-Patriarch),		1706-1763.
62.	Petros II,	?-1406.	92.	*Israel* (Anti-Patriarch),		1763-1765.
63.	Karapet,	1406-1411	93.	Hovhannes X,		1763-1786.
64	David VIII.	1411-1411.	94.	Simeon V,		1794-1810.
65.	Matheos III,	1412-1440.	96	Sarguis II Hassan-Djalahantz,		1794-1815
66.	Athanasius,	1440-1441				
67.	Grigor I,	1441-?		—	—	died 1828.

II. PATRIARCHS

Patriarchs of Jerusalem

1	Abraham I,	637-669	17	Abraham IV,	1295-?
2	Grigor I Ezekielan,	669-696.	18	Arakel,	1218-1230.
3	Gueorg,	696-708	19	Hovhannes II of Erzerum,	1230-1238.
4.	Mkrtitch I,	708-730.	20	Karapet I of Jerusalem,	1238-1254.
5	Hovhannes I,	730-758.	21.	Hakob I,	1254-1281.
6.	Stephanos,	758-774.	22.	Sarguis I,	1281-1313.
7.	Eghia,	774-797.	23	Astvatzatour I,	1313-1317.
	. . .	797-885.	24	David I	1317-1321.
8.	Abraham II,	835-916.	25	Poghos I,	1321-1331.
	. . .	916-981.	26.	Vardan,	1331-1341.
9.	Grigor II,	981-1006.	27.	Hovhannes III,	1341-1353.
10.	Arsene,	1006-1038.	28.	Barsegh,	1353-1358
	. . .	1038-1090.	29.	Crigor III,	1358-1366.
11.	Simeon,	1090-1109.	30.	Mkrtitch II,	1366-1381.
12.	Movses,	1109-1133.	31.	Hovhannes IV of Poland,	1381-1385
13	Essai I,	1133-1152.	32	Grigor IV of Egypt,	1385-1390.
14.	Sahak I,	1152-1180.	33	Essai II.	1390-1393
15.	Abraham III of Jerusalem,	1180-1191.	34.	Sarguis II,	1395-1417.
16.	Minas I,	1191-1205.	35.	Poghos II of Garni,	1417-1419.

— 413 —

#	Name	Dates	#	Name	Dates
36.	Martyros I of Egypt,	1419-1430.	56	Minas II of Amid,	1689-1701.
37.	Essai III,	1430-1439.		—	1703-1704.
38.	Hovhannes V,	1441-1445.	57.	Galoust, *coadjutor*,	?-1701.
39	Abraham V,	1445-1454.	58.	Avetik,	1701-1703.
40.	Mesrop,	1454-1461.		—	1704-1705.
41.	Petros I,	1461-1476.	59.	Grigor VI "Pitzak"	1705-1707.
42.	Mkrtitch III,	1476-1479.	60.	Matheos of Caesarea,	1705-1706.
43.	Hovhannes VI,	1479-1491.	61.	Martyros IV,	1706-1706.
44	Martyros II of Brusa,	1491-1501.	62	Michael of Kharput	1706-1707.
45	Petros II,	1501-1507.	63.	Sahak II of Aboutchek,	1707-1707.
46.	Sarguis III,	1507-1523			1708-1714.
47.	Astvatzatour II of Mardin,	1523-1544.	64.	Hovhannes VIII of Smyrna,	1707-1708.
	—	1564-1568.	65.	Hovhannes IX of Gandzak,	1714-1715.
48.	Philippos,	1544-1564.	66.	Grigor VII of Chirvan	
49.	Andreas of Mardin,	1566-1595.		"Cheghthaiakir",	1715-1749.
50.	David II of Mardin,	1595-1615.	67.	Hakob II Nalian,	1749-1752
51.	Grigor IV Margarian		68.	Theodorus I,	1752-1761.
	"Baron-Ter"	1615-1647.	69.	Karapet II of Gandzak,	1761-1768.
52.	Astvatzatour III of		70.	Poghos III of Van,	1768-1775.
	Taraun,	1647-1666.	71.	Hovakim of Kanaker,	1775-1793.
	—	1667-1668.	72	Petros III of Tokat,	1793-1800.
	—	1670-1672	73.	Theodorus II of Van,	1800-1819.
53.	Eghiazar of Aintab,	1666-1667.	74	Gabriel of Nicodemia,	1819-1840.
	—	1668-1669.	75.	Zacharia Ter-Grigorian,	1840-1846.
	—	1672-1682.	76.	Kirakos Mnatzakanian,	1846-1850.
54	Martyros III of Kafa,	1669-1670.	77	Hovhannes X Movsessian,	1850-1860.
	—	1682-1684	78.	Essai IV Karapetian,	1864-1885
55	Hovhannes VII of Constantinople,	1684-1691.	79	Haruthioun Vehapetian,	1885-1910.

PATRIARCHS OF CONSTANTINOPLE

#	Name	Dates	#	Name	Dates
1.	Hovakim of Brusa,	1461-1478.	18.	Zacharia I of Van,	1626-1631.
2.	Nikoghaios,	1478-1489.		—	1636-1639.
3.	Karapet I,	1489-1509.	19.	David,	1639-1641.
4.	Martyros I,	1509-1526.		—	1643-1644.
5.	Grigor I,	1526-1537.		—	1644-1649.
6.	Astvatztour I,	1537-1550		—	1650-1651.
7.	Stephanus I,	1550-1561.	20	Kirakos of Erivan,	1641-1642.
8.	Tiratour,	1561-1563.	21.	Khatchatour I of Sivas,	1642-1643.
	—	1596-1599.	22.	Thomas II of Aleppo,	1644-1644.
9	Hakob I,	1563-1573.		—	1657-1659.
10.	Hovhannes I of Diarbekir,	1573-1581.	23	Eghiazar of Aintab,	1651-1652.
11	Thomas I,	1581-1587.	24	Hovhannes IV of Moghni,	1652-1655.
12.	Sarguis I of Zeitoun,	1587-1590.	25	Martyros II of Kafa,	1659-1660
	—	1592-1596.	26	Ghazar of Sivas,	1660-1663.
13	Hovhannes II,	1590-1591.	27	Hovhannes V,	1663-1664.
14.	Azaria of Julfa,	1591-1592.		—	1665-1667.
15	Melchisedech I of Garni,	1599-1600	28	Sarguis II of Rodosto,	1664-1665.
16	Hovhannes III of Constantinople,			—	1667-1670.
		1600-1601	29.	Stephanus II of Meghri,	1670-1674.
	—	1610-1611	30.	Hovhannes VI of Amassia,	1674-1675
	—	1621-1623	31.	Andreas of Constantinople,	1675-1676
	—	1631-1636.	32.	Karapet II of Caesarea,	1676-1679
17	Grigor II of Caesarea,	1601-1608.		—	1680-1681.
		1611-1621		—	1681-1684.
		1623-1626.		—	1686-1687.

	— —	1688-1689	56.	Daniel of Surmeli,	1799 1800
33.	Sarguis III.	1679-1680	57.	Hovhannes XI of Baibourt,	1801-1802
34.	Thoros of Constantinople,	1681-1681		— —	1802-1813
	— —	1687-1688	58	Grigor IV,	1801-1802
35.	Ephrem,	1684 1686	59.	Abraham of Tatheve,	1813-1815
	— —	1694-1698	60	Poghos I, Grigorian,	1815-1823
	— —	1701-1702	61	Karapet III of Balat,	1823 1831
36	Khatchatur II,	1688-1688	62.	Stephanos III, Zacharian "Aghavni",	1831-1839
37.	Matheos I of Caesarea,	1692-1694		— —	1840-1841
38	Melchisedech II "Soubhi",	1698-1699	63.	Hakobos Serobian	1839-1840
	———	1700-1701		— —	1848-1858
39	Mekhithar,	1699-1700			
40.	Avetik,	1702-1703	64	Astvatzatur II of Constantinople,	1841-1844
	— —	1704-1706	65.	Matheos II, Tchoukadjian,	1844-1848
41.	Galoust of Amassia,	1703-1704	66.	Gueorg II, Kerestidjian,	1858-1860
42	Nerses I of Balat,	1704-1704	67.	Sarguis IV, Couyounmdjian,	1860-1861
43.	Martyros III of Erzindjan,	1706-1706		Stephanos Maghakian, locum tenens,	1861-1863
44	Michael of Kharput,	1706-1707	68	Poghos II, Taktakian,	1863-1869
45.	Sahak of Aboutchek,	1707-1707	69.	Ignatios Kakmadjian,	1869 1869
	— —	1708-1714	70.	Mkrtitch Khrimian	1869-1873
46	Hovhannes VII of Smyrna,	1707-1708	71	Nerses II. Varjapetian,	1874-1884
47.	Hovhannes VIII of Gandzak,	1714 1715	72	Harouthioun Vehapetian,	1885-1888
48	Hovhannes IX of Bitlis "Kolot",	1715-1741	73.	Khoren Achekian	1888-1894
49	Hakob II, Nalian,	1741-1749	74.	Matheos III, Izmirlian,	1894-1896
	— —	1752-1764			1908-1908
50	Prokhoron of Silistria,	1749-1749	75.	Maghachia Ormanian,	1896-1908
51.	Minas of Eghine,	1749-1751	76.	Eghiche Tourian,	1909-1911
52.	Gueorg I,	1751-1752	77	Hovhannes XIII, Archaruni,	1912-1913
53.	Grigor III, Basmadjian,	1764-1773	78	Zavene Eghaian, present patriarch,	1913
54	Zacharia II of Kaghizman,	1773-1781			
	— —	1782-1799			
55.	Hovhannes X of Hamadan,	1781-1782			

* * *
* *
*

LIST OF ILLUSTRATIONS

Chapter I.

The two Ararats, view taken from the Araxes valley	15
The city of Samosata and the Euphrates, allegorical figure on an old coin	30
Map: region of Lake Van	31
Map: position of the Armenian plateau compared to neighboring countries	34
Map: the Armenian stronghold	35
Map: Armenia in Roman times	41
Map: provinces of Greater Armenia	43
Map of the regions of western Asia inhabited by the Armenians	46
Map of Cilicia	47
The river Cydnus, allegorical figure on an old coin	48
The river and city of Tarsus, allegorical figure on a coin of Emperor Commodus	48
The river Pyramis, allegorical figure on an old coin	48
The city of Anazarbus, allegorical figure on an old coin	49

Chapter II.

Map: Armenia and adjoining countries, according to Herodotus	51
Map: Migrations of the Armenians	52
Coins ascribed to Croesus, king of Lydia	55
Vannic winged bull	58
Map: Armenia and neighboring countries according to the Assyrians	60
Ethnography of western Asia, from Genesis chapter X	62
Hieroglyphic inscription at Ani	68
Pagan Bas-relief at Bagrevant near Bayazid	71
Double golden daric of the Achaemenids	73
Coin of the Achaemenean satrap Pharnabazus	75
Tetradrachma of Alexander the Great	78
Tetradrachma of Seleucus I Nicator	79
Tetradrachmas of Antiochus the Great	81
Coin of Sames, king of Commagene	81
Coin of Charaspes, king of Armenia	83
Coin of Arsames, king of Armenia	83
Coin of Abdissares, king of Armenia	84
Coin of Xerxes, king of Armenia	84

Chapter III.

Effigy of King Tigranes II the Great, from a tetradrachma in the British Museum	85
Tetradrachma of Mithidrates the Great	86
Drachma of the Parthian king Mithidrates II	88
Tetradrachma of the Parthian king Orodes I	88
Aureus of Sulla	89
Map: Kingdoms of the Pontus and Armenia during the wars with the Romans	92
Coin of Antiochus Theos, king of Commagene	93
Tetradrachma of the Parthian king Phraat III	94
Tetradrachma of king Tigranes II of Armenia	98
Bronze coin of Tigranes II	99
Coin of the Parthian king Mithidrates III	100
Coin of king Artavazd III of Armenia	103
Drachma of the Parthian ruler Pacorus I	103
Tetradrachma of Phraat IV, Arsacid king of Persia	104
Denarius of Mark Antony and Cleopatra, ARMENIA DEVICTA	105
Coin of Tigranes II, king of Armenia	107
Denarius of Augustus, ARMENIA CAPTA	108
Coin of Tigranes III, king of Armenia	108
Coin of Tigranes III, king of Armenia, with his sister Erato	109

Chapter IV.

Drachma of Onones or Vodones as king of Persia	110
Imitation of a denarius of Augustus struck in Transcaucasia	110
Coin of Augustus and Artavazd V	111
Coin of Abgar XI of Osrhoene and Gordian III	112
Denarius of Germanicus with, reverse, the crowning of Artaxias	113
Coin of Antiochus IV Epiphanus with Iotapé	114
Coin of Antiochus IV Epiphanus, king of Commagene	114
Coin with head of Iotapé, sister and wife of Antiochus IV Epiphanus	115
Silver coin of Lucius Verus showing captive Armenia	116
Bronze coin showing Lucius Verus giving Armenia a king	116
Coin of Antoninus Pius showing him crowning the king of Armenia	116
Coins of Emperor Trajan commemorating his Armenian campaigns	117
Tetradrachma of Vologeses I, Arsacid king of Persia	117
Statue of Tiridates, king of Armenia (Louvre Museum)	119
Drachma of Artaxerxes I, first Sassanid king of Persia	120
Coin of Artaban V, last of the Arsacid kings of Persia	120
The Zoroastrian Fire-Temple, reverse of a tetradrachma of the rulers of Persis	121
St Gregory from a miniature of the 10th century	123
Drachma of the Sassanid type of the Georgian Eristhaw Gourgen	129
Drachma of the Sassanid type of the Georgian Eristhaw Stephanos I	130
Drachma of Sapor I, Sassanid king of Persia	131
Coin of Vabalath, son of Zenobia, queen of Palmyra	132
Coin of Zenobia, queen of Palmyra	132
Gold coin of Chosroes II Sassanid king of Persia	133
Armenian inscription at Ani (A.D 662)	134

— 418 —

Chapter V.

Map: Arab Empire	137
Coin of the last Sassanid king of Persia, Yezdedjerd IV	138
Coin of Constans II, Byzantine emperor	139
Coin of Justin II, Byzantine emperor	140
Coin of Justinian II, Byzantine emperor	141
Coin of the Ommiad Caliph Abd-el-Melek	141
Ruins of the Castle of Ani	144
Sketch-Map of the site of the city of Ani	146
Coin of Basil I, Byzantine emperor	149
Castle of Khochab in Kurdistan	150
Armeno-Byzantine capital from Etchmiadzin	152

Chapter VI.

Map of the Ararat region	155
Coin of Leo the Philosopher, Byzantine emperor	156
View of the fortress of Van	159
Plan of the former city of Melazkert	160
Coin of Constantine XI Porphyrogenetus	162
Miniature painting from an Armenian Gospel-book A D 966	162
Tomb of king Ashot III the Charitable, at Horomos Monastery near Ani	164
Map: the Armenian kingdoms of the 10th century	165
Coin of David Curopalatus, king of Georgia (993-1001)	166
View of the ramparts & chief gate of the city of Ani	166
View of the castle of Ani taken from outside the city	167
View of Ani cathedral	169
Coin of Bagrat IV, king of Georgia, (1026-72)	170
Coin of Giorgi II, king of Georgia (1072-89)	171
Gold solidus of Emperor Basil II	171
Coin of Gorigé, king of Albania (1046-1082)	172
Gold solidus of Emperor Michael IV the Paphlagonian	176
Gold solidus of Emperor Constantine XII Monomachus	177
Coin of the Ortokid Sultans of Mardin	180
Tombstone of Hairapet, Bishop of Siuniq	186

Chapter VII.

Map of Cilicia	187
Coin of Emperor Nicephorus Phocas	189
Coin of John Zimisces	189
Castle of Lampron in Cilicia	190
Coin of Alexis I Comnenus	191
Plan of the ruins of Aias	191
Plan of Megarsus	192
Plan of Alaya	192
Plan of Sidé	193
Coin ascribed to the Armenian rulers of Asia Minor	193
Coin of unnamed baron of New Armenia	194
Coin of Thoros, baron of Armenia	194
Coin of Tancred of Antioch	196
Coin of Baldwin of Edessa	198

— 419 —

Coin of Alexis I Comnenus	198
Coin of Raymond of Poitiers, prince of Antioch	199
Coin of Emperor John II Comnenus	199
Coin of Emperor Manuel I Comnenus	200
View of Castle of Anazarbus (Cilicia)	204
Coin of Eimad-ed Din Zangui, Sultan of Iconium	205
Coin of Rokn-ed-Din Masaoud, Sultan of Iconium	205
Coin of Emperor Andronicus I Comnenus	205
Coin of Richard of Marasch	206
Plan of the Castle of Monté (Cilicia)	207
Coin of Amaury I, king of Jerusalem	207
Coin of Sultan Nur-ed-Din Mahmoud	208
Coin of El Salih-Ismail, Zenguid Atabek of Aleppo	208
Gold coin of Emperor Michael Ducas	209
Coin of Kilidj-Arslan II, sultan of Iconium	210
Coin of Emperor Isaac Angelus	211
Coin of Bohemond III of Antioch	212
Coin of Saladin (Salah-ed-Din)	212
Coins of John of Brienne and the Holy Sepulchre	213
Map: Latin principalities of the East	214
Coin of Leo II, baron of New Armenia	214
Coin of Isaac Ducas Comnenus, despot of Cyprus	215
Coin of Guy of Lusignan, first king of Cyprus	215
St. Nerses (from the Armenian iconography)	216
Signature of Leo I, first king of New Armenia	218
Handwriting of St. Nerses of Lampron on a Greek MS	219
Coin of Emperor Alexis Comnenus	220
Coin of Henry of Champagne	220
Seal of Raymond-Rupen	221
Coin of Tripoli, without ruler's name	221

Chapter VIII.

Effigy of Leo I, king of New Armenia	222
Coins of king Leo I	223
Gold Bulla of king Leo I	224
Gold coin of Hugh I, king of Cyprus	224
Coin of Bohemond IV, prince of Antioch	225
Coin of Raymond-Rupen, prince of Antioch	225
Coin of Theodore Lascaris, Emperor of Nicaea	226
Imitations by the Crusaders of Moslem coins	226
Coin of Kaikhosrou, Sultan of Iconium	228
Coin of Soleiman-Shah, Sultan of Iconium	228
Effigy of Hetum I, king of New Armenia	230
Coin of Hetum I, king of New Armenia	230
Coins with names of Hetum I and Sultans of Iconium	231
Handwriting of Hetum I	232
Coin of Hetum I and Isabel	233
Seal of Constantine I, patriarch of Partzerpert	233
Coin of Rousoudan, queen of Georgia	233
Coin of Kaikobad I, Sultan of Iconium	234
Coin of Kaikhosrou II, Sultan of Iconium	234
Coin of Mango-Khan	235
Coin of David V, king of Georgia, and Mango Khan	235
Coin of Houlago	235

Coin of Michael VIII Palaeologus, Byzantine emperor	236
Coins of Leo II, king of New Armenia	236
Coins of Emperor Andronicus II	238
Signature of king Leo II	240
Coins of Hetum II, king of New Armenia	241
Seal of Brother Ian (Hetum II)	241
Lead Bulla of Thoros	242
Coins of Sempad, king of New Armenia	242
Coins of Constantine II. king of New Armenia	243
Map. Empire of Nicaea	244
Coins of Leo III, king of New Armenia	245
Coins of Ochin, king of New Armenia	246
Coins of Henry II of Lusignan, king of Cyprus	247
Coins of Leo IV, king of New Armenia	248
Leo IV of Armenia administering justice, contemporary miniature painting	249
Escutcheons of Tarsus	249
Coin of Emperor Michael IX Palaeologus	251
Coin of Emperor John V Palaeologus	251
Coin of Emperor Andronicus III Palaeololgus	251
Coin of Guy of Lusignan (Constantine II), king of New Armenia	252
Coins of Constantine III, king of New Armenia	253
Coin of Dieudonné of Gozon, Grand Master of Rhodes	253
Coin of Peter I, king of Cyprus	254
Coins of Constantine IV, king of New Armenia	257
Coins of Leo V. of Lusignan, king of New Armenia	259
Coin of Peter II of Lusignan, king of Cyprus	260
View of the ruins of the city and castle of Gorigos	260
Tombstone at Nicosia	261
Plan of the port of Gorigos	261
View of Castle of Gorigos	262
Castle of Châhi-Maran (Cilicia)	263
Ruins of the fortress of Sis	267
Escutcheon on tombstone of Leo V of Lusignan, king of New Armenia	272
Tomb of Leo V of Lusignan, at St. Denis	272
Seal and signature of king Leo V of Lusignan	274

Chapter IX.

Coin of Giorgi III, king of Georgia, with Al Moktafy	277
Coin of Djelal-ed-Din, Sultan of Charesm	279
Coin of David V. Solsan, king of Georgia	279
Coin of Arghoun-Khan and Demetri II of Georgia	279
Coin of Ghazan-Khan and Wakhtang III, king of Georgia	279
Coin of Bagrat V, king of Georgia	280
Coin of Giorgi VIII, king of Georgia	280
Georgian coin (uncertain) 14th century	280
Coins of Ereklé, king of Georgia	284
Map: Russia's advances in Armenia	286
Russian coin of Georgia	286

Chapter X.

Coins of Emperor Mauricius Tiberius	316
Coin of Mauricius Tiberius, Constantine and Theodosius	317
Coin of Heraclius I, as Consul	318

— 421 —

Coin of Heraclius I, as Emperor ... 318
Coin of Heraclius I, Heraclius Constantine, and Eudoxia ... 318
Coin of Heraclius, Heraclius Constantine, & Heracleonas ... 319
Coin of Heracleonas, David Tiberius, and Constans II ... 319
Coin of Heraclius Constantine and Heracleonas ... 319
Coin of Heraclius I, Heraclius Constantine, & Martina ... 319
Coin of Heracleonas alone ... 319
Coin of Constans II and Constantine Pogonatus ... 320
Coin of Constans II, Constantine Pogonatus, Heraclius and Tiberius ... 320
Coin of Constans II, Heraclius, and Tiberius ... 320
Coin of Constantine IV Pogonatus ... 320
Coin of Filepicus Bardanes ... 321
Coin of Artavazdus and Constantine V ... 321
Coin of Artavazdus and Nicephorus ... 322
Coin of Leo V the Armenian and Constantine VII ... 322
Coin of Leo V the Armenian alone ... 322
Coin of Basil I, alone ... 322
Coin of Basil I and Constantine IX ... 322
Coin of Emperor Leo the Philosopher ... 323
Coin of Leo VI and Alexander ... 323
Coin of Leo VI and Constantine X ... 323
Coin of Alexander alone ... 323
Coin of Constantine X and Zoé ... 323
Coin of Constantine X and Romanus I ... 323
Coin of Constantine X and Romanus II ... 324
Coin of Romanus I alone ... 324
Coin of Romanus I, Constantine X, and Christophorus ... 324
Coin of Romanus II alone ... 324
Coin of Romanus II and Basil II ... 325
Coin of Empress Theophanon ... 325
Coin of Basil II and Constantine XI ... 325
Coin of John Zimisces ... 325
Coin of Constantine XI alone ... 325
Coin of Theodora, wife of Constantine XII ... 326
Coin of Theodora and Michael III ... 326
Narses and Theodora (Mosaic at Ravenna) ... 327
Sarcophagus of Isaac the Armenian ... 328
Architectural design on the Church at Safar ... 337

CHAPTER XI.

Armenian Pharagir Writing ... 338
Armenian carved stone. Ergathagir writing ... 340
Armenian Ergathagir writing of 10th cent. (966) ... 342
Armenian Ergathagir writing of 10th cent. (989) ... 343
Armenian Notragir writing, most recent form (1596) ... 344
Armenian Bolorgir writing ... 345
Portrait of Monsignor Khrimian ... 360
The Island of St. Lazarus at Venice ... 363
Stamp of the Armenian printer Hakob (Venice 1513) ... 364
Page from the Calendar published at Venice in 1513 by the Armenian printer Hakob ... 366
The Armenian printer Abgar of Venice presenting his psaltery to Pope IV (1565) ... 367
Plan of the Church of St Gregory (Zvartsnots), near Etchmiadzin ... 372

— 422 —

Plan of the present monastery of Etchmiadzin	373
View of the Cathedral of Etchmiadzin	373
Plan of the Cathedral of Etchmiadzin	374
View and plan of the church of St. Ripsimé at Valarsapat	374
Monastery of St. Varag at Van	375
Church of St. Stepanos and monastery of Maghard	375
Monastery of Nirek	376
Church of St. George at Ani	377
Church of Akhtamar, near Van	378
Lion carved on the ramparts of Ani	379
Christ, the Virgin, and St. Gregory (stone carving at Ani)	379
Tombstones at Ani	380
Armenian tombstones	382
Descent from the Cross, (wooden carving in Etchmiadzin treasure-house)	383
Carved door of Sevan monastery	383
Falling Asleep of the Virgin, from Armenian iconography	384
Miniature painting on Sissouan MS dated 1330	384
Animals fighting (from Armenian iconography)	385
The Virgin (miniature painting on MS of king Hetum II)	385
Silver coin of Gourgen, Eristhaw of Georgia	386
Coin of Bagrat IV, king of Georgia	386
Coin of Giorgi II, king of Georgia	386
Coin of Giorgi III, king of Georgia, and Al Moktafy	387
Coin of Roussoudan, queen of Georgia	387
Coin of Giorgi VIII, king of Georgia	388
Reliquary at Etchmiadzin	389
The Island and Monastery of Lake Sevan (Russian Armenia)	396
Dragon (from Armenian iconography)	398

* * *
* *
*

CONTENTS

Dedication 5
Preface 7
Foreword 9

Chapter I.

Physical features of Armenia. — Geography. — Generalities 15-49

Ararat, 15 — The Alagheuz, 16 — The Gheuk-tchaï or Sevanga, 20 — The Araxes. 21. — The plain of Erivan, 22. — The Qara-bagh and the Qara-dagh, 24. — The plain of Moughan, 27. — Azerbaidjan, 28. — Persian Kurdistan, 29 — The Erzerum plateau, 30. — Lazistan and the Pontic Alps, 32. — Climate of the Armenian plateau, 34. — The Armenian stronghold, 35 — Southern Armenia, 37. — Turkish Kurdistan, 38. — Western Armenia, 39 — Frontiers of Armenia, 41. — The provinces of Armenia, 43. — Greater and Lesser Armenia, 45. — New Armenia or Sissouan, 45 — The three Armenias, 49.

Chapter II

Origin of the Armenian people — Sojourn of the Armeno-Phrygians in Thrace. — Their crossing into Asia. — Their march to the Ararat country. — Conquest of the Erzerum plateau. — The Haïkian patriarchs — The legendary dynasty. — Median ascendancy — The kingdom of Armenia under Achaemenean suzerainty. — The Macedonian conquest — The dynasty of Phraataphernes — Rule of the Seleucids of Syria. 50-84

Armenian beginnings, 51 — The Armeno-Phrygians of Herodotus, 52. — The Armenians of the 12th to the 8th century B.C, 53 — The Iranians in the 8th century B C, 54. — The Urartaeans not the ancestors of the Armenians, 55. — Armenian traditions concerning the kingdom of Urartu, 58 — Migration of the Armenians, 59. — Legendary dynasties, 62. — The invasion of the Scythians, 65. — Conquest of Armenia by Haïk, 65. — The Armenian language, 67 — The religion of the Armenians in ancient times, 69. — Armenia subdued by the

— 425 —

Persian Achaemeneans, 72. — The Anabasis of the Ten Thousand through Armenia, 75. — The Alexandrian conquest, 78. — Armenia under Alexander's successors, 79. — Erivan founded, 79. — Ervand (Orontes), governor of Armenia, 79. — Artaxias, king of Armenia, 81 — Zariadras, 82. — Numismatic records, Charaspes, Arsames, Abdissares, and Xerxes, kings of Armenia, known only from their coins, 83. sq. —

Chapter III.

Reign of Tigranes II the Great, — Lucullus and Pompey in Armenia. — The country divided by the Romans. — The last kings of the dynasty of Artaxias. 85-109

Artavazd II, 86. — Tigranes II the Great, 87. — Mithidrates V. defeated by Sulla, 89 — Lucullus, 90. — Battle of Tigranocerta, 91. — Recall of Lucullus, 94. — Pompey in Armenia, 95. — Submission of Tigranes II, 96 — Armenia under Tigranes II, 98. — Marcus Crassus in Asia, 100. — Artavazd III, 100. — Defeat of Crassus, 101. — Mark Antony in Asia, 104. — Alexander, son of Antony and Cleopatra king of Armenia, 107 — Artashes II, 107. — Last successors of Artaxias, 108. — Tigranes III and Tigranes IV, 108.

Chapter IV.

The foreign dynasty (A.D. 2-53) — The Arsacids of Armenia (A.D 53-429). — Tiridates II the Great (A.D. 217-238). — Conversion of Armenia to Christianity. — Saint Gregory the Illuminator. 110-136

Ariobarzanes, 110. — Artavazd V, 111. — Tigranes V, 111. — Erato, 111. — Vonones, 111. — Artashes III, 112 — Archak I, 112. — Mithidrates, 112. — Rhadamistus, 112. — Tiridates I, 115. — Corbulo, 116 — Tigranes VI, 116 — Exedares, 117. — First Arsacids of Armenia, 118 — Tiridates II (Chosroes I), 118. — Accession of the Sassanids to the Persian throne, 226. — Tiridates III and St. Gregory the Illuminator, 124. — Conversion of Armenia to Christianity, 124. — Founding of the Patriarchal See of Etchmiadzin, 127. — The Armenian Church, 130. — Artavazd VI, 132 — Chosroes II, Tiran, Archak II, Pap, Varazdat, Archak III, Chosroes III, Vrampachouh, 132 — St Sahak and St. Mesrop 133. — Invention of Writing, 133. — Last Arsacid kings of Armenia, 135. — The Marzpans, 135. — Vardan Mamikonian, 135. — Vahan Mamikonian, 136.

Chapter V.

The Arab conquest — Armenia a province of the Empire of the Caliphs. 137-152

End of the Sassanid Empire, Yezdedjerd IV, 138. — Abd-er-Raham enters Armenia, 139. — Struggle between the Byzantines and Arabs in Armenia, 140. — Arab government set up in Georgia and Armenia, 142. — Ashot, governor of Armenia for the Arabs, 143. —Description of the site of Ani, 144 — Ashot, "prince of princes", (king of Ani), 148. —

Chapter VI.

The Dynasty of the Bagratids 153-186

Origin of the Bagratids, 153. — Ashot I, 154. — Sembat I, 157. — Khatchik-Gaghik, king of Vaspurakan, 159. — Ashot II, king of Ani, 161. — Abas, 163. — Ashot III, 163. — Division of Armenia into seven kingdoms, 165 — Sembat II, 167. — Gaghik I, 168 — Sembat III, 172. — Arrival of the Turks in Armenia, 173. — Armenian principality of Sivas, 174. — Gaghik II, 176. — Exile of Gaghik II, 177. — Assassination of Gaghik II, 179. — Taking of Ani by the Seljuk Turks, 182. — Rôle of the Armenian nobility, 184.

Chapter VII.

The Barony of New Armenia 187-221

Revolt of Rupen, 188. — Cilicia, 190. — Constantine I and Thoros I, barons, 194 — Arrival of the Second Crusade, 195 — Leo I, baron, 198 — Captivity of Leo I, 200 — Thoros II, baron, 201. — Mleh, baron, 209. — Rupen II, baron, 211. — Leo II, baron, 212. — Arrival of the Third Crusade, 212

Chapter VIII.

The Kingdom of New Armenia 222-274

Leo I, king of Armenia, 222. — The Court of Armenia, 227. — The Commerce of the Armenians, 228. — Isabel, queen, 231 — Hetum I, king of Armenia, 232. — Leo II, king of Armenia, 237. — Hetum II. 240. — Thoros, 242. — Sempad and Constantine, usurpers, 242 — Return of Hetum II to power, 244. — Leo III, 245. — Ochin, 246. — Leo IV, 247. — Guy of Lusignan (Constantine II), 250 — Constantine III, 253. — Constantine IV, 255 — Leo V. of Lusignan 258. — Leo V in Cyprus, 260. — Crowning of Leo V, 265 — Siege of Sis, 266. — Taking of Sis by the Moslems, 269 — Capitulation of the Castle of Sis, 269 — Captivity of Leo V., 270 — Liberation of Leo V, 271. — Death of Leo V, 271.

Chapter IX.

Armenia, after the loss of its independence 275-314

Moslems' attitude to Christians in conquered countries, 275. — Turkish domination in Armenia, 278 — The Mongols in Armenia, 278 — Persian rule, 281. — The Armenians appeal to Europe, 282 — Peter the Great and Catherine, 283 — Conquest of Upper Armenia by Russia, 285 — Treaty of Adrianople, 287. — Zeitoun, 290 — Treaty of San Stefano, 291. — Congress of Berlin, 292 — Cyprus Agreement, 293. — The causes of the massacres, 296. — Armenian nobility in the 20th century, 298 — The Patriarchs, 300 — The Young Turks, 303 — The massacres, 304. — The population of the Ottoman Empire, 313. — The Armenian population, 313.

Chapter X.

The Armenians outside of Armenia. — The population of Armenia and of the Armenian Colonies 315-337

The Armenian Emperors of Byzantium, 315. — Mauricius Tiberius, 317. — Flavius Heraclius I, 318. — Constans II, 320. — Constantine IV Pogonatus, 320. — Justinian II, 321. — Tiberius IV, 321 — Filepicus Bardanes, 321. — Artavazdus, 321. — Leo V the Armenian, 322 — Michael III and Basil I, 322. — Alexander, 323. — Constantine X. Porphyrogenetus, 323. — Romanus I, 324. — John Zimesces, 325. — Constantine XI Porphyrogenetus, 325. — Armenian Empresses and Princesses, 326. — The Armenian officials of the Greek Empire, 326 — The Bagratid dynasty of Georgia, 327 — The Armenians in Persia and Constantinople, 328. — The Armenians in Poland, 330. — The Armenians in western Europe, 333 — The Armenians in India and the Far-East, 334 — The Armenians in Venice, the Mekhitharists, 334. — The Armenians in Russia, 334. — Russian administration of the Armenians, 335. — The Armenians in America, 336.

Chapter XI.

Literature, Science, and Art among the Armenians 338-391

Ancient writing of Asia, 338. — Armenian writing, 340 — Mesrop, 341 — Ancient Armenian literature, 345. — Moses of Khoren, 351. — Liturgical poetry, 352 — Secular poetry, 353. — Armenian troubadours, 355. — Modern Armenian literature, 356 — Armenian versification, 362 — The Sciences, 363. — Printing, 364. — Newspapers and Reviews, 364. — Music, 368. — The Stage, 370 — Architecture and Sculpture, 370. — Frescoes and Icons, 381. — Illumination of Manuscripts, 381. — Coining of money in Georgia, 385. — The industrial arts, 389. — Dancing, 391.

Chapter XII.

Events in Armenia, since the fall of the Czar's government in Russia (1917-1918) 392-397

* * *
* *
*

APPENDICES

CHRONOLOGY. — *Remotest times.* — Legendary data. 401. — *Historical data, Earliest times*, 402. — *First Period of Independence.* 402 — *Rule of the Seleucids*, 402. *Second period of Independence*, Dynasty of Artaxias, 402. — *Foreign Dynasty*, 402. — Arsacids of Armenia, 403. — *Persian Rule*, Marzpans or Governors-General, 403. — *Governors-General of Byzantine Armenia*, 404. — *Arab rule*, Ostikans or Governors-General, 405. — *Third Period of Independence*, Dynasty of the Armenian Bagratids, 407. — *Fourth Period of Independence*, Dynasty of the Rupenians in New Armenia. I, the Barons, II the Kings, 407-8.

ECCLESIASTICAL CHRONOLOGY. — Catholici of Etchmiadzin. 409. — Catholici of Cilicia, 411. — Catholici of Akhthamar, 412. — Catholici of Aghouan, 412. — Patriarchs of Jerusalem, 413 — Patriarchs of Constantinople, 414.

* * *
* *
*